Lecture Notes in Computer Science 10282

Commenced Publication in 1973
Founding and Former Series Editors:
Gerhard Goos, Juris Hartmanis, and Jan van Leeuwen

More information about this series at http://www.springer.com/series/7409

Gabriele Meiselwitz (Ed.)

Social Computing and Social Media

Human Behavior

9th International Conference, SCSM 2017
Held as Part of HCI International 2017
Vancouver, BC, Canada, July 9–14, 2017
Proceedings, Part I

 Springer

Editor
Gabriele Meiselwitz
Towson University
Towson, MD
USA

ISSN 0302-9743   ISSN 1611-3349   (electronic)
Lecture Notes in Computer Science
ISBN 978-3-319-58558-1   ISBN 978-3-319-58559-8   (eBook)
DOI 10.1007/978-3-319-58559-8

Library of Congress Control Number: 2017939717

LNCS Sublibrary: SL3 – Information Systems and Applications, incl. Internet/Web, and HCI

Printed on acid-free paper

This Springer imprint is published by Springer Nature
The registered company is Springer International Publishing AG
The registered company address is: Gewerbestrasse 11, 6330 Cham, Switzerland

Foreword

The 19th International Conference on Human–Computer Interaction, HCI International 2017, was held in Vancouver, Canada, during July 9–14, 2017. The event incorporated the 15 conferences/thematic areas listed on the following page.

A total of 4,340 individuals from academia, research institutes, industry, and governmental agencies from 70 countries submitted contributions, and 1,228 papers have been included in the proceedings. These papers address the latest research and development efforts and highlight the human aspects of design and use of computing systems. The papers thoroughly cover the entire field of human–computer interaction, addressing major advances in knowledge and effective use of computers in a variety of application areas. The volumes constituting the full set of the conference proceedings are listed on the following pages.

I would like to thank the program board chairs and the members of the program boards of all thematic areas and affiliated conferences for their contribution to the highest scientific quality and the overall success of the HCI International 2017 conference.

This conference would not have been possible without the continuous and unwavering support and advice of the founder, Conference General Chair Emeritus and Conference Scientific Advisor Prof. Gavriel Salvendy. For his outstanding efforts, I would like to express my appreciation to the communications chair and editor of *HCI International News*, Dr. Abbas Moallem.

April 2017   Constantine Stephanidis

HCI International 2017 Thematic Areas and Affiliated Conferences

Thematic areas:

- Human–Computer Interaction (HCI 2017)
- Human Interface and the Management of Information (HIMI 2017)

Affiliated conferences:

- 17th International Conference on Engineering Psychology and Cognitive Ergonomics (EPCE 2017)
- 11th International Conference on Universal Access in Human–Computer Interaction (UAHCI 2017)
- 9th International Conference on Virtual, Augmented and Mixed Reality (VAMR 2017)
- 9th International Conference on Cross-Cultural Design (CCD 2017)
- 9th International Conference on Social Computing and Social Media (SCSM 2017)
- 11th International Conference on Augmented Cognition (AC 2017)
- 8th International Conference on Digital Human Modeling and Applications in Health, Safety, Ergonomics and Risk Management (DHM 2017)
- 6th International Conference on Design, User Experience and Usability (DUXU 2017)
- 5th International Conference on Distributed, Ambient and Pervasive Interactions (DAPI 2017)
- 5th International Conference on Human Aspects of Information Security, Privacy and Trust (HAS 2017)
- 4th International Conference on HCI in Business, Government and Organizations (HCIBGO 2017)
- 4th International Conference on Learning and Collaboration Technologies (LCT 2017)
- Third International Conference on Human Aspects of IT for the Aged Population (ITAP 2017)

Conference Proceedings Volumes Full List

1. LNCS 10271, Human–Computer Interaction: User Interface Design, Development and Multimodality (Part I), edited by Masaaki Kurosu
2. LNCS 10272 Human–Computer Interaction: Interaction Contexts (Part II), edited by Masaaki Kurosu
3. LNCS 10273, Human Interface and the Management of Information: Information, Knowledge and Interaction Design (Part I), edited by Sakae Yamamoto
4. LNCS 10274, Human Interface and the Management of Information: Supporting Learning, Decision-Making and Collaboration (Part II), edited by Sakae Yamamoto
5. LNAI 10275, Engineering Psychology and Cognitive Ergonomics: Performance, Emotion and Situation Awareness (Part I), edited by Don Harris
6. LNAI 10276, Engineering Psychology and Cognitive Ergonomics: Cognition and Design (Part II), edited by Don Harris
7. LNCS 10277, Universal Access in Human–Computer Interaction: Design and Development Approaches and Methods (Part I), edited by Margherita Antona and Constantine Stephanidis
8. LNCS 10278, Universal Access in Human–Computer Interaction: Designing Novel Interactions (Part II), edited by Margherita Antona and Constantine Stephanidis
9. LNCS 10279, Universal Access in Human–Computer Interaction: Human and Technological Environments (Part III), edited by Margherita Antona and Constantine Stephanidis
10. LNCS 10280, Virtual, Augmented and Mixed Reality, edited by Stephanie Lackey and Jessie Y.C. Chen
11. LNCS 10281, Cross-Cultural Design, edited by Pei-Luen Patrick Rau
12. LNCS 10282, Social Computing and Social Media: Human Behavior (Part I), edited by Gabriele Meiselwitz
13. LNCS 10283, Social Computing and Social Media: Applications and Analytics (Part II), edited by Gabriele Meiselwitz
14. LNAI 10284, Augmented Cognition: Neurocognition and Machine Learning (Part I), edited by Dylan D. Schmorrow and Cali M. Fidopiastis
15. LNAI 10285, Augmented Cognition: Enhancing Cognition and Behavior in Complex Human Environments (Part II), edited by Dylan D. Schmorrow and Cali M. Fidopiastis
16. LNCS 10286, Digital Human Modeling and Applications in Health, Safety, Ergonomics and Risk Management: Ergonomics and Design (Part I), edited by Vincent G. Duffy
17. LNCS 10287, Digital Human Modeling and Applications in Health, Safety, Ergonomics and Risk Management: Health and Safety (Part II), edited by Vincent G. Duffy
18. LNCS 10288, Design, User Experience, and Usability: Theory, Methodology and Management (Part I), edited by Aaron Marcus and Wentao Wang

Social Computing and Social Media

Program Board Chair(s): **Gabriele Meiselwitz, USA**

- Rocio Abascal Mena, Mexico
- Sarah Omar AlHumoud, Saudi Arabia
- Areej Al-Wabil, Saudi Arabia
- James Braman, USA
- Cesar Collazos, Colombia
- Habib Fardoun, Saudi Arabia
- Cristóbal Fernández Robin, Chile
- Panagiotis Germanakos, Cyprus
- Carina S. Gonzalez Gonzales, Spain
- Sara Hook, USA
- Ali Shariq Imran, Norway
- Rushed Kanawati, France
- Tomas Kincl, Czech Republic
- Styliani Kleanthous, Cyprus
- Carsten Kleiner, Germany
- Niki Lambropoulos, Greece
- Soo Ling Lim, UK
- Fernando Loizides, UK
- Hoang Nguyen, Singapore
- Anthony Norcio, USA
- Elaine Raybourn, USA
- Christian Rusu, Chile
- Christian Scheiner, Germany
- Stefan Stieglitz, Germany
- Giovanni Vincenti, USA
- José Viterbo Filho, Brazil
- Evgenios Vlachos, Denmark
- Yuanqiong (Kathy) Wang, USA
- June Wei, USA
- Brian Wentz, USA

The full list with the Program Board Chairs and the members of the Program Boards of all thematic areas and affiliated conferences is available online at:

http://www.hci.international/board-members-2017.php

HCI International 2018

The 20th International Conference on Human–Computer Interaction, HCI International 2018, will be held jointly with the affiliated conferences in Las Vegas, NV, USA, at Caesars Palace, July 15–20, 2018. It will cover a broad spectrum of themes related to human–computer interaction, including theoretical issues, methods, tools, processes, and case studies in HCI design, as well as novel interaction techniques, interfaces, and applications. The proceedings will be published by Springer. More information is available on the conference website: http://2018.hci.international/.

General Chair
Prof. Constantine Stephanidis
University of Crete and ICS-FORTH
Heraklion, Crete, Greece
E-mail: general_chair@hcii2018.org

http://2018.hci.international/

Contents – Part I

Social Issues in Social Media

Contents – Part II

Opinion Mining and Sentiment Analysis

Social Data and Analytics

User Experience and Behavior in Social Media

Investigating Arab DHH Usage of YouTube Videos Using Latent Variables in an Acceptance Technology Model

Lamia Abdul Aziz Bin Husainan, Hanan Ali AL-Shehri$^{(\boxtimes)}$,
and Muna Al-Razgan

Information Technology, King Saud University, Riyadh, Saudi Arabia
Lamo0o_198@hotmail.com, hlnaanly12@hotmail.com,
malrazgan@ksu.edu.sa

Abstract. YouTube is one of the more powerful tools for self-learning and entertaining globally. Uploading and sharing on YouTube have increased recently as these are possible via a simple click. Moreover, some countries, including Saudi Arabia, use this technology more than others. While there are many Saudi channels and videos for all age groups, there are limited channels for people with disabilities such as Deaf and Hard of Hearing people (DHH). The utilization of YouTube among DHH people has not reached its full potential. To investigate this phenomenon, we conducted an empirical research study to uncover factors influencing DHH people's motivations, perceptions and adoption of YouTube, based on the Technology Acceptance Model (TAM). The results showed that DHH people pinpoint some useful functions in YouTube, such as the captions in English and the translation in Arabic. However, Arab DHH people are not sufficiently motivated to watch YouTube due to the fact that the YouTube time-span is fast and DHH personnel prefer greater time to allow them to read and understand the contents. Hence, DHH people tend to avoid sharing YouTube videos among their contacts.

Keywords: Social media · Acceptance technology model · YouTube · Deaf and hard of hearing people

1 Introduction

The Internet and its advanced technologies facilitate searching for various knowledge areas in very a short time and this allows self-learning or e-learning through online services and technologies [1]. One of the technologies that facilitate self-learning is YouTube. YouTube is a video-sharing website and application where the users can search, upload, share and view many types of videos, including educational videos, entertainment videos and Vlog videos [1, 2]. YouTube was launched in 2005 and purchased by Google in 2006. Since this time, YouTube has become one of the most powerful Internet technologies and has acquired millions of videos [2]. According to 2015 Arab social media report [3], in Saudi Arabia 6% of total users preference is YouTube, 40% are current subscribers to YouTube, and 70% access it on daily basis. In addition, the Ministry of Communications and Information Technology's website in

© Springer International Publishing AG 2017
G. Meiselwitz (Ed.): SCSM 2017, Part I, LNCS 10282, pp. 3–12, 2017.
DOI: 10.1007/978-3-319-58559-8_1

Saudi Arabia specify that, seven million Saudis watched YouTube clips at a rate of 105,900 h daily in 2016 [4].

Moreover, one of the benefits of YouTube that makes it stand out from other technologies is that the audiences are not only non-disabled people but also people with special needs, especially deaf and hard of hearing (DHH) people. DHH people not only share videos that contain sign language but also, they can understand other videos through captions, which provide textual versions of the dialog or voices. In Saudi Arabia, there are approximately 1.5 million people with disabilities, which comprise 7% of the population [5]. The number of disabled people is expected to increase in the future as 50% of the cases were caused by marriages between relatives [6].

Arab DHH people, especially in Saudi Arabia, there is still an ambiguity in the acceptance of YouTube. Therefore, it is necessary to conduct research that intensively investigates factors influencing YouTube acceptance in self-learning for Arab DHH people. In addition, there is a need to determine the relationship between DHH people's YouTube use and personal factors such as YouTube perceived usefulness (PU), YouTube perceived ease of use (PEOU), attitude toward YouTube (AT), and behavioral intention (BI).

In this study, we focus on understanding the antecedents of YouTube usage as self-learning for Arab DHH people In Saudi Arabia, and assess how the factors of interest interact with each other using the Technology Acceptance Model (TAM). TAM is a well-known theoretical model that helps in explaining and predicting user behavior of information technology [7].

This study is structured as follows: The research problem is stated in the next section, followed by a presentation of the objectives of the study. Next, the study hypotheses are presented related to the latent variables of acceptance of the technology model. Subsequently, related studies are presented in the literature review section. Next, the methodology of the study is established and specified which consists of: the study setting, data collection instruments, design of the study process, and data analysis procedures. Then, the findings of this study are summarized and a meaningful analysis based on DHH people's comments, as well as on regression models, is provided. Finally, conclusion is provided.

2 Research Problem

YouTube was launched in 2011 in Saudi Arabia [2] and some DHH users have embraced the technology while others have not. DHH people have experienced low motivation toward the use and adoption of this technology in their self-learning. This investigation is about understanding reasons for the lower rate of YouTube usage in self-learning for DHH people. The level of acceptance and the causes of resistance must be identified to provide insights to encourage awareness of YouTube as a self-learning technology. Based on previous studies [7, 8] motivation was generally determined by PEOU and PU [8]. Although similar attempts have been made in previous research, to the best of our knowledge, there are no studies that have examined the specific factors simultaneously, as external variables influencing YouTube acceptance as postulated in TAM. We hope this study will provide additional insights into PEOU, PU, AT and BI relationships and their role in YouTube usage.

3   Research Objectives

In this study, we use the TAM model to determine the variables, which most significantly affect the acceptance of YouTube among DHH people. Thus, the objective is to analyze the relationship of DHH people with YouTube usage while offering some videos that could be classified as educational. The selected constructs are perceived usefulness, perceived ease of use, user attitude, and behavioral intention. In Table 1, shows variables in this study, we then indicate the number of items (questions) used to measure each variable along with its theoretical support, and last we provide references from previous studies.

Table 1. Variables of TAM Model

Variables	Definition	Previous studies
Perceived ease of use (PEOU)	Measures the degree to which a person believes YouTube usage will be free of effort	[7, 8]
Perceived usefulness (PU)	Measures the degree to which a person believes YouTube usage will enhance job performance	[7, 8]
Attitude toward (AT)	Measures DHH people's attitude toward YouTube	[7, 8]
Behavioral intention (BI)	Measures DHH people's behavior to using and sharing YouTube links in the future	[7, 8]

4   Research Hypotheses

The purpose of our study is to investigate DHH people's acceptance of YouTube videos using the following variables: perceived usefulness, perceived ease of use, user attitude and behavioral intention. We asked several questions to find out the variables that have an impact on DHH acceptance of YouTube videos as learning media. Then, we have derived the following hypotheses (see Fig. 1):

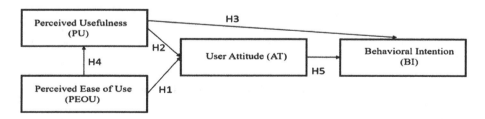

Fig. 1. Technology Acceptance Model of YouTube

Perceived Ease of Use (PEOU)
H1: Perceived ease of use (PEOU) will positively influence DHH people's attitude towards YouTube.

Perceived Usefulness (PU)
H2: Perceived Usefulness (PU) will positively influence DHH people's attitude towards YouTube.

H3: Perceived Usefulness (PU) will positively influence DHH people's behavioral intention to use YouTube.

Perceived Ease of Use (PEOU) and Perceived Usefulness (PU)
H4: Perceived Ease of Use (PEOU) will positively influence Perceived Usefulness (PU) of YouTube.

Attitude (AT) and Behavioral Intention (BI)
H5: Attitude towards YouTube will positively influence users' behavioral intention to use YouTube.

5 Literature Review

The literature addressing the acceptance of technology has undergone a significant increase in recent years. Moreover, there is much research studying the usage of YouTube as a tool for self-learning purposes.

There are several studies that use the TAM model as a way to investigate acceptance of any information system. In [9] the authors investigated the acceptance model of (university) course websites. They used constructs of perceived usefulness and perceived ease of use to assess university students' acceptance of course websites as an effective learning tool. A survey instrument was distributed to 450 university students and a total of 403 usable responses were obtained. They implemented exploratory and confirmatory factor analyses using structural equation modeling techniques. This was subsequently used to fit and validate the Course Website Acceptance Model (CWAM) designed for their study. Their model indicated a good fit to the data. The causal relationships between the constructs considered by this model were well supported, accounting for 83% of the total variance in the course website acceptance and usage.

Moreover, the authors in [10] examined the motivations, perceptions and adoption of users towards a taxi-hailing app based on the Technology Acceptance Model (TAM). A survey instrument was distributed to 208 taxi-hailing app users in a large metropolitan setting. The survey was about their patterns of usage, demographic, perceptions about the technology, and their behavioral intentions to use the online taxi-hailing service. The results confirmed that users' perceptions are significantly associated with their intentions to use mobile phones. Moreover, perceived usefulness is the strongest determinant of users' attitudes and intentions towards the taxi-hailing app, followed by perceived ease of use.

The following two studies [11, 12] and were related to deaf students' needs in accessing online resources. In [11], the target student group was deaf or hard of hearing (DHH) students in science, technology, engineering and mathematics (STEM). The authors studied the general challenges that were faced by DHH people when using social media. The main finding was that DDH person has challenges associated with Accessible Media that is available on the Internet. They found that rules for captioning only pertain to those videos originally aired on TV, which means that videos produced for online access may not have captioning. The automatic captioning option on You-Tube is one solution that is often offered. However, in many cases captioning is inaccurate, which is especially problematic when viewing technical content with specialized vocabulary. Following these findings, STEM has created an online community, using off-the-shelf social media tools to promote socialization opportunities and to share accessible STEM-related media with its participants.

The authors in [12] tested if YouTube's auto-generated captions meet deaf students' needs. They assessed a particular type of video. These videos were weekly informal news updates created by individual professors for their online classes. The authors' goal was to see if automatic captions are sufficiently accurate to meet the needs of deaf students. They analyzed 68 min of video captions and 525 phrase -level errors were found. On average, there were 7.7 phrase errors per minute. The results confirmed that auto-generated captions are too inaccurate to be used exclusively.

The study in [1] examined the use of YouTube as a learning resource in higher education using the TAM model. The authors developed scales to measure the different variables of TAM for YouTube as a learning resource. They investigated a sequence of qualitative and quantitative experiments, which resulted in valid scales and a reliable model. Furthermore, they investigated an additional construct, which was exploratory factor analysis (EFA) to identify new factors that may explain the intention to use YouTube as a learning resource. They found that (PU), (PEU), (UA), and (BI) were important constructs for YouTube users. The findings of the study were used as a basis for further research.

6 Research Methodology

We adopt the Technology Acceptance Model (TAM) to test DHH people's acceptance toward YouTube. Our aim was to validate our hypothesis of DHH people's YouTube usage among Arab DHH personnel. We distributed survey questions among Arab DHH people that were aligned with the questionnaires in reference [1].

Based on the previous studies, we focused on the antecedents of constructs that demonstrated the influence of usefulness, ease of use, user attitude and behavioral intension on the usage of YouTube as self-learning in our study. We also focused on (1) understanding the personal factors that influence YouTube usefulness and which play an important role in the acceptance or rejection of the technology and (2) examining the relationship among (PU), (PEOU), (AT) and (BI).

The following subsections will present the TAM experiment and its results for Arab DHH people's acceptance toward YouTube.

6.1 TAM Model Experiment

This study measured a sample of Arab DHH people's acceptance of YouTube videos for learning and entertainment. The chosen videos contained sign language and captions that were designed for DHH people to increase their knowledge and information.

Thus, the measures to be assessed in this study were as follows:

- Perceived Usefulness of YouTube for DHH people.
- DHH people's Attitude to YouTube.
- Perceived Ease of Use of YouTube for DHH people.
- Behavioral Intention of DHH people with YouTube.

6.2 TAM Experiment Description and Material

We distributed an online survey for the TAM experiment using a Google docs form. The survey had three main sections. The first section contained general questions that measured the awareness of YouTube usage and options. The second section requested Arab DHH people to watch three YouTube videos designed specifically for them (videos that contained sign language and captions), and to measure their understanding, they were asked questions about these videos. The third section consisted of questions that measured DHH people's acceptance of YouTube videos. We also included an open-ended question to collect participant opinion and feedback. The experiment lasted between 15–20 min.

6.2.1 Participants

We recruited 8-DHH female participants to conduct our experiments. One of whom was less than 17 years old, two of whom were more than 30 years old, and five of whom were between 17 and 30 years old. All of them were deaf or hard of hearing people and all of them were YouTube users.

6.2.2 Data Analysis and Results

We entered the survey data in SPSS Version 16 software to perform further analysis using Cronbach's alpha regression and descriptive statistics. The reliability analysis was conducted in order to check the internal validity and consistency of the items used for each factor. The results of the reliability analysis are presented in Table 2. According to Nunnally (1978), the questionnaire used for the various factors of YouTube usage was judged to be a reliable measurement instrument, with the Cronbach's alpha scores all above 0.7.

Table 2. Internal consistency reliability testing

Cronbach's alpha	Cronbach's alpha based on standardized items	N of items
0.794	0.776	19

In Table 3, detail the Cronbach's alpha calculation for each factor by listing the factors (PU, AT, PEOU, and BI) that were measured in this experiment. All the coefficients exceed 0.70. Thus, all of these four measures were deemed acceptable and valid.

Table 3. Cronbach's alpha

Factor	Items	Cronbach's alpha (average)
Perceived usefulness (PU)	6	0.78
Attitude (AT)	6	0.77
Perceived ease of use (PEOU)	5	0.79
Behavioral intention (BI)	4	0.79

6.2.3   Reliability Statistics

Furthermore, we conducted correlation analysis among the variables as shown in Table 4. The aim of the correlation matrix is to avoid multicollinearity among the variables and to build an accurate regression model. A high correlation value indicates redundancy among the input variables, as observed in PU. Table 4 shows that the correlations between the PEOU, PU, AT and BI are positive and significant. This confirms the original hypothesis made in the literature concerning the Technology Acceptance Model. PU is more influenced by PEOU than by AT, and least influenced by BI, since PEOU has the highest score, which is 0.244. AT is more influenced by PU than by BI and least influenced by PEOU since PU has the highest score, which is 0.255. PEOU is more influenced by PU than by AT and least influenced by BI since PU has the highest score, which is 0.126. BI is more influenced by AT than by PU and least influenced by PEOU since AT has the highest score, which is 0.208. As shown in Table 4, the PU variable has the most impact on the other factors.

Table 4. Correlation matrix

Factor	PU	AT	PEOU	BI
PU Pearson correlation (average)	1	0.241	0.244	0.043
AT Pearson correlation (average)	0.255	1	0.026	0.208
PEOU Pearson correlation (average)	0.126	0.026	1	0.038
BI Pearson correlation (average)	0.043	0.208	0.010	1

6.3   Hypotheses Testing

A standard regression analysis was performed between the dependent variable (one of each of the variables) and the independent variables (the remaining variables). Analysis was performed using SPSS regression as shown in Table 5. This table presents the result of simple regression of the interaction variables. The first column refers to the hypothesis, the second refers to the dependent variables, and the third column refers to the independent variables. Also, the table includes values for multiple regression analyses for each hypothesis along with its validation result.

Table 5. Direct effect between independent constructs

Hypothesis	Dependent variables	Independent variables	R2	F-value	β	P-value	Validation
H1	AT	PEOU	**.644**	4.514	−.355	**.293**	Not supported and the influence is not significant. (β = −.355, p > 0.05)
H2		PU			**.905**	**.030**	Supported and the influence is significant. (β = .905, p < 0.05)
H3	BI	PU	.444	1.985	.462	**.394**	Not supported and the influence is not significant. (β = −.462, p > 0.05)
H4	PU	PEOU	.220	1.688	.469	.242	Supported but the influence is not significant. (β = .469, p > 0.05)
H5	BI	AT	.444	1.985	.929	**.120**	Supported and the influence is not significant. (β = .929, p > 0.05)

As shown in Table 5, the value of R square for H1 and H2 indicates that the two predictors (PU, PEOU) explained 64.4% of the variation in attitudes to use. This indicates that this model is a rational one, although there are other unknown factors, which may impact the users' attitude to use YouTube, which are not accounted for in this model.

The standardized coefficients (β) show that Perceived Usefulness (β = 0.905) has larger impact than the Perceived Ease of Use (β = −0.355) where β is a positive value for PU and a negative value for PEOU. Also, the results indicate that PU has a significant impact on AT since the score is less than 0.05, and PEOU does not have a significant impact on AT since the score is more than 0.05. Hence, if DHH people feel that YouTube is useful for them then they are more likely to use it. On other hand, if DHH people feel that YouTube will be easy to use and reduce the effort of learning, they will be likely to adopt it. Subsequently, a linear regression model was also used to test H3 and H5, which are the impact of Perceived Usefulness and Attitude on users' behavioral intention towards YouTube.

As shown in Table 5, the results confirmed H3 that Perceived Usefulness (PU) had a negative and not significant effect on Behavioral Intention (BI), with β = −0.462, Significant = 0.394 (more than p = 0.12). While Attitude Toward (AT) had a positive and not significant influence on the dependent variable BI, with β = 0.929,

Sig = 0.120. If the DHH person recognizes that YouTube has some useful functions, they perceived that these functions would be shareable to other DHH people.

Finally, another linear regression model was used to investigate the influence of Perceived Ease of Use (PEOU) on Perceived Usefulness (PU) H4. The results showed an R Square value of 0. 220 which is low; this indicated that PEOU explained only 22.0% of the variation in PU. Based on the Standardized coefficient value (β = 0.469), Perceived Ease of Use (PEOU) had a positive but not significant impact on Perceived Usefulness (PU), with β = 0.469, Significant = 0.242 (more than 0.05). Also, the deaf recognized that YouTube has some useful functions, but they perceived that this application is not intuitive for them to use.

In summary of the four hypotheses, Perceived Usefulness (PU) had a negative impact on Behavioral Intention (BI), this was followed by a strong positive influence of Perceived Usefulness (PU) on Attitude Toward (AT) using YouTube. Perceived Ease of Use (PEOU) had a negative impact on users Attitude Toward (AT) YouTube. Finally, users' attitude had a negative impact on their Behavioral Intention (BI).

Some of the DHH participants' Comments:

> "I find YouTube useful and it provides much functionality but not for all topics."
> "I like it as a tool to watch useful videos, especially if it offers Edit Arabic caption."
> "I think YouTube's Auto-generated Captions does not meet deaf students' needs."
> "I share videos that have understandable caption."
> "I don't know caption is existing before, and I will use it in the future."

6.4   Key Findings and Recommendations

The results of the TAM model experiment showed that DHH people pinpoint some useful functions in YouTube, such as the captions in English and the translation to Arabic. However, Arab DHH people are not motivated enough to watch YouTube because it is lacking Arabic videos for DHH people. Due to the fact that the YouTube time-span is fast for DHH people, they prefer a slower time-span to allow them to read the captions and understand the content of the videos. Hence, DHH people avoid sharing YouTube videos among their contacts except if the videos were from DHH care institutions. In addition, 75% of the participants did not know about the auto-caption and edited-caption features that YouTube provides for some of its videos. Also, for the participants who knew about them, they gave their opinions of the need to improve these and the need to have auto-captions for Arabic videos. This is to allow them to watch and understand the content of Arabic videos rather than just watching English videos that have Arabic captions translated from English captions on YouTube.

7   Conclusion

Since YouTube has become one of the self-learning resources for individuals, and the huge usage of YouTube in Saudi Arabia, there is still an ambiguity regarding DHH people's acceptance of YouTube. Thus, this study has attempted to uncover this ambiguity by adopting the TAM model, which is a well-known theoretical model that helps to explain and predict user behavior related to information technology [7].

The results of the TAM experiment showed that DHH people identify some useful functions in YouTube, such as the captions in English and the translation to Arabic. However, Arab DHH people are not excited to watch YouTube because of the lack of Arabic videos designed for DHH people.

Some of results of interest from this study are:

– 76 out of 80 of the DHH people in King Saud University female students cannot read and write Arabic as well as other institutions. Therefore, they are not an audience of YouTube.
– 75% of the participants did not know about the auto-caption and edited-caption features that YouTube provides for some of its videos.
– DHH people need more time more than non-disabled people to read and understand video captions using their smartphone. Therefore, there is a need to implement the slow time-span of YouTube videos in Android and iOS platforms on smartphones.

References

1. Chintalapati, N., Daruri, V.S.: Examining the use of YouTube as a learning resource in higher education: scale development and validation of TAM model. Telemat. Inf. (2016)
2. History of YouTube. En.wikipedia.org https://en.wikipedia.org/wiki/History_of_YouTube. Accessed 05 Jan 2017
3. Dubai School of Government's Governance and Innovation Program. Arab Social Media Report, Arab Social Media Influencers Summit, Dubai (2015)
4. Over 18 million users of social media programs and applications in Saudi Arabia, Ministry of Communications and Information Technology (2016). http://mcit.gov.sa/En/MediaCenter/Pages/News/News-22032016_982.aspx. Accessed 04 Jan 2017
5. Alsaggaf, A.: 1.5 million of disabilities in Saudi Arabia are celebrating Disability Day, Al Madina Newspaper (2014)
6. Almubark, S.: The Deafs in SA are between 350 and 450 thousand people, Al-Riyadh Newspaper (2014)
7. Park, S.: An analysis of the technology acceptance model in understanding University students' behavioral intention to use e-Learning. Educ. Technol. Soc. 12(3), 150–162 (2009)
8. Bousbahi, F., Alrazgan, M.: Investigating IT faculty resistance to learning management system adoption using latent variables in an acceptance technology model. Sci. World J. 2015, 1–11 (2015)
9. Ignatius, J., Ramayah, T.: An empirical investigation of the course website acceptance model (CWAM). Int. J. Bus. Soc. 6, 69–82 (2005)
10. Liu, Z.Y.: An Analysis of Technology Acceptance Model-Exploring user acceptance and intension of taxi-hailing app in Shanghai (2015)
11. Elliot, L.B., Easton, D., McCarthy, J., Murray, R. Tavernese, A.: Creating an Online Community of Practice: The Deaf and Hard of Hearing Virtual Academic Community
12. Parton, B.S.: Video captions for online courses: do YouTube's auto-generated captions meet deaf students' needs? J. Open Flex. Distance Learn. 20(1), 8–18 (2016)

Can the Success of Mobile Games Be Attributed to Following Mobile Game Heuristics?

Reham Alhaidary[(✉)] and Shatha Altammami

King Saud University, Riyadh, Saudi Arabia
reham.alhaidary@gmail.com, Shaltammami@ksu.edu.sa

Abstract. The mobile game industry is increasing in market share and becoming saturated with hundreds of products. This rises competition to gain user's satisfaction for fun and easy to use mobile games. In fact, the main concern of mobile game development is the usability due to smart phones restrictions (screen size, processing power, storage, etc.). To identify such usability problems, heuristic evaluation is applied. In this paper, we evaluated a popular mobile game, "Hay day", using heuristic evaluation conducted by six evaluators to examine 44 heuristics. The results of this study provide insights to game developers in order to improve usability.

Keywords: Heuristics evaluation · Usability · Mobile games

1 Introduction

With the widespread of mobile phones, game applications became one of the main entertainment methods. This expand in game industry led researches and game developers to study the reasons behind games success, which they discovered to be dependent on users' first experience (Delone and McLean 2003). Mobile users get their first impression after interacting with the game thought its interface. However, the interface efficiency alone does not determine the game success, because there are other factors like amusement and challenge which must be present to grab user's interest (Federoff 2002). Therefore, to produce successful games, developers need to focus on 'user experience', a term coined by Federoff to describe game usability. It can be defined as the degree to which a player is able to learn, control, and understand a game (Pinelle et al. 2008). There are three areas of game usability, which are game interface, game play, and game mechanics. Evaluation methods for game usability varies and they range from interviews, questionnaires or observation. However, the most common method to evaluate game usability is through heuristic evaluation.

In this paper, we attempt to evaluate one of the popular mobile game (Rajanen and Nissinen 2015), "Hay Day", using heuristics evaluation from the literature to measure the correlation between the success of mobile games and its application of these heuristics, and we suggest improvements when applicable. The paper proceeds as follows. First, we discuss the background of usability evaluation and an overview of heuristics specifically designed for games. Second, we explain the methodology used to

© Springer International Publishing AG 2017
G. Meiselwitz (Ed.): SCSM 2017, Part I, LNCS 10282, pp. 13–21, 2017.
DOI: 10.1007/978-3-319-58559-8_2

undergo this study. Third, the results are presented and discussed. Finally, we conclude the implication of this study.

2 Background

Usability is the main factor for ensuring the success of a system. In order to identify usability issues, usability evaluation is performed at different stages of system development (Nielsen 1994). There are different usability evaluation methods. One of the most common methods in Human Computer Interaction (HCI) field is heuristic evaluation. It was first introduced by Nielsen and Molich in 1990. Later in 1994, Nielsen introduced a set of 10 usability heuristics to evaluate interfaces of software. However, because of the unique characteristics of mobile games, there is a need to include additional heuristics that specifically measure the usability in mobile games.

Several researchers have used Nielsen's measures as a basis for mobile game heuristics evaluation. For example, Federoff (2002) developed a set of 40 heuristics for game usability, some of them were based on Nielsen's heuristics. The heuristics was divided into three categories: game interface, game mechanics and game play. Desurvire et al. (2004) developed the HEP – Heuristic Evaluation for Playability – which identifies four game heuristic categories: game play, game story, game mechanics, game usability. In a follow-up study, a refined list called Heuristics of Playability (PLAY) is introduced with three categories. The first category is game play; while the second includes coolness, entertainment, humor, or emotional immersion. The third category covers usability and game mechanics (Desurvire and Wiberg 2009). Pinelle et al. (2008) proposed 10 heuristics to identify usability issues in video games focusing on single user issues. In addition, Hochleitner et al. (2015) proposed a framework for video games consist of 49 heuristics categorized into two sets: game play/game story, virtual interface.

Most of video games requires multiplayers, which makes the interaction between the players more challenging. Pinelle et al. (2009) developed 10 networked game heuristics (NGH) to evaluate multiplayer game usability. These measures support coordination, communication and social interactions between the players. In addition, Korhonen and Koivisto (2006) introduced playability heuristics for multiplayer mobile games. The model consists of three modules: Game Usability, Mobility, and Gameplay.

3 Methodology

The most popular heuristics developed for game design are presented in the following papers (Desurvire et al. 2004; Federoff 2002; Pinelle et al. 2008). Desurvire and Federoff studies have strong similarities where they focus on player engagement and fun. However, they do not consider usability in detail. Therefore, Pinelle found a gap in their study and introduced similar heuristics for video game with usability as the focus. Although, previously mentioned studies were designed for video games, applying them on mobile games may not cover all aspects. Therefore, Korhonen and Koivisto (2006) proposed a model focused on mobile games.

In this study, we have consolidated heuristics models from (Desurvire et al. 2004; Pinelle et al. 2008; Korhonen et al. 2006). To conduct the study, we follow a technique used in a previous study on "Farmville", where they identified 5 objectives. However, since "Hay Day" is a mobile game we add a sixth objective for mobility.

1. The game should have mechanisms that facilitate the player's learning process and general gameplay.
2. The game should be easy and enjoyable to play but have some complexity to engage the player.
3. The player should be able to identify his actions in the game and respective feedback.
4. The game should be graphically appealing without overriding game play and be customizable.
5. The game should be accessible to any person or player.
6. The game should be suited for mobility.

After defining the objectives and supporting heuristics, evaluators are chosen to undergo the study. The literature suggests three to five evaluators, each spend time to test the game interface and produce a list of heuristic violations (Nielsen 1994). In this study, we used six evaluators, three users who are familiar with the game, while the other three have no experience with the game. Table 1 shows evaluators details.

Table 1. Evaluators details

	Gender	Age	Game experience
Evaluator 1	Female	27	Yes
Evaluator 2	Female	18	Yes
Evaluator 3	Male	34	Yes
Evaluator 4	Male	34	No
Evaluator 5	Male	20	No
Evaluator 6	Female	15	No

According to Nielson, *heuristic evaluation involves having a small set of evaluators examine the interface and judge its compliance with recognized usability principles (the "heuristics")* (Nielsen 1994). The evaluation session goes as follow: each evaluator examines the interface several times and goes through all the elements. Then, he\she is asked to evaluate the game by answering yes (Y) or no (N) to a list of usability heuristics.

4   Results and Discussion

The results of the evaluation show that 23 of the 44 heuristics were verified as shown in Tables 2, 3, 4, 5, 6 and 7. The first objective is concerned about game mechanism and the player's learning process and general gameplay. It was analyzed with 12 heuristics, 4 of them were verified as shown in the table below with the green highlights. All the

Table 2. Objective 1 evaluation

Heuristic	Objective 1	Evaluators					
		1	2	3	4	5	6
H1	Tutorial provided at beginning of the game	Y	Y	Y	Y	Y	Y
H2	Tutorials are repeatable.	Y	N	Y	Y	N	N
H3	Help is clear and informative.	Y	Y	Y	Y	Y	Y
H4	Match between system and real world.	Y	Y	Y	Y	Y	N
H5	Customizable controls.	Y	Y	Y	Y	N	Y
H6	Errors are prevented with warnings and messages.	N	Y	Y	Y	Y	Y
H7	Player is involved quickly and easily.	Y	Y	Y	Y	Y	Y
H8	Game gives hints and suggestions.	Y	N	Y	Y	Y	Y
H9	A game manual is not required to play.	Y	Y	Y	Y	Y	Y
H10	Non-playable content can be skipped.	Y	Y	Y	Y	Y	N
H11	Information is displayed in various forms.	Y	Y	Y	N	Y	Y
H12	Player has full control over game.	Y	Y	Y	Y	Y	N

Table 3. Objective 2 evaluation

Heuristic	Objective 2	Evaluators					
		1	2	3	4	5	6
H1	Game difficulty can be changed.	N	N	N	N	N	N
H2	There are multiple game goals.	Y	Y	Y	Y	N	Y
H3	Game is balanced: no definite way to win.	Y	Y	Y	Y	Y	Y
H4	Challenge, strategy, and pace are in balance.	Y	Y	Y	Y	N	Y
H5	Game gives rewards.	Y	Y	Y	Y	Y	Y
H6	The first-time experience is encouraging.	Y	Y	Y	Y	N	Y
H7	Game is re-playable.	Y	Y	Y	Y	Y	Y
H8	Player does not rely on memory to play.	Y	Y	Y	Y	Y	Y
H9	Player experiences fairness of outcomes.	Y	Y	Y	Y	Y	Y
H10	There are no repetitive or boring tasks.	N	N	N	N	N	N
H11	The player sees the progress in the game and can compare the results	Y	Y	Y	Y	Y	Y

evaluators agreed that tutorials are provided in the beginning of the game; however, three of them think that tutorials cannot be repeated again. The remaining seven heuristics have 5 positive responses with one negative response. For "Errors are prevented with warnings and messages" heuristic, one evaluator did not agree with that, she stated that network errors are not recognized immediately which lead to losing the

Table 4. Objective 3 evaluation

Heuristic	Objective 3	Evaluators					
		1	2	3	4	5	6
H1	Player score/status is identifiable	Y	Y	Y	Y	Y	Y
H2	Feedback provided through sound.	Y	Y	Y	Y	Y	Y
H3	All feedback is immediate.	Y	Y	Y	Y	Y	Y
H4	There are multiple forms of feedback.	Y	Y	Y	Y	Y	Y

Table 5. Objective 4 evaluation

Heuristic	Objective 4	Evaluators					
		1	2	3	4	5	6
H1	Interface is consistent in color & typography.	Y	Y	Y	Y	Y	Y
H2	Screen layout is efficient and visually pleasing.	Y	Y	Y	Y	Y	Y
H3	The player understands the terminology and art used in the game.	Y	Y	Y	Y	Y	Y
H4	All relevant information is displayed.	Y	Y	Y	Y	Y	Y
H5	The interface is non-intrusive.	Y	N	N	Y	Y	Y
H6	Navigation is consistent, logical, and minimalist.	Y	Y	Y	Y	Y	Y
H7	The game story supports the gameplay and is meaningful.	Y	Y	Y	Y	Y	Y
H8	Visual and audio effects arouse player interest.	Y	Y	Y	Y	N	Y
H9	Audio, video and graphics settings are customizable.	Y	Y	Y	N	Y	N

session. Figure 1 shows a screenshot of the game interface, with the settings button on the top left, and Fig. 2 shows the settings menu.

The second objective, game should be easy and enjoyable to play but have some complexity to engage the player, has 11 heuristics. Overall, 6 heuristics were verified, 2 were not verified, and 3 heuristics have different answers. The first heuristic concerned about changing the game difficulty, all evaluators agreed that the player cannot change the difficulty at all. In addition, all evaluators think that the game has repetitive and boring tasks. For heuristic H4, one evaluator who is new to the game finds it hard at the beginning.

The third objective focuses on identifying player's actions in the game and respective feedback. This objective was analyzed with four heuristics. All the heuristics

Table 6. Objective 5 evaluation

Heuristic	Objective 5	Evaluators					
		1	2	3	4	5	6
H1	Icons size are adjustable	N	N	N	Y	Y	Y
H2	Game has accessible language	Y	Y	Y	Y	Y	Y
H3	Game actions description can be turned on/off	N	N	N	Y	N	N
H4	The player cannot make irreversible errors	Y	Y	Y	N	N	Y

Table 7. Objective 6 evaluation

Heuristic	Objective 6	Evaluators					
		1	2	3	4	5	6
H1	The game and play sessions can be started quickly.	Y	Y	N	Y	Y	Y
H2	The game accommodates with the surroundings.	Y	Y	Y	Y	Y	N
H3	Interruptions are handled reasonably.	Y	Y	Y	Y	Y	Y
H4	The Player can easily turn the game off and on, and be able to save games in different states.	Y	Y	Y	Y	Y	Y

Fig. 1. Screenshot of "Hay Day" main interface.

were verified by evaluators. They agreed that the game provides multiple forms of feedback (written or by sound or visual feedback) and they can identify their score clearly.

Objective four states that the game should be graphically appealing without overriding game play and be customizable. Six heuristics were verified for this objective; evaluators approved that the interface is visually pleasing with its colors and

Fig. 2. Screenshot of the "Settings" menu

typography, all information needed is shown, and game has clear and understandable navigation, terminology and art. The remaining three heuristics received diverse answers. Two evaluators did not agree that the interface is non-intrusive. While one evaluator did not find the video and audio effects appealing to his personal taste. For the last heuristic, two evaluators did not agree that graphics settings are customizable.

Objective five measures the game accessibility to any person or player was analyzed with four heuristics. Only one heuristic was verified while the remaining heuristics received different answers. The experienced evaluators disagreed that icon size can be changed while first time evaluators stated they could zoom in or out to adjust icon size. Most evaluators disagreed that game description can be turned off. However, one experienced evaluator stated description messages has a close button, which can be pressed to remove the message instantly.

The last objective measures game mobility with four heuristics to verity game can be played anywhere anytime. Two heuristics were verified, "Interruptions handled reasonably" and "game can be easily turned on or off". One evaluator does not agree that the game accommodate with the surrounding, in which animals in the game emit unexpected sounds that may cause embarrassment to the player. However, other evaluators mentioned the game sound can be disabled when the player is in public places. For the remaining heuristic, evaluators stated that game-lunching time depends on the internet speed. However, game developers have no control on internet connectivity.

Based on the above evaluation, percentage of heuristics verified for each objective is calculated in the below table. Objective 3 was 100% verified, while most heuristics in objective 2 and 4 were verified. However, objectives 1 and 5 had few heuristics verified. This result is compared to the statistics obtained from the Google play market for "Hay Day" where the number of downloads exceeds eight million and rating reaches 4.5. We conclude that if a mobile games do not satisfy some usability heuristics, it does not necessarily lead to an unsuccessful product (Table 8).

Table 8. Percentage of heuristics verified for each objective

Objective	% of heuristics verified
1	33%
2	55%
3	100%
4	67%
5	25%
6	50%

5   Conclusion

This study evaluates "Hay Day" mobile game by using six objectives, consisting of 44 heuristics. Six evaluators were chosen to carry out this study. The results show that 23 heuristics were verified. Only one objective was fully verified "objective 3: the player should be able to identify his actions in the game and respective feedback." Based on our results, we provide some suggestions to improve the game. Half of evaluators did not know that tutorials are repeatable; this might be because the tutorials are in the help section. It is better to make tutorials accessible from the settings section. Some evaluators think that interface is intrusive, icons on the sides are blocking some of the content. In addition, most of evaluators agreed that actions description cannot be turned on/off, some of the tasks are repeated which make it boring. We suggest providing the player the ability to opt-out such actions.

It is evident that first time evaluators were not able to verify certain heuristics due to their lack of experience. For example, the game accommodate with the surrounding was not verified because the evaluator thinks the sounds emitted may cause embarrassment in public. However, the game provides options in the settings as shown in Fig. 2, which allows the user to turn off animal sounds, and another option to turn off music. Moreover, another evaluator, who used the game for the sake of this study, did not find it interesting, which may have affected his evaluation since he did not agree that first time experience is encouraging and visual, audio effects arouse his interest.

Although not all heuristics were verified, only 2 received consensus negative evaluation, while the rest 19 heuristics received diverse answers. This suggests that "Hay Day" developers have considered most heuristics to accomplish a positive user experience. In fact, not complying with all usability heuristics does not necessarily lead to lower ratings. This is reflected in the statistics showing the number of downloads that exceeds eight million and excellent user ratings. However, heuristics evaluation presented in this study shows that there is room for improvement specifically to enhance the experience of first time users.

Acknowledgements. We would like to express our gratitude to the evaluators for the valuable time they dedicated to this study.

References

Delone, W.H., McLean, E.R.: The Delone and McLean model of information systems success: a ten-year update. J. Manag. Inf. Syst. **19**(4), 9–30 (2003)

Desurvire, H., Caplan, M., Toth, J.A.: Using heuristics to evaluate the playability of games. In: Proceedings of the CHI 2004 Extended Abstracts on Human Factors in Computing Systems, pp. 1509–1512 (2004). https://doi.org/10.1145/985921.986102

Desurvire, H., Wiberg, C.: Game usability heuristics (PLAY) for evaluating and designing better games: the next iteration. In: Ozok, A.A., Zaphiris, P. (eds.) OCSC 2009. LNCS, vol. 5621, pp. 557–566. Springer, Heidelberg (2009). doi:10.1007/978-3-642-02774-1_60

Federoff, M.A.: Heuristics and Usability Guidelines for the Creation and Evaluation of Fun in Video Games (2002)

Hochleitner, C., Hochleitner, W., Graf, C., Tscheligi, M.: A heuristic framework for evaluating user experience in games. In: Bernhaupt, R. (ed.) Game User Experience Evaluation. HIS, pp. 187–206. Springer, Cham (2015). doi:10.1007/978-3-319-15985-0_9

Korhonen, H., Koivisto, E.M.I.: Playability heuristics for mobile multi-player games Playability heuristics for mobile games. In: Proceedings of the 8th Conference on Human-Computer Interaction with Mobile Devices and Services (2006). https://doi.org/10.1145/1306813.1306828

Nielsen, J.: Enhancing the explanatory power of usability heuristics. In: Proceedings of CHI 1994, pp. 152–158 (1994)

Pinelle, D., Wong, N., Stach, T.: Heuristic evaluation for games: usability principles for video game design. In: Proceedings of the SIGCHI Conference on Human Factors in Computing Systems, pp. 1453–1462 (2008)

Pinelle, D., Wong, N., Stach, T., Gutwin, C.: Usability heuristics for networked multiplayer games. In: Proceedings of the ACM 2009 International Conference, pp. 169–178 (2009)

Rajanen, M., Nissinen, J.: A survey of game usability practices in Northern European game companies. Association for Information Systems (Nr 6) (2015)

The Collective Impression of Saudis' Perceptions of Entertainment

Noura Alomar[✉] and Alaa Alhumaisan[✉]

College of Computer and Information Sciences,
King Saud University, Riyadh, Saudi Arabia
{nnalomar,aalhumaisan}@ksu.edu.sa

Abstract. The diversity of human perceptions of entertainment coupled with the continuous emergence of new modes of entertainment have raised a challenge in offering the entertainment environment that is properly aligned with the public interest. Entertainment preferences are known to be shaped by a combination of individuals' social and cultural background, instability in economic situation, and generational differences. In the Saudi context, many cultural considerations have created a multitude of preferences with regards to accepting newly emerged or imported entertainment methods, particularly due to the distinctive nature of the Saudi cultural context and the complexity of perceptual factors that contribute to shaping individuals' preferences in the Saudi community. In this paper we propose to utilize visual surveys as a mean for collecting and quantifying urban perceptions of entertainment, with the hope of revealing the current challenges and envisioning the potential directions of improvement. We employ visual surveys as a data collection tool to understand how people's defined expectations, prior experiences and demographic variables relate to their perceptions with regards to preferred entertainment modes. It is our hope that this research work will open the door toward utilizing the availability of crowdsourcing techniques for comparing and contrasting urban perceptions in other different cultures and contexts.

1 Introduction

Contrary to traditional data collection approaches, crowdsourcing has enabled the active participation of citizens in decision planning processes by opening the door toward simplifying the challenging task of understanding the complexities underlying human perceptions. Crowdsourcing-based data collection techniques have also made it possible to obtain the knowledge required for constructing a filtered view of urban perceptions while allowing the interpretation of cultural, social and economic factors that contributed to shaping these perceptions as well as individuals' personal experiences and opinions [1–6]. That is, these techniques have facilitated building an accumulative picture of perceptions while allowing the data collection process to span geographical and cultural boundaries [7].

In this paper, we employ crowdsourcing as a human-centered data collection approach to obtain a unified view of entertainment perceptions for local populations in

© Springer International Publishing AG 2017
G. Meiselwitz (Ed.): SCSM 2017, Part I, LNCS 10282, pp. 22–31, 2017.
DOI: 10.1007/978-3-319-58559-8_3

Saudi Arabia. We present the first research attempt that quantifies the entertainment-related perceptions of people in the Saudi context. Using perception data collected by crowdsourcing the task of rating paired images in a visual survey, we show the effectiveness of crowdsourcing as a tool for uncovering differences of entertainment perceptions in Saudi Arabia, a culture representing people of diverse backgrounds, experiences and cultural beliefs.

One of the main properties of the Saudi culture, as suggested by Hofstede's theory of cultural dimensions, is that it is a collectivistic culture meaning that its individuals work for the welfare of the social group for which they belong [8]. Given this and the fact that people in Saudi Arabia have different social and cultural norms, we expect collecting perceptual data on people living in different areas in Saudi Arabia via visual surveys to help in revealing and quantifying the perceptual differences of various Saudi cultural groups. We also aim to investigate whether the highly masculine nature of the Saudi society has any clear effects on individuals' perceptions of entertainment.

While the psychology literature has unveiled many factors that explain cross-cultural human behavior and perception, the study of inter-cultural features that explain perceptions of residents in Arabic countries is still yet to be explored. In particular, we note that despite the multi-cultural nature of the Saudi environment, the question of what effects does this cultural diversity have on individuals' values and preferences remains open. Despite the fact that these preferences can be studied from a variety of different perspectives, we utilize the fact that formulation of entertainment preferences in individuals' minds is resulted from the intersection of a multitude of dimensions, including the consideration of personal preferences and the acceptability of new entertainment options, for demonstrating the effectiveness of crowdsourcing in unrolling the complexities of these human factors. Thus, for each specific sub-cultural group in Saudi Arabia, we aim to show the factors that could contribute to defining what makes an entertainment option more or less preferred than the other available options. Synthesizing our observations on each group also makes it possible to draw some generalizations that are applicable for the Saudi culture as a whole and at the same time identify the perceptual similarities and differences between all the sub-cultural groups in question.

Our overarching goal is not only to provide insights for urban planners and designers in the Saudi context but also to demonstrate the ability of crowdsourcing-based visual ratings to capture quantified subjective judgments of people regardless of the complex features of their cultures, their social backgrounds or demographics. Therefore, the contributions of the present research effort are: (1) building a human-centered crowdsourcing platform for eliciting perception data in the Saudi context that is based on a new image data set of many entertainment modes, (2) exploiting entertainment as a way for uncovering the perceptual indicators of citizens and residents in Saudi Arabia, and (3) proposing a data collection model that could be generalized for gaining an improved understanding of perceptual responses on a society level while considering the subjective properties of individuals who collectively contribute to shaping the big picture of the society's overall impression.

2 Related Work

Prior work has demonstrated the effectiveness of online crowdsourced visual surveys as a technique for facilitating the collection of perception data on a large scale and enabling the interpretation and evaluation of urban impressions from multiple dimensions [1, 7]. This technique was exploited by a number of researchers for gathering data about urban perceptions of places and relating people's aggregate impressions with economic, social, demographic and cultural factors [1–3, 7]. For instance, Quercia et al. constructed a visualized map representing the collective recognizability of places in London based on the subjective responses collected via a crowdsourcing game [3]. The analysis of the perception data gathered by Quercia et al. facilitated establishing a quantified subjective ranking of the main regions in London according to the recognizability ratings obtained from the respondents [3]. Quercia et al. also demonstrated how the conducted analyses helped them uncover the correlation between a respondent's evaluation of the recognizability of a place and his/her country of residence [3]. In another research effort that crowdsourced the task of judging the beauty of London's streets, pairwise image ratings collected from a large pool of respondents helped researchers understand the role played by the aesthetic and visual features of urban environments on shaping public perceptions [2].

Salesses et al. also outsourced the task of rating images on a larger scale to explain the differences in public perceptions in a number of cities and relate the obtained quantified data to participants' social and demographic variables [1]. Using a similar approach, Ruiz-Correa et al. grounded the study of youth perceptions of outdoor environments on data gathered through crowdsourced visual surveys [9]. Particularly for indoor environments, other researchers built a characterization of place ambiance based on the analysis of image ratings gathered from Amazon Mechanical Turk crowd workers [7]. Based on the results of the experiment conducted in crowdsourcing setting, Santani and Gatica-Perez also demonstrated the applicability of using images of indoor places as stimuli for understanding the psychological factors that contribute to shaping place perceptions and examining the differences in collective impressions on a large scale [7]. Aggregate impressions of people gathered using crowdsourcing platforms were also utilized in other research attempts to particularly explore what drive people to feel unsafe in urban places [4, 10]. For instance, Traunmueller et al. found that safety perceptions of cities are affected primarily by people's familiarity of places [10]. In another interesting research effort, a platform named *Streetsmart* was particularly built to gather safety ratings about people depicted in images rather than focusing on perceptual dimensions of places [4].

The above mentioned research efforts clearly show that the scalability of image-based crowdsourced surveys enabled capturing detailed insight on people's impressions and obtaining contextualized understanding of social perceptions from multiple perspectives. Despite the tremendous advantages of this data collection approach, there exists no study that utilizes this approach for particularly understanding the collective perceptions of the local populations in Saudi Arabia. We also note that prior work has mostly focused on studying perceptual factors independently without giving considerable attention to studying the effects of the interaction of social, cultural and personal factors on shaping individuals' preferences and perceptions. Unlike previous studies, we crowdsource visual surveys for uncovering the factors that contribute to shaping entertainment-related perceptions and demonstrating the effect placed by the interaction between these factors on public perceptions in the Saudi context, a problem that has not been tackled in the preceding studies.

3 Research Methodology

We followed a structured research methodology that facilitated collecting and analyzing perception data of the participants in systematic manner (see Fig. 1). The methodology we followed for conducting this study was inspired by Salesses et al. work [1]. As the focus of this study is on uncovering the differences in perceptions of entertainment methods in the Saudi culture, we started by preparing a dataset of images, sourced from Google images, representing a wide spectrum of entertainment options.

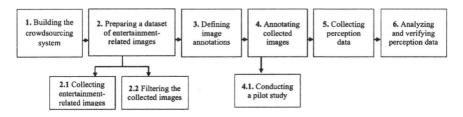

Fig. 1. The research methodology

While selecting images included in the dataset, we excluded those images that included aspects that could distract the participant from focusing on the presented entertainment option or point the participant to a specific answer rather than the other. For instance, images that included large textual descriptions or drawings were excluded. We also made sure that all images considered in the study are not of variable quality levels to avoid the possibility of not preferring an image because of its bad resolution or clarity. We also considered having more than one image of one place with different factors included in the image (e.g., having the same image in different times of the day) as this helped us study the effect of these factors on viewers' perceptions. At the end of the image collection phase, we had a dataset containing 1200 different images (see Table 1).

We then manually inspected the collected images and annotated them with labels indicating the entertainment options depicted in the image. We chose to cover a variety of entertainment elements and labeled the collected images accordingly. We also made sure that all image labels are evenly distributed across our dataset to avoid the bias resulted from having more images belonging to a particular category compared to the others. For each image, our annotations indicated whether the image represents indoor entertainment activities (e.g., shopping malls, arcades, and cafes), outdoor entertainment

Table 1. Sample of the images included in the dataset

options (e.g., parks, resorts and beaches), sports activities and special cultural and social events. We also placed labels indicating if the entrainment method depicted in the image is electronic (e.g., video games) or kinetic.

These annotations were then used to facilitate extracting the different dimensions that characterize entertainment-related perceptions in each Saudi region. As we aim to elicit users' perceptions through their image choices and since images were annotated while taking into consideration a variety of dimensions that are contributive to shaping individuals perceptions, we note that the majority of the collected images were representative of multiple entertainment preferences, depending on the inclusion of an image of human subjects, whether the image shows a sport or cultural activity and the type of entertainment option that it depicts (e.g., video games vs kinetic games). For instance, in Table 1, the choice of images **(a)**, **(h)**, **(i)** and **(l)** could mean that the participant tend to prefer outdoor entertainment options over those which exist in indoor environments. On the other hand, preferring images **(e)**, **(g)** and **(h)** signals that a user's tendency to accept non-cultural events over cultural ones is not probable. We also gave special attention to sport activities and heritage places as depicted in images **(a)** and **(d)**, respectively. After annotating all the images in the dataset, we recruited a number of students and faculty members from the College of Computer and Information Sciences at King Saud University and some social media sites for a pilot study that aimed at validating that the images included in the crowdsourcing platform capture and depict the entertainment properties in question.

The collected images were then plugged into the crowdsourcing platform built for the purpose of collecting subjective ratings on how preferable a particular entertainment mode is by allowing the random presentation of these images for each user in a visual survey form. In our crowdsourcing platform, we included one question as a basis for the visual survey which is: *"Which place looks more entertaining, fun or relaxing?"* (Figure 2 shows the crowdsourcing platform used to collect urban perceptions of entertainment in the Saudi context). A link to the developed web-based platform was then distributed to Saudi residents via social networking and instant messaging platforms such as Twitter and WhatsApp in order to collect perception data needed for the study. For each user, we collected demographic data relating to his/her gender, age group, educational background and the particular Saudi region in which he/she resides (i.e., eastern region, central region, northern region and western region). We also noted whether a participant is a Saudi citizen or a Saudi resident to explore the perceptual differences between Saudis and non-Saudis. While analyzing the collected data, we related participants' demographic and personal properties with our perception-related observations. We also noted the differences in perceptual factors between individuals belonging to different Saudi Arabian regions or cultural groups. This was followed by conducting interviews in-person with individuals belonging to these different groups in order to verify the results of the conducted analyses and gain insights on the applicability of applying crowdsourcing to capture a holistic view of entertainment-related impressions in the Saudi context.

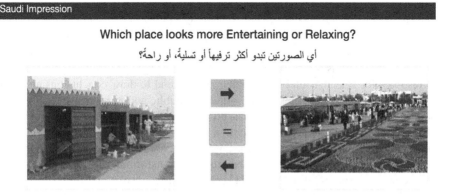

Fig. 2. Visual surveys in **Saudi-Impression** crowdsourcing system

3.1   Quantifying Perceptions

To measure users' perceptions, users' clicks were considered to give each image a weight scaling from 0 to 10, with 0 being indicative of the lowest preference and 10 the highest. The method was adapted from a similar approach proposed by Salesses et al. to quantify users' perceptions in urban areas [1]. In the crowdsourcing system, images were displayed in pairs in which both images were chosen randomly and some would be significantly attractive or superior compared to the other. For each image, the total number of image clicks was taken into account (see Eqs. 1 and 2), where Wi and Li refer to the win score and loss score of image i respectively. For a given image i, Wi, li, and ti refer to the number of win clicks, the number of loss clicks, and the number of equality clicks for the image, respectively.

$$W_i = \frac{w_i}{(w_i + l_i + t_i)} \tag{1}$$

$$L_i = \frac{l_i}{(w_i + l_i + t_i)} \tag{2}$$

The wins and losses of other paired images were also taken into account to validate each image's weight (see Eq. 3). Where Qi is the accumulated weight of an image i, niw is the total number of images i was preferred over in the pairwise comparison, nil is the total number of images that were preferred over i in the pairwise comparison, ji is the subset of images i was preferred over, and j2 is the subset of images preferred over image i. Finally, the $\frac{10}{3}$ and +1 are to scale the weight in the range 1–10.

$$Q_i = \frac{10}{3}\left(W_i + \frac{1}{n_i^w}\sum_{j_1=1}^{n_i^w} W_{j_1} - \frac{1}{n_i^l}\sum_{j_2=1}^{n_i^l} L_{j_2} + 1 \right) \tag{3}$$

4   The Role of Visual Analytics in the Study

With the introduction of social media and internet of things, large amounts of complex data and information is increasingly being made available by the public, representing a rich resource for scientists and stakeholders who intend to draw conclusions and view problems from the eye of beneficiaries within the public audience. However, the large amounts and high heterogeneity of data poses a challenge relating to analyzing and understanding data volumes in an effective way. Visual analysis has therefore been shown effective at enhancing human analyzing capabilities by exploiting computer intelligence. Visualization is simply, the study of transforming data and information into interactive visual representations [11]. Iterative, interactive and dynamic integration of human intelligence with data analysis creates a novel analysis dimension, namely, visual analytics [12].

In the context of visualizing urban perceptions, visual analysis was utilized with the aim to reveal hidden patterns and represent the structures and distributions of raw perception data. It facilitates obtaining global understanding of entertainment preferences while correlating entertainment variables between different regions or sub categorize or sub groups. For the purpose of visualizing perception data collected for the present study, a number of visualization techniques could be employed for discovering the differences in perception among different Saudi cultural contexts while uncovering the common themes in perception between different Saudi regions or different generations. Grounding the visualization of collected perception data on the Q-scores recorded for each image and relating these scores with the personal and demographic variables collected from each participant is expected to help in understanding how different cultural groups prioritize entertainment modes. This would also provide urban planners with a tool that informs their design of entertainment modes in each sub-cultural group while allowing users to grasp complex properties effortlessly.

It is also noteworthy to mention that since *Saudi Impression* is a real-time online tool, instant visualization will allow the observation of how collective perceptions of Saudis change over time by giving the capability to present real-time visualization of perceptions. For instance, point-based visualization could be used to plot information about the participants, while representing each individual by a single dot in the Saudi region on the map where the participants belong to and with the color of the dot being the indicator of the age group or the gender of the participant. The advantage of the dot-based visualization is that it provides the viewer with the ability to observe the state of every single object independently. But when the data accumulates for many objects as time passes, dot-based representations could become infeasible as the visualization becomes complex and hard to understand [13]. A good alternative could be using heatmap to illustrate the integrated amount of a large number of objects on the Saudi map [13].

Furthermore, the perceptions of the respondents from each Saudi region could be reflected on cartograms with each cartogram representing the perceptions of individuals belonging to each geographical region, with the dark shade representing low Q-score values and the lighter shade being reflective of high Q-score values. Region-based representation is suitable for showing the relevant preference of each region compared to its neighbors by revealing hidden macro-patterns [14]. On the other hand, it is incapable to analyze micro patterns so it is commonly used in combination with other techniques that can go to more detailed levels.

Bubble charts could be used to display the set of Q-scores with each bubble corresponding to different entertainment mode and the size of the bubbles representing the mean Q-score values. For instance, the analysis of responses from the large and industrial cities in the Central and Eastern regions of Saudi Arabia, where the majority of the population are youth, could reflect that sport activities and indoor entertainment are more preferred than other types of entertainment (see Fig. 3). On the other hand, outdoor entertainment could outperform other types of entertainment in the Southern region of Saudi Arabia due to the moderate weather.

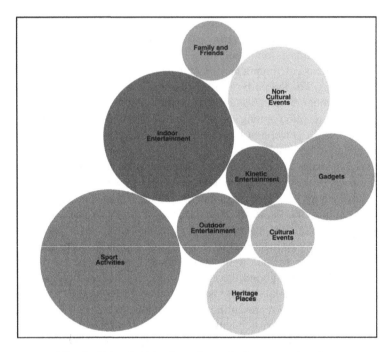

Fig. 3. Using bubble charts for analyzing perception data

5   Conclusion, Limitations and Future Work

The aim of this work is not only to understand the Saudi view of entertainment and explore the potential areas of improvements in entertainment but also to provide a tool that can be easily generalized to read the audience visual perceptions on any topic and in turn anticipate those perceptions in measurable deliverables to the beneficiaries, whether they are from the public, business or government. The rationale of using a visual survey for reading audience perceptions in an area like entertainment is that entertaining facilities have properties, such as ambiance, natural surroundings and social interactions that cannot be collectively measured by the traditional approaches which takes only tradable factors into account. The strength of the pair-image comparison approach comes from the flexibility to be applied on any topic with pre-collected related images and proposing any question of interest. It also has the advantage of simplicity where participants involved with different demographics whether they are tech savvy youth or non-technology oriented elderly they all have the capability to participate and even enjoy the game like questionnaire. It also allows reaching a reasonable characterization of individuals' preferences and encompassing the whole range of factors affecting the perceptions of individuals even if they belong to different cultural groups or geographical regions.

In the course of this study, a number of limitations have raised that allow for future enhancements. First, since the sample pictures were sourced from Google images, we lacked the full control of the quality or resolution which may affect the user perception of the image content. In some cases, the angle of the image may put the focus or distract the viewer from observing some image contents. In future work, we aim to collect a dataset of manually taken images where we can unify the ambiance of sample images. This piece of research contributes to set a crowdsourcing approach to understand the collective public perception of participants who are not physically located or interacting with the objects under study. A flexible approach which can be generalized on any topic with a set of images that satisfies measurable dimensions.

References

1. Salesses, P., Schechtner, K., Hidalgo, C.A.: The collaborative image of the city: mapping the inequality of urban perception. PLoS ONE **8**, 1–12 (2013)
2. Quercia, D., O'Hare, N.K., Cramer, H.: Aesthetic capital: what makes london look beautiful, quiet, and happy? In: Proceedings of the 17th ACM Conference on Computer supported Cooperative Work & Social Computing (2014)
3. Quercia, D., Pesce, J.P., Almeida, V., Crowcroft, J.: Psychological maps 2.0: a web engagement enterprise starting in London. In: Proceedings of the 22nd International Conference on World Wide Web (2013)
4. Traunmueller, M., Marshall, P., Capra, L.: Crowdsourcing safety perceptions of people: opportunities and limitations. In: Liu, T.Y., Scollon, C., Zhu, W. (eds.) Social Informatics. LNCS, vol. 9471, pp. 120–135. Springer, Cham (2015). doi:10.1007/978-3-319-27433-1_9
5. Alsaleh, M., Alomar, N., Alarifi, A.: Smartphone users: understanding how security mechanisms are perceived and new persuasive methods. PloS One **12**(3), e0173284 (2017)
6. Al-Ageel, N., Al-Wabil, A., Badr, G., AlOmar, N.: Human factors in the design and evaluation of bioinformatics tools. Procedia Manuf. **3**, 2003–2010 (2015)
7. Santani, D., Gatica-Perez, D.: Loud and trendy: Crowdsourcing impressions of social ambiance in popular indoor urban places. In: Proceedings of the 23rd ACM international conference on Multimedia (2015)
8. Alomar, N., Wanick, V., Wills, G.: The design of a hybrid cultural model for Arabic gamified systems. Comput. Hum. Behav. **64**, 472–485 (2016)
9. Ruiz-Correa, S., Santani, D., Gatica-Perez, D.: The young and the city: Crowdsourcing urban awareness in a developing country. In: Proceedings of the First International Conference on IoT in Urban Space (2014)
10. Traunmueller, M., Marshall, P., Capra, L.: when you're a stranger: evaluating safety perceptions of (un) familiar Urban places. In: Proceedings of the Second International Conference on IoT in Urban Space (2016)
11. Liu, S., Cui, W., Wu, Y., Liu, M.: A survey on information visualization: recent advances and challenges. Vis. Comput. **30**(12), 1373–1393 (2014)
12. Cook, K.A., Thomas, J.J.: Illuminating the path: the research and development agenda for visual analytics. IEEE Computer Society, Richland (2005)
13. Chen, W., Guo, F., Wang, F.-Y.: A survey of traffic data visualization. IEEE Trans. Intell. Trans. Syst. **16**, 2970–2984 (2015)
14. Zheng, Y., Wu, W., Chen, Y., Qu, H., Ni, L.M.: Visual analytics in Urban computing: an overview. IEEE Trans. Big Data **2**, 276–296 (2016)

Getting Interrupted? Design Support Strategies for Learning Success in M-Learning Applications

Upasna Bhandari[✉] and Klarissa Chang

Department of Information Systems, School of Computing,
National University of Singapore, Singapore, Singapore
upasna.bhandari@u.nus.edu.sg, changtt@comp.nus.edu.sg

Abstract. This study explores how interruption support from a design stand-point can impact learning and resumption success with mobile applications. Building upon memory for goals theory, we propose that metacognitive support and interactive immediacy are two interruption support features that can increase user's learning and resumption success. We also propose that these effects are moderated by the task complexity that user is achieving with the app. We aim to find a fit between task and feature that will guide developers and designers to support users during interruptions. The proposed hypothesis will be tested with laboratory experiments.

Keywords: Mobile applications · Memory for goals · Cognitive load · Interruptions

1 Introduction

Global market for mobile learning products and services will reach \$37.60 billion in 2020[1] with revenues doubling in more than 66 countries (Lim and Churchill 2016).

Mobile learning, also referred to as m-learning (Biggs and Justice 2011) is defined as learning with the use of mobile or portable devices anywhere and at any time (Costabile et al. 2008; Deegan 2015; Sinclair 2011). By introducing new and unique ways of learning, m-learning is now replacing traditional learning facets and improves learning performance (Sinclair 2011; Wang and Shen 2012). It has reached a mature stage and became "mainstream" in countries such as the United States, Japan, South Korea, Singapore, and in Northern Europe (Sanakulov and Karjaluoto 2015). Mobile network connectivity provides fast access to current learning materials and enables quick communication and collaboration among the users (Biggs and Justice 2011; Sinclair 2011). However, poorly designed systems that do not incorporate learning environment present certain challenges. Often times which leads to decreased learning performance. These challenges can range from technical issues (slow performance, poor internet connection etc.), general usability issues (Deegan 2015), design of learning materials (Wang and Shen 2012), and also the *learner's environment* (Deegan 2015). While usability and designing appropriate material has received considerable

© Springer International Publishing AG 2017
G. Meiselwitz (Ed.): SCSM 2017, Part I, LNCS 10282, pp. 32–43, 2017.
DOI: 10.1007/978-3-319-58559-8_4

attention, much less focus has been paid to learning environment (Hoehle and Venkatesh 2015; Adipat et al. 2011).

Deegan emphasizes that the main source of possible distractions and interruptions for the learner exists in the environment (Deegan 2015). According to a study, interruptions impose a higher cognitive load on the learner and, thus, impair his or her learning performance (Costa and McCrae 1990). With increased cognitive load also comes less efficiency and accuracy while performing tasks (Wickens et al. 2000; Albers and Kim 2000). Furthermore, the ability to resume the main task post interruption is impaired by interruption characteristics. It was found that 41% of tasks remain un-resumed after interruptions (Mark et al. 2005). Some task takes up to 25 min to be resumed (Mark et al. 2005). Thus mobile applications that are designed for mobile learning have to address the issue of interruptions faced learning. Therefore, our main research question is:

RQ: *What are the design requirements of learning based mobile applications that support interruptions for higher learning success?*

Design is one of the main components of learning environments. Gamification has been a major influence in the education context (Nah et al. 2014; Nah et al. 2013). Studies have looked at interface aesthetics (Bhandari and Chang 2014; Cyr et al. 2006; Sonderegger and Sauer 2009), color and menu icons (Sonderegger et al. 2012), and graphics (Wells et al. 2011), but enough focus has not been paid on design from an interruption perspective. One of the major design guideline for developers by Apple is to be prepared for interruptions (Apple 2012). Very few studies have synthesized the existing body of research on learning interruptions in order to derive theory-based IS design recommendations.

Our study looks at long term use of technology and since interruptions have known to effect task performance (Speier et al. 2003), decision making (Speier et al. 1999; Xia and Sudharshan 2002), usage (Rennecker and Godwin 2005) and thus is of extreme important to the area of information systems. By exploring design principles specifically for m-learning domain we are contributing to the theory of interruptions for learning success and practically guiding developers to design for interruptions.

The paper proceeds as follows: we discuss relevant prior literature in the next section. After that we present research model and hypothesis. Post that we discuss research methodology and finally present the potential contributions.

2 Theoretical Background

2.1 M-Learning

Learning has been defined in literature as *"the acquisition and development of memories and behaviors, including skills, knowledge, understanding, values, and wisdom"* (Deegan 2015). Psychology take a different perspective and defines it as commitment of changes to the long-term memory (Craik and Lockhart 1972; Eysenck and Keane 2000).

Even though research in the domain of mobile technologies an devices and it associated theories has been progressing, it is very disparate (Alrasheedi et al. 2015). Scope dependency is a major factor in defining learning (Alrasheedi et al. 2015; Trifonova and Ronchetti 2003). Since e-leering was the predominant domain when studying learning the definition is also heavily borrowed dorm this discipline. It can also be described as fusion of E-Learning and mobile technologies: "mobile devices are a natural extension of e-learning" (Kossen 2001).

Thus we adapt the definition of mobile learning by (Deegan 2015), who defines it as learning with the aid of mobile or portable devices anywhere and at any time. Mobile devices are often connected to a mobile network and, thus, enable an on-demand access to learning materials and collaboration with other learners (McQuiggan et al. 2015).

2.2   Interruption and Interruption Complexity

Interruption is defined as an *"externally-generated, randomly occurring, discrete event that breaks continuity of cognitive focus on a primary task"* (Botha et al. 2010; Coraggio 1990). In order to understand the design guidelines for learning based mobile apps it is important to understand what factors lead to decreased performance in learning and how to counteract them. Interruptions in e-learning environment and m-learning environments are quite unique. While in e-leering interruptions can be more task based, in m-learning lot of interruptions are environment based. For e.g. halting the learning process due to noisy background or having a phone in between and resuming subsequent task on the mobile device. M-leaning has its advantages in the form of freedom and portability in learning and choosing the environment, the inherent issues remain. This causes extra cognitive load on the learner as he needs to recuperate from these environmental interruptions (Botha et al. 2010; Deegan 2015; Costabile et al. 2008).

When considering in depth what kind of negative effect interruptions has on lining we can refer o study by Morgan et al. 2009 where they categorized the negative effects into following broad categories: forgetting to resume from an interruption, delays in resumption of the primary task, decreased efficiency, decreased accuracy, and stress elevation (Morgan et al. 2009). Even when user intends to resume the task after being interrupted t is in most cases unsuccessful (Einstein et al. 2003). A study showed that because of delay in retrieval of required information, the task resumption is enhanced (Hodgetts and Jones 2006). Resumption of a task can be measured by the time lag between interruption of primary task and resumption of primary task. This effects performance and accuracy (Eyrolle and Cellier 2000) (Flynn et al. 1999). Study also showed that the effect of interruption could be seen in elevated levels of mental stress (Zijlstra et al. 1999).

According to Botha, interruptions decrease the learner's attention span. In this context, this paper defines interrupted learning as learning that occurs at irregular intervals, each of which receives only a short attention span by the learner (Botha et al. 2010).

2.3 Designing for Interruptions: Memory for Goals

We store information in two forms of memory: namely short term memory and long term memory. Information that we perceive with our perceptual senses is stored in short term memory. However information that receives our attention passes from short term to long term memory. Tasks that occur at regular interval can eventually be stored in long-term memory, while small interruptions like a phone call while reading, knock in the door while playing a game are short term interruptions (Paas et al. 2004; McQuiggan et al. 2015).

In terms of executing complex task requiring cognitive resources short term memory is not the adequate part of memory to be used, the long term working memory is more useful to retrieve and then process the information required for completing cognitive complex task. (Eysenck and Keane 2000; Shrager et al. 2008). Distractions have been found to interrupt the primary task and thus take up working memory resources (Sweller 1988).

Memory for Goals (MFG) is "a theory of cognitive control that explains goal memory in terms of general declarative memory constructs, such as activation and associative priming, rather than using a special goal memory or control structure, such as a goal stack" (Altmanna and Trafton 2002). Goals stored in the memory compete for higher control of cognitive resources. Decision of which goals gets activated depends on which goal holds the highest instantaneous activation value. Activation is a function of total number of times an item from memory has been retrieved in given time frame and the length if the above mentioned timeframe. Thus it is combining usage history and the current requirements together so that the cognitive system can deal with memory decay and keep the information needed alive.

Specifically for interruptions, the memory for goals theory suggests that there are two important ways of reducing memory decay with respect to goals: rehearsal and using environmental cues. Rehearsal is done in two ways, retrospection (e.g., "What was I doing till now?") or in a prospection (e.g., "What was I about to do?") (Altmanna and Trafton 2002). Both are important, however people prefer to use prospective introspection when needed (Trafton et al. 2003). Another factor that can help in activation of a goal in our model is to prime using external mnemonics. External cues when added, they further add to the activation to any goals with which they are associated (Dodhia and Dismukes 2009). This expansion of activation is added to the activation produced using heuristics. This is based on assumption that the goal will have decayed during the interval of the interruption. Studies have shown that system designers should keep "interaction chains" (the number of interface actions that lead to a goal or sub goal) quite short (Oulasvirta and Saariluoma 2006). The amount of time is not guided by theory, but 20 s currently used by designers.

3 Research Model and Hypothesis

3.1 External Mnemonics/Metacognitive Processes Support

Using prospective memory theory framework, it can be inferred that reminders causes a person to explicitly encode an intention to resume, which should facilitate performance

(Trafton et al. 2003). Studies found that the use of a blue dot cue improves performance upon resumption of the task (Finstad et al. 2006). People who are constantly interrupted by to real-time interruptions and tasks that need prospective memory can great benefit from reminders. To set free working memory resources, the mobile application should provide an implementation of an external prospective memory (Einstein et al. 2003; Morgan et al. 2009) (Fig. 1) .

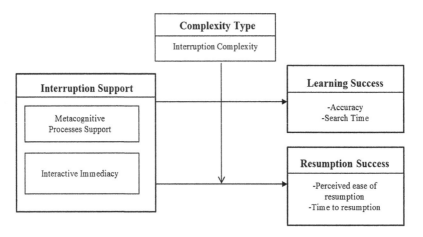

Fig. 1.   Research framework

Consistent with this predictions studies found that reminders facilitate resumptions. Resumption is defined as abandoning/attending the interruption task and returning to primary task (Dodhia and Dismukes 2009; Dismukes 2010). The external prospective memory is an information storage which the learner can use to outsource information – in contrast to reminder cues relatively high quantities – from his working memory for a later use (McDaniel et al. 2004). Following the above, we hypothesize:

H1 (a): *For information browsing via mobile applications, design features supporting external mnemonic will lead to increase in learning success.*

H1 (b): *For information browsing via mobile applications, design features supporting external mnemonic will lead to increase in resumption success.*

3.2   Contextual Cues/Interactive Immediacy

Memory for goals theory explains that when the learner's environment alters or there is little information from environmental context, the goal will be more difficult to resume (Altmanna and Trafton 2002). However, highlighting the context via environmental cues can facilitate resumption. The theory provides a very specific process description: the environmental cue adds activation to the goal that was suspended by the interruption. For example, a user is switching between two tasks (e-mail and making a graph in Microsoft excel). When switching to the graphing task after an interruption, it would be helpful to present some environmental or contextual cues (Dodhia and Dismukes 2009). To aid in reorientation in such a scenario information like "tasks already completed", "next task to do" is helpful.

This is in line with activation based memory for goals model which focuses in the resumption of an interrupted task. By activating the specific goal needed to ensure resumption of primary task this framework highlights the importance of contextual cues (Altmanna and Trafton 2002). For e.g. three colors coded arrows can show the user's previous three steps: light red (top arrow) to bright red (bottom arrow). This type of color order has been shown to be a natural way of presenting ordered and quantitative data (much like task statistics) for task performance (Spence et al. 1999; Breslow et al. 2009). Interface facilitation in earlier empirical work has been strongly recommended to support resumption (Trafton et al. 2003), although the task was quite different from traditional office work. This is supported by the memory for spatial location paradigm where participants generally are able to return to the location of where they left for.

Following the above our hypothesis is proposed as follows:

H2 (a): *For information browsing via mobile applications, design features supporting contextual cues will lead to* increase in learning success.

H2 (b): *For information browsing via mobile applications, design features supporting contextual cues will lead to increase in resumption success.*

Memory of goals theory suggests that the length of interruption can determine how adversely it impacts the outcome. The more complex an interruption the more rehearsal or external cues it will be needed to slow down the decay. Also that includes higher external mnemonics to support resumptions. It was found that subtle external mnemonics like cursor pointing to last point of action was ineffective. This calls for combining design strategies that can combat the effect of complex interruptions (Trafton et al. 2003). Finally, as the complexity of interruption during browsing task increases (e.g., frequency of interruption, duration of interruption etc.), the need for information scents to help locate desirable information will be stronger (Coraggio 1990). As discussed earlier, we predict that interruption complexity positively moderates the individual effect of external mnemonic and contextual cues on users' learning performance and perception. Therefore, we expect that as interruption complexity increases, the effect of adding integrated adaptation of external mnemonic and contextual cues to basic design will be stronger than that of adding external mnemonic and contextual cues separately. Our hypothesis is proposed as follows:

H3: *The greater the interruption task complexity, the greater the positive effect of adding* **both** *external mnemonic and contextual cues, as compared to adding* **only** *one of them on*

(a) *Learning success*
(b) *Resumption success*

4 Research Methodologies and Data Analysis

4.1 Design Principles for Interruptions in M-Learning

This is a research-in-progress paper that uses an experiment to examine influence of interface design guided by memory for goals theory and interruption theory on learning success. Majority of users use mobile application simply for content viewing. These applications are popularly known as "content aggregators". They provide magazine style interface to view information in articles. Users also browse through multiple pages in mobile learning applications. These are more goal-oriented applications. The information contained can vary from text, images, hyperlinks etc. Supporting for interruptions is a challenging task for both these categories of learning applications. In this study we focus on the first type of applications simply because they are more affected by lack of support for interruptions, as intrinsic motivation to resume the task is low. Also they are more popular type of applications.

We first analyzed learning based applications in the appstore from category *"Education"*. (https://itunes.apple.com/us/genre/ios-education/id6017?mt=8). We excluded free applications from our set, as it is much harder to control for quality in this category. Meta level design requirements were extracted specific to interruptions in m-learning, which then resulted in design considerations corresponding to these meta-requirements. The aim is to ensure that our selection of interruption support principles as guided by memory for goals theory and prospective framework theory map to the real world scenario. The meta-level design requirements are mapped to the extant literature and broadly divided in to two categories (a) meta-cognitive process support and (b) interactive immediacy.

4.2 Experiments

We aim to test the hypothesis in laboratory experiments with a $2 \times 2 \times 2$ factorial design. Interruption support design factors: meta-cognitive support (high/low) and interactive immediacy (high/low) is within subject factor. Interruption complexity (high/low) will be a between subjects factor. Participants will be asked to perform multiple tasks while manipulating levels of interruption design support. A different mobile application is used for each of the conditions. These applications will be experimentally designed guided by literature and current app development design guidelines. We intend to use repeated measures ANOVA to analyze the effect of interruption support design and interruption complexity. We will also check for Bonferroni multiple comparison because it is a robust multiple comparisons method suited for within-subjects design (Maxwell and Delaney 2000).

Dependent and Independent Variables. For manipulating meta-cognitive support, we follow studies mentioned in Table 1. Information is broken down into easy reading chunks rather than long running paragraphs. No scrolling is involved in condition of high meta-cognitive support (all the information is contained in one page). Easy navigation capabilities are provided and are placed at the bottom rather than at the top.

Table 1. Design guidelines synthesized from existing literature and existing mobile applications applying them.

Design Considerations for Learning Based Mobile Application	Conceptualization (Based on Literature and Existing Design Practices)	Design Strategies (SAT UP)
Metacognitive Processes Support (External Mnemonics) (McQuiggan et al. 2015; Morgan et al. 2009) (Sweller 2006) (Einstein et al. 2003)	Having information being broken into condensed chunks to enhance selective user attention allocation can assist preparing for resumption from interruption. Unwanted information is not displayed. Relevant information in condensed chunks is displayed due to limited screen size. Elements in the interface design need to be consistent and simple to reduce extra cognitive load. • *Notifications are provided for supporting resumptions from interruptions.*	Image 1
Interactive Immediacy (Contextual Cues) (McQuiggan et al. 2015) (Cypher 1986) (Franke et al. 2002) (Morgan et al. 2009)	Designing mobile application to have interactive features facilitating learning through interaction and providing feedback for user actions. An interruption can be followd by a history of the interruption characteristics. When the interruption happened, how long it lasted etc. Along with this, pre interruption tasks and post interruption tasks can be displayed. The user should have the possibility to re-assess important information he overlooked or neglected. • *When user returns to the main task, information is presented for easy access of tasks already completed and the upcoming tasks to aid in resumption.*	Image 2

Source for Image 1 and 2: https://itunes.apple.com/sg/app/sat-up-new-sat-test-preptutoring/id582 725370?mt=8

For interactive immediacy, intention based reminder cues are presented as user finishes the interruption task. Lack of such reminders would be the low manipulation of immediacy feedback. Also external mnemonics like a colored arrow is provided referring to steps completed further steps to be completed and corresponding details.

In this study users are asked to find answers to simple fact based questions (Adipat et al. 2011). Accuracy is the objective measures which captures whether the number of correct responses. Search time is measured as time taken to finish the task. Time to resumption is the lag between suspension of primary task and resuming form interrupted task. After the user finished the task on his/her assigned application, they proceed to fill a survey-based questionnaire measuring perceived ease of resumption. Perceived ease of resumption is subjective measure capturing how easily they think they resumed the primary task.

5 Contributions

The study has contributions to both theory and practice. Theoretically we develop a unique set of design factors specific to learning on mobile platforms using memory for goals theory. Further interruption theory is used to understand complexity as a potential moderator for the relationship between interruption design principles and learning success. Practical contributions include guiding practitioners to understand how to tackle interruptions as a major source of hindrance in learning on mobile apps. Also design principles like meta-cognitive support features and immediacy are useful for developers in ensuring long term learning success for their mobile applications.

References

Adipat, B., Zhang, D., Zhou, L.: The effects of tree-view based presentation adaptation on mobile web browsing. MIS Q. **35**(1), 99–122 (2011)

Albers, M.J., Kim, L: User web browsing characteristics using palm handhelds for information retrieval. In: Professional Communication Conference. Proceedings of 2000 Joint IEEE International and 18th Annual Conference on Computer Documentation (IPCC/SIGDOC 2000), pp. 125–135. IEEE (2000)

Alrasheedi, M., Capretz, L.F., Raza, A.: A systematic review of the critical factors for success of mobile learning in higher education (University students' perspective). J. Educ. Comput. Res. **52**(2), 257–276 (2015)

Altmanna, E.M., Trafton, J.G.: "Memories for goals: an activation-based model" [Cognitive Science 26 (2002) 39–83]. Cogn. Sci. **26**(2), 233 (2002)

Barnaghi, P.M., Kareem, S.A.: Ontology-based multimedia presentation generation. In: TENCON 2005 IEEE Region 10, pp. 1–5. IEEE (2005)

Bhandari, U., Chang, K.: Role of Emotions and Aesthetics in ICT Usage for Underserved Communities: A Neurois Investigation (2014)

Biggs, B., Justice, R.: M-Learning: the next evolution. Chief Learn. Officer **10**(4), 38–41 (2011)

Botha, A., Herselman, M., van Greunen, D.: Mobile user experience in a mlearning environment. In: Proceedings of the 2010 Annual Research Conference of the South African Institute of Computer Scientists and Information Technologists, pp. 29–38. ACM (2010)

Breslow, L.A., Trafton, J.G., Ratwani, R.M.: A perceptual process approach to selecting color scales for complex visualizations. J. Exp. Psychol. Appl. **15**(1), 25 (2009)

Chen, Y., Ma, W.-Y., Zhang, H.-J.: Detecting web page structure for adaptive viewing on small form factor devices. In: Proceedings of the 12th International Conference on World Wide Web, pp. 225–233. ACM (2003)

Coraggio, L.: Deleterious Effects of Intermittent Interruptions on the Task Performance of Knowledge Workers: A Laboratory Investigation (1990)

Costa Jr., P.T., McCrae, R.R.: Personality: another'hidden factor'is stress research. Psychol. Inq. 1(1), 22–24 (1990)

Costabile, M.F., De Angeli, A., Lanzilotti, R., Ardito, C., Buono, P., Pederson, T.: Explore! possibilities and challenges of mobile learning. In: Proceedings of the SIGCHI Conference on Human Factors in Computing Systems, pp. 145–154. ACM (2008)

Coyle, J.R., Thorson, E.: The effects of progressive levels of interactivity and vividness in web marketing sites. J. Advertising 30(3), 65–77 (2001)

Craik, F.I., Lockhart, R.S.: Levels of processing: a framework for memory research. J. Verbal Learn. Verbal Behav. 11(6), 671–684 (1972)

Cypher, A.: The Structure of Users' Activities. In: User Centered System Design, pp. 243–263 (1986)

Cyr, D., Head, M., Ivanov, A.: Design aesthetics leading to M-Loyalty in mobile commerce. Inf. Manag. 43(8), 950–963 (2006)

Deegan, R.: Complex mobile learning that adapts to learners' cognitive load. Int. J. Mob. Blended Learn. (IJMBL) 7(1), 13–24 (2015)

Dismukes, R.K.: Remembrance of things future: prospective memory in laboratory, workplace, and everyday settings. Rev. Hum. Factors Ergon. 6(1), 79–122 (2010)

Dodhia, R.M., Dismukes, R.K.: Interruptions create prospective memory tasks. Appl. Cogn. Psychol. 23(1), 73–89 (2009)

Einstein, G.O., McDaniel, M.A., Williford, C.L., Pagan, J.L., Dismukes, R.: Forgetting of intentions in demanding situations is rapid. J. Exp. Psychol. Appl. 9(3), 147 (2003)

Eyrolle, H., Cellier, J.-M.: The effects of interruptions in work activity: field and laboratory results. Appl. Ergon. 31(5), 537–543 (2000)

Eysenck, M.W., Keane, M.T.: Cognitive Psychology: A Student's Handbook. Taylor & Francis, Abingdon (2000)

Finstad, K., Bink, M., McDaniel, M., Einstein, G.O.: Breaks and task switches in prospective memory. Appl. Cogn. Psychol. 20(5), 705–712 (2006)

Flynn, E.A., Barker, K.N., Gibson, J.T., Pearson, R.E., Berger, B.A., Smith, L.A.: Impact of interruptions and distractions on dispensing errors in an ambulatory care pharmacy. Am. J. Health Syst. Pharm. 56, 1319–1325 (1999)

Franke, J.L., Daniels, J.J., McFarlane, D.C.: Recovering context after interruption. In: Proceedings 24th Annual Meeting of the Cognitive Science Society (CogSci 2002), pp. 310–315 (2002)

Harvey, N., Bolger, F.: Graphs versus tables: effects of data presentation format on judgemental forecasting. Int. J. Forecast. 12(1), 119–137 (1996)

Hodgetts, H.M., Jones, D.M.: Contextual cues aid recovery from interruption: the role of associative activation. J. Exp. Psychol. Learn. Memory Cogn. 32(5), p. 1120 (2006)

Hoehle, H., Venkatesh, V.: Mobile application usability: conceptualization and instrument development. MIS Q. 39(2), 435–472 (2015)

Jiang, Z., Benbasat, I.: The effects of interactivity and vividness of functional control in changing web consumers' attitudes. In: ICIS 2003 proceedings, p. 93 (2003)

Kossen, J.S.: When E-Learning Becomes M-Learning. Palmpower Magazine Enterprise Edition (6) (2001)

Lim, C.P., Churchill, D.: Mobile Learning. In: Interactive Learning Environments (2016)

Mark, G., Gonzalez, V.M., Harris, J.: No task left behind?: examining the nature of fragmented work. In: Proceedings of the SIGCHI Conference on Human Factors in Computing Systems, pp. 321–330. ACM (2005)

Maxwell, S., Delaney, H.: Early Designing Experiments and Analyzing Data. Erlbaum, Mahwah (2000)

McDaniel, M.A., Einstein, G.O., Graham, T., Rall, E.: Delaying execution of intentions: overcoming the costs of interruptions. Appl. Cogn. Psychol. **18**(5), 533–547 (2004)

McQuiggan, S., McQuiggan, J., Sabourin, J., Kosturko, L.: Mobile Learning: A Handbook for Developers, Educators, and Learners. Wiley, Hoboken (2015)

Morgan, P.L., Patrick, J., Waldron, S.M., King, S.L., Patrick, T.: Improving memory after interruption: exploiting soft constraints and manipulating information access cost. J. Exp. Psychol. Appl. **15**(4), 291 (2009)

Nah, F.F.-H., Eschenbrenner, B., Zeng, Q., Telaprolu, V.R., Sepehr, S.: Flow in gaming: literature synthesis and framework development. Int. J. Inf. Syst. Manag. **1**(1–2), 83–124 (2014)

Nah, F.F.-H., Telaprolu, V.R., Rallapalli, S., Venkata, P.R.: Gamification of education using computer games. In: Yamamoto, S. (ed.) HIMI 2013. LNCS, vol. 8018, pp. 99–107. Springer, Heidelberg (2013). doi:10.1007/978-3-642-39226-9_12

Oulasvirta, A., Saariluoma, P.: Surviving task interruptions: investigating the implications of long-term working memory theory. Int. J. Hum.-Comput. Stud. **64**(10), 941–961 (2006)

Paas, F., Renkl, A., Sweller, J.: Cognitive load theory: instructional implications of the interaction between information structures and cognitive architecture. Instr. Sci. **32**(1), 1–8 (2004)

Press Releases. Markets and Markets.com http://www.marketsandmarkets.com/Market-Reports/mobile-learning-market-73008174.html

Rennecker, J., Godwin, L.: Delays and interruptions: a self-perpetuating paradox of communication technology use. Inf. Organ. **15**(3), 247–266 (2005)

Sanakulov, N., Karjaluoto, H.: Consumer adoption of mobile technologies: a literature review. Int. J. Mob. Commun. **13**(3), 244–275 (2015)

Sears, A., Shneiderman, B.: Split menus: effectively using selection frequency to organize menus. ACM Trans. Comput.-Hum. Interact. (TOCHI) **1**(1), 27–51 (1994)

Shrager, Y., Levy, D.A., Hopkins, R.O., Squire, L.R.: Working memory and the organization of brain systems. J. Neurosci. **28**(18), 4818–4822 (2008)

Sonderegger, A., Sauer, J.: The influence of laboratory set-up in usability tests: effects on user performance, subjective ratings and physiological measures. Ergonomics **52**(11), 1350–1361 (2009)

Sonderegger, A., Zbinden, G., Uebelbacher, A., Sauer, J.: The influence of product aesthetics and usability over the course of time: a longitudinal field experiment. Ergonomics **55**(7), 713–730 (2012)

Speier, C., Valacich, J.S., Vessey, I.: The influence of task interruption on individual decision making: an information overload perspective. Decis. Sci. **30**(2), 337–360 (1999)

Speier, C., Vessey, I., Valacich, J.S.: The effects of interruptions, task complexity, and information presentation on computer-supported decision-making performance. Decis. Sci. **34**(4), 771–797 (2003)

Spence, I., Kutlesa, N., Rose, D.L.: Using color to code quantity in spatial displays. J. Exp. Psychol. Appl. **5**(4), 393 (1999)

Sundar, S.S., Kim, J.: Interactivity and persuasion: influencing attitudes with information and involvement. J. Interact. Advertising **5**(2), 5–18 (2005)

Sweller, J.: Cognitive load during problem solving: effects on learning. Cogn. Sci. **12**(2), 257–285 (1988)

Sweller, J.: Discussion of 'emerging topics in cognitive load research: using learner and information characteristics in the design of powerful learning environments'. Appl. Cogn. Psychol. **20**(3), 353–357 (2006)

Trafton, J.G., Altmann, E.M., Brock, D.P., Mintz, F.E.: Preparing to resume an interrupted task: effects of prospective goal encoding and retrospective rehearsal. Int. J. Hum.-Comput. Stud. **58**(5), 583–603 (2003)

Trifonova, A., Ronchetti, M.: Where is mobile learning going. In: Proceedings of World Conference on E-Learning in Corporate, Government, Healthcare, and Higher Education, pp. 1794–1801 (2003)

Vessey, I.: Cognitive fit: a theory-based analysis of the graphs versus tables literature. Decis. Sci. **22**(2), 219–240 (1991)

Wang, M., Shen, R.: Message design for mobile learning: learning theories, human cognition and design principles. British J. Educ. Technol. **43**(4), 561–575 (2012)

Wells, J.D., Parboteeah, V., Valacich, J.S.: Online impulse buying: understanding the interplay between consumer impulsiveness and website quality. J. Assoc. Inf. Syst. **12**(1), 32 (2011)

Wickens, C.D., Gempler, K., Morphew, M.E.: Workload and reliability of predictor displays in aircraft traffic avoidance. Transp. Hum. Factors **2**(2), 99–126 (2000)

Xia, L., Sudharshan, D.: Effects of interruptions on consumer online decision processes. J. Consum. Psychol. **12**(3), 265–280 (2002)

Zijlstra, F.R., Roe, R.A., Leonora, A.B., Krediet, I.: Temporal factors in mental work: effects of interrupted activities. J. Occup. Organ. Psychol. **72**(2), 163–185 (1999)

World of Streaming. Motivation and Gratification on Twitch

Daniel Gros$^{(\boxtimes)}$, Brigitta Wanner, Anna Hackenholt, Piotr Zawadzki, and Kathrin Knautz

Heinrich Heine University Düsseldorf, Dusseldorf, Germany
{daniel.gros, brigitta.wanner, anna.hackenholt,
piotr.zawadzki, kathrin.knautz}@hhu.de

Abstract. Within the gaming industry, live-streaming is becoming very popular as a form of online entertainment. Especially the so called social live streaming services (SLSSs) as a new type of social media have established in the last few years.

Subsequently a new web topic-specific live streaming service solely for streaming video games has emerged. One of the most prominent and current examples is Twitch.tv which provides the opportunity for streamers to broadcast a game and react to viewers' comments just-in-time. The viewers however watch the stream with the option to communicate either with the streamer or with other participants through a chat.

The main goal of this study is to determine the motivation and behavior of Twitch users. Therefore, a research model including research questions has been developed. This model contains the dimensions 'Information', 'Entertainment' and 'Socialization' which were investigated in relation to the average time spent on Twitch as well as potential expenses. The data for the analysis originates from a developed questionnaire (n = 791) and provides interesting results. One of the key findings reveals a connection between the time and money users spend on Twitch. Of particular note is also the significance of the dimension 'Socialization'.

Keywords: Streaming · Social live streaming services · Twitch · Use · Gratification · Motivation · Money · Media usage

1 Introduction

One of the most prominent examples for social live streaming services is Twitch with collectively more than 459,000 years-worth of video [1]. These streams mainly deal with video games that are broadcasted.

Nowadays, more and more internet users not only consume information but also actively produce it. Toffler characterized this type of user as "prosumers" [2]. Consumers, producers and prosumers use streaming platforms. Concerning Twitch, consumers only watch streams, producers solely stream and prosumers do both. Users who only watch streams are called viewers and users who stream and sometimes also watch streams are streamers. Besides streaming, a major part is real-time communication

© Springer International Publishing AG 2017
G. Meiselwitz (Ed.): SCSM 2017, Part I, LNCS 10282, pp. 44–57, 2017.
DOI: 10.1007/978-3-319-58559-8_5

through chatting. Twitch has become an integral component of the viewers' life as they are watching it progressively on a daily basis. In 2015, 421,6 min were monthly watched per viewer (for comparison, YouTube 291 min.) and users who watch Twitch on their smartphone make up 35% of all users every month [1, 3]. The usage of Twitch is free of charge; however, viewers have the possibility to subscribe to a specific streamer, to donate to a streamer or a good cause. Over $17,400,000 were raised for different charities in 2015 [1]. The popularity of Twitch has risen not only in the United States but also in Germany. Twitch is ranked on place 48 of the most visited websites in Germany[1].

With growing usage of streaming platforms like Twitch, the motivation of this paper is to look closer at the reasons why and how Twitch is used in Germany and why some of the users spend money on it even though it is free of charge in general. Since Twitch and other streaming platforms are a rather new phenomenon for the gaming industry, research is still sparsely conducted. This paper will explore the motivation for using Twitch regarding the time and money spent on it.

2 Related Work

Along with the gaming industry, a new type of social media has been established in the last few years. Social live streaming services (SLSSs) are defined by specific characteristics: synchrony, real-time broadcasting of the users' own program, usage of their own devices, interactions between the audience and the broadcaster and lastly the possibility of a gratification system [4]. This new form of online entertainment developed into one of the main entertainment media [5, 6]. As Cheung and Huang [7] point out, recent social studies reveal a considerable number of casual players who favor watching games on a livestream rather than playing themselves. The popularity of SLSSs and the growing gaming industry in general have been ascertained and treated in previous studies [5, 8].

To determine the motivation of why people consume different types of media – including SLSSs – is one of the biggest area in communication and media science [9]. One of the most prominent approach to answer this question is the Uses and Gratification theoretical perspective [10–12]. This approach intents to answer which gratifications the audience gains by consuming a specific type of media [13]. The main difference to other approaches is that the audience is not passively consuming the media, but rather actively consuming it to satisfy one's own needs [14]. In the beginning of the seventies, McQuail et al. [15] established four usual motivations to satisfy needs by using media: developing and portraying of individuality, seeking for information, entertainment, and socialization. These motivations were adapted and customized by other researches over the years. Hsu et al. [16] used these motivations to explain the use for social media. Developing one's own personality underlines the need to self-portrayal and seeking of information forms the basis of requesting new information, which can be satisfied by using social networks. The gratification of

---

[1] www.alexa.com/siteinfo/twitch.tv.

entertainment belongs to the demand of joy by using the media and to fulfill the need of socialization, social networks are used to be in touch with others.

Twitch in general, especially concrete influential factors considering the different motivations to use it, is still a new area which needs to be explored further. Since SLSSs are a new type of social networks, the motivations based on the Uses and Gratification theory can be adapted and be further developed for Twitch as well.

The gratification of self-portrayal is the basis for the usage by streamers. One of the main reasons to create content and the need to portray oneself is to entertain or inform others, but mainly to evoke reactions [17]. The form of reactions differs from streamer to streamer. Some want to build a community and enjoy the social interactions, some want to get acknowledgment for what they are doing and be praised [8].

Viewers on Twitch can find new information about games, strategies and methods, which can satisfy the need for seeking information [18]. Twitch offers different functions for the user to seek out information: by viewing a stream and learning from the streamer or by communicating with other viewers, as they may have new information as well.

Along to watching the stream, the streamer himself can contribute to the entertainment need of the viewer. This sort of entertainment can be compared to watching TV shows or movies [19]. Furthermore, Twitch offers tournaments and other eSports events, which can be compared to traditional sport events [20]. Along with positive afflicted entertainment, there is also negative afflicted entertainment while watching streams. To critize a streamer in a negative way or trolling him can also be described as a form of entertainment for the troll [21].

Based on a multidisciplinary framework Gandolfi [24] identified different types of streams, e.g. "the professional" which is reliant on the streamers performance skills and contains partial interaction with viewers. Twitch is a platform where viewers can not only interact with the streamer e.g. through the chat, but also with other viewers. These interactions can fulfill the need of socialization by getting in touch with other users who share the same interests. Although the communication takes place online, friendships can develop between the viewers based on their shared opinion and likes [22]. In addition to that, building of communities is also common. McMillan and Chavis [23] described the feeling to belong to a community as a corporate feeling. Members of a community share an abandonment and pursue similar objectives like the need for affiliation, integration of new members, sharing of emotions and socialization [23].

The motivations based on the Uses and Gratification theory focus on satisfying the needs of the viewer or user of the medium. But one of the characteristics of a SLSS is that there is a possibility to reward the streamer as well [4]. There are different approaches to reward a streamer. On the one hand a viewer can reward the streamer simply by watching the stream, since the invested time is a resource as well. Twitch is used approximately more than 20 h per week by half of its users [1, 25]. On the other hand, a viewer can reward and support the streamer by spending money. Viewers have the possibility to make a one-time donation where the amount of the money is not determined or they can commit to a monthly subscription for $4.99. Most of the time, the streamer acknowledges the support and mentions the viewers who just spend money by name (Fig. 1).

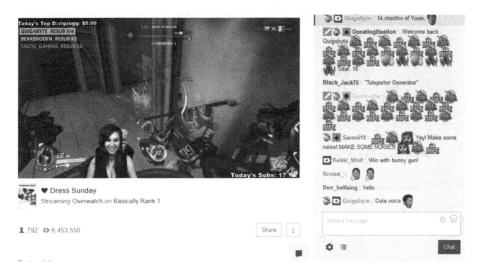

Fig. 1. Screenshot of a Twitch channel

Therefore, not only the streamer is rewarded, but the viewer is also rewarded by the interaction with the streamer. This leads to the question if the viewer's action is selfless and based on the goal to support the streamer or if the viewer wishes to receive a reward in return. As of today, this study differs from others by combining the motivations to use Twitch with the fact if money or time was already spent as a type of gratification.

3 Methods

To investigate the success of Twitch about motivation, money and usage time, the following research questions emerged from the previous literature and ideas.

RQ1: What are the most popular motivations to use Twitch?
RQ2a: How does the motivation differ if money was spent?
RQ2b: How does the motivation differ by analyzing the average usage time?
RQ3: Are usage time and money correlating with each other?

These questions have guided the development of the research model (Fig. 2). Based on the model, a questionnaire was developed to answer the research questions. On the one hand the questionnaire was distributed to measure why and how much Twitch is used and on the other hand whether the participants already spent money on it. Results are focusing on the exploration of the motivations of Twitch users who only use it as a viewer.

To avoid an unequal distribution among different countries, only German individuals were asked to fill in the questionnaire. A pretest with ten German participants was carried out. While answering the questions, problems could be found and corrected.

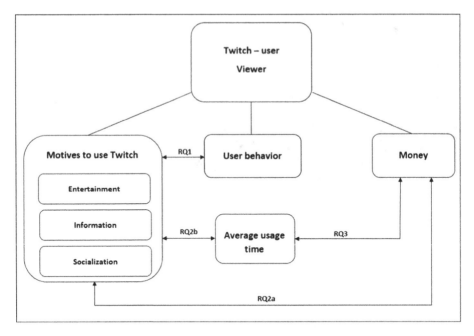

Fig. 2. Research model

The questionnaire was available online from December 30th, 2015 until February 15th, 2016, and was disseminated on the authors' Facebook walls as well as in several Facebook groups, forums – especially Reddit[2] because of its wide scope among users – and on Twitter through corresponding hashtags. Additionally, through the private message function Twitch streamers were asked to distribute the questionnaire in their stream and the chat. Answering the questionnaire took approximately 10 to 15 min. The questionnaire is composed of 23 items in total.

To measure the time users spent on Twitch, the participants had to state the average number of hours they use the platform every week. The information, if money was already given in form of a donation or subscription, was part of the questionnaire.

In order to answer the research questions, the different reasons to use Twitch regarding time and money spent on the platform are analyzed. Hence, all investigations of this study are based on the viewers. In addition to that, chosen demographic facts are considered.

The main part "Motivations to use Twitch" is separated into the three subparts, based on the uses and gratification theory [16], namely Entertainment, Information and Socialization (Fig. 2). Self-presentation as an aspect has been excluded, because this study focuses solely on the viewers who cannot represent themselves like streamers. In the questionnaire, the items in *Information* deal with different aspects as involving information – e.g. getting or possessing information – including items like using

---

[2] https://www.reddit.com/.

Twitch to have something to talk about with friends [7] or to learn new gaming techniques [20, 26]. While the items in *Entertainment* include reasons for using Twitch for pleasure, e.g. being entertained [5, 20] or to avoid boredom [27], but also negative reasons like criticizing streamers [28]. The subpart *Socialization* consists of reasons based on solidarity and getting in touch with others, for example, using the chat [8, 20, 26] or trolling other users [29]. However, Socialization also includes reasons to use Twitch to get in touch with streamers.

For every item of the three categories, a five-point Likert scale was used. The participants were informed that the answer options have the same distance on a scale of sentiments: "Strongly Disagree" (1), "Disagree" (2), "Undecided" (3), "Agree" (4) and "Strongly Agree" (5). To test the internal consistency of our 16 answer options, which specify the reasons to use Twitch, Cronbach's Alpha was calculated [30].

For further investigations, new variables were created by summing up every item for each category. This means that Entertainment and Information can have a minimum value of 5 and a maximum value of 25 as there are five items with values from 1 to 5, while Socialization has a minimum of 6 and a maximum of 30 as there are six items. To be able to compare the new variables with each category, the summed up values were divided by the respective number of items.

By presenting the average values of the five-point Likert scale for the different reasons for using Twitch, RQ1 can be answered. Important factors, like the usage time of a user and the willingness to financially support a streamer may be an influential key factor. Therefore, RQ2 focusses on the influence of the factor money (RQ2a) as well as time (RQ2b) and is answered by investigating the resulting motivations. At last, comparisons between usage time and money are made in order to answer RQ3.

4   Results

Overall, 791 people filled in the questionnaire. The first two questions intended to investigate whether the participants know Twitch and if they use it. 695 (87.9%) are acquainted with the live-streaming platform. Twitch is used by 603 (86.6%) of them. Further results are all based on the Twitch users.

For all test items regarding the motivation to use Twitch Cronbach's Alpha (α) was 0.770, which is an indicator for an "Acceptable" internal consistency and a "mo-tivationable goal" [31].

4.1   Motivations of Twitch Users

To answer RQ1, the different motivations why people use Twitch are analyzed by calculating the arithmetic mean (Table 1).

The highest arithmetic mean for the category *Entertainment* is the particular motivation to be entertained with a value of 4.56. The next motivations in a descending order are: to follow gaming events with a value of 3.95, to have an alternative for television with 3.74 and to avoid boredom with 3.48. The only answer with an average below 2 is criticizing a streamer in a negative way (1.19).

Table 1. Motivations to use Twitch

I use Twitch...	Average
Entertainment	
to be entertained. (E)	4.56
to follow tournaments and events. (E)	3.95
as an alternative or addition for TV. (E)	3.74
to avoid boredom. (E)	3.48
to criticize a streamer in a negative way. (E)	1.19
Socialization	
to communicate with other viewers through the chat. (S)	2.23
to play with other users. (S)	2.13
to be part of a community. (S)	2.10
to support a streamer financially. (S)	1.86
to get in touch with a streamer. (S)	1.80
to troll/annoy other users. (S)	1.35
Information	
to learn new gaming strategies and techniques. (I)	3.46
to be up-to-date. (I)	2.57
to look up a walkthrough of a game. (I)	1.90
to be able to talk about it with my friends. (I)	1.60
to obtain information about hardware. (I)	1.52

(E) = *Entertainment*, (C) = *Sozialization*, (I) = *Information*; N = 603

For the category *Socialization,* there is no average higher than 3. The highest arithmetic mean is 2.23 with the motivation to communicate with others. Using Twitch to play together with other viewers (which has a mean of 2.13), and using it to be part of a community (with 2.10) have an average above 2, while the remaining three answers are below 2.

For the category *Information* the answer that is most agreed to is using Twitch for learning new gaming strategies or techniques with an arithmetic mean of 3.46. Using Twitch to be up-to-date is the second highest answer with an arithmetic mean of 2.57. All of the remaining answers have an arithmetic mean below 2.

To see which category has the highest mean overall, three new variables are used. *Socialization* has a mean of 1.91. *Information* has an average overall mean of 2.21 while *Entertainment* has the highest mean of 3.39.

4.2   Influence of Money and Usage Time Regarding Motivation

About one third of the participants (31.5%, n = 190) have already spent money on Twitch. In addition to that, they were asked what kind of payment they made: donation, subscription or both. While 22.6% (n = 43) donated to a streamer and 31.6% (n = 60) subscribed, most of them did both (45.8%, n = 87). Apart from that, they were asked to specify the motivations for their payment. With 92.1% (n = 175), the main motivation is to support a streamer financially.

The next most common motivation is to have the advantages of a donation or subscription (25.3%, n = 48). There are different advantages users could receive from streamers, which were also noticed in the observations. Most of the advantages of a donation or subscription reveal benefits for viewers, for example, the usage of the chat or the communication with streamers. In most streams, the streamer mentions a viewer who subscribed or made a donation during the stream. Some of the monitored streamers even play a song to put focus on the new donation or subscription. Additionally, most streamers express their gratitude verbally on stream immediately. Most of the small streamers do not offer many advantages like mentioning the viewer who spends money, while paying viewers from a mid-sized streamer also have influence on the chat. Donors or subscribers of more popular streamers are not only mentioned, they also have an influence on the current game and also the opportunity for exclusive chats. Moreover, subscribers have the chance to get into an exclusive chat that is only available for them. As a consequence, the chat for paying viewers is not spammed.

Nearly none of the participants are willing to pay for more or better prizes in draws and contests (1.6%, n = 3). Motivations given via the free text field were mostly about charity events. Furthermore, the new variables were utilized to see how the average changes after selecting participants who already spend money from those who did not (RQ2a). *Entertainment* has the highest mean of 3.56 for Twitch users who already spend money on it. The motivation with the highest mean for participants who did not spend money on Twitch is also *Entertainment* with 3.31. An overview of the different arithmetic means is shown in Table 2.

Table 2. Average of the summed up variable regarding money

	Information	Entertainment	Socialization
Money spent	2.25	3.56	2.45
No money spent	2.19	3.31	1.66
Difference (Δ)	0.06	0.25***	0.79***

***p ≤ .001, N = 603

As a result, the highest difference between the summed up variable regarding if money was spent or not is for the category *Socialization* (Δ = 0.79). Due to the fact that *Socialization* stood out the most, a closer look on the six items has been taken (Table 3).

The biggest gap is 1.19 for supporting a streamer, followed by communicating with others (0.96). Furthermore, the highest arithmetic mean for users who already spent money is 2.89 (communicating with other viewers through the chat). For those who did not spend money on Twitch, the highest arithmetic mean is 1.93 with the same motivation.

Beside the money the users rated their average usage time of Twitch with a number of hours. Participants were split up evenly into five groups regarding their average usage time. The first group is based on those who spend 0 to 1 h (n = 100) per week on Twitch, followed by 2 to 3 h (n = 123), 4 to 9 h (n = 138), 10 to 18 h (n = 121) and more than 18 h (n = 121).

Table 3. Mean of money spent on Twitch regarding *Socialization* motivations

	Did you already spend money on Twitch?		
I use Twitch to...	Yes	No	Difference
be part of a community	2.74	1.81	0.93***
communicate with other viewers through the chat	2.89	1.93	0.96***
troll/annoy other users	1.52	1.27	0.25***
support a streamer financially	2.67	1.48	1.19***
get in touch with a streamer/to get his attention	2.28	1.57	0.71***
play together with other users	2.62	1.91	0.71***

***$p \leq .001$, N = 603

To answer RQ2b '*How does the average time spent on Twitch per week influence the motivations to use it?*' the arithmetic means of the three superior motivations to watch Twitch were compared in regard of the time the participants spend on Twitch per week. For each of the five groups concerning the time, the most important motivation to use Twitch is the *Entertainment* factor (Fig. 3). *Socialization* is the motivation with the highest difference between the participants who spend only up to one hour a week on Twitch and those who spent more than 18 h on the platform (1.35 to 2.27).

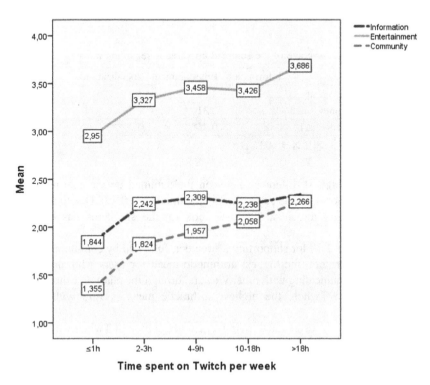

Fig. 3. Motivations to use Twitch by usage time

For a better and more detailed investigation how the time spent on Twitch corre-lates with the motivations to use it, further analysis was carried out. Through this, a closer look at the single answer options of *Socialization, Information* and *Entertain-ment* is taken.

Table 4 shows a more detailed view of the different motivations to use Twitch. In this table, the correlations of the particular motivations and the usage time are repre-sented. The main motivation to watch Twitch is to be entertained for most of the participants. This is independent of the average time they spent on Twitch ($\varnothing = 4.56$). Getting entertained is also represented in Table 4. The results of the correlation between the named motivation and the usage time give: $r_s = 0.27$. Thus, there is a positive correlation between the time participants spend on the platform and the usage motivation to be entertained. According to the Table 4, the highest correlation for the *Entertainment* aspect is between the motivation to use Twitch as an alternative for television and the usage time ($r_s = 0.38$).

Table 4. Correlations between the usage time and the motivations to use Twitch

Motivations to use Twitch	Spearman's-Rho (r_s)
Socialization	
I use Twitch to be part of a community	0.35***
I use Twitch to communicate with other viewers through the chat	0.27***
I use Twitch to support a streamer financially	0.31***
I use Twitch to play with other users	0.22***
Entertainment	Spearman's Rho (r_s)
I use Twitch as an alternative or addition for TV	0.38***
I use Twitch to be entertained	0.27***

***$p \le .001$; **$p \le .01$; *$p \le .05$, N = 603

In regard to *Socialization,* more motivations show higher rank correlations with the usage time. The correlation between the motivation to use Twitch to communicate with others through the chat and the usage time is $r_s = 0.27$, to use Twitch to support a streamer financially ($r_s = 0.31$) and to use Twitch to play with other users ($r_s = 0.22$). The strongest correlation is between usage time and the motivation to use Twitch to be part of a community ($r_s = 0.35$). These correlations show that the more hours the par-ticipants spend on Twitch every week, the more Socialization-based the motivation is.

4.3   Correlation of Money and Usage Time

By comparing participants who spent money in combination with their stated time spent on Twitch per week, RQ3 is answered (Fig. 2). Most of the donators and sub-scribers are assigned to the groups that watch Twitch 10–18 h (30%, n = 57) or more than 18 h (33%, n = 63). In comparison to that, participants who do not spend money on Twitch use it infrequently on a weekly basis.

In Fig. 4 a constant increase of users who already spent money on Twitch is noticed depending on the time these users spent on the platform.

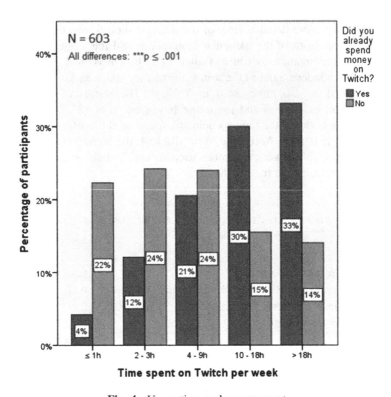

Fig. 4. Usage time and money spent

5   Discussion, Limitations and Outlook

The area of social live streaming services is a fast-growing domain and therefore deeply interesting to investigate. Particularly Twitch has a high number of users who spend time and money on the platform and produce content which leads to high traffic numbers.

The main goal of this investigation was to identify the motivation for Twitch usage, especially regarding the time and money aspect. The motivation to use Twitch has been divided into the aspects of *Socialization*, *Entertainment* and *Information* whereby every category contained multiple (motivation) items. The main purpose regarding the data of the questionnaire was to compare the relative importance of the items and based on the classification into the three mentioned categories some superior differences have been determined. With the users' feedback certain motivations appeared to be the most approved, which afterwards have been analyzed in relation to the time and money spent. As a consequence, it was possible to detect some correlations between the three categories and the factors time and money.

The general motivations of Twitch usage are discussed in RQ1. Overall the motivations of being entertained (*Entertainment*) and learning new gaming strategies or techniques (*Information*) prove to have the highest approval. Taking a closer look at the results, differences between people who spend money on Twitch by making a donation or subscription and those who do not can be determined. Those differences give an answer to RQ2a. Regardless of whether participants spent money on Twitch, the main motivation for using the platform is *Entertainment*.

In contrast to *Entertainment,* the *Socialization* aspect seems to have an impact on the decision to donate or subscribe on Twitch, as assumed in RQ2a. Most of the advantages of donations and subscriptions are *Socialization*-based, for example, exclusive emoticons for the chat, the possibilities to communicate with the streamer through a donation message or exclusive chats and games. In addition to that, $17.4 million were collected for charity in 2015. Participants justify their payments mostly to support the streamer or to do some charity. Self-interested reasons do not seem to be important for the paying viewers. Reasons could be related to a study from Dunn et al. about 'Spending Money on Others Promotes Happiness'. For example, viewers who want to be in a community need to use the chat in order to socialize [32].

Analogous to the money aspect in RQ2a, the time spent on Twitch in particular is analyzed through RQ2b. Moreover, the approval of motivations to use Twitch (in terms of *Socialization*, *Entertainment* and *Information*) increase with the time spent on Twitch. The *Socialization* aspect shows the most interesting outcomes, especially the high difference between people who use Twitch excessively and those who use it rarely (0.91). With those findings, RQ2b can be answered, as people who are part of a community on Twitch need to spend more time on the platform in order to socialize or in other words: the more hours the participants spend on Twitch, the more *Socialization*-based is the motivation.

RQ3 aims to investigate whether there are correlations between the factors money and time. After analyzing the time and money separately (RQ2a & RQ2b), RQ3 aims to reveal possible correlations between both factors. On the one hand a high ratio of the participants who spent money on Twitch were assigned to groups with a high usage time and on the other hand participants who did not spend money on Twitch used the platform unfrequently on a weekly basis. Therefore, the more time a user spends on the platform, the more likely money will be spent through a donation or a subscription.

During the development of the questionnaire only German participants and streamers were chosen to avoid an unequal distribution among different countries. Since solely German people were surveyed, it would be interesting to see if there are differences in other countries.

In this study only 16.9% (n = 102) of the participants are female. As it may seem imbalanced, this represents a realistic distribution of Twitch users [33, 34].

It is needed to be mentioned that only parts of the results of the questionnaire are presented. For instance, questions about the importance of the interaction between viewer and streamer or about the usability aspect are excluded in this study in order to not exceed the given limits. Furthermore, some of the correlations are slight and should therefore not be overestimated.

It would be of interest to do further research on Twitch and the impact on its users. Our model could possibly be altered into different areas, such as the usability aspect of

Twitch, to get more information about viewers' and streamers' behavior. Concerning this, it would be interesting to analyze the results of the remaining questions which are not included in this study. As the *Socialization* aspect seems to have a big influence on Twitch users it would be interesting to investigate how users are interacting. In this context, the role of the streamer needs to be examined, too. Since this paper only investigates the motivations to use Twitch as a viewer it would be interesting to compare these motivations with those of active players (and others, who do neither watch nor stream through SLSSs). These findings could lead to a new model which could be either compared or included into the current research model presented in this paper.

Lastly, a comparison between users of other existing platforms, like hitbox[3] or YouTube Gaming[4], would be of interest to examine differences regarding the usage.

References

1. Twitch: Welcome Home: The 2015 Retrospective. https://www.twitch.tv/year/2015
2. Toffler, A.: The Third Wave. Bantam Books, New York (1981)
3. Twitch: Welcome Home: The 2014 Retroperspective. https://www.twitch.tv/year/2014
4. Scheibe, K., Fietkiewicz, K., Stock, W.G.: Information behavior on social live streaming services. J. Inf. Sci. Theory Pract. **4**(2), 6–20 (2016)
5. Kaytoue, M., Silva, A., Cerf, L., Meira, W., Raïssi, C.: Watch me playing, i am a professional: a first study on video game live streaming. In: Proceedings of the 21st International Conference on World Wide Web - WWW 2012 Companion, pp. 1181–1188. ACM Press, New York (2012)
6. Pires, K., Simon, G.: YouTube live and twitch : a tour of user-generated live streaming systems. In: Proceedings of the 6th ACM Multimedia Systems Conference, pp. 225–230. ACM Press, New York (2015)
7. Cheung, G., Huang, J.: Starcraft from the stands: understanding the game spectator. In: Proceedings of the 2011 Annual Conference on Human Factors in Computing Systems - CHI 2011, pp. 763–772. ACM Press, New York (2011)
8. Hamilton, W.A., Garretson, O., Kerne, A.: Streaming on twitch: fostering participatory communities of play within live mixed media. In: Proceedings of the 32nd Annual ACM Conference on Human Factors in Computing Systems - CHI 2014, pp. 1315–1324. ACM Press, New York (2014)
9. Sjöblom, M., Hamari, J.: Why do people watch others play video games? An empirical study on the motivations of Twitch users. Comput. Hum. Behav. (2016, in press). http://dx.doi.org/10.1016/j.chb.2016.10.019
10. Katz, E., Blumler, J.G., Gurevitch, M.: Utilization of mass communication by the individual. In: The Uses of Mass Communications: Current Perspectives on Gratification Research, pp. 19–32. Sage, Beverly Hills (1974)
11. Ruggiero, T.E.: Uses and gratification theory in the 21st century. Mass Commun. Soc. **3**, 3–37 (2000)
12. Katz, E., Gurevitch, M., Haas, H.: On the use of the mass media for important things. Am. Sociol. Rev. **38**, 164–181 (1973)

---

[3] www.hitbox.tv.

[4] https://gaming.youtube.com.

13. Schenk, M.: Publikums- und Gratifikationsforschung. In: Medienwirkungsforschun, pp. 651–753. Mohr Siebeck, Tübingen (2007)
14. Meyen, M.: Mediennutzung: Mediaforschung, Medienfunktionen, Nutzungsmuster. UTB/UVK, Stuttgart/Konstanz (2004)
15. McQuail, D., Blumler, J.G., Brown, J.R.: The television audience: a revised perspective. In: Sociology of Mass Communications: Selected Readings, pp. 135–165. Penguin, Middlesex (1972)
16. Hsu, M.-H., Chang, C.-M., Lin, H.-C., Lin, Y.-W.: Determinants of continued use of social media: the perspectives of uses and gratifications theory and perceived interactivity. Inf. Res. **20**, 1 (2015). Paper 671, http://www.informationr.net/ir/20-2/paper671.html
17. Bowmann, S., Willis, C.: We Media: How Audiences are shaping the Future of News and Information. The Media Center at The American Press Institute, Reston (2003)
18. Foster, S.R., Esper, S., Griswold, W.G.: From competition to metacognition. In: Proceedings of the SIGCHI Conference on Human Factors in Computing Systems - CHI 2013, pp. 99–108. ACM Press, New York (2013)
19. Smith, T., Obrist, M., Wright, P.: Live-streaming changes the (video) game. In: Proceedings of the 11th European Conference on Interactive TV and Video - EuroITV 2013, pp. 131–138. ACM Press, New York (2013)
20. Edge, N.: Evolution of the gaming experience: live video streaming and the emergence of a new web community. Elon J. Undergrad. Res. Commun. **4**(2), 33–39 (2013)
21. Hardaker, C.: Trolling in asynchronous computer-mediated communication: From user discussions to academic definitions. J. Politeness Res. **6**(2), 215–242 (2010)
22. Woermann, N., Kirschner, H.: Online livestreams, community practices, and assemblages. Towards a site ontology of consumer community. Adv. Consum. Res. **43**, 438–442 (2015)
23. McMillan, D.W., Chavis, D.M.: Sense of community: a definition and theory. J. Community Psychol. **14**, 6–23 (1986)
24. Gandolfi, E.: To watch or to play, it is in the game: the game culture on Twitch.tv among performers, plays and audiences. J. Gaming Virtual Worlds **8**(1), 63–82 (2016)
25. Twitch Advertising - Audience
26. Burroughs, B., Rama, P.: The eSports Trojan Horse: Twitch and streaming futures. J. Virtual Worlds Res. **8**(2), 1–5 (2015)
27. Heaven, D.: Dark cloud: how life online has changed ownership. New Sci. **217**(2910), 34–37 (2013)
28. Lange, P.G.: What is your claim to flame? First Monday **11**(9) (2006). http://dx.doi.org/10.5210/fm.v11i9.1393
29. Raes, T.C.M.: Twitch TV: Motives and Interaction, A Consumer Perspective (Master Thesis). Aalborg University/Faculty of Humanities, Aalborg/Denmark (2015)
30. Cronbach, L.J.: Coefficient alpha and the internal structure of tests. Psychometrika **16**, 297–334 (1951)
31. Gliem, J.A., Gliem, R.R.: Calculating, interpreting, and reporting Cronbach's alpha reliability coefficient for Likert-type scales. In: 2003 Midwest Research to Practice Conference in Adult, Continuing, and Community Education, pp. 82–88. The Ohio State University, Columbus (2003)
32. Dunn, E.W., Aknin, L.B., Norton, M.I.: Spending money on others promotes happiness. Science **319**(5870), 1687–1688 (2008)
33. Sundén, J., Malin, S.: Gender and Sexuality in Online Game Cultures: Passionate Play. Routledgel, New York (2012)
34. Williams, D., Martins, N., Consalvo, M., Ivory, J.D.: The virtual census: representations of gender, race and age in video games. New Media Soc. **11**(5), 815–834 (2009)

Do Members Share Knowledge in Facebook Knowledge Groups?

Li-Ting Huang[1,2(✉)] and Ming-Yang Lu[1]

[1] Department of Information Management, Chang Gung University, No. 259,
Wenhua 1st Rd., Guishan District, Taoyuan City 33302, Taiwan (R.O.C.)
lthuang@mail.cgu.edu.tw, jambjer@gmail.com
[2] Division of Physical Medicine and Rehabilitation,
Chang Gung Memorial Hospital in Linkuo, No. 5, Fu-Hsing Street,
Guishan District, Taoyuan City 33302, Taiwan (R.O.C.)

Abstract. People are getting used to interact with friends, search information, and even go shop on Facebook. It is reported that there are 1.4 billion users and 0.86 billion active users per day on Facebook. Many knowledge groups are created on Facebook for sharing knowledge and exchanging opinions and experiences. This study expects to figure out determinants influencing members' sharing behavior of contribute their own knowledge in Facebook Knowledge Groups based on the perspective of psychological ownership. Research model is developed based on the perspective of psychological ownership and the justice theory. An online survey was conducted for data collection. Three hundred and sixty-two usable data were analyzed. Results show that organization psychological ownership positively affects members' knowledge sharing behavior. Trust towards other members and relational embeddedness of knowledge groups positively affect organization psychological ownership. Relational embeddedness and perceived equity towards knowledge groups positively affect members' trust towards other members. The construct of equity is a secondary order constructs and consists of distributive, procedural, interpersonal, and information justice. All four sub-dimensions are significant. Results show that interpersonal equity is especially important and the importance of other three dimensions is almost the same. Implications are discussed.

Keywords: Knowledge sharing · Psychological ownership · Trust · Relational embeddedness · Justice

1 Introduction

People are getting used to interact with friends, search information, and even go shop on Facebook. It is reported that there are 1.4 billion users and 0.86 billion active users per day on Facebook. Many knowledge groups are created on Facebook for sharing knowledge and exchanging opinions and experiences. Facebook Knowledge Groups indicate an organization consisted of members who have a common interest, hobby or objective. Facebook Knowledge Groups are a specific space for members' interaction, discussion, and learning, who are interested in a dedicated domain. Members in a Facebook Knowledge Group could share information, links, pictures, videos, post

© Springer International Publishing AG 2017
G. Meiselwitz (Ed.): SCSM 2017, Part I, LNCS 10282, pp. 58–70, 2017.
DOI: 10.1007/978-3-319-58559-8_6

opinions and response to other members' posts. One or some administrators could manage a Facebook Knowledge Groups.

Pi et al. [26] indicated that members are more willing to share their know-how with other members in a Facebook Knowledge Group in which members perceived a good sharing and reciprocal atmosphere. O'Bannon et al. [22] showed that existence of groups of Facebook could facilitate members' sharing knowledge behavior and increase members' intention to join discussion in groups. Park et al. [25] demonstrated that members in a community are willing to contribute to this community because they would like to pursue self – achievement. Choi [8] showed that the more active members behave, the more effective members acquire knowledge in a knowledge group. However, similar to other communities, some members love to share something with others, but others do not. They dive in knowledge groups and only browse other members' posts and do not actively share their knowledge. This study expects to figure out determinants influencing members' sharing behavior of contribute their own knowledge in Facebook Knowledge Groups based on the perspective of psychological ownership.

This issue is getting attention in literatures because environments of social media are different from general organizational environments. The members in a general organizational environment are usually familiar with each other and are driven to share knowledge by external motives, such as economical rewards, promotion, job security, or expected benefits in the future. However, members in Facebook knowledge groups do not know other members well and do not receive any external benefits from sharing knowledge with other members although they have common interesting and objectives. A Facebook Knowledge group is an informal and loose organization. Members in Facebook Knowledge groups may be defensive and hesitate to share their own knowledge because they have no close relationship and do not trust other members. So, it is important that members in a virtual community perceive high organization psychological ownership and identify themselves with this community. Under this circumstance, members are more willing to share knowledge because they trust this community and they hope this community could be improved. Even there is no external reward, and promotion on jobs, members will not compete with other members for their own benefits. Hence, we would like to explore factors which prompt users in Facebook knowledge groups to share their know-how with other unknown members in the same groups.

In general, members in Facebook Knowledge Groups perceive fair payoff, well-defined and clear regulatory, open and transparent information, friendly and kind relationship among members, share understanding of dedicated knowledge, cooperative problem solving, they will be gradually devoted themselves into this community, be an integral part of this community, and look forward to promoting growth and development of this community. That is organization psychological ownership. Organization psychological ownership is usually applied in organization-level studies. Sieger et al. [28] demonstrated that the influence of psychological ownership, equity and satisfaction on employees' commitment and loyalty. However, we proposed that a Facebook Knowledge Group is an informal organization. A Facebook Knowledge Group shares some common features with a formal organization, such as initiators, administrators, rules and regulation, shared value, common objectives, and so on. It is appropriate that applying this concept in the context of virtual communities for figure out members' knowledge sharing behavior.

Members in a Facebook Knowledge group are unfamiliar with others, so it is difficult that members have high identity to this community. Trust will be the first step to enhance members' identification. Maintaining trust is dependent on intensive interaction, good relationship, impartial treatment, positive reciprocal, a harmonious circumstance, as well as mutual inclusiveness and esteem. According, this study focus on the influence of environmental and atmospherics factors on user' behavior of sharing knowledge in Facebook knowledge groups. We propose that the higher closeness among members, the higher probability members share their knowledge. We aim to figure out antecedents of closeness relationship and identification towards a community. Hence, we intend to answer the following research questions in this study.

1. Does organization psychological ownership toward a virtual community increase members' knowledge sharing behavior in a virtual community?
2. Do members' trust in a virtual community and their relational embeddedness of virtual community directly affect organization psychological ownership?
3. Is members' perceived equity in a virtual community critical their perceived trust in a virtual community?

2   Conceptual Background and Hypotheses

Research model is developed based on the perspective of psychological ownership and the equity theory. Organizational psychological ownership, relational embeddedness, trust and justice, which members perceive in a community, are major affection related to environmental atmospherics factors. Organizational psychological ownership is the most important determinant of members' knowledge sharing behavior. Relational embeddedness and trust increase members' organizational psychological ownership. Justice and relational embeddedness improves members' trust towards members in a Facebook knowledge group.

2.1   Knowledge Sharing

Knowledge sharing in an organization could increase organizational competence. Literatures investigated factors of knowledge sharing and show that interaction and identification in an organization are important. For example, Pi et al. [26] examine the influence of extrinsic motivation, social and psychological forces, and social networking sharing culture on intention to sharing knowledge sharing on Facebook groups. Results of Pi et al.'s [26] study shows that reputation and sense of self-worth positively affect attitude towards knowledge sharing. Social networking sharing culture, indicating atmospherics of circumstance and including fairness, identification and openness, is critical to intention to sharing knowledge sharing. Li et al. [21] indicated that employees' commitment increases their organization psychological ownership and in turn employees are more willing to share their own knowledge with others. Chiu et al. [6] demonstrated that trust, reciprocity, shared language and share vision influence members' willingness of knowledge sharing in a professional virtual community. They indicated that members in a professional virtual community have common objectives and interests, mutual communication, as well as share knowledge and information. Zhang and Jiang [32] indicated that knowledge receivers' capability and attitude toward learning and relationship between members influence individual's knowledge sharing behavior. Hence, this study expects to explore the influence of closeness and trust among members on knowledge sharing behavior in Facebook Knowledge Group.

2.2 Organization Psychological Ownership

Psychological ownership indicated that an individual thinks one target, such as objects, ideas, processes, and even another person, is belonged to him [27]. Literatures show that psychological ownership is the determinant of employees' attitude and behavior in an organization. Chiang et al. [5] indicated that employees who have psychological ownership towards a company brand, they will take more effort to promote this brand, perform organizational citizen behavior towards this brand, and even do exclusion behavior towards competitive brands. Olckers and Du Plessis [23] indicated that employees with high psychological ownership are willing to do more for pursuing organizational performance and continuously work for the organization without equivalent return. van Dyne and Pierce's [30] study shows psychological ownership positively influence employees' attitude, increase their organizational citizen behavior, and raise their intention of knowledge sharing in an organization. Li et al. [21] further classified psychological ownership into organization and knowledge psychological ownership and explores influence of these two ownerships on knowledge sharing. Their study shows that members with high organization psychological ownership are more willing to share knowledge, but members with high knowledge psychological ownership hesitate to share knowledge [21]. Following the line of literatures, members in Facebook knowledge groups think they are a part of this community, they are belonged to this community, and identity to this community, they are more willing to contribute to this community for pursuing growth of this community. Hence, we propose hypothesis 1.

H1: Organization psychological ownership is positively associated with knowledge sharing behavior.

2.3 Relational Embeddedness

Uzzi [29] defined relational embeddedness as social attachments between two organizations or improvements of co-development of a belonging relationship. Relational embeddedness is usually measured by frequency of interaction, degree of closeness, level of reciprocity, or duration of a relationship. The degree of closeness of relationship and quality of interaction is important to members' behavior in social network sites [20]. Zhang et al. [31] indicated that frequent communication, long-term interaction, and continuous reciprocity increase closeness among members in a community, and in turn enhance organization psychological ownership. Feeley et al. [13] mentioned that relational embeddedness is a primary factor of members' contribution behavior. Following the line of literatures, relational embeddedness, that is good interaction and close relationship among members, could benefit all members and are inclined to generate positive feedback to a community. Members with high relational embeddedness tend to be devoted to their belonged community and view their belonged community as theirs. Members in Facebook knowledge groups interact with other members by clicking the Like button, sharing information, writing a post, writing a comment, or helping others and then deeply connect to other members. Members are getting more intimacy, build a close relationship, and then view themselves as a part of this Facebook knowledge group. Hence, we propose hypothesis 2.

H2:   Relational embeddedness is positively associated with organization psychological ownership.

Chen et al.'s [4] study demonstrated that relational embeddedness is positively affect trust. Panteli and Sockalingam's [24] study also demonstrated that building a good relationship by collaborative development; communication, interaction, and planning could push two organizations into high level of trust. Following this line, members in Facebook Knowledge groups maintain good friendship by continuous and intense interaction. They tend to believe that other members will be good to them based on past experience and then have confidence on other members. Hence, we propose hypothesis 3.

H3:   Relational embeddedness is positively associated with trust.

2.4   Trust

Gefen [15] indicated that trust is the fundamental of interaction among people and it is gradually developed by continuous interaction. Doney and Cannon [11] proposed four dimensions of trust, including competency, benevolence, integrity, and predictability. Competency is for lowering uncertainty of knowledge, benevolence is an expectancy of fair trade, integrity is an impartial behavior, and predictability is an expectancy of sticking in commitment on a trade and principals of interaction. Divya and Srinivasan [10] indicated that interpersonal trust affects employees' attitude and behavior toward an organization, their morale at work, as well as their perceived possessiveness toward an organization. When a member with high interpersonal trust, they are more willing to work in a sincere manner, do positive things for the sake of an organization, and devoted themselves into this organization as their own business. Members in Facebook Knowledge groups will have high identification towards these groups and are willing to do a share of efforts for these groups, if they have confidence with other members and believe that other members do not take advantage on them. Hence, we propose hypothesis 4.

H4:   Trust is positively associated with organization psychological ownership.

2.5   Equity Theory

Adams [1] proposed the equity theory and defined equity as an individual's perception of equilibrium on payoff between himself and others in an exchange relationship.

Chiu et al.'s [7] study shows positive relationship of trust and equity, as well as of trust and repurchase intention. Equity consists of distributive justice, procedural justice, interpersonal justice, and information justices [9].

Distributive justice is defined as an individual's perception of just payoff. For example, members in a virtual community evaluate the balance of efforts and return, such as acceptance of their opinion or numbers of responses, etc. If they think it is unfair, they perform negative emotions or behaviors towards other members in this community. If they think they get the corresponding return, they will believe other members. Distributive justice is positively influence trust [2, 17]. Procedural justice is defined as a sense of fairness to the process or policy. In a virtual community, if administrators could deal with policy and procedural conflicts or problems carefully, members' negative feelings or images could be reduced [19]. Fang et al. [12] indicated that members in an organization who perceive distributive and procedural justice tend to trust other members and then help other members actively derived from altruism. Knonvsky and Pugh [19] indicated that interpersonal justice encourage communication among members and maintain a stable exchange relationship. Members in a virtual community who perceived interpersonal justice tend to perform conscientious behavior and trust in other members [12]. Maintain good interaction and building a harmonious environment in a community could raise the trustworthiness among members. Informational justice indicates that information is not distort and is equally transmitted to every member in a community. Informational justice is positively influence trust [18]. Colquitt et al.'s [9] study shows that information justice decrease confusion and misunderstanding among members in a virtual social community. If members could receive the true meaning of information and then they do not make effort to conjecture or guess other members' meanings in Facebook Knowledge groups, they will tend to believes members in a community and this community.

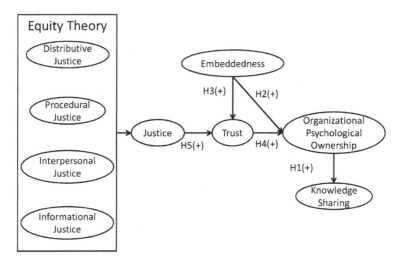

Fig. 1. Research framework

If members in Facebook Knowledge groups get balanced payoff, clearly know the procedure of conflicts resolution, perceive friendly atmospherics, get mutual assistance, receive accurate and complete information, as well as perceived respects from others, they will have confidence on this environment and believe other members. Hence, we propose the hypothesis 5.

H5:   Distributive justice, procedural justice, interpersonal justice, and information justices are positively associated with trust.

3   Research Methods

3.1   Operationalization and Instrument Design

The instruments for constructs were adapted from literature and revised to fit our research context. All items were anchored on seven-point Likert scales, from strong disagreement to strong agreement. The operational definition is shown in Table 1. A short interview with several colleagues and experts and a pre-test were carried out to ensure face validity and content validity for the compliant questionnaires. The Conrach's Alpha test was conducted for ensuring reliability data collected from the pre-test. Cronbach's Alpha of constructs was all above 0.7.

Table 1. Operationalization for constructs and numbers of measurement items

Construct	Definition	Number of items	Sources
Distributive justice	The extent that members in a community could get the relative return when they contribute to this community [12]	4	Fang and Chiu [12]
Procedural justice	The extent that regulation or policy in a community is equally applied to all members and administrators of a community could provide solutions for members when controversy or problems are happened [12]	4	Fang and Chiu [12]
Interpersonal justice	The extent that members in a community could be treated as a manner of equity, no cheating, and esteem [12]	5	Fang and Chiu [12]
Informational justice	The extent that members in a community could acquire sufficient, clear, definite and updated information happened in this community [12]	3	Fang and Chiu [12]
Trust	The extent that members in a community interact with other members as a manner of integrity and benevolence [15]	4	Gefen et al. [15]
Relational embeddedness	The extent to closeness members in a community interact with other members, such as maintaining intense connection and collaboration [31]	4	Zhang et al. [31]
Organization psychological ownership	The extent that members in a community have high degree of identity towards this community and think they are parts of this community [16]	3	Han et al. [16]
Knowledge sharing behavior	The extent that members in a community are willing to and make efforts to share their own knowledge and answer questions asked by other members [26]	4	Pi et al. [26]

3.2   Data Collection

This study employed an online questionnaire for data collection. Respondents should be members of knowledge groups on Facebook. The survey request to solicit participation was launched on the Internet and uploaded to the survey forum on "PTT (ptt. cc)," knowledge groups on Facebook. Participants were self-selected for this study via the posted messages. Respondents are asked for answering questions in accordance with one Facebook knowledge group which they most frequently visit. A sweepstakes was held to increase survey responses. In order to motivate potential respondents to fill out the questionnaire, volunteers will be given a possibility to win a prize after completion of the questionnaire. During two weeks, 362 records were identified for data analysis.

4   Data Analysis and Results

4.1   Measurement Model

The measurement model is assessed by confirmatory factor analysis using SmartPLS 3.0. The "justice" is a secondary order constructs and consists of distributive, procedural, interpersonal, and information justice. All constructs which are reflective constructs are included in confirmatory factor analysis, including distributive, procedural, interpersonal, and information justice, trust, relational embeddedness, organization psychological ownership, and knowledge sharing behavior. Factors loadings of indicators are all above the acceptable level of 0.6 and significant ($p <= 0.01$), ranging from 0.659 to 0.939. It reveals the acceptance of construct validity. The reliability and convergent validity are acceptable as compared the threshold suggested by Bagozzi and Yi [3]: 0.7 and 0.5 respectively, as shown in Table 2. The discriminant validity is acceptable based on the rule that the correlations between any two distinct construct are lower than the square root of the average variance extracted of these constructs [14], as shown in Table 3.

Table 2. Reliability and convergent validity

	Cronbach's Alpha	Composite reliability	Average variance extracted
Distributive justice	0.921	0.944	0.808
Procedural justice	0.791	0.864	0.615
Interpersonal justice	0.893	0.923	0.708
Informational justice	0.859	0.914	0.780
Trust	0.917	0.941	0.800
Relational embeddedness	0.864	0.908	0.711
Organization psychological ownership	0.837	0.902	0.754
Knowledge sharing behavior	0.921	0.944	0.809

Table 3. Discriminant validity

	DJ	PJ	IPJ	IFJ	Trust	RM	OPO	KS
DJ	**0.899**	–	–	–	–	–	–	–
PJ	0.357	**0.883**	–	–	–	–	–	–
IPJ	0.413	0.78	**0.841**	–	–	–	–	–
IFJ	0.447	0.400	0.414	**0.899**	–	–	–	–
Trust	0.331	0.337	0.310	0.624	**0.868**	–	–	–
RM	0.526	0.607	0.571	0.378	0.327	**0.784**	–	–
OPO	0.395	0.345	0.353	0.674	0.641	0.371	**0.894**	–
KS	0.439	0.501	0.593	0.643	0.536	0.505	0.568	**0.843**

Note 1: DJ: Distributive Justice; PJ: Procedural Justice; IPJ:
Interpersonal Justice; IFJ: Informational Justice; RM: Relational
Embeddedness; OPO: Organization Psychological Ownership; KS:
Knowledge Sharing Behavior
Note1: **represents correlation is significant at the 0.01 level
(2-tailed)
Note2: Diagonal represents square root of AVE of each construct

4.2   Hypotheses Testing

The structure model is analyzed by Structural Equation Model (SEM) calculated by
SmartPLS 3.0. The results of main effect are presented in Fig. 2 and all hypotheses are
supported. Results show that interpersonal justice is most important among four
dimensions. Organization psychological ownership positively affects members'
knowledge sharing behavior. Trust towards other members and relational embeddedness
of knowledge groups positively affect organization psychological ownership. Relational
embeddedness and perceived justice towards knowledge groups positively affect

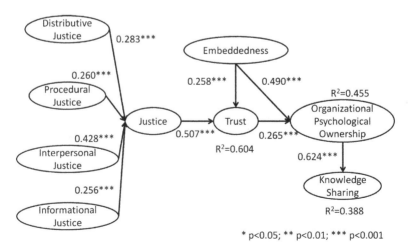

Fig. 2. Structural model – main effects

members' trust towards other members. The explained variance of trust, organization psychological ownership and knowledge sharing behavior are 60.4%, 45.5% and 38.8%. The value of R square of three constructs show good explanatory power of antecedents. Especially, organization psychological ownership is critical to knowledge sharing.

5 Discussion and Implications

5.1 Conclusions

This study aims to investigate factors of members' knowledge sharing behavior in knowledge groups on Facebook based on the perspective of psychological ownership. We focus on members' perception towards the knowledge group on Facebook, which are cumulated by daily interaction in a community, including perceived equity, trust, relational embeddedness and organization psychological ownership. Four main findings are drawn from results. **First**, members perceived organization psychological ownership is critical to their knowledge sharing in a knowledge group on Facebook. Members' high identification towards a community lead them to be devoted themselves into helping other members. Members who perceived high organization psychological ownership will try to do more for advance overall knowledge level of members in their belonged community, so they are much willing to share their own knowledge, discuss with others members, as well as help other members for solving problems. **Second**, relational embeddedness and trust are important determinants of organization psychological ownership. Especially, the influence of relational embeddedness on organization psychological ownership is almost double to of trust. In addition, relational embeddedness is positively affect trust. It shows that high intensity of interaction and long-term and satisfied relationship among members leads them to have a sense of belonging and then think themselves as an integral part of their belonged community. Meanwhile, the good relationship and interaction also increase their trust towards members in this community, decrease their self-protection, and feel comfort when interact with others. And then, members' confidence in others deepens their belief that they are identical to this community. **Third**, equity is critical to trust. The influence of equity on trust is almost twice in comparison with relational embeddedness. It shows that members' perceived trust not only comes from a satisfied and long-term relationship, but also comes from their perceived equity during interacting with other members and participating activities in a community. When members perceived equity in a community, they will have a faith that they will not be cheated, taken advantages, or abused. They can feel easy and comfortably when they are surfing and posting in this community. Perceived equity consists of distributed, procedural, interpersonal and informational justice. It shows that members perceives good equity only when they think the payoff is fair, information is opened and transparent, the regulations is unequivocal, as well as members are mutual respect and have an equal state. Especially, interpersonal justice is the most important one. **Fourth**, the explanatory powers of determinants on trust and organization psychological ownership are good, 60.4%, 45.5% respectively. It shows that members will totally trust in the community and members if they love to interact with other members, take much time on this community, as well as be treated equally in compare with other members' treatment. In addition, trust and relational embeddedness are important to organizational psychological ownership. It shows that a positive spiral up association of relational embeddedness and trust determines members' perceived organizational psychological ownership.

5.2 Academic Implications

According to these findings, there are three academic implications. **First**, organizational psychological ownership exert its influence on knowledge sharing in online social communities. Although members in a Facebook knowledge group are unfamiliar to each other and there is no external rewards or benefit foe sharing knowledge, members who are devoted into this group are willing to sharing their know-how and help others. **Second**, results in this study are similar to Zhang et al.'s [31] study, which indicated that relational embeddedness in a brand community positively influences organization psychological ownership towards a brand community and in turn increase members' willingness to promoting this brand. Feeley et al. [13] indicated that relational embeddedness increase members' identification of a community. Our study demonstrates the importance of relational embeddedness, since relational embeddedness and trust determine the level of organization psychological ownership, in addition, relational embeddedness increase members' trust. **Third**, perceived equity improves members' trust in a community and members. Results in this study are similar to Chiu et al.'s [7] and Fang et al.'s [12] studies. According to their studies, distributed, procedural, interpersonal, and information justice are all important to trust in context of online auction websites and virtual communities. Our study especially treat perceived equity as a secondary construct and find out the relative importance of four dimensions on perceived equity on Facebook. It shows that interpersonal equity is especially important and the importance of other three dimensions is almost the same. The reason may be due to invisibility and unfamiliarity of members in a knowledge group on Facebook. So, the feeling of being treated equally is particularly sensitive and important when interacting with other members. Only when members feel comfortable and being respected, they will trust in other members in a knowledge group on Facebook.

5.3 Practical Implications

Our findings lead to suggestions for managers. **First**, maintaining a close relationship in a Facebook knowledge group is critical to promoting knowledge sharing behavior. Relational embeddedness and trust, which are members' affective responses towards members and group belongs, increase positive influence users' organizational psychological ownership. Administrators of a Facebook knowledge group could hold activities or games which could increase interaction, discussion or cooperation among members. Feelings of a sense of belongings and identification could increase members' willingness to share knowledge. **Second**, building a justice environment, creating harmonious and open-minded circumstance in a Facebook knowledge group could raise members' belongings and closeness in a Facebook knowledge group. Interpersonal justice is especially important to maintain a justice environment. Hence, administrators should pay attention on maintain friendly interaction, and prevent any offensive interaction, as well as try the best to equally deal with any dispute.

References

1. Adams, J.S.: Inequity in social exchange. Adv. Exp. Soc. Psychol. **2**, 267–299 (1965)
2. Ambrose, M.L., Schminke, M.: Organization structure as a moderator of the relationship between procedural justice, interactional justice, perceived organizational support, and supervisory trust. J. Appl. Psychol. **88**, 295–305 (2003)
3. Bagozzi, R.P., Yi, Y.: On the evaluation of structural equation models. Acad. Mark. Sci. **16** (1), 74–94 (1988)
4. Chen, Y.H., Lin, T.P., Yenb, D.C.: How to facilitate inter-organizational knowledge sharing: the impact of trust. Inf. Manag. **51**(5), 568–578 (2014)
5. Chiang, H.H., Chang, A., Han, T.S., McConville, D.: Corporate branding, brand psychological ownership and brand citizenship behaviour: multilevel analysis and managerial implications. J. Gen. Manag. **39**(1), 55–80 (2013)
6. Chiu, C.M., Hsu, M.H., Wang, E.T.G.: Understanding knowledge sharing in virtual communities: an integration of social capital and social cognitive theories. Decis. Support Syst. **42**(3), 1872–1888 (2006)
7. Chiu, C.M., Huang, H.Y., Yen, C.H.: Antecedents of trust in online auctions. Electron. Commer. Res. Appl. **9**(2), 148–159 (2010)
8. Choi, A.: Use of facebook group feature to promote student collaboration. In: 2013 ASEE Southeast Section Conference (2013)
9. Colquitt, J.A.: On the dimensionality of organizational justice: a construct validation of a measure. J. Appl. Psychol. **86**, 386–400 (2001)
10. Divay, K., Srinivasan, P.T.: Psychological ownership: it's relationship with interpersonal trust and work outcomes. In: Twelfth AIMS International Conference on Management (2014)
11. Doney, P.M., Cannon, J.P.: An examination of the nature of trust in buyer-seller relationships. J. Mark. **61**(2), 35–51 (1997)
12. Fang, Y.H., Chiu, C.M.: In justice we trust: exploring knowledge-sharing continuance intentions in virtual communities of practice. Comput. Hum. Behav. **26**(2), 235–246 (2010)
13. Feeley, T.H., Moon, S.I., Kozey, R.S., Slowe, A.S.: An erosion model of employee turnover based on network centrality. J. Appl. Commun. Res. **38**, 167–188 (2010)
14. Fornell, C., Larcker, D.F.: Evaluating structural equation models with unobservable variables and measurement error. J. Mark. Res. **36**(10), 1246–1255 (1981)
15. Gefen, D.: E-commerce: the role of familiarity and trust. Int. J. Manag. **28**(6), 725–738 (2000)
16. Han, T.S., Chiang, H.H., Chang, A.: Employee participation in decision making, psychological ownership and knowledge sharing: mediating role of organizational commitment in Taiwanese high-tech organizations. Int. J. Hum. Resour. Manag. **21**(12), 2218–2233 (2010)

17. Hubbell, A.P., Chory-Assad, R.M.: Motivating factors: perceptions of justice and their relationship with managerial and organizational trust. Commun. Stud. **56**, 47–70 (2005)
18. Kernan, M.C., Hanges, P.J.: Survivor reactions to reorganization: antecedents and consequences of procedural, interpersonal, and informational justice. J. Appl. Psychol. **87**, 916–928 (2002)
19. Knonvsky, M., Pugh, D.: Citizenship behavior and social exchange. Acad. Manag. J. **37**, 656–669 (1994)
20. Lee, H.J., Lee, D.H., Taylor, C.R., Lee, J.H.: Do online brand communities help build and maintain relationships with consumers? A network theory approach. J. Brand Manag. **19**, 213–227 (2011)
21. Li, J., Yuan, L., Ning, L., Li-Ying, J.: Knowledge sharing and affective commitment: the mediating role of psychological ownership. J. Knowl. Manag. **19**(6), 1146–1166 (2015)
22. O'Bannon, B.W., Beard, J.L., Britt, V.G.: Using a facebook group as an educational tool: effects on student achievement. Comput. Sch. **30**(3), 229–247 (2013)
23. Olckers, C., Du Plessis, Y.: Psychological ownership as a requisite for talent retention: the voice of highly skilled employees. Eur. J. Int. Manag. **9**(1), 52–73 (2015)
24. Panteli, N., Sockalingam, S.: Trust and conflict within virtual inter-organizational alliances: a framework for facilitating knowledge sharing. Decis. Support Syst. **39**(4), 599–617 (2005)
25. Park, N., Kee, K.F., Valeneuela, S.: Being immersed in social networking environment: Facebook groups, uses and gratifications, and social outcome. Cyber Psychol Behav. **12**(6), 729–732 (2009)
26. Pi, S.M., Chou, C.H., Liao, H.L.: A study of facebook groups members' knowledge sharing. Comput. Hum. Behav. **29**(5), 1971–1979 (2013)
27. Pierce, J.L., O'Driscoll, M.P., Coghlan, A.M.: Environment structure and psychological ownership: the mediating effects of control. J. Soc. Psychol. **144**(5), 507–534 (2004)
28. Sieger, P., Bernhard, F., Frey, U.: Affective commitment and job satisfaction among non-family employees: investigating the roles of justice perceptions and psychological ownership. J. Family Bus. Strategy **2**(2), 78–89 (2011)
29. Uzzi, B.: Social structure and competition in interfirm networks: The paradox of embeddedness. Adm. Sci. Q. **42**(1), 33–35 (1997)
30. van Dyne, L., Pierce, J.L.: Psychological ownership and feelings of possession: Three field studies predicting employee attitudes and organizational citizenship behavior. J. Organ. Behav. **25**(4), 439–459 (2004)
31. Zhang, J.Y., Nie, M., Yan, B.S., Wang, X.D.: Effect of network embeddedness on brand-related behavior intentions: Mediating effects of psychological ownership. Soc. Behav. Pers. **42**(5), 721–730 (2014)
32. Zhang, X., Jiang, J.Y.: With whom shall i share my knowledge? A recipient perspective of knowledge sharing. J. Knowl. Manag. **19**(2), 277–295 (2015)

Assessing Symptoms of Excessive SNS Usage Based on User Behavior and Emotion

Analysis of Data Obtained by SNS APIs

Ploypailin Intapong[1(✉)], Saromporn Charoenpit[2],
Tiranee Achalakul[3], and Michiko Ohkura[4]

[1] Graduate School of Engineering and Science,
Shibaura Institute of Technology, Tokyo, Japan
nb15508@shibaura-it.ac.jp
[2] Faculty of Information Technology,
Thai-Nichi Institute of Technology, Bangkok, Thailand
saromporn@tni.ac.th
[3] Department of Computer Engineering,
King Mongkut's University of Technology Thonburi, Bangkok, Thailand
tiranee.ach@mail.kmutt.ac.th
[4] College of Engineering, Shibaura Institute of Technology, Tokyo, Japan
ohkura@sic.shibaura-it.ac.jp

Abstract. The use of social networking sites (SNSs) continues to dramatically increase. People are spending unexpected and unprecedented amounts of time online. Excessive and compulsive use of them has been categorized as a behavioral addiction. This research is conducted to assess the symptoms of excessive SNS usage by studying user behavior and emotion in SNSs. We designed a data collection application and developed a tool for collecting data from questionnaires and SNSs by APIs. The data were collected at the Thai-Nichi Institute of Technology (TNI), Thailand from 177 volunteers. We introduce our analysis of data obtained by SNS APIs by focusing on Facebook and Twitter. We used modified IAT and BFAS to measure SNS addiction. The Facebook and Twitter results, including a combination with questionnaires, were analyzed to identify the factors associated with SNS addiction. Our analytic results identified potential candidates of the key components of SNS addiction.

Keywords: Social Networking Sites · SNS · Social network addiction · User behavior

1 Introduction

Digital technology plays an important role in daily life. Social Networking Sites (SNSs) have exploded as a popular type of communication where groups virtually meet and interact with others who share similar interests [1].

In January 2016, a summary of SNS usage from WeAreSocial reported that the total population is about 7.4 billion while about 3.4 billion are active SNS users, which

© Springer International Publishing AG 2017
G. Meiselwitz (Ed.): SCSM 2017, Part I, LNCS 10282, pp. 71–83, 2017.
DOI: 10.1007/978-3-319-58559-8_7

equal almost 30% of the world's population actively use SNSs [2]. In Thailand, over 50% of population is active SNS users. In addition, a survey of Thai Internet users by ETDA [3] reported that 96% use SNSs. The top three most popular SNSs are YouTube, Facebook, and Line [3]. The average daily SNS use was almost three hours [2]. Unfortunately, some people spend too much time on SNSs and use them in potentially deleterious ways. Many studies [1] have warned about the negative consequences of excessive SNS usage, including the risk of addictive behavior.

This research studied user behavior and emotion related to SNS usage to assess the symptoms of excessive SNS usage. We divided our research into the following four main stages:

1. Collect SNS user behavior data
2. Clarify the characteristic of SNS usage and their relationships
3. Estimate user emotions of SNS usage using biological signals
4. Detect symptoms of excessive SNS usage

In the first stage, we previously designed and developed a data collection application as a tool for collecting SNS user behavior data from questionnaires and SNSs by APIs [4, 5]. The questionnaires gathered user experiences with SNSs. Modified IAT and BFAS were employed as part of a questionnaire to measure SNS addiction. APIs were used for directly retrieving data from SNSs. The data were collected at the Thai-Nichi Institute of Technology (TNI), Thailand from 177 volunteers. Figure 1 illustrates the procedures for collecting the SNS data.

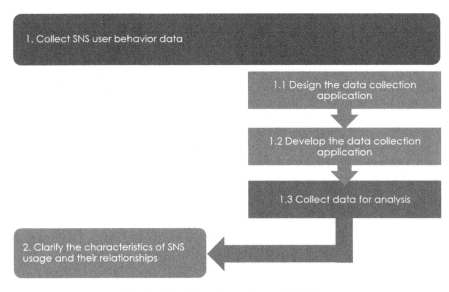

Fig. 1. Procedures for collecting SNS data

The second stage is in progress. The data obtained by the application will be analyzed to clarify the characteristics of SNS usage and their relationships. In a previous study [6], the data obtained by questionnaires were analyzed to find the factors associated with SNS addiction. However, that approach was insufficient for capturing every aspect of the users. Therefore, in this article, we introduce the analysis of data obtained by SNS APIs, including a combination with questionnaire data to improve data analysis for identifying the factors associated with SNS addiction.

The analytic results will be applied for detecting the symptoms of excessive SNS usage and developing prevention strategies for increasing the awareness of excessive SNS usage.

2 SNS Addiction

Many studies have argued that excessive SNS usage can cause various negative consequences such as relational, performance, health-related, and emotional problems, including the risk of addiction. The excessive and compulsive use of SNSs has also been linked to behavioral addictions [7].

Internet addiction is one type of behavioral addiction. Young [8, 9] identified five types of internet addiction: computer addiction, information overload, net compulsion, cyber-sexual addiction, and cyber-relationship addiction. SNS addiction falls in the last category [1]. Since Facebook has become one of the world's most commonly used Internet sites, addiction to it may be a specific form of Internet addiction [10].

SNS addiction shares similarities with other behavioral addictions [1, 7]. Kuss and Griffiths [1] argued that the symptoms of SNS addiction resemble the symptoms of other addictions. The following are the addiction components from a biopsychosocial perspective [10]:

(1) Salience: behavioral, cognitive, and emotion preoccupation
(2) Mood modification: engagement that modifies/changes emotional states
(3) Tolerance: increased amount of time spent on it
(4) Withdrawal: unpleasantness when the use is restricted
(5) Conflict: relationship problems with family and friends because of usage
(6) Relapse: failure to avoid use

3 Method

This study aims to explore the key components for SNS addiction by clarifying the characteristic of SNS usage and their relationships. We experimentally collected data from undergraduate students in Thailand to determine SNS usage variables and the relationships between them. The data were collected at the Thai-Nichi Institute of Technology (TNI).

3.1   Data Collection Application

We designed a data collection application and developed a tool for collecting SNS data from questionnaires and SNSs by APIs [4, 5]. Our application can be accessed through a web browser, i.e., Google Chrome. Its architecture design is shown in Fig. 2, and the data obtained by it are shown in Fig. 3.

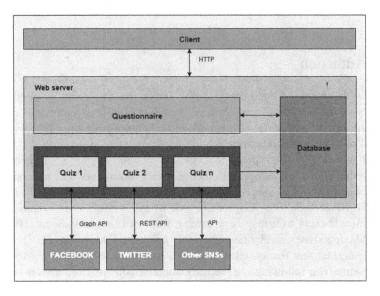

Fig. 2. Architecture design

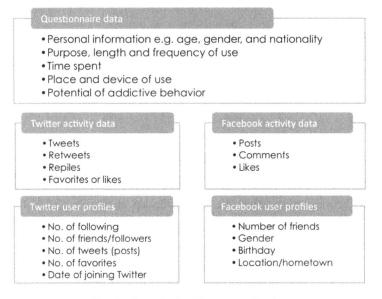

Fig. 3. Data obtained by our application

3.2   Questionnaire

Questionnaire is one part of our data collection application that gathers user SNS experiences [4]. Our questionnaire is divided into three parts: (1) personal information, (2) SNS usage, and (3) SNS addiction. In the third part, we used IAT [11] and BFAS [10] to reflect the addictive behaviors.

Internet Addiction Test. The internet addiction test (IAT) is a 20-item questionnaire [11] that measures the characteristics and behaviors associated with compulsive Internet use. IAT is scored on a 6-point Likert scale and results in four levels: none, mild, moderate, and severe.

Bergen Facebook Addiction Scale. The Bergen Facebook addiction scale (BFAS) is a six-item questionnaire developed [10] to assess Facebook addiction in epidemiology studies and clinical trials. It is scored on a 5-point Likert scale and broken down into normal and excessive users.

Our questionnaire was originally implemented in English. IAT and BFAS were modified for SNSs by retaining the original concepts and cut-off scores. In this experiment, we translated the questionnaire into Thai. We used the Thai version of IAT by Weerachatyankul [12] and the Thai version of BFAS (Thai-BFAS) by Phanasathit et al. [13] and modified them for SNS.

3.3   SNS APIs

We directly retrieved SNS data through SNS APIs. Each SNS provides a different API. First, we focused on retrieving data from Facebook and Twitter.

Graph APIs. Facebook provides Graph APIs [14] for accessing its data based on HTTPs for various purposes. Most requests require an access token, which is "an opaque string that identifies a user, app or page" [14], which is generally obtained in the OAuth authentication process.

REST APIs. Twitter provides REST APIs for accessing its data. A REST API is designed to take a number of requests to perform a number of tasks and for smaller stream samples. The REST API identifies Twitter applications and users using OAuth authentication, and the response data are in the JSON formation [15].

We implemented Facebook and Twitter quizzes that asked such questions as "How often do you tweet?" as part of our data collection application. When users complete the quizzes, the data are retrieved by APIs [16].

3.4   Session Identification

Session identification categorizes the different activities performed by each user and segments them into individual access sessions. If the activities are not connected to previous activities or there is more than a 30-minute delay (based on previous empirical findings [17]) between the activities, then it is defined as a different session.

To estimate the time spent on SNSs, we used a session identification approach. We organized the data retrieved from Facebook and Twitter as the sequences of activities with action times (Table 1). We segmented the session and calculated the duration between its first and last activities. For user AAAA in Table 1, the two activities were considered the same session (A) with a 14-minute-time difference. For user BBBB, the four activities were considered the same session (B). BBBB's sessions lasted nine minutes.

Table 1. Example of sequence of SNS activities

#	User ID	Action type	Action time	Time difference (minutes)	Session ID
1	AAAA	post	2016-08-26 10:21:51	N/A	A
2	AAAA	reply	2016-08-26 10:36:38	14	A
3	BBBB	comment	2016-09-01 10:17:04	N/A	B
4	BBBB	reply	2016-09-01 10:18:13	1	B
5	BBBB	reply	2016-09-01 10:19:17	1	B
6	BBBB	reply	2016-09-01 10:23:50	4	B
7	BBBB	reply	2016-09-01 10:27:18	3	B

With session identification, we calculated the following variables from the Facebook and Twitter data:

- Frequency of use (times/day)
- Time spent (minutes/time)
- Length of use (minutes/day)

3.5 Experimental Procedure

The following are the experimental procedures:

1. Instructor introduces an overview of the research and the data collection application.
2. Instructor distributes the instruction documents to the participants and explains the experiment's procedure.
3. Participants access the application by a web browser and follow the procedures in the document.
   (a) Participants complete Twitter quiz and/or Facebook quiz, based on which the account they use.
   (b) Participants answer the questionnaires.

Participants read and accepted the terms of agreement before they did the quizzes and answered the questionnaires.

4   Results

We did our experiment with 177 volunteers who were undergraduate students in the faculty of Information Technology, the Thai-Nichi Institute of Technology. Their ages ranged from 17 to 26 ($\bar{x}$ = 21.17, SD = 1.64).

4.1   Facebook

Facebook Usage. 99 participants granted us data-access to their Facebook accounts: 65 males and 34 females. The data were retrieved by Graph APIs in a three-month period. Facebook usage is summarized in Table 2.

Table 2. Facebook usage in three-month period

Variables	Median	Mean	SD
Friends	636.00	836.60	828.09
Time spent (mins/time)	15.46	15.38	6.62
Frequency of use (times/day)	1.33	1.41	0.38
Length of use (mins/day)	21.82	22.88	13.15
User feed usage (time)			
Posts	49.00	84.55	91.13
Comments	12.00	20.29	21.51
Replies	36.00	101.08	154.03
Tagged posts	5.00	7.46	7.61
Type of post (time)			
Status updates	7.00	18.98	29.07
Photos	19.00	39.66	48.93
Videos	4.00	10.58	13.74
Links	8.00	15.29	20.38
Ratio of usage period			
06:00–09:00	0.6	0.08	0.08
09:00–12:00	0.18	0.19	0.14
12:00–13:00	0.06	0.07	0.06
13:00–18:00	0.40	0.43	0.24
18:00–24:00	0.70	0.80	0.50
After midnight	0.10	0.14	0.15

The average usage frequency was 1.41 times per day, and the average amount of time spent on Facebook was 15.38 min per session and 22.88 min per day. The most common activities on the user feeds were replying ($\bar{x}$ = 101.08), followed by posting ($\bar{x}$ = 84.55). The ratio of posting types was 22% for status updates, 47% for photos, 13% for videos, and 18% for links.

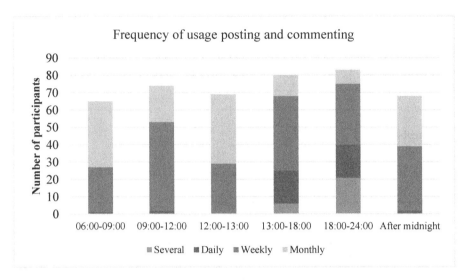

Fig. 4. Frequency of usage posting and commenting

Figure 4 shows the usage activities: posting, commenting, and replying. Facebook users did them several times during the 13:00–18:00 (6.06%) and 18:00–24:00 (21.21%) time periods. They also did these activities daily, except for the 12:00–13:00 period. Chi-square analysis results indicated significant differences among each usage period ($p < 0.05$).

Facebook Usage and SNS Addiction. We analyzed the data obtained from Facebook (including the combination with data from questionnaires [6]) to find factors associated with SNS addiction. Since the normality test on Facebook variables resulted in negative outcomes, a non-parametric test was used. The IAT and BFAS results from the questionnaires were used for measuring SNS addiction based on the reasonable results from a previous study [6].

According to the definition of the original IAT level, we named participants as *excessive* users if their scores appeared in each level of Internet addiction (mild, moderate, and severe) and the others as *normal* users. The original BFAS also classified users this way.

To examine the relationship of SNS addiction with Facebook variables, the Mann-Whitney U Test was employed. As shown in Table 3, the ratio of usage during the 18:00–24:00 period was significantly different for both the IAT level ($z = -2.376$, $p < 0.05$) and the BFAS level ($z = -1.966$, $p < 0.05$). Moreover, the ratios of posting status updates ($z = -2.305$, $p < 0.05$) and videos ($z = -1.974$, $p < 0.05$) were significantly different for the IAT level.

To identify how excessive and normal users differ, we applied logistic regression analysis to both the IAT and BFAS results to determine the importance of the effective variants used to distinguish excessive from normal users. The results are shown in Table 4.

Table 3. Mann-Whitney U test for variables from Facebook

Variables	Z-Value	
	IAT	BFAS
Ratio of posts		
Status updates	*−2.305	
Videos	*−1.974	
Ratio of usage period		
18:00–24:00	*−2.376	*−1.966

$p < 0.05$

Table 4. Logistic regression analysis for variables from Facebook

Variables	IAT (β)	BFAS (β)
User feed usage		
Comments and replies	*−0.018	*−0.016
Posts, comments, and replies (times/day)	*0.274	*0.195
Ratio of posts		
Videos	*−5.777	−2.791
Ratio of usage period		
18:00-24:00	*2.561	*2.902
Constant	−1.317	−1.110
Correct percentage	68.5%	66.3%

$p < 0.05$

For both IAT and BFAS, the following variables distinguish excessive from normal users:

- number of comments and replies in a three-month period
- number of daily activities (posting, commenting, replying)
- the ratio of usage during 18:00–24:00 period

The ratio of posting video was another effective variant for IAT.

4.2 Twitter

Twitter Usage. 36 participants granted us data-access to their Twitter accounts: 19 males and 17 females. The data were retrieved by REST APIs over a three-month period. A summary of the Twitter usage is shown in Table 5.

The average usage frequency was 2.02 times per day, and the average time spent on Twitter was 14.71 min per session and 40.13 min per day. The average number of years using Twitter was 3.47 years. Twitter activities were tweets ($\bar{x} = 258.81$), retweets ($\bar{x} = 166.78$), and replies ($\bar{x} = 62.28$).

Table 5. Twitter usage in three-month period

Variables	Median	Mean	SD
Time spent (mins/time)	12.17	14.71	10.34
Frequency of use (times/day)	1.34	2.02	1.61
Length of use (mins/day)	16.92	40.13	57.27
Profile			
Year Twitter use began	4.00	3.47	2.02
Followers	55.00	129.14	227.16
Friends	164.50	206.22	194.50
Statistics of use	1,309.00	10,921.56	20,175.06
Statistics of favorites	164.50	490.25	671.15
Usage (time)			
Tweets	34.00	258.81	581.35
Retweets	35.50	166.78	239.37
Replies	4.00	62.28	169.48
Ratio of usage period			
06:00–09:00	0.14	0.17	0.18
09:00–12:00	0.05	0.09	0.13
12:00–13:00	0.00	0.03	0.04
13:00–18:00	0.18	0.21	0.17
18:00–24:00	0.20	0.22	0.15
After midnight	0.26	0.28	0.19

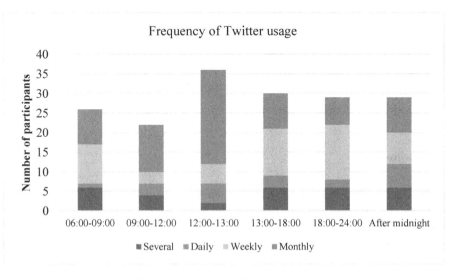

Fig. 5. Frequency of Twitter usage

According to Fig. 5, Twitter users engaged in daily activities on it during all periods. After midnight was the top period in which 33.33% of Twitter users engaged in daily activities. Chi-square analysis results indicated that the periods between 13:00–18:00 and after midnight were significantly different from other periods ($p < 0.05$).

Twitter Usage and SNS Addiction. The data obtained from Twitter (including the combination with the data from questionnaires [6]) were analyzed to find the factors associated with SNS addiction. Since the normality test on Twitter variables resulted in negative outcomes, we used a non-parametric test. The IAT and BFAS results from the questionnaires were used for measuring SNS addiction.

To examine the relationship of SNS addiction with the Twitter variables, we used the Mann-Whitney U test and logistic regression analysis. The analytic results indicated no significant differences between the Twitter variables and IAT. On the contrary, the results from both the Mann-Whiney U test and logistic regression analysis indicated a significant difference between the ratio of usage after midnight and BFAS.

5 Discussion

In this study, over half of our participants were Facebook users, 20% were Twitter users, and 18% used both Facebook and Twitter. Our descriptive analysis results indicated that the Facebook and Twitter usages are different.

- Facebook users spent about 23 min/day posting, commenting, and replying, while Twitter users spent about 40 min/day on similar activities: tweets, retweets, and replies.
- The number of interactions on Facebook was fewer than on Twitter.
- A majority of the activities for Facebook users was responding to content, while for Twitter users, it was sharing content with others.
- The Twitter users did activities on Twitter several times for all of the time periods, while Facebook users did activities on Facebook several times during the 13:00–18:00 and 18:00–24:00 time periods.

Key Components for SNS Addiction. Since the Facebook and Twitter platforms and usages are different, we separately analyzed the data from them (including the combination from the questionnaire data) to find the factors associated with SNS addiction.

As for the Facebook variables, the Mann-Whitney U test and logistic regression analysis for both IAT and BFAS indicated that the Facebook variables differing excessive users from normal users. All of the variables that influence BFAS also influenced IAT. As for the Twitter variables, the Mann-Whitney U test and logistic regression analysis indicated that no variables can distinguish between excessive and normal users for IAT. On the contrary, the ratio of usage after the midnight period was the Twitter variable that separated excessive users from normal users for BFAS.

Based on this study's results, the following are the candidates of the key components for SNS addiction:

- the amount of activity (posting, commenting, and replying) on Facebook
- the ratio of posting videos on Facebook
- the ratio of usage on Facebook in the 18:00–24:00 period
- the ratio of usage on Twitter after the midnight period

Similarly, some candidates in this finding correspond with the results from our previous study [6].

Restriction of SNS APIs. SNS APIs are insufficient to capture all of the activities in Facebook and Twitter, especially reading and the time of action like/favorite. Graph APIs limit access to Facebook data even if users grant permission for it. The data on a user's timeline can only be retrieved through APIs. REST APIs limit the number of request operations and response data. As a result, the data obtained by APIs are insufficient to describe all of the aspects of user behavior in Facebook and Twitter and cannot be retrieved over long-time periods. However, using APIs is the most common way to directly retrieve data from SNSs, and users are noticed about data-access.

To improve data analysis, future work will use an alternative method, for example, web log analysis.

6 Conclusion

This research is conducted to assess the symptoms of excessive SNS usage by studying user behavior and emotion in SNSs. We collected data from undergraduate students in Thailand, retrieved them from Facebook and Twitter (including a combination of data from questionnaires), and statistically analyzed them to clarify SNS usage behaviors and factors associated with SNS addiction. This study's analytical results identified the candidates of key components of SNS addiction.

However, employing SNS APIs is insufficient to capture all Facebook and Twitter activities due to the restriction of APIs. Therefore, further studies will employ web log analysis including the combination with questionnaires and SNS APIs to improve data analysis.

Finally, we will apply our analytic results for detecting the symptoms of excessive SNS usage and use our research's outcome for developing prevention strategies to increase the awareness of the risks of excessive SNS usage.

Acknowledgements. We thank Pannee Lumwanwong and Sirirat Weerachatyanukul, the lecture of School of Information Technology and Innovation, Bangkok University, Thailand for IAT-Thai version. We also thank the students of Thai-Nichi Institute of Technology for the participants

References

1. Kuss, D.J., Griffiths, M.D.: Online social networking and addiction-a review of the psychological literature. Int. J. Environ. Res. Public Health **8**(9), 3528–3552 (2011)
2. We Are Social (2016). http://wearesocial.net
3. Electronic Transactions Development Agency (ETDA), Ministry of Digital Economy and Society, Thailand. Thailand Internet User Profile (2016). https://www.etda.or.th/publishing-detail/thailand-internet-user-profile-2016-th.html
4. Intapong, P., Achalakul, T., Ohkura, M.: Collecting data of SNS user behavior to detect symptoms of excessive usage: design of data collection application. In: International Symposium on Affective Science and Engineering (ISASE), pp. 1–7 (2016)
5. Intapong, P., Achalakul, T., Ohkura, M.: Collecting data of SNS user behavior to detect symptoms of excessive usage: development of data collection application. In: Soares, M., Falcão, C., Ahram, T. (eds.) Advances in Ergonomics Modeling, Usability & Special Populations, vol. 468, pp. 88–99. Springer, Cham (2016)
6. Intapong, P., Charoenpit, S., Achalakul, T., Ohkura, M.: Assessing symptoms of excessive SNS usage based on user behavior and emotion: analysis of data obtained by questionnaire. In: International Symposium on Affective Science and Engineering (ISASE) (2016, in press)
7. Andreassen, C.S.: Online social network site addiction: a comprehensive review. Curr. Addict. Rep. **2**(2), 175–184 (2015)
8. Young, K.: The research and controversy surrounding internet addiction. Cyberpshchol. Behav. **2**, 381–383 (1999)
9. Young, K.,: Internet addiction: symptoms, evaluation, and treatment. In: Innovations in Clinical Practice: A Source Book, vol. 17, pp. 19–31 (1999)
10. Andreassen, C.S., Torsheim, T., Brunborg, G.S., Pallesen, S.: Development of a Facebook addition scale. Psychol. Rep. **110**(2), 501–517 (2012)
11. Young, K.: The emergence of a new clinical disorder. Cyberpshchol. Behav. **1**(3), 237–244 (1998)
12. Weerachatyanukul, S.: Effect of internet addiction on students' academic performance of the second year students, faculty of business administration Bangkok University. HCU J. **18**(36), 47–63 (2015)
13. Phanasathit, M., Manwong, M., Hanprathet, N., Khumsri, J., Yingyeun, R.: Validation of the Thai version of Bergen Facebook Addiction Scale (Thai-BFAS). J. Med. Assoc. Thai. = Chotmaihet Thangphaet **98**, S108–S117 (2015)
14. Facebook Developers. https://developers.facebook.com/
15. Twitter Deveopers. https://dev.twitter.com/
16. Intapong, P., Achalakul, T., Ohkura, M.: Collecting data of SNS user behavior to detect symptoms of excessive usage: technique for retrieving SNS data. In: International Conference on Business and Industrial Research, pp. 275–282 (2016)
17. Spiliopoulou, M., Mobasher, B., Berendt, B., Nakagawa, M.: A framework for the evaluation of session reconstruction heuristics in web-usage analysis. Informs J. Comput. **15**(2), 171–190 (2013)

Research on the Social Experience of Mobile Internet Products

Tian Lei[(⊠)] and Sijia Zhang

Department of Industrial Design,
Huazhong University of Science and Technology, Wuhan, China
andrew.tianlei@hust.edu.cn

Abstract. There are many factors affecting the social experience of the product, such as the contents, UI design, interactive mode and communication method. Taking Wechat and Weibo as examples, this paper studies the influencing mechanism of social experience of the product which leads to group indifference by questionnaire survey. The questionnaire involves five aspects including target users' characteristics, product contents, ways of social interaction, privacy and security mechanisms and the review mechanism. The results indicate that: (1) If the positioning of products is different, the arrangement and the design of the products are different as well as the social experience produced; (2) if the audiences are different, the content structure of products and the social interactive methods are different, so is the social experience generated; (3) the bigger the product's freedom is, the bigger the negative social experience is; (4) the bigger the number of phenomenal user is, the easier the negative social experience of product produces. In brief, in the product of mobile internet products, the commercial positioning, the scope of audience, the freedom degree and the number of phenomenal user are the four key factors which affect the product's social experience.

Keywords: Mobile internet product · Social experience · User experience

1 Background

With the rapid development of mobile Internet, more and more users are involved in the use of mobile applications as social media. Social media is "a group of Internet-based applications that build on the ideological and technical foundations of Web 2.0, and that allow the creation and exchange of user generated content" [1]. Typical social media Products include: instant messaging services like Wechat and QQ, social networking services like Renren and Facebook, microblog services like Weibo and Twitter [2]. In the 39th China Internet development statistics report on CNNIC shows: Until the December 2016, China's Internet users reached 731 million, of which mobile phone users occupy the 95.1% of entire Internet users [3]. Mobile Internet promotes China's economy, culture, education, life, social intercourse develop towards sharing, intelligence, scene oriented and value oriented. It has become an important media for the dissemination of all kinds of major public events. However, with the penetration of mobile applications in the various aspects of people's daily environment, the negative

© Springer International Publishing AG 2017
G. Meiselwitz (Ed.): SCSM 2017, Part I, LNCS 10282, pp. 84–93, 2017.
DOI: 10.1007/978-3-319-58559-8_8

social experience of products is gradually increasing, especially the phenomenon of group indifference. How to avoid this kind of negative social experience is an urgent event which needs to solve the problems cooperating with all aspects of society.

2 Literature Review

For mobile Internet products, good social experience will not only let users feel the information superiority, the sense of time as well as sense of freedom while using the mobile, but also enhances the users' viscosity feeling and brings positive energy and a sense of harmony to society. Liu and Ma took China's famous mobile Internet applications - Weibo as the research object, proposed the spread model of the social experience of the Internet product, that is latent, growth, spread, outbreak, decay and death [4]. Each stage will have a different impact on the user. Some of the effects are due to the upgrading of products, such as product content updates, changes in the design of the interface, the changes in the way of interaction as well as the expansion of the transmission path, etc. For example, due to the upgrading of products it is leading the users appear the barrier in the style of use and habits, which most users have a language attack on function and interactive product interface, namely social experience of negative product. It may also be because of the differences of products in the information architecture, interface design style, and so on, so as to produce the gap in the effectiveness of social experience. For example, Chen found through a comparative study that due to the different modes of communication between Weibo and Wechat in the dissemination of information, resulting in negative social experience when the product appears, the molecular fission as a way to spread [5]. The Weibo is faster than the one to one mode for the spread of Wechat.

The user's cultural background, the acceptance of the information content, the different degree of social relations, and the authenticity of the product information itself, as well as the difference of transparent degree can also cause effect and direction of social experience of different products. For example, Liu and Ma by using the method of complex network, explored the dissemination of negative social experience effect in different fields, when users paid attention to the information content and the acceptance [4]. Chang takes the user relationship as the breakthrough point, and discusses the negative social experience effect of the mobile product when the disadvantaged group releases negative information in the social relationship [6]. Due to the weak relationship provides most of the information, and online most of the audience and the weak relationship exist a certain distance between the parties in space and time. It is not clear to understand the specific situation in a state of "pluralistic ignorance", so most people keep a calm, surrounded, suspicious, guessing state to the information. A lot of people cannot accurately and timely response to the surface concern, but also they cannot correctly interpret the reaction of others, resulting in a negative social experience of the product - "group apathy".

This paper will present the China Mobile Internet social mainstream products - "Wechat" and "Weibo" as an example, it researches the results in negative social experience by means of questionnaire, especially the influence mechanism of the group indifference to this phenomenon.

3 Questionnaire Survey

3.1 Methods

This research investigates the influence mechanism of the two mobile Internet social mainstream products of negative social experience in China from the target population characteristics, product content, social interaction, privacy and security mechanisms and the review mechanism. The object of the study was 60 young people aged 18–25 years, who were often using these two mobile social media. There are 31 persons who have bachelor's degree, 22 persons who have master's degree, and 6 persons who have degree under the bachelor, as well as a doctorate.

3.2 Questionnaires

See Table 1.

Table 1. The questionnaire about the social experience of mobile internet products

No.	Questions
Q1	What is your educational background?
Q2	What is your view about the degree of involving new, strange and special things, and breaking news in Weibo and Wechat?
Q3	What is your opinion about the degree of involving info about chicken soup in Weibo and Wechat?
Q4	How often do you interact with strangers in Weibo and Wechat?
Q5	How often do you interact with relatives, friends, colleagues and other acquaintances in Weibo and Wechat?
Q6	Have you met internet trolls in Weibo and Wechat?
Q7	What is your perspective of filtering the bad info (violence, pornography, rumors) in Weibo and Wechat?
Q8	How often do you receive the negative info?
Q9	Have you met usability problems frequently in Weibo and Wechat?
Q10	How often do you publish your personal info in Weibo and Wechat?
Q11	What is your perception of the info's propagation speed in Weibo and Wechat?
Q12	What is your opinion about the degree of concerning the same info in Weibo and Wechat?

4 Analysis and Conclusions

(1) The products' positioning is different, therefore, the information involved in it is different, which generates the different social experience. The position of Weibo is the people who are related or unrelated to the users while the one of Wechat is the people

that have a certain relationship with the users. Therefore, the type of information involved in Weibo is more extensive than Wechat's, and it is more likely for Weibo to involve such information as new, novel, special and breaking news. However, for Wechat, it concentrates more on health care, life philosophy and users' life pictures. Table 2 verifies this view. Two Apps have a significant difference on the two problems–"What is your opinion about the degree of involving new, strange and special things, and breaking news in Weibo and Wechat?" and "What is your opinion about the degree of involving Info about chicken soup in Weibo and Wechat?". In the first problem, the average score of Weibo is higher than Wechat, and in the second problem, Wechat's score is higher than Weibo, seen in Table 3.

Table 2. ANOVE of the degree of the certain information types involved in Weibo and Wechat

		Sum of squares	df	Mean square	F	Sig.
Degree of involving new, strange and special things, and breaking news	Between groups	16.133	1	16.133	10.983	.001
	Within groups	173.333	118	1.469		
	Total	189.467	119			
Degree of involving info about chicken soup	Between groups	9.075	1	9.075	5.326	.023
	Within groups	201.050	118	1.704		
	Total	210.125	119			

Table 3. Score comparison of the degree of the certain information types involved in Weibo and Wechat

		N	Mean	Std. deviation	Std. error
Degree of involving new, strange and special things, and breaking news	Weibo	60	3.63	1.178	.152
	Wechat	60	2.90	1.245	.161
	Total	120	3.27	1.262	.115
Degree of involving Info about chicken soup	Weibo	60	3.10	1.189	.153
	Wechat	60	3.65	1.412	.182
	Total	120	3.38	1.329	.121

By the correlation analysis between the data of "What is your opinion about the degree of involving new, strange and special things, and breaking news in Weibo and Wechat?" and the data of" What is your opinion about the possibility of negative social experience appearing in Weibo and Wechat?", we found that at the level of $\alpha = 0.01$, there was a significant correlation between the above two items, whose correlation coefficient was 0.308. This indicates that the wider the product's position is, the greater the possibility of the negative social experience is (Table 4).

(2) The products' audience is different, so their Information Architecture and interactive ways are different, which lead to the different social experience. Table 5 shows that there is a significant correlation between "How often do you interact with strangers in Weibo and Wechat?" and "How often do you interact with relatives,

Table 4. Correlation analysis between products' information types and possibility of the negative social experience

		Degree of receiving new, strange, special and entertaining info	Possibility of negative social experience appearing
Degree of receiving new, strange, special and entertaining info	Pearson correlation	1	.308**
	Sig. (2-tailed)		.001
	N	120	120
Possibility of negative social experience appearing	Pearson correlation	.308**	1
	Sig. (2-tailed)	.001	
	N	120	120

**Correlation is significant at the 0.01 level (2-tailed).

Table 5. Comparison of the audience's familiarity degree to users

		Sum of squares	df	Mean square	F	Sig.
Communicate with strangers	Between groups	16.875	1	16.875	9.525	.003
	Within groups	209.050	118	1.772		
	Total	225.925	119			
communicate with acquaintance	Between groups	110.208	1	110.208	82.525	.000
	Within groups	157.583	118	1.335		
	Total	267.792	119			

friends, colleagues and other acquaintances in Weibo and Wechat?" It indicates that there is a difference in communicating with strangers and a discrepancy in communicating with acquaintance in interactive activities (such as add friends, chat, comment, forward and like).

Figure 1 shows that in Weibo the function of forwarding is particularly prominent and the one of chatting is relatively weak, while in Wechat the chatting function is quite well and the forwarding function is weaker. It is roughly consistent with our speculation that Weibo is more inclined to browse and forward information for strangers, and strangers can also see the comments each other just because it has a wider audience. And the Wechat's audience is the person who has a definite relationship with the user, so Wechat is designed for communicating with each other, and only friends can see each other's comments. Thus, the more powerful the forwarding function of the product is, the greater the effectiveness of its social experience is; the stronger the chatting function is, the less the effectiveness of its own social experience is.

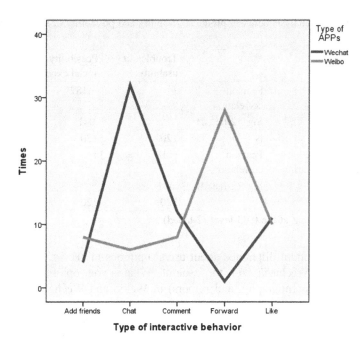

Fig. 1. Comparison of the frequency of products' interactive behavior

(3) The freedom of the product is closely linked to its social experience. Tables 6 and 7 show that there is a significant difference in the two products' usability, and a few use obstacles arise in Weibo. These obstacles in usability not only partly limits users' freedom of interaction but also affect the possibility of negative social experience's occurrence. And there is a weak correlation relationship between them, too, shown in Table 8. This manifests that the usability of products affects the production of undesirable social experience.

Table 6. Comparison of the means of products' usability

	N	Mean	Std. error
Weibo	60	3.15	.157
Wechat	60	2.57	.164
Total	120	2.86	.116

Table 7. ANOVA of the products' usability

	Sum of squares	df	Mean square	F	Sig.
Between groups	10.208	1	10.208	6.605	.011
Within groups	182.383	118	1.546		
Total	192.592	119			

Table 8. Correlation analysis between products' usability and possibility of the negative social experience

		Troubles in usability	Possibility of negative social experience appearing
Troubles in usability	Pearson correlation	1	−.187*
	Sig. (2-tailed)		.041
	N	120	120
Possibility of negative social experience appearing	Pearson correlation	−.187*	1
	Sig. (2-tailed)	.041	
	N	120	120

*Correlation is significant at the 0.05 level (2-tailed).

There is an important difference about users' opinions in "Have you met internet trolls in Weibo and Wechat?", so is the issue of "What is your opinion of filtering the bad info (violence, pornography, and rumors) in Weibo and Wechat?" The result is given in Table 9. The subjects think that the freedom degree of Wechat is lower (that is, the perception of filtering bad information is high), so it is less likely to meet internet trolls and surely the possibility of negative social experience is also low. However, the freedom degree of Weibo is high, that is, the perception of filtering bad information is low, therefore it is more likely to meet internet trolls and the possibility of negative social experience is relatively bigger, shown in Fig. 2.

Table 9. ANOVA of the products' freedom degree

		Sum of squares	df	Mean square	F	Sig.
Meet with internet trolls	Between groups	42.008	1	42.008	23.795	.000
	Within groups	208.317	118	1.765		
	Total	250.325	119			
Perception of filtering bad information	Between groups	14.008	1	14.008	10.023	.002
	Within groups	164.917	118	1.398		
	Total	178.925	119			

(4) The more the phenomenal users are, the higher the possibility of the negative social experience appearing is Fig. 3 shows that Weibo is more likely to produce a negative social experience than Wechat, which is related to the difference in concerning the phenomenal users, seen in the Table 10. In Weibo, users pay more attention to the famous persons than in Wechat, from which we can conclude that the number of phenomenal users may be higher than in Wechat.

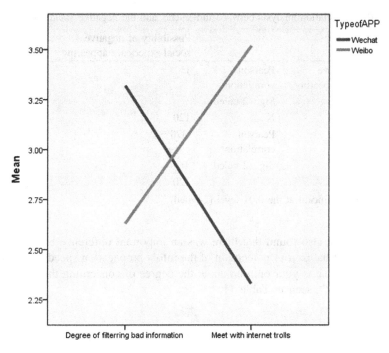

Fig. 2. Comparison of the means of products' freedom degree

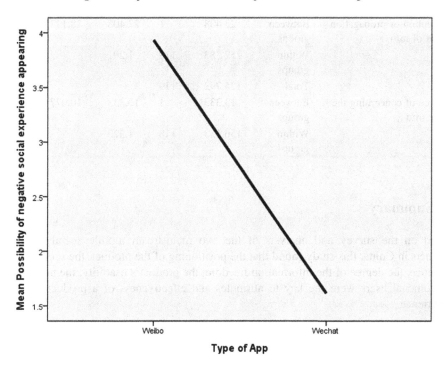

Fig. 3. Comparison of the possibility of the negative social experience

Table 10. Correlation analysis between influencers and the negative social experience

		Possibility of negative social experience appearing	Concern influencers
Possibility of negative social experience appearing	Pearson correlation	1	.370**
	Sig. (2-tailed)		.000
	N	120	120
Concern influencers	Pearson correlation	.370**	1
	Sig. (2-tailed)	.000	
	N	120	120

**Correlation is significant at the 0.01 level (2-tailed).

In addition, we also found that there was an important difference between Weibo and Wechat in "What is your perception of the info's propagation speed in Weibo and Wechat?" and "What is your opinion about the degree of concerning the same info in Weibo and Wechat", seen in Table 11.

Table 11. ANOVA of the info's propagation speed and the degree of concerning the same Info

		Sum of squares	df	Mean square	F	Sig.
Perception of propagation speed of info	Between groups	23.408	1	23.408	18.127	.000
	Within groups	152.383	118	1.291		
	Total	175.792	119			
Degree of concerning the same info	Between groups	13.333	1	13.333	10.077	.002
	Within groups	156.133	118	1.323		

5 Summary

Based on the survey and analysis of the two mainstream mobile social network products in China, this study found that the positioning of the product, the scope of the audience, the degree of the information freedom, the product's usability, the number of phenomenal users were the key to attributes and effectiveness of a product's social experience.

References

1. Kaplan, A.M., Haenlein, M.: Users of the world, unite! The challenges and opportunities of social media. Bus. Horiz. **53**(1), 59–68 (2010)
2. Gan, C., Wang, W.: Weibo or weixin? Gratifications for using different social media. In: Li, H., Mäntymäki, M., Zhang, X. (eds.) I3E 2014. IAICT, vol. 445, pp. 14–22. Springer, Heidelberg (2014). doi:10.1007/978-3-662-45526-5_2
3. China Internet Network Information Center. Statistical Report on Internet Development (in China). http://www.cnnic.net.cn/hlwfzyj/hlwxzbg/hlwtjbg/201701/t20170122_66437.htm
4. Liu, Y., Ma, Y.: The behavior analysis of product negative word-of-mouth spread on sina weibo. In: Zu, Q., Hu, B. (eds.) HCC 2016. LNCS, vol. 9567, pp. 284–295. Springer, Cham (2016). doi:10.1007/978-3-319-31854-7_26
5. Chen, Y.D.: Wechat to micro-blog: complementary rather than alternative to news and writing. China Acad. J. Electron. Publ. House **PP**, 31–33 (2013)
6. Chang, H.: How to activate the user's emotion in the social network to eliminate the ignorance and indifference. In: PA2012 Conference, pp. 3–7 (2012)

The Impact of Texting Interruptions on Task Performance

Scott McCoy[1], Eleanor Loiacono[2(✉)], and Shiya Cao[2]

[1] College of William and Mary, Williamsburg, USA
scott.mccoy@mason.wm.edu
[2] Worcester Polytechnic Institute, Worcester, USA
{eloiacon,scao2}@wpi.edu

Abstract. Texting has become ubiquitous in today's society. The high rate of cellular and wireless coverage across the globe coupled with the ease and low cost of some smartphones has made staying in touch easy—some might say too easy. Texting apps allow people to communicate with friends and family whenever and wherever they want, but these interruptions are not always at opportune moments and can be distracting. This paper discusses preliminary results of ongoing research into the effects of texting on task performance. In particular, data was collected using three treatment groups (zero, three, and six text messages). via WhatsApp during a reading comprehension task. The results reveal that high levels of interruptions affect task performance.

Keywords: Social media · WhatsApp · Texting · Task performance

1 Introduction

Interruptions due to social media notifications and texting have become a way of life for many, especially the youth of today. A survey of Johnson & Wales University found interesting results on student texting behavior. The sample (N = 48) consisted of

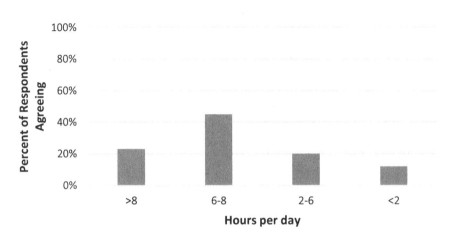

Fig. 1. Hours per day checking social media by college students

© Springer International Publishing AG 2017
G. Meiselwitz (Ed.): SCSM 2017, Part I, LNCS 10282, pp. 94–102, 2017.
DOI: 10.1007/978-3-319-58559-8_9

males (n = 26) and females (n = 22) who were administered a student perception questionnaire on how social media affects college students. The results of the survey questionnaire indicated that 45% of the people admitted that they spent 6–8 h per day checking social media sites, while 23% spent more than 8 h; 20% spent 2 to 4 h and only 12% spent less than 2 h on this task (see Fig. 1, [1]).

Therefore, understanding the impact of these frequent interruptions presented via social media in our daily lives is worthy of further investigation. The purpose of this research is to investigate the impact such interruptions have on a person's task performance.

2 Literature Review

Previous research has established the significance of interruptions on work performance. Some researchers worked on the impact on performance due to different types of tasks; other researchers worked on the impact on performance due to different types of interruption.

In particular, Baron [2] clarified the definition of simple tasks, which referred to well-learned tasks such as simply to write numbers as they appeared on the page (number copying); while complex and counter instinctual tasks are more difficult such as reverse letter copying.

Speier et al. [3] investigated the effects of interruptions on decision-making performance with college level coursework in different information-presenting modes. They revealed that interruptions facilitate performance of simple tasks but impede performance of complex tasks. For simple tasks, interruptions focus a decision maker's attention on important cues resulting, in general, in both increased decision accuracy and shorter decision time.

Payne [4] found that simple tasks require processing fewer cues (pieces of data) than complex tasks. Therefore, decision makers have ample cognitive resources to process simple tasks when interruptions occur and therefore do not need to change the way in which they process information. On the other hand, when processing complex tasks, decision makers minimize their expenditure of scarce cognitive resources, uncritically examining both relevant and irrelevant cues [2]. In addition, when performing simple tasks, individuals may perceive that the task "is too easy" and therefore do not dedicate their full attention and processing capabilities to performing the task at hand. Instead, they may think about other work-related (e.g., creative problem-solving on another task, creating a mental "to do" list) or personal issues.

Lee and Duffy [5] indicated that interruption frequency was also limited to three times per task because task performance had not changed significantly at more than three times per task and subjects showed unintended annoyance, which can possibly affect the task performance. In the pilot experiment, more than three interruptions per task was also tested, but too many interruptions in a task resulted in a severe decrease in task performance due to frustration and lack of motivation, not due to the effects of interruptions.

3   Research Question and Model

This research focuses on the question: *How does texting affect performance?* Based on previous research, the research model (see Fig. 2) shows texting frequency as a mediator. Task (reading) performance is thought to decrease as the number/frequency of interruptions of texting increases.

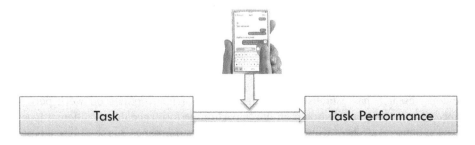

Fig. 2. Research model

4   Research Method

Since the study was looking at the impact of different levels of interruptions presented via a social media app, in this case WhatsApp, on reading comprehension/performance, a controlled lab environment was chosen. Participants were randomly assigned to one of three groups as they registered for the study. Each group received a different number of interruptions (0 for the control group, 3 messages for treatment group 1, and 6 messages for treatment group 2) (see Table 1).

Table 1. Treatment groups

Group	Treatment description	No. of subjects
1. Control	**No level of interruption:** received 0 message interruptions	39
2. Treatment 1	**Low level of interruption:** received 3 message interruptions	29
3. Treatment 2	**High level of interruption:** received 6 message interruptions	35

Upon entering the lab, all subjects were told to take a seat wherever they felt comfortable. Researchers ensured that the subject had WhatsApp on their cell phone and felt comfortable using it (see Fig. 3). The researcher then asked the participant for their WhatsApp name to add to the group texts. They were told to attend to any texts they received from WhatsApp while performing the task (see Fig. 4).

4.1   Sample

The overall sample consisted of 103 college students from a Chilean university. The students consisted of 57 males and 46 females. Their average age was 20.19. Subjects'

Fig. 3. WhatApp screen sample

Fig. 4. Study procedure

average number of hours spent per week using different social media apps were as follows: 0.10 h for Text messaging, 3.65 h for Instant messenger, 3.77 h for Email, 14.40 h for Facebook, and 23.04 h for WhatsApp (see Table 2).

Table 2. Demographic information

Gender	Male = 57
	Female = 46
Age	Average = 20.19
Average hours per week using:	
Text messaging	0.10
Instant messenger	3.65
Email	3.77
Facebook	14.40
WhatsApp	23.04

4.2 Task

After all subjects were seated, the researchers gave the subjects the study website address and provided further instructions. The subjects were given a survey site URL, where they would first answer several questions regarding their social media usage (see Fig. 5). They would then answer specific questions related to their experience with WhatsApp (see Fig. 6). Once all had completed the preliminary questions, the group was instructed to start reading a passage on the "No Smoking Law" and answer comprehension questions (see Fig. 7) related to the reading based on their memory. (They were not able to refer back to the passage).

WhatsApp

https://web.whatsapp.com

Sección 1 — Preguntas Demográficas--Demographics

Estas preguntas son importantes porque nos ayudan a ver si distintos tipos de personas responden el cuestionario de manera distinta. NO son utilizadas para identificar a ninguna persona.

1-1. ¿Cuántos años tiene? ____

1-2. ¿Cuál es su sexo?
Masculino / Femenino

how many hours

Por favor, indique el número de HORAS a la semana que utiliza las siguientes tecnologías, en el recuadro contiguo a cada una.	
1.8 Mensaje de Texto (SMS)	
1.9 Mensajería instantánea (MSN Messenger, Google Talk, u otros)	
1.10 E-mail	
1.11 Facebook	
1.12 WhatsApp	

How many times a week

Por favor, indique el número de VECES a la semana que utiliza las siguientes tecnologías, en el recuadro contiguo a cada una.	
1.13 Mensaje de Texto (SMS)	
1.14 Mensajería instantánea (MSN Messenger, Google Talk, u otros)	
1.15 E-mail	
1.16 Facebook	
1.17 WhatsApp	

Rank order from most simple to most complex to use

Por favor, ordene las siguientes tecnologías según su complejidad, de la menos compleja (1) a la más compleja (5). Recuerde asignar un grado DISTINTO a cada tecnología.	1	2	3	4	5
1.18 Mensaje de Texto (SMS)					
1.19 Mensajería instantánea (MSN Messenger, Google Talk, u otros)					

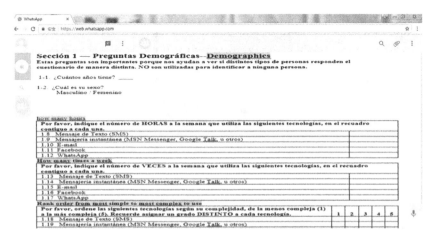

Fig. 5. The question sample of social media usage

WhatsApp

https://web.whatsapp.com

Sección 2 — Uso de WhatsApp—Using whatsapp

Por favor, indique el grado en el cual usted está en Acuerdo o Desacuerdo con las siguientes afirmaciones, según apliquen al uso de WhatsApp desde su Celular. Estamos interesados SOLO en el uso de WhatsApp a través de Celulares.

SECCIÓN 2-1: TECNOLOGÍAS DE MENSAJERÍA INSTANTÁNEA TAM measures: EOU, USEFUL, USE	Muy en Desacuerdo V. disagree			Indiferente			Muy de Acuerdo V. agree
1. Me es fácil desarrollar habilidades en el uso de WhatsApp	1	2	3	4	5	6	7
2. Considero fácil de utilizar la tecnología de WhatsApp	1	2	3	4	5	6	7
3. El aprendizaje de la operación de tecnologías de WhatsApp me es fácil	1	2	3	4	5	6	7
4. Pienso que es fácil lograr que las tecnologías de WhatsApp hagan lo que quiero que hagan	1	2	3	4	5	6	7
5. El uso de tecnologías de WhatsApp hace que mi efectividad aumente	1	2	3	4	5	6	7
6. Creo que las tecnologías de WhatsApp son útiles	1	2	3	4	5	6	7
7. El uso de tecnologías de WhatsApp hace que mi productividad aumente	1	2	3	4	5	6	7
8. El uso de tecnologías de WhatsApp hace que mi desempeño mejore	1	2	3	4	5	6	7
9. En la actualidad soy un usuario intensivo de tecnologías de WhatsApp USE-heavy user	1	2	3	4	5	6	7
10. Actualmente uso tecnologías de WhatsApp frecuentemente	1	2	3	4	5	6	7
11. Las tecnologías de WhatsApp son simples de usar	1	2	3	4	5	6	7

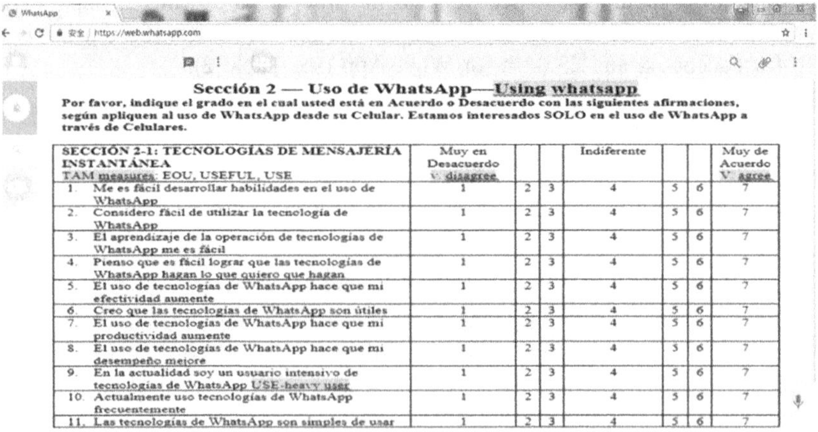

Fig. 6. The question sample of experience with WhatsApp

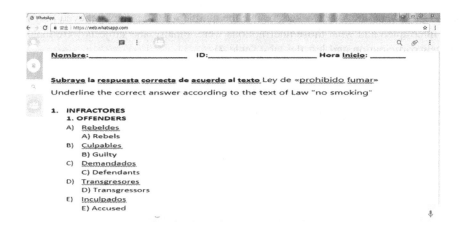

Fig. 7. The question sample of reading task

During the time that students were reading the passage, they were sent text messages through WhatsApp. They were not required to respond, but were simply asked to read them. The interruptions (see Fig. 8) were spaced equally—approximately 1 min apart. As seen in Table 3, the minimum time for completing the task was five minutes, while the maximum time was 18 min.

We removed outliers of those with no value of time-taking and with very high score of performance as well.

After completing the reading task, the subjects were asked to rate: (1) how mentally demanding the task was, (2) how much time pressure they felt, (3) how well they feel they met the objective of the task, (4) how much they felt insecure, discouraged, irritated, tensed, or worried during the task (see Fig. 9). Next, in order to understand how they perceived interruptions, they were asked if they were interrupted during the

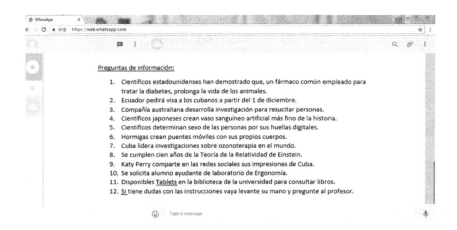

Fig. 8. WhatsApp interruption text

task. If they were, they were asked to state the number of times they believed they had been interrupted and what those interruptions were. Finally, the subjects were thanked for their participation and left the lab (Table 4).

Table 3. Task completion (time)

Treatment	Minutes			
	Mean	Max	Min	Median
No interruption	8.8	11	5	9
3 messages	11.74	18	6	12
6 messages	9.97	15	5	10

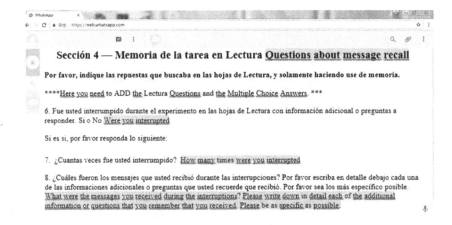

Fig. 9. The question sample after completing reading task

Table 4. Task completion (reading comprehension score)

Treatment	Mean	Std. deviation
No interruption	4.11	1.30
3 messages	4.62	0.81
6 messages	3.90	1.21

5   Results

The result of research indicated that values of scores differ statistically between the groups receiving 3 messages and 6 messages; values of scores also differ statistically between the groups receiving 3 messages and 0 messages; while values of scores do not differ statistically between the groups receiving 6 messages and 0 messages (Table 5).

Table 5. Treatment T-test results

Treatment comparison	T-value	P-value
0 to 3 messages	−2.007	0.048*
3 to 6 messages	2.933	0.005*
0 to 6 messages	0.689	0.493

*Significant at .05

6 Discussion

We assumed a negative relationship between frequency of texting and reading performance. The preliminary results showed that the performance of people receiving 3 messages was statistically better than those receiving 6 messages and receiving 3 messages was statistically better than that receiving 0 message. The reason behind people receiving 3 messages to perform statistically better than those receiving 6 messages is that more than three interruptions per task resulted in a severe decrease in task performance due to frustration and lack of motivation [5]. The reason behind people receiving no messages to not perform better than those receiving 3 messages is that interruptions facilitate performance on simple tasks and inhibit performance on complex tasks; while too simple tasks distract people's attention so that the performance is not going well [4].

7 Conclusions and Future Research

7.1 Conclusions

Based on the above analysis, preliminary results indicated that low frequency of interruptions facilitate performance, while high frequency of interruptions impede performance. Interruptions such as texting do affect students' reading performance (Table 6).

Table 6. Preliminary research implications

Interruptions	Performance
Low frequency and simple interruptions	↑
High frequency and complicate interruptions	↓

7.2 Future Research

In our future research, we want to work on several parts. First, we want to investigate focus group. We'll pick out focus group to investigate them, including picking out people who did very well and did very poorly in the test, also some middle of the road.

Second, we want to conduct more dependent variables analysis. These variables may include number of hours a week using WhatsApp, complexity using WhatsApp, difficulty of the reading task, etc.

Third, we want to see the impact of frequency of texting on a broader range of tasks (such as more complicated tasks) and the impact on performance with a time lag as well.

Third, we want to do more complex tests, such as not just texting messages but also texting questions that need to be answered and not only looking at reading performances but also looking at writing performances and other study performances.

Fourth, we want to expand the range of subjects. We are considering to do future research in group work, different age groups, and diverse cultural environment, etc. Also, variability of impact on performance in a variety of work settings and a variety of work tasks vs academic setting/tasks is worth to study on.

References

1. Qingya, W., Wei, C., Yu, L.: The Effects of Social Media on College Students. MBA Student Scholarship (2011)
2. Baron, R.S.: Distraction-conflict theory: progress and problems. Adv. Exp. Soc. Psychol. **19**, 1–39 (1986)
3. Speier, C., Vessey, I., Valacich, J.S.: The effects of interruptions, task complexity, and information presentation on computer-supported decision-making performance. Decis. Sci. **34** (4), 771–797 (2003)
4. Payne, J.W.: Contingent decision behavior. Psychol. Bull. **92**, 382–402 (1982)
5. Lee, B.C., Duffy, V.G.: The effects of task interruption on human performance: a study of the systematic classification of human behavior and interruption frequency. Hum. Factors Ergon. Manuf. Serv. Ind. **25**(2), 137–152 (2015)

Improving Engagement Metrics in an Open Collaboration Community Through Notification: An Online Field Experiment

Ana Paula O. Bertholdo[1]([⊠]), Claudia de O. Melo[2], and Artur S. Rozestraten[3]

[1] Department of Computer Science, University of São Paulo, São Paulo, Brazil
`ana@ime.usp.br`
[2] Faculty of Technology, University of Brasília, Brasília, Brazil
`claudiam@unb.br`
[3] Faculty of Architecture and Urbanism, University of São Paulo,
São Paulo, Brazil
`artur.rozestraten@usp.br`

Abstract. Open collaboration communities depend on contributors. To foster users' engagement with collaborative systems, it is necessary to consider features related to engagement attributes, such as awareness, control, novelty, and feedback, among others. However, it is not trivial to develop a feature that effectively improves engagement, considering specific contexts. This study analyzes the notification feature with respect to its effectiveness on increasing users' engagement in open collaboration communities. We conducted an online field experiment in a real setting, analyzing the engagement of two homogeneous user groups: pre- and post-implementation of a notification feature. We measured users' engagement using recency, frequency, duration, virality, and ratings metrics. There was an improvement in frequency, recency, and duration of users after inserting the notification feature. Considering the virality metric, there were changes in the behavior of users that accessed the notification interface, but there was neither influence of the notification on the virality metric from accesses through Facebook or Google+, nor on the ratings from comments and evaluations of system contents. Our results indicate an improvement of the user's engagement, as four of the five engagement metrics had positive results.

1 Introduction

Communities that enable open collaboration rely on collaborators [8,19]. It is essential to have active contributors for sustainability reasons. Enhancing online community engagement is an approach to motivate members to contribute [2], as well as improve usability. Engaged users are motivated, and perceive themselves to be in control over the interaction [17]. Engagement is a category of user experience characterized by attributes of feedback, challenge, positive affect, aesthetic and sensory appeal, attention, variety/novelty, interactivity, and control perceived by the user [17]. Feedback is an engagement attribute related to the

© Springer International Publishing AG 2017
G. Meiselwitz (Ed.): SCSM 2017, Part I, LNCS 10282, pp. 103–116, 2017.
DOI: 10.1007/978-3-319-58559-8_10

need for collaborative awareness of what is happening in the online environment. It helps to provide a common ground [6], a shared background of understanding that supports user interaction. As users need to understand how their actions affect the system and the other community members with whom they relate [5], notifications are usually designed to efficiently provide current and relevant information [4,5].

In remote collaboration, it is difficult to understand what the current focus of attention of the individuals is. People often fail to realize when common ground is non-existent or insufficient during online collaboration [4,5].

A variety of features have been developed to allow people to maintain online awareness of interesting information, for instance, notification systems. Knowledge gain from notifications can help users to plan future tasks, interact with others socially, and conclude simple tasks in a timely manner [5]. Notification improves the awareness of what is happening in the system, but does the use of notifications increase engagement with open collaboration online communities?

In this paper, we studied the effects of notification on user engagement in an open collaborative system. The research objective was to understand if the notification would interfere with the users' engagement of an open collaboration system for architecture image sharing (http://arquigrafia.org.br). The notification was the first feature inserted intending to contribute to engagement, seeking to improve the feedback of each action the user performs with the system and, consequently, supporting the awareness of what happens in the collaborative environment.

2   Awareness and Notification

People working collaboratively must establish and maintain awareness of one another's intentions, actions and results. Connecting individuals, peers, and social groups as part of their own feedback loops with technology has a great potential of learning, motivation and creativity [3].

Notification systems are typically triggered by user's task events, such as mail alerts and status updates. Therefore, they typically support awareness of the collaborator presence, tasks, and actions, helping to keep people aware of events beyond their current interactions. In many cases, the notification functionality supports collaborative awareness [5].

Carroll [4] presents a conceptual model of communities based on community identity; participation and awareness; and social networks, in which participation and awareness are directly related to engagement. Users need notification systems that keep them informed about: (i) what is happening to the objects they care about; (ii) what actions are being taken with such objects to access or to modify them, and (iii) who is performing these actions. Relevant information could be a discrete event or a series of events [5,16].

The success of notification systems depends on supporting the attention between tasks, while simultaneously allowing a utility evaluation by accessing additional information. Notifications should ideally cause minimal user distraction with respect to his/her primary task [13]. However, some notification systems are designed to attract user's attention and get them to perform a task, such as reminding a commitment. Examples of notification systems include instant messaging, system and user status updates, e-mail alerts, and news [14].

The benefit of notifications depends on the content of the message, its structure, style, and relationships between messages. The benefit might also vary among users and situations. Therefore, a notification can result in user ratings completely different from the perceived benefit [21].

According to Sousa *et al.* [20], personal and business relationships are built on systems that aggregate a variety of contexts and configurations, establishing new interaction scenarios that bring together into a common space the technology, applications, and users. This space becomes an aggregator of individuals and actions that enable certain behaviors, such as sharing, definition of new connections, as well as proposals of learning and participation of each individual involved [12].

In this context, Millen and Patterson [15] argue that shared online spaces need to be designed to support social engagement. Notification is particularly an important design feature. In addition, there is a negative impact of prolonged silence in the system, as it exhibits the inactivity of the community. Daily and ongoing activities are important to sustain community participation and it is important that members become aware of this activity.

3 Related Work

A large body of literature seeks to describe the factors that contribute to a specific online behavior, such as the frequency of participation by message posts [15]. Carroll *et al.* [5] studied a virtual school system to identify key aspects of awareness in collaborative situations, understand usability issues, and explore how notification systems can be designed. When analyzing integrated event logs, they found that the interaction flow with notification systems has an impact on the ability users have to collaborate and to be aware in the system. As a result, the authors presented notification design strategies to better support collaborative activities.

Vastenburg *et al.* [21] present the results of a controlled laboratory study of ten participants performing routine household activities. They subjectively assessed factors that were expected to influence the acceptability of notifications. All user activities and notifications were controlled. The results showed that adjusting the message intrusion level may improve the acceptability of notifications and that users' activities at the time of notification do not influence acceptability.

Millen and Patterson [15] investigated the effects of email notification on social engagement from the activity logs. They concluded that users are almost twice as likely to return to the site when they receive a notification alert. They also found evidence that increasing the number of messages contained in the alert is useful for promoting community engagement.

McCrickard *et al.* [13] evaluated the use of animated text in secondary displays in notification systems looking for the balance between attention and utility. They described two empirical investigations focused on the three often conflicting design objectives: interruption of primary tasks, reaction to specific notifications, and comprehension of information over time. The researchers concluded that the slow fade appears to be the best secondary display animation type tested.

Our research is focused on the analysis of engagement, before and after the insertion of the notification functionality, during the process of developing a collaborative system that has problems of engagement with users.

4   Online Field Experiment

Online field experiments, often called A/B testing, are built into the context of an online community under study. They do not allow for a direct manipulation of the treatment nor need to assign subjects at random to either control or treatment conditions. In general, online field experiments select a random sample of an online community's population for participation, divide participants into groups and then observe or measure the participants' outcomes [18].

Online field experiments usage has grown substantially in recent years, mostly in the industry, in a world in which the traces of social interactions are increasingly available online [18]. They are popular in multiple fields, such as computer science, economics, public finance, industrial organization, human-computer interactions, computer-supported collaborative work, and e-commerce [7].

The overall goal of our online field experiment is to investigate whether notifications increase engagement in open collaboration online communities. Particularly, we planned the experiment in the context of the Arquigrafia online community.

Arquigrafia is a public, nonprofit digital collaborative community dedicated to disseminating architectural images, with special attention to the Brazilian architecture (www.arquigrafia.org.br). The main objective of the community is to contribute to the study, teaching, research, and diffusion of architectural and urban culture, by promoting collaborative interactions among people and institutions.

Arquigrafia needs to foster a community around Architecture images and information. The analysis of subjective architectural issues on images will only generate relevant results when a mass of users engages to build a collective intelligence on architecture and urbanism. For this reason, it is a suitable project to carry out the experiment.

We use the GQM approach [1] to document our goal. Therefore, we state the overall experimental goal as:

Analyze the notification feature
For the purpose of its evaluation
With respect to its effectiveness on increasing users' engagement in open collaboration online communities
from the viewpoint of the researcher
in the context of the Arquigrafia open collaboration online community.

We thus aim to answer the following research question (RQ): *Do notifications increase engagement in open collaboration online communities?*

Engagement can be best analyzed by a series of interrelated metrics which are combined to form a whole. The relative proportion, or importance, of each of these metrics will vary depending on the type of business being considered [22]. These metrics can be aggregated as an engagement score:

Recency is about the time gap between the last visit to the present.
Frequency is about the number of user accesses to the system.
Duration is about how long users spend time in each connection.
Virality is about how many other users are influenced by a certain user to engage with the object.
Ratings is a user evaluation in terms of quality, quantity, or some combination of both.

The metrics are used to measure user engagement with the system before (Period 1) and after (Period 2) inserting a new notification feature. The period considered (Period 1 + Period 2) was *14 June 2015 to 10 August 2015*.

Table 1 describes the periods considered in this experiment.

Table 1. Periods before and after inserting the notification feature

Periods	Dates
Period 1 (Pre-insertion group)	June 14 to June 27
Period 2 (Post-insertion group)	July 28 to August 10

The **recency metric** was obtained by means of the difference between the last and the second to last access in days. Therefore, even though the user has used the system more than once during a day, the recency only counts 1 day if he had an access the previous day. Therefore, the lower the recency, the greater the interest the user had in returning to the system in a short time.

For this experiment, the recency was calculated from the beginning of each period; otherwise, Period 2 would be harmed with higher results of recency than Period 1. Both periods have stored data only since the insertion of logs from June 14; therefore, we have no recency data for many users that accessed the system in Period 1, because Period 1 started on June 14. For this reason, we balanced both periods starting recency calculation at the beginning of each period.

The **frequency metric** was calculated with the number of accesses to the system for different moments of the day (frequency per day); and with the number of access days of each user (frequency in days). For the first case, if the user accessed the system five times within an hour, we still consider only one access because it happened within one hour of the day analyzed. Therefore, the frequency per day was calculated with the number of accesses in the period divided by the number of days of each period, 14 days. The maximum number of accesses is equal to 24 hours per day * 14 days or 336 accesses in each period. For the frequency in days, we count the number of days a user accessed the system in both periods.

The **duration metric** presents the time of each user access in seconds, showing the difference between the last and the last but one access dates. Analogously, as with the frequency metric, the duration is also grouped by day and hour. The results of duration metric in each period are calculated by means of the average of access durations of a user in the period.

The **virality metric** was analyzed calculating accesses to the system via posts on Facebook and Google+ social networks and by the pages accessed from the notification functionality. This metric allows a deeper analysis of the impact of notification, as it tracks users accessing content in a system they would not know otherwise.

For the **ratings metric**, we considered the functions of comments and evaluations in the system. Comment functionality allows users to express their opinions about shared content, and may add new data or add value to content in the system. The evaluation functionality is an area the user has to analyze by means of quantitative parameters of the shared content in the system.

Similarly to other studies on online engagement [9,10], we purposefully designed the experiment as an online field experiment, in a real existing open collaboration system, rather than in a laboratory setting.

Event logs were inserted in the system to collect real usage data. User actions were logged into .log files. We wrote an algorithm (in the Java programming language) to convert each row from the .log files into data organized in a .csv file. These files, in turn, were converted into SQL queries to insert the content into a MySQL database. To retrieve the notification engagement metrics, it was necessary to evaluate external events from both development process and code updates, as well as events involving new users accessing the system, such as the new users logging because of the usability tests.

In Period 1, the system did not have the notification feature and it had the first version of the action logs system. In Period 2, the system had a new notification feature, which was inserted after a remote usability test between June 29 and July 14, but focused on other features.

The notification feature inserted in Period 2 was an improvement over a previous version. In this release, it was possible to group notifications related to the same object shared by an author (system user). For instance, in the previous version, if ten users commented on a single content shared by a certain user in the system, the system displayed ten different notifications to the author. In the second version, only one notification appears informing that ten users commented on a specific content. In both versions, it was possible to access the notified content from the notification interface.

Originally, 33,855 events of logged users were analyzed, with 1422 events from 89 users of Period 1 and 32,433 events from 1096 users of Period 2. We believe that the increase of users in Period 2 occurred as a consequence of a remote usability test. For this reason, we deleted the data of users that accessed the system during the test period aiming to withdraw the influence of the usability test in the analysis.

Besides, for building a comparable data set, we deleted users' data that appeared in only one of the periods considered in the experiment. Therefore, we analyzed the behavior of the same users in the 2 periods, each period with the same number of days: 14 days. After the data cleaning, each period has 31 users. Period 1 has 321 events and Period 2 has 11,654 events performed by the same users as in Period 1. Therefore, we were able to compare the behavior of two homogeneous user groups pre- and post-implementation of the notification feature, Period 1 and Period 2, respectively. The relevant information was recovered from MySQL database and was exported to CSV files, which were used as data sources for the R tool. In the R tool, we performed statistical analysis to validate the data set relevance. We are considering a statistical significance of 0.05. If the p-value is less than 0.05, there is evidence to claim that the data sets differ significantly. The Shapiro-Wilk normality test rejected the hypothesis that data from Periods 1 and 2 come from a normal population. Therefore, we used the Wilcoxon rank sum test, a non-parametric statistical hypothesis test, to perform data analysis.

The analysis was divided into two periods: before and after the insertion of the notification feature. We created MySQL views for each period to facilitate retrieving metric values from users that accessed the system in each period. We also generated graphs (boxplot) from the statistical analysis to facilitate the results visualization. Our SQL scripts enable standardized and automated retrieval of metrics, enabling replication of the analysis performed at any time. The notification feature implemented in the system was intended to display to users their status as well as the status of their objects in the system. For example, notifying the user that people have commented on some content shared by him/her. The feature also enables the user to know who the users who followed him/her are, which can promote the expansion of their contacts. Note that the notification feature can be viewed by any user logged in, regardless of whether they have notifications about their status at that time or not. In this case, the user receives a message that he/she does not have notifications yet, which is an indication that he/she needs to perform actions on the system. The next sections present the results for each of the five engagement metrics considered.

5   Results and Discussion

Table 2 presents statistical results for metrics frequency and duration. For metrics recency, virality and ratings, enough evidence lacks to compare Periods 1 and 2. The results of Table 2 are discussed in further detail in the next subsections.

Table 2. Statistical results for the experiment.

Metrics	W	p-value	Mean (Period 1)	SD (Period 1)	Mean (Period 2)	SD (Period 2)
Frequency per day	19	2.229e-11	0.14	0.17	4.22	6.51
Frequency in days	3.5	8.146e-13	1.09	0.53	11.35	3.56
Duration in seconds	314	0.01308	211.05	445.91	210.75	425.47

5.1   Frequency and Duration Metrics

For the frequency per day, in Period 1, 31 users had frequency average between 0.07 and 0.64 accesses per day. In Period 2, the 31 users accessed the system between 0.14 and 21.35 times per day. The average number of accesses per day was 0.14 accesses for Period 1 with standard deviation (SD) of 0.17; and 4.22 accesses for Period 2 with standard deviation of 6.51. The p-value for periods comparison was 2.229e-11, from Wilcoxon rank sum test. Figures 1(a) and (b) summarize the average number of accesses of users per day for the 14 days of each period.

For the frequency in days, in Period 1, 30 users had frequency of 1 day of access and only 1 user had frequency of 4 days of access. In Period 2, 27 users accessed the system between 9 and 14 days and 4 users accessed the system between 2 and 4 days. The average number of access days is 1.09 for Period 1 with standard deviation of 0.53; and 11.35 days of access for Period 2 with standard deviation of 3.56. The p-value for periods comparison was 8.146e-13, from Wilcoxon rank sum test. Figures 2(a) and (b) summarize the number of users access days for the 14 days of each period. Our data suggests that Period 2 presented an improvement in the frequency of accesses of users, for both types of frequency, considering the same 31 users, after the insertion of the notification feature.

For the duration metric, in Period 1, 22 users had duration average nearly 0 s, which represents only the access to the home page, without taking any action on the system; 2 users had duration average between 11 and 77 s; 5 users had duration average between 462.41 and 937.66 s; and 2 users had duration between 1134 and 1875 s. In Period 2, 10 users had duration average nearly 0 s (up to 0.09); 2 users had duration average between 0.5 and 2.51 s; 9 users had duration average between 21.42 and 65.29 s in the period; 6 users had duration average between 124.29 and 226.03 s; and 4 users had duration average between 1255.80 and 1326.34 s. Period 1 had average access duration of 211.05 s with standard deviation of 445.91.

For Period 2, the average duration was 210.75 s with standard deviation of 425.47. The comparison between Period 1 and Period 2 resulted in a p-value of 0.01308 for the **duration metric**, from Wilcoxon rank sum test. Although the duration in seconds remained small in Period 2, for users data without outliers - up to 226.03 s -, there was an increase of short accesses, as if the users were checking something new in the system, which is directly related to the

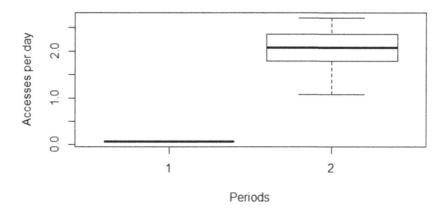

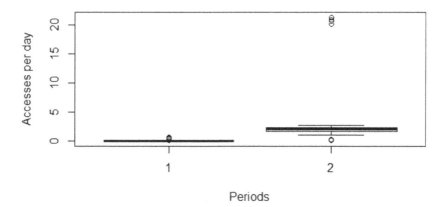

Fig. 1. Average number of accesses per day for Periods 1 and 2.

notification entry informing them of novelty. In the duration metric, the outliers data from Period 1 increased the duration average but they did not represent most users of Period 1. 70% of the users had a duration average of nearly 0 s in Period 1, whereas in Period 2, 32% of the users had the same duration of nearly 0 s (up to 0.09) or 38% to also consider durations between 0.5 and 2.51 s. The results are summarized in Figs. 3(a) and (b). Our data suggests that there was a slight improvement in duration metric after the insertion of the notification, especially when the variation in duration in seconds is analyzed among the same users considered in both periods, according to Fig. 3.

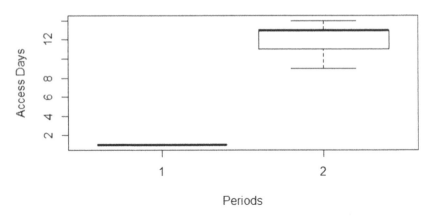

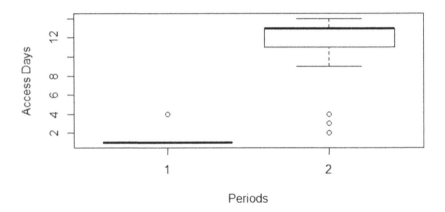

Fig. 2. Number of access days for Periods 1 and 2.

5.2 Recency, Virality and Ratings Metrics

In Periods 1 and 2, the virality from Facebook and Google+ was 0. For the virality from notification, six users accessed other system pages starting from the notification feature. The average of virality from notification was 2 in Period 2, ranging from 2 to 3 accesses to other pages from the notification, from the six users that received notifications. For the ratings metric from comments, Period 1 had no comments, while Period 2 had 1 user comment. For the ratings metric from evaluations of photos, the two periods had no evaluations performed.

It is worth noting that the pages considered for the virality metric calculation indicate the content pages of the system that were accessed by users from the notification, as pages of users' profile. The notifications view is available to all logged-in users, but only users who received comments about their shared content

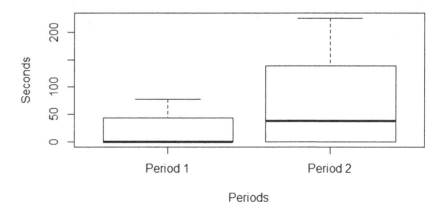

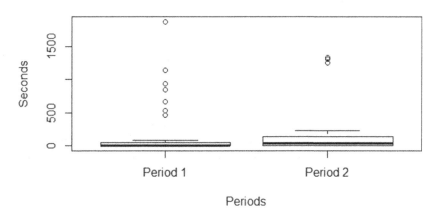

Fig. 3. Average duration in seconds for Periods 1 and 2.

or users who had new followers received notifications. The user who shared the content is notified with the identification of who the user was and what action he/she performed (e.g., posting a comment).

Considering the periods under analysis, access to pages from the notification started in Period 2. Only the six users who received notifications from users who followed them could have access to pages from the notification interface. The six users that received notifications are among the longest and most frequent users. However, there was no influence of the notification on the virality metric from accesses through Facebook or Google+, as well as on the from comments and evaluation of system contents.

For the recency metric, in Period 1, thirty users accessed the system once and they have no previous access data because we started the action logging in Period 1; therefore, it is not possible to calculate their recency. Only 1 user had recency equal to 1 day. However, the access dates ranged between June 20 and June 27. Therefore, it is possible to conclude that the recency of the thirty users was higher than 6 days in Period 1. In Period 2, the 31 users had recency between 1 and 3 days, 24 of them with recency equal to 1. Therefore, our data suggests that Period 2 presented an improvement in the recency of users.

5.3 Discussion

The analysis of the engagement metrics was performed in an open collaboration system that depends on the users' interaction, so that urban architectural elements can be jointly shared and analyzed by the community. For this reason, engagement is a central concept for the sustainability of the system. However, Arquigrafia was facing user engagement problems, the reason why we chose it for our study.

There were no other activities in the system that could lead to increased frequency, duration or recency of users in the system. The number of uploads, ratings and comments about photos was small to influence the user behavior. The only external event that occurred was the usability test between Periods 1 and 2, but all users who accessed the system during the test period were removed from the analysis. For this reason, our data suggest that the notification improved the frequency and the recency of the same group of users from Period 1 to Period 2 and the notification caused a slight improvement in the duration of users in the system.

The results are in agreement with the conclusions obtained by Millen and Patterson [15], who stated that the presence of a notification service resulted in increased site activity, especially total sessions per day. In addition, Millen and Patterson reported that ongoing daily activities are important to sustained participation in a community, and the members need be made aware of the activities. According to Carroll *et al.* [5], notification systems provide common ground essential for collaborative work since they have an impact on the ability users have to collaborate and to be aware of the system. Consequently, notification systems can increase users participation and awareness, which are directly related to engagement.

One limitation in the experiment was the data sample size. Each group was analyzed with data collected in a 14-day period, with 31 users in each period. This approach is also encouraged by Kohavi *et al.* [11]. Despite this sample limitation, we believe that our approach is valuable because it brings insights about the research question before investing in larger studies.

6   Conclusion

We conducted an online field experiment in an open collaboration community for 28 days. Our study analyzed the relationship between the notification implementation and user engagement behavioral outcomes. We aimed to investigate whether notifications increase users' engagement in the context of Arquigrafia, a digital collaborative community focused on the diffusion of architectural images. The major original contribution of this paper was to explore, in a real setting, the engagement of two homogeneous user groups: pre- and post-implementation of a notification feature. We measured users' engagement using recency, frequency, duration, virality, and ratings metrics.

There was a significant improvement in frequency and recency of users and a slight improvement in the duration after the insertion of the notification, considering the same users in both periods. For the virality from notification, there were changes in the behavior of users that accessed the notification interface, but there was no influence of the notification on the virality metric from accesses in Facebook or Google+, nor on the ratings from comments and evaluations of system contents. Regarding our Research Question (*Do notifications increase engagement in open collaboration online communities?*), our results indicate an improvement in the user's engagement, as four of the five engagement metrics had positive results.

This work points to the need for some future studies. The next step is to conduct a large-scale online field experiment to be able to test hypotheses about the relationship between the notification feature and user engagement. This would also increase results generalizability. Finally, future studies may aim to evaluate additional features that might influence users' engagement in open collaboration communities.

Acknowledgments. This research has been supported by FAPESP, Brazil, proc. 2015/06660-8 and proc. 2012/24409-2.

References

1. Basili, V.R., Trendowicz, A., Kowalczyk, M., Heidrich, J., Seaman, C.B., Jürgen Münch, H., Rombach, D.: Aligning Organizations Through Measurement - The GQM+Strategies Approach. The Fraunhofer IESE Series on Software and Systems Engineering. Springer, Cham (2014)
2. Bista, S.K., Nepal, S., Colineau, N., Paris, C.: Using gamification in an online community. In: 2012 8th International Conference on Collaborative Computing: Networking, Applications and Worksharing (CollaborateCom), pp. 611–618. IEEE (2012)
3. Burleson, W.: Developing creativity, motivation, and self-actualization with learning systems. Int. J. Hum.-Comput. Stud. **63**(4), 436–451 (2005)
4. Carroll, J.M.: The Neighborhood in the Internet: Design Research Projects in Community Informatics. Routledge, London (2014)
5. Carroll, J.M., Neale, D.C., Isenhour, P.L., Rosson, M.B., McCrickard, D.S.: Notification and awareness: synchronizing task-oriented collaborative activity. Int. J. Hum. Comput. Stud. **58**(5), 605–632 (2003)
6. Carston, R.: Herbert H. Clark, Using Language, pp. xi+ 432. Cambridge University Press, Cambridge (1996). J. Linguist. **35**(01), 167–222 (1999)
7. Chen, Y., Konstan, J.: Online field experiments: a selective survey of methods. J. Econ. Sci. Assoc. **1**(1), 29–42 (2015)

8. Forte, A., Lampe, C.: Defining, understanding, and supporting open collaboration: lessons from the literature. Am. Behav. Sci. **57**(5, SI), 535–547 (2013)
9. Hamari, J.: Do badges increase user activity? A field experiment on the effects of gamification. Comput. Hum. Behav. (2015, in press)
10. Hamari, J., Shernoff, D.J., Rowe, E., Coller, B., Asbell-Clarke, J., Edwards, T.: Challenging games help students learn: an empirical study on engagement, flow and immersion in game-based learning. Comput. Hum. Behav. **54**, 170–179 (2016)
11. Kohavi, R., Deng, A., Frasca, B., Walker, T., Ya, X., Pohlmann, N.: Online controlled experiments at large scale. In: Proceedings of 19th ACM SIGKDD International Conference on Knowledge Discovery and Data Mining, pp. 1168–1176. ACM (2013)
12. Kolko, J.: Endless nights-learning from design studio critique. Interactions **18**(2), 80–81 (2011)
13. McCrickard, D.S., Catrambone, R., Chewar, C.M., Stasko, J.T.: Establishing trade-offs that leverage attention for utility: empirically evaluating information display in notification systems. Int. J. Hum. Comput. Stud. **58**(5), 547–582 (2003)
14. McCrickard, D.S., Czerwinski, M., Bartram, L.: Introduction: design and evaluation of notification user interfaces. Int. J. Hum. Comput. Stud. **58**(5), 509–514 (2003)
15. Millen, D.R., Patterson, J.F.: Stimulating social engagement in a community network. In: Proceedings of 2002 ACM Conference on Computer Supported Cooperative Work, pp. 306–313. ACM (2002)
16. Neuwirth, C.M., Morris, J.H., Regli, S.H., Chandhok, R., Wenger, G.C.: Envisioning communication: task-tailorable representations of communication in asynchronous work. In: Proceedings of ACM CSCW 1998 Conference on Computer Supported Cooperative Work, pp. 265–274. Association for Computing Machinery (1998)
17. O'Brien, H.L., Toms, E.G.: What is user engagement? A conceptual framework for defining user engagement with technology. J. Am. Soc. Inf. Sci. Technol. **59**(6), 938–955 (2008)
18. Parigi, P., Santana, J.J., Cook, K.S.: Online field experiments. Soc. Psychol. Q. **80**(1), 1–19 (2017)
19. Qureshi, I., Fang, Y.: Socialization in open source software projects: a growth mixture modeling approach. Org. Res. Methods **14**, 208–238 (2010)
20. Sousa, S., Lamas, D., Dias, P.: Value creation through trust in technological-mediated social participation. Technol. Innov. Educ. **2**(1), 1 (2016)
21. Vastenburg, M.H., Keyson, D.V., De Ridder, H.: Considerate home notification systems: a user study of acceptability of notifications in a living-room laboratory. Int. J. Hum.-Comput. Stud. **67**(9), 814–826 (2009)
22. Zichermann, G., Cunningham, C.: Introduction - Gamification by Design: Implementing Game Mechanics in Web and Mobile Apps, 1st edn., p. xiv. O'Reilly Media, Sebastopol (2011). ISBN 1449315399

What Happens When Evaluating Social Media's Usability?

Virginica Rusu[1], Cristian Rusu[2], Daniela Quiñones[2(✉)],
Silvana Roncagliolo[2], and César A. Collazos[3]

[1] Universidad de Playa Ancha de Ciencias de la Educación, Valparaíso, Chile
virginica.rusu@upla.cl
[2] Pontificia Universidad Católica de Valparaíso, Valparaíso, Chile
{cristian.rusu,silvana.roncagliolo}@pucv.cl,
danielacqo@gmail.com
[3] Universidad del Cauca, Popayán, Colombia
ccollazo@unicauca.edu.co

Abstract. The paper presents a study on the perception of 16 evaluators over a set of usability heuristics for smartphones - SMASH. All participants were asked to perform a heuristic evaluation of the mobile version of Facebook. Later on a survey was conducted based on the standard questionnaire that we developed. Evaluators perceive SMASH as an appropriate instrument to evaluate social media's usability, and they intent to use it in future evaluations.

Keywords: Usability · Heuristic evaluation · Usability heuristics · Social media · Facebook

1 Introduction

The ISO 9241-210 defines usability as "the extent to which a system, product or service can be used by specified users to achieve specified goals with effectiveness, efficiency and satisfaction in a specified context of use" [1]. Lewis identifies two approaches on evaluating usability: (1) summative, "measurement-based usability", and (2) formative, "diagnostic usability" [2].

Heuristic evaluation is one of the most popular usability evaluation methods [3]. Generic or specific heuristics may be used. Generic heuristics are familiar to evaluators and therefore easy to apply, but they can miss specific usability issues. Specific heuristics can detect relevant domain related usability issues.

The paper presents a study on the perception of 16 evaluators over a set of usability heuristics for smartphones - SMASH [4]. All participants were asked to perform a heuristic evaluation of the mobile version of Facebook. Later on a survey was conducted based on a standard questionnaire that we developed. Section 2 briefly reviews the concepts of usability and its evaluation. Section 3 describes SMASH, the set of usability heuristics that we used. Section 4 presents the survey on evaluators' perception after evaluating the mobile version of Facebook. Section 5 highlights conclusions and future work.

© Springer International Publishing AG 2017
G. Meiselwitz (Ed.): SCSM 2017, Part I, LNCS 10282, pp. 117–126, 2017.
DOI: 10.1007/978-3-319-58559-8_11

2 Usability and Usability Evaluation

Known for decades, the usability concept is still evolving. A widely accepted usability definition was proposed by the ISO 9241 standard back in 1998 [5]. The ISO 9241 standard was updated in 2010 [1], but a new revision started briefly after, in 2011 [6].

There is no general agreement on either usability definition or its dimensions, but several aspects are recurrent in all definitions: effectiveness, efficiency, satisfaction, and the context of use. The ISO 9241 current approach relates usability to user and business requirements: effectiveness means success in achieving goals, efficiency means not wasting time, and satisfaction means willingness to use the system [6].

Usability evaluation does not limit to measuring effectiveness, efficiency and satisfaction. Several classifications were proposed for usability evaluation methods. Usually methods are classified as: (1) empirical usability testing, based on users' participation [7], and (2) inspection methods, based on experts' judgment [8].

Heuristic evaluation is arguably the most common usability inspection method. Usability specialists (evaluators) analyze every interactive element and dialog following a set of established usability design principles called heuristics [3]. Generic or specific heuristics may be used. Generic heuristics, as Nielsen's ones, are familiar to evaluators and therefore easy to apply; however they are not universally suitable, and can miss specific usability issues. Specific heuristics can detect relevant usability issues related to the application area.

We developed sets of specific usability heuristics for smartphones [4], touchscreen-based mobile applications [9], grid computing applications [10], virtual worlds [11], interactive digital television [12], transactional web applications [13], driving simulators [14], u-Learning applications [15], and cultural aspects [16], among others. We used a methodology that we proposed backed in 2011 [17]. The methodology is currently under review; some changes have been already proposed [18].

We systematically conduct studies on evaluators' perception over generic (Nielsen's) and specific usability heuristics. We developed a standard questionnaire, concerning 4 dimensions: D1 - *Utility*, D2 - *Clarity*, D3 - *Ease of use*, D4 - *Necessity of additional checklist*. All dimensions are evaluated using a 5 points Likert scale. The studies offer an important feedback for both teaching and research. Some results have been published [19, 20].

3 A Set of Usability Heuristics for Smartphones

We developed a set of usability heuristics for smartphones - SMASH [4]. It includes 12 heuristics and it is based on a set of usability heuristics for touchscreen-based mobile applications [9]. SMASH heuristics are briefly described below.

> SMASH1 - *Visibility of system status*: The device should keep the user informed about all the processes and state changes through feedback and in a reasonable time.
> SMASH2 - *Match between system and the real world*: The device should speak the users' language instead of system oriented concepts and technicalities. The device

should follow the real world conventions and display the information in a logical and natural order.

SMASH3 - *User control and freedom*: The device should allow the user to undo and redo his/her actions, and provide clearly pointed "emergency exits" to leave unwanted states. These options should be available preferably through a physical button or equivalent.

SMASH4 - *Consistency and standards*: The device should follow the established conventions, allowing the user to do things in a familiar, standard and consistent way.

SMASH5 - *Error prevention*: The device should hide or deactivate unavailable functionalities, warn users about critical actions and provide access to additional information.

SMASH6 - *Minimize the user's memory load*: The device should offer visible objects, actions and options in order to prevent users from having to memorize information from one part of the dialog to another.

SMASH7 - *Customization and shortcuts*: The device should provide basic and advanced configuration options, allow definition and customization of shortcuts to frequent actions.

SMASH8 - *Efficiency of use and performance*: The device should be able to load and display the required information in a reasonable time and minimize the required steps to perform a task. Animations and transitions should be displayed smoothly.

SMASH9 - *Esthetic and minimalist design*: The device should avoid displaying unwanted information overloading the screen.

SMASH10 - *Help users recognize, diagnose, and recover from errors*: The device should display error messages in a language familiar to the user, indicating the issue in a precise way and suggesting a constructive solution.

SMASH11 - *Help and documentation*: The device should provide easy-to-find documentation and help, centered on the user's current task and indicating concrete steps to follow.

SMASH12 - *Physical interaction and ergonomics*: The device should provide physical buttons or the equivalent for main functionalities, located in positions recognizable by the user, which should fit the natural posture (and reach) of the user's dominant hand.

4   Evaluating Facebook's Usability: Evaluators' Perception

We made an experiment with 16 undergraduate Computer Science students at Pontificia Universidad Católica de Valparaíso, Chile. They performed a heuristic evaluation of the mobile version of Facebook, based on SMASH. They all had (low) previous experience in heuristic evaluations, based on Nielsen's heuristics. They were all frequent users of Facebook, mainly in its mobile version.

After performing the heuristic evaluation, all participants were asked to rate SMASH heuristics, based on a standard questionnaire, using a 5 points Likert scale. The average scores are presented in Table 1.

Table 1. Average scores of evaluators' perception on SMASH

	D1 - utility	D2 - clarity	D3 - ease of use	D4 - necessity of additional checklist
SMASH1	4.44	4.00	3.31	3.81
SMASH2	3.81	3.44	3.25	4.13
SMASH3	3.81	3.56	3.25	4.38
SMASH4	4.06	3.75	3.25	4.06
SMASH5	4.31	3.75	3.44	4.38
SMASH6	3.81	3.56	3.06	4.06
SMASH7	3.63	3.44	3.50	4.25
SMASH8	4.00	3.75	3.38	4.06
SMASH9	4.31	3.94	3.81	4.00
SMASH10	4.19	3.75	3.31	4.06
SMASH11	3.75	4.06	3.81	4.00
SMASH12	3.88	3.87	3.43	3.94
Average score by dimension	4.00	3.74	3.40	4.09

When evaluating Facebook, SMASH heuristics are perceived as useful (average score 4.00) and clear (average score 3.74). However, they are perceived as not quite easy to use (average score 3.40), and therefore there is a necessity of additional checklist (average score 4.09).

SMASH1 - *Visibility of system status* is perceived as the most useful heuristic (4.44); it is also perceived as clear (4.00), and the necessity of additional checklist is the lowest one (3.81). SMASH9 - *Esthetic and minimalist design* is also positively perceived: useful (4.31), clear (3.94), and easy to use (3.81). On the opposite side, SMASH7 - *Customization and shortcuts* is perceived as the less useful (3.63) and less clear (3.44) heuristic; the necessity of additional checklist is high (4.25).

Some heuristics are perceived as useful, relatively clear, but not quite easy to use: SMASH4 - *Consistency and standards*, SMASH5 - *Error prevention*, SMASH8 - *Efficiency of use and performance*, and SMASH10 - *Help users recognize, diagnose, and recover from errors*. Their associated necessities of additional checklist are quite high.

On the other hand, even if it is perceived as clear and easy to use, heuristic SMASH11 - *Help and documentation* is not perceived as really useful. That is probably because evaluators are so familiar with Facebook; they do not feel the need for help and documentation when using this particular social network.

As observations' scale is ordinal, and no assumption of normality could be made, the survey results were analyzed using nonparametric statistics tests. In all tests $p \leq 0.05$ was used as decision rule. Spearman ρ tests were performed to check the hypothesis:

- H_0: $\rho = 0$, the dimensions Dm and Dn are independent,
- H_1: $\rho \neq 0$, the dimensions Dm and Dn are dependent.

Table 2 shows the correlations between dimensions when all 12 SMASH heuristics are considered. There is a very strong significant correlation between dimensions D2 – *Clarity* and D3 - *Ease of use*. As expected, when heuristics are perceived as clear, they are also perceived as easy to use. There are no other significant correlations.

Table 2. Spearman ρ test when all SMASH heuristics are considered

	D1 - utility	D2 - clarity	D3 - ease of use	D4 - necessity of additional checklist
D1	1	Independent	Independent	Independent
D2		1	0.802	Independent
D3			1	Independent
D4				1

We also performed Spearman ρ tests for each heuristic (Tables 3, 4, 5, 6, 7, 8, 9, 10, 11, 12, 13 and 14). There are only two very strong significant correlations: (1) between dimensions D1 – *Utility* and D3 - *Ease of use*, in the case of SMASH1 - *Visibility of system status*, and (2) between dimensions D1 – *Utility* and D2 – *Clarity*, in the case of SMASH2 - *Match between system and the real world*. There are few strong or moderate correlations. The most recurrent correlation occurs between dimensions D2 – *Clarity* and D3 - *Ease of use* (for 7 out of 12 heuristics).

Table 3. Spearman ρ test for SMASH1

	D1 - utility	D2 - clarity	D3 - ease of use	D4 - necessity of additional checklist
D1	1	0.510	0.864	Independent
D2		1	0.663	Independent
D3			1	Independent
D4				1

Table 4. Spearman ρ test for SMASH2

	D1 - utility	D2 - clarity	D3 - ease of use	D4 - necessity of additional checklist
D1	1	0.816	Independent	Independent
D2		1	0.776	Independent
D3			1	Independent
D4				1

Table 5. Spearman ρ test for SMASH3

	D1 - utility	D2 - clarity	D3 - ease of use	D4 - necessity of additional checklist
D1	1	Independent	Independent	Independent
D2		1	Independent	Independent
D3			1	Independent
D4				1

Table 6. Spearman ρ test for SMASH4

	D1 - utility	D2 - clarity	D3 - ease of use	D4 - necessity of additional checklist
D1	1	Independent	Independent	Independent
D2		1	0.752	Independent
D3			1	Independent
D4				1

Table 7. Spearman ρ test for SMASH5

	D1 - utility	D2 - clarity	D3 - ease of use	D4 - necessity of additional checklist
D1	1	Independent	Independent	Independent
D2		1	Independent	Independent
D3			1	Independent
D4				1

Table 8. Spearman ρ test for SMASH6

	D1 - utility	D2 - clarity	D3 - ease of use	D4 - necessity of additional checklist
D1	1	Independent	Independent	Independent
D2		1	0.683	Independent
D3			1	Independent
D4				1

Table 9. Spearman ρ test for SMASH7

	D1 - utility	D2 - clarity	D3 - ease of use	D4 - necessity of additional checklist
D1	1	Independent	Independent	Independent
D2		1	0.556	Independent
D3			1	Independent
D4				1

Table 10. Spearman ρ test for SMASH8

	D1 - utility	D2 - clarity	D3 - ease of use	D4 - necessity of additional checklist
D1	1	Independent	Independent	Independent
D2		1	Independent	Independent
D3			1	Independent
D4				1

Table 11. Spearman ρ test for SMASH9

	D1 - utility	D2 - clarity	D3 - ease of use	D4 - necessity of additional checklist
D1	1	Independent	0.576	Independent
D2		1	0.549	Independent
D3			1	Independent
D4				1

Table 12. Spearman ρ test for SMASH10

	D1 - utility	D2 - clarity	D3 - ease of use	D4 - necessity of additional checklist
D1	1	0.599	Independent	Independent
D2		1	0.659	Independent
D3			1	Independent
D4				1

Table 13. Spearman ρ test for SMASH11

	D1 - utility	D2 - clarity	D3 - ease of use	D4 - necessity of additional checklist
D1	1	0.554	Independent	Independent
D2		1	Independent	Independent
D3			1	Independent
D4				1

Table 14. Spearman ρ test for SMASH12

	D1 - utility	D2 - clarity	D3 - ease of use	D4 - necessity of additional checklist
D1	1	Independent	0.662	Independent
D2		1	Independent	Independent
D3			1	Independent
D4				1

We asked participants three additional questions; responses were evaluated using a 5 points Likert scale. Average scores are presented in Table 15.

Table 15. Overall perception on SMASH when evaluating social media's usability

Question	Average score
Q1 – *Easiness*: How easy was to perform the heuristic evaluation of Facebook?	3.00
Q2 – *Intention*: Would you use SMASH when evaluating social media in the future?	3.88
Q3 – *Completeness*: Do you think SMASH covers all usability aspects for social media?	3.94

Even if evaluators do not think the heuristic evaluation of Facebook was an easy task, they do perceive SMASH as an appropriate instrument to evaluate social media's usability, and they intent to use it in future evaluations.

We also performed a Spearman ρ test to check the correlation between Q1, Q2, Q3, and D1, D2, D3, D4. Results are presented in Table 16.

Table 16. Spearman ρ tests for Q1, Q2, Q3, and D1, D2, D3, D4

	Q1 – easiness	Q2 – intention	Q3 – completeness	D1 - utility	D2 - clarity	D3 - ease of use	D4 - necessity of additional checklist
Q1	1	Independent	Independent	Independent	Independent	0.570	Independent
Q2		1	Independent	Independent	Independent	Independent	Independent
Q3			1	0.517	Independent	Independent	0.542
D1				1	Independent	Independent	Independent
D2					1	0.802	Independent
D3						1	Independent
D4							1

Correlations between dimensions D were analyzed above. As we already mentioned, there is only one very strong significant correlation, between dimensions D2 – *Clarity* and D3 - *Ease of use*.

Analyzing other correlations, we noticed that:

• Q1 – *Easiness* is moderately correlated with D3 – *Ease of use*. When SMASH are perceived as easy to use, the heuristic evaluation is also perceived as easy to perform.

• Q3 – *Completeness* is moderately correlated with dimensions D1 – *Utility*, and D4 - *Necessity of additional checklist*. When evaluators perceived SMASH as useful, they also feel is an appropriate/complete tool. But they also think that SMASH could be complemented with an additional checklist.

5 Conclusions

Evaluating specific applications' usability is still challenging. Social media is not an exception. Even a well know inspection method, as heuristic evaluation, is hard to perform by novice evaluators. As generic heuristics can miss specific usability issues, we usually prefer to use specific heuristics, which can detect relevant domain related usability issues.

16 undergraduate Computer Science students performed a heuristic evaluation of the mobile version of Facebook, based on a set of 12 usability heuristics that we developed (SMASH). SMASH targets smartphone applications in general, but it seems to work well when evaluating social media. Evaluators do not perceive the heuristic evaluation of Facebook as an easy task, probably because they were using SMASH for

the very first time. However, they think SMASH is an appropriate instrument to evaluate social media's usability, and they intent to use it in future evaluations.

We surveyed evaluators' perception on SMASH based on 4 dimensions: D1 - *Utility*, D2 - *Clarity*, D3 - *Ease of use*, D4 - *Necessity of additional checklist*. There is only one strong significant correlation between dimensions D2 and D3, when all 12 heuristics are considered; when heuristics are perceived as clear, they are also perceived as easy to use. Correlation between dimensions D2 and D3 was also the most recurrent one identified in a previous study [20]. When performing Spearman ρ tests for each heuristic, no patterns could be identified.

As future work, we intend to complement the study with a qualitative approach, based on data collected through surveys and interviews.

References

1. ISO 9241-210: Ergonomics of human-system interaction — Part 210: Human-centred design for interactive systems. International Organization for Standardization, Geneva (2010)
2. Lewis, J.: Usability: lessons learned… and yet to be learned. Int. J. Hum.-Comput. Inter. **30** (9), 663–684 (2014)
3. Nielsen, J., Mack, R.L.: Usability Inspection Methods. John Wiley & Sons, New York (1994)
4. Inostroza, R., Rusu, C., Roncagliolo, S., Rusu, V., Collazos, C.: Developing SMASH: a set of SMArtphone's uSability heuristics. Comput. Stand. Interfaces **43**, 40–52 (2016)
5. ISO 9241-11: Ergonomic requirements for office work with visual display terminals (VDTs) – Part 11: Guidance on usability. International Organization for Standardization, Geneva, (1998)
6. Bevan, N., Carter, J., Harker, S.: ISO 9241-11 revised: what have we learnt about usability since 1998? In: Kurosu, M. (ed.) HCI 2015. LNCS, vol. 9169, pp. 143–151. Springer, Cham (2015). doi:10.1007/978-3-319-20901-2_13
7. Dumas, J., Fox, J.: Usability testing: current practice and future directions. In: Sears, A., Jacko, J. (eds.) The Human – Computer Interaction Handbook: Fundamentals, Evolving Technologies and Emerging Applications, pp. 1129–1149. Taylor & Francis, New York (2008)
8. Cockton, G., Woolrych, A., Lavery, D.: Inspection – based evaluations. In: Sears, A., Jacko, J. (eds.) The Human – Computer Interaction Handbook: Fundamentals, Evolving Technologies and Emerging Applications, pp. 1171–1189. Taylor & Francis, New York (2008)
9. Inostroza, R., Rusu, C., Roncagliolo S., Rusu V.: Usability heuristics for touchscreen-based mobile devices: update. In: First Chilean Conference on Human - Computer Interaction (ChileCHI2013), pp. 24–29. ACM International Conference Proceeding Series (2013)
10. Roncagliolo, S., Rusu, V., Rusu, C., Tapia, G., Hayvar, D., Gorgan D.: Grid computing usability heuristics in practice. In: 8th International Conference on Information Technology: New Generations (ITNG2011), pp. 145–150. IEEE Computer Society Press (2011)
11. Rusu, C., Muñoz, R., Roncagliolo, S., Rudloff, S., Rusu, V., Figueroa A.: Usability heuristics for virtual worlds. In: The Third International Conference on Advances in Future Internet (AFIN2011), pp. 16–19. IARIA (2011)
12. Solano, A., Rusu, C., Collazos, C., Arciniegas, J.: Evaluating interactive digital television applications through usability heuristics. Ingeniare **21**(1), 16–29 (2013)

13. Quiñones, D., Rusu C., Roncagliolo S.: Redefining usability heuristics for transactional web applications. In: 11th International Conference on Information Technology: New Generations (ITNG2014), pp. 260–265. IEEE Computer Society Press (2014)
14. Campos, A., Rusu, C., Roncagliolo, S., Sanz, F., Galvez, R., Quiñones, D.: Usability heuristics and design recommendations for driving simulators. Adv. Intell. Syst. Comput. **448**, 1287–1290 (2016)
15. Sanz, F., Galvez, R., Rusu, C., Roncagliolo, S., Rusu, V., Collazos, C., Cofré, J.P., Campos, A., Quiñones, D.: A set of usability heuristics and design recommendations for u-Learning applications. Adv. Intell. Syst. Comput. **448**, 983–993 (2016)
16. Diaz, J., Rusu, C., Collazos, C.: Experimental validation of a set of cultural-oriented usability heuristics: e- Commerce websites evaluation. Comput. Stand. Interfaces **50**, 160–178 (2017)
17. Rusu, C., Roncagliolo, S., Rusu, V., Collazos C.: A methodology to establish usability heuristics. In: The Fourth International Conference on Advances in Computer-Human In-teractions (ACHI2011), pp. 59–62. IARIA (2011)
18. Quiñones, D., Rusu, C., Roncagliolo, S., Rusu, V., Collazos, C.: Developing usability heuristics: a formal or informal process? IEEE Lat. Am. Trans. **14**(7), 3400–3409 (2016)
19. Rusu, C., Rusu, V., Roncagliolo, S., Apablaza, J., Rusu, V.Z.: User experience evaluations: challenges for newcomers. In: Marcus, A. (ed.) DUXU 2015. LNCS, vol. 9186, pp. 237–246. Springer, Cham (2015). doi:10.1007/978-3-319-20886-2_23
20. Rusu, C., Rusu, V., Roncagliolo, S., Quiñones, D., Rusu, V.Z., Fardoun, H.M., Alghazzawi, D.M., Collazos, C.A.: Usability heuristics: reinventing the wheel? In: Meiselwitz, G. (ed.) SCSM 2016. LNCS, vol. 9742, pp. 59–70. Springer, Cham (2016). doi:10.1007/978-3-319-39910-2_6

On User eXperience in Virtual Museums

Cristian Rusu[1], Virginia Zaraza Rusu[1], Patricia Muñoz[1],
Virginica Rusu[2], Silvana Roncagliolo[1], and Daniela Quiñones[1(✉)]

[1] Pontificia Universidad Católica de Valparaíso, Valparaíso, Chile
{cristian.rusu, silvana.roncagliolo}@pucv.cl,
rvzaraza90@hotmail.com,
patricia.alej.munoz@gmail.com, danielacqo@gmail.com
[2] Universidad de Playa Ancha de Ciencias de la Educación, Valparaíso, Chile
virginica.rusu@upla.cl

Abstract. User eXperience (UX) evaluation is a challenging task, especially for newcomers and when evaluating domain related aspects. Usability and UX in virtual museums is one of our current research topics. We focused on identified users' needs, on developing a set of specific usability heuristics, and a methodology to asses UX in virtual museums. We conducted several experiments, mainly with graduate and undergraduate students in Tourism and Computer Science. The paper presents a UX study on Pre-Columbian Museum portal.

Keywords: User eXperience · Usability · Virtual museums · Co-discovery

1 Introduction

Usability is a basic attribute in software quality. There is still no clear and generally accepted usability definition; usability's complex nature is hard to describe in a unique definition. The current ISO 9241-210 definition of usability refers to "the extent to which a system, product or service can be used by specified users to achieve specified goals with effectiveness, efficiency and satisfaction in a specified context of use" [1].

User eXperience (UX) goes beyond the three generally accepted usability's dimensions: effectiveness, efficiency and satisfaction. The ISO 9241-210 standard defines UX as a "person's perceptions and responses resulting from the use and/or anticipated use of a product, system or service" [1].

The UX concept is very popular nowadays. To move from usability to UX is a tendency; even the former "Usability Professionals Association" (UPA) redefined itself as "User Experience Professionals Association" (UXPA). Most authors consider UX as an extension of the usability concept; others still use the terms usability and UX indistinctly [2].

Measuring effectiveness, efficiency and satisfaction does not represent the only way of evaluating usability. Two major conceptions on usability have been pointed out: (1) summative, focused on metrics, "measurement-based usability", and (2) formative, focused on usability problems detection and associated design solutions, "diagnostic usability" [3].

© Springer International Publishing AG 2017
G. Meiselwitz (Ed.): SCSM 2017, Part I, LNCS 10282, pp. 127–136, 2017.
DOI: 10.1007/978-3-319-58559-8_12

Evaluating UX is more challenging than evaluating usability. If usability is a subset of UX that means usability evaluation methods are also able to evaluate some UX aspects. But how can we evaluate other UX aspects? Almost 90 UX evaluation methods are described at www.allaboutux.org [4].

Usability and UX in virtual museums is one of our current research topics. We identified a set of users' needs, we developed a set of specific usability heuristics, and we proposed a methodology to asses UX in virtual museums. The results are yet to be published. We used as case studies a well-known virtual museum, such as Google Cultural Institute [5], but also a local (Chilean) one, the Pre-Columbian Museum [6]. We conducted several experiments, mainly with graduate and undergraduate students in Tourism and Computer Science.

The paper presents a UX study on Pre-Columbian Museum. Section 2 reviews the concepts of usability, UX and their evaluation. Section 3 refers to usability and UX evaluation of virtual museums. Section 4 describes a co-discovery experiment on Pre-Colombian Museum. Section 5 highlights conclusions and future work.

2   Usability and UX

A well-known usability definition was proposed by the ISO 9241 standard back in 1998 [7]. The ISO 9241 standard was updated in 2010 [1]. Yet a new revision started briefly after, in 2011 [8]. It proves once again the evolving nature of the usability concept.

Literature refers to usability dimensions as "attributes", "factors" or "goals". Several aspects are recurrent in all definitions, as well and in ISO standards: effectiveness, efficiency, satisfaction, and the context of use. As Bevan, Carter and Harker highlight, the ISO 9241 current approach directly relates usability to user and business requirements: effectiveness means success in achieving goals, efficiency means not wasting time and satisfaction means willingness to use the system. Three main lessons learned since 1998: (1) the importance of understanding UX (2) the "measurement-based" usability approach is not enough, and (3) the need to explain how to take account negative outcomes that could arise from inadequate usability [8].

As usability, UX does not limit to software systems; it also applies to products and services. The ISO 9241-210 standard considers that UX "includes all the users' emotions, beliefs, preferences, perceptions, physical and psychological responses, behaviors and accomplishments that occur before, during and after use" [1]. The "User Experience White Paper" aims to "bring clarity to the UX concept" [9]. It highlights the multidisciplinary nature of UX, which has led to several definitions of and perspectives on UX, each approaching the concept from a different point of view: from a psychological to a business perspective, and from quality centric to value centric. Rather than intending to give a unique UX definition, the document mentions the wide collection of definitions available at www.allaboutux.org.

Usability evaluation methods are basically classified as: (1) empirical usability testing, based on users' participation [10], and (2) inspection methods, based on experts' judgment [11].

Evaluating UX is more challenging and arguably overwhelming for newcomers. Almost 90 UX evaluation methods are described at www.allaboutux.org and the list will probably still grow up [4]. If we consider usability as a subset of UX that means usability evaluation methods are also able to evaluate some UX aspects. But how can we evaluate other UX aspects?

3 Evaluating the Usability and UX in Virtual Museums

3.1 Virtual Museums

The International Council of Museums (ICOM) defines a museum as "a non-profit, permanent institution in the service of society and its development, open to the public, which acquires, conserves, researches, communicates and exhibits the tangible and intangible heritage of humanity and its environment for the purposes of education, study and enjoyment" [12]. Several characteristics established by the ICOM definition are strengthened by a virtual museum; probably the most important one is the public access.

Virtual museums evolved from digital media in the pre-internet era, to on-line museums and immersive digital museums. As MacDonald points out, the virtual museum experience delivered through museum websites is a critical concern for museum professionals [13]. Sylaiou, Liarokapis, Kotsakis and Patias indicate that digitizing museums' collections should have a double purpose: (1) to preserve the cultural heritage, but also (2) to make the information content accessible to the wider public in an "attractive" manner [14].

A basic feature of a virtual museum is the on-line collection. However, it seems to also be among the least popular features of a museum website [15, 16]. Museum experts usually attribute this low popularity to a lack of interest, but a poor UX may also decrease users' interest.

Usability and UX in virtual museums is one of our current research topics. We identified a set of users' needs [17], we developed a set of specific usability heuristics [18], and we proposed a methodology to asses UX in virtual museums [19]. The work we have done is only available in Spanish, locally, at Pontificia Universidad Católica de Valparaíso, Chile. We used as case studies Google Cultural Institute [5] and the Pre-Columbian Museum [6].

We conducted several experiments, mainly with graduate and undergraduate students of programs from two areas:

- Tourism - students from Universidad de Playa Ancha, Valparaíso, Chile,
- Computer Science - students from Pontificia Universidad Católica de Valparaíso, Valparaíso, Chile).

3.2 Heuristic Evaluation: Evaluators' Perception

We conducted several heuristic evaluations on Google Cultural Institute, based on Nielsen's heuristics [20]. 33 Computer Science undergraduate and 15 Computer

Science graduate students were involved as evaluators. Then, all of them participated in a survey. We developed a standard questionnaire that assesses evaluators' perception over a set of usability heuristics, concerning 4 dimensions: D1 - *Utility*, D2 - *Clarity*, D3 - *Ease of use*, and D4 - *Necessity of additional checklist*. All dimensions were evaluated using a 5 points Likert scale.

Results were analyzed in a previous work [21]. The number of correlations within the four surveyed dimensions is low.

In the case of graduate students, there are no significant differences between the evaluators with and without previous experience, excepting the dimension D4 - *Necessity of additional checklist*.

In the case of undergraduate students the perception is rather different:

- there are no significant differences between the evaluators with and without previous experience for dimension D1 – *Utility* and D4 - *Necessity of additional checklist*;
- there are significant differences between the two groups of evaluators in the case of dimension D2 – *Clarity* and D3 – *Ease of use*.

Nielsen's heuristics are not perceived as one would expect, even when evaluators have previous experience in their use. The study offered relevant information particularly for the development of a new set of usability heuristics for virtual museums [18]. We definitely recommend the use of specific heuristics instead of generic heuristics, when evaluating the usability of virtual museums.

3.3   UX Evaluation

Evaluating the UX in virtual museums is challenging. There are certainly UX aspects beyond usability's dimensions. Specific domain characteristics have to be considered when selecting an evaluation method. "Traditional" usability evaluation methods may be used, but also specific UX methods.

We analyzed the pros and cons of all methods proposed by Allaboutux.org [4]. We tested several methods: co-discovery, thinking aloud, controlled observations, emo-cards, semi-structured experience interviews, valence method, heuristic evaluation, card sorting, and formal experiments. We also conducted a communicability evaluation experiment. We proposed and partially validated a (preliminary) methodology to asses UX in virtual museums [19].

Applying a single evaluation method offers a limited perspective and results. If time and resources are available, several methods should be used: quantitative and qualitative, inspections and user tests, usability and UX oriented methods.

4   The Pre-colombian Museum: A Co-discovery Experiment

Co-discovery is a user testing method also referred as "co-discovery learning" or "constructive interaction". As it offers valuable user thinking/thoughts insides, it is also a suitable UX method. Two users explore a (software) product together, freely discussing about it, while performing specific tasks.

The evaluation protocol is quite similar to the thinking aloud method, when a single user expresses his/her thoughts while performing the specified tasks. However, when two users are working together is more natural to comments what they are doing, than in a single user scenario.

4.1 Methodology

The experiment took place in the Usability Laboratory of the School of Informatics Engineering at Pontificia Universidad Católica de Valparaíso, Chile, in October 2016. It was conducted by two UX experts. One has a MSc in Computer Science, the other one is an architect, currently studying Psychology. They both have a Diploma in UX. The Pre-Colombian museum was evaluated, based on a pre-defined set of tasks.

The participants worked in pairs, performing the tasks without interruptions and distractions. During the experiment the participants were observed by the evaluators through a polarized glass that allows the vision in a single direction. Cameras were placed in each room to record the comments made by each couple, and their facial expressions during the experiment, also recording the display of theirs computer screens.

At first, each participant signed a confidentiality agreement which indicated the conditions of the test. Afterwards, they were shown the website to be evaluated and were informed about the different stages of the test.

In the first stage each user had to complete a preliminary questionnaire, to collect general data: sex, age, level of education and information regarding experience in portals similar to the product that will be evaluated.

In a second stage a list of tasks to accomplish was provided to each pair of participants: the search of elements in different sections of the website, the selection of news, and the playback of an audio. Participants were asked to comment aloud their opinions regarding the website, the fulfillment of the requested tasks, and any other significant elements.

After completing the tasks, a third stage consisted of a questionnaire of perception that had to be completed individually, aiming to measure the ease of task completion, accessibility of the sought information, orientation within the site, ease of navigation, effectiveness of results, level of satisfaction with the portal, and intention to reuse the site. In addition three open questions were asked, related to navigation difficulties, the most and the least preferred elements of the virtual museum.

4.2 The Pre-test Questionnaire

The preliminary questionnaire consisted of 5 questions whose objective was to identify broadly the profile of the user and his/her previous experience visiting virtual museums. 8 users participated, 5 males and 3 females, of age ranging from 23 to 37 years. They were all graduate students of a Master program in Computer Science.

Half of the users (4) reported no experience in visiting virtual museums, while the other half had already visited a similar site. 3 students visited the Google Cultural

Institute web site, and another one visited the Metropolitan Museum of New York web site; they had a general notion about virtual museums, but they indicated that (almost) never visit such type of portals.

4.3   The Test

The first task consisted of finding elements of different materiality belonging to one of the collections of objects of the site. 100% of the participants did it, approaching the time limit period (5 min), showing some delays in the process of distinction of elements by materiality. When returning to the main menu (activity that was part of the task), the users showed confusion regarding the different icons and signage that allowed to fulfill such function; only 25% of the users correctly achieved it. However they did not performed the task in the pre-established time limit. Therefore no pair of users was able to perform the task properly, and within the pre-assigned time period.

The second task consisted of selecting and printing a news item. Although all users completed it, only 50% managed to do it within the pre-established time (3 min). Common problems were lack of orientation within the site and delays in finding the appropriate section and the printing function.

The third task required to play an audio. It was executed by 100% of the participants within the assigned time period (5 min). However, there where difficulties to reproduce the audio in the first instance; some of the users tried to download it, or to configure the audio options. Only 25% of the users returned to the main menu, which was one of the task requirements.

The fourth task asked to identify a freely chosen element for each of the exhibition views of the virtual museum. Although it was completed by all participants, 25% of them surpassed the time limit assigned (5 min), experiencing problems in finding the required destination. One of the pairs of users even had to use the website's search option, instead of following the indicated sequence of steps. Some users experienced confusion between denominations of different options and sections (identical denominations but with different destinations, and complications in distinguishing between "rooms" and "views"). The task was fully accomplished by 75% of the users.

Analyzing the above results, we may highlight the failure in the subtasks of returning to the main menu, either because of the lack of attention to read the instructions or lack of guidance within the portal, along with exceeding the pre-established time limit. Only 25% of the users managed to return to the main menu, as required in the first and in the third task; all users had managed to comply with the rest of the instructions.

Analyzing the reasons that markedly reduced the success rate, the failures and delays mentioned above were not so much due to the difficulty of the task itself. They were related to the lack of orientation within the site, the troubles in finding sections and functions, the confusion between similar signage, and the complications to remain inside of a certain navigation route, caused by deviations of the system to other tabs and links. However, most of the subtasks (finding elements, printing news and audio playback functions) were performed by all participants. In some cases, routes other than those indicated in the task specification were followed; however this was not perceived as a failure in the execution of the task, because the evaluation was emphasized on the ability of an intuitive navigation that can respond to the user's needs, more than on obeying instructions.

4.4   The Post-test Questionnaire

The post-test questionnaire aimed to analyze the perceived level of difficulty in the accomplishment of the tasks and the conformity with the evaluated site. It included 8 questions based on a 5 points Likert scale, and 3 open questions.

Regarding the difficulty in completing the tasks, half of the participants (4 users) considered that it was difficult to complete them, while for the remaining half, it seemed neutral (2 users) or easy (2 users). Regarding the difficulty in finding the required information, more than half of the participants perceived it as difficult (5 users), being appreciated by the rest as neutral (2 users) or easy (1 user). As for the orientation level within the portal, most participants affirmed feeling little (4 users) or very little oriented (2 users), while the rest (2 users) considered it neutral. With respect to navigation difficulties through the collections of the virtual museum, more than half of the users considered it difficult (5 users), the rest seeing it as easy (1 user) or very easy (2 users).

Thus, throughout the evaluation, it was evident that participants encountered several difficulties and lack of orientation through the process of task execution, information identification and navigation in general. Most of the users who had previously visited other virtual museums tended to assign a high level of difficulty to the above mentioned aspects. It suggests that, compared to other similar websites, the Pre-Colombian portal presents sever usability problems, mainly related to a disorganized structure and difficult navigation.

The search effectiveness oscillated between effective (3 users), neutral (2 users) and ineffective (3 users). It was the item that showed more variety, possibly because involved personal judgements of a more subjective nature.

Regarding the level of satisfaction with the information available in the site, more than half of the participants evaluated it as little satisfactory (4 users) or totally unsatisfactory (1 user); only 3 users considered it satisfactory. The conformity with the use of the portal in general, was of little satisfaction for half of the participants (4 users), being for the remaining half neutral (2 users) or satisfactory (2 users). Finally, more than half of the users (5 users) stated that they would not use the portal again, while the rest (3 users) were neutral in this aspect. There is a prevalence of a low level of satisfaction with the Pre-Colombian virtual museum, being mainly manifested in the majority of the users with previous experiences in similar sites, probably because they had higher expectations for this type of portals.

Among the aspects that made the navigation difficult, the participants emphasize the lack of orientation due to the existence of multiple menu types, the complexity of perceiving and distinguishing some sections and options, as well as their location. They also mentioned that the deviation to new tabs generates confusion within the navigation route that was intended to be followed. In addition, they underlined problems to understand the information structure and its utility in some cases. They also indicated some difficulties in using the audio playback function.

These same aspects were highlighted as less preferred by participants: lack of orientation through the website, lack of structure, excessive menus and annoying new windows, poor visibility of some functions, difficulties to find certain types of information (objects' description), and some useless data. In addition, more specific problems were mentioned, such as troubles in the audio's playback, existence of sites and images without associated information, redundant information, inconsistency in translation from Mapuche (a local ethnic language) to Spanish and vice versa, and lack of minimalism.

As favorite elements of the portal, users highlighted the pertinence, variety and quality of textual, visual and auditory information, the graphic and chromatic aesthetics of the interface. Other appreciated aspects were the possibilities of interactive tours through the exhibition halls (being perceived as didactic) and the availability of a menu in English.

4.5 Remarks on Users Emotions

Throughout the evaluation, the pairs of users expressed different emotions in response to the various elements and situations they encountered during their navigation through the Pre-Colombian portal. First of all, there were general feelings of confusion about the logic and structure of the site, about a multitude of similar options, being difficult to differentiate from each other, and about the usefulness of information, as well as the lack of adequate feedback regarding URL changes and the location within the site, which generated the prevalence of a sense of disorientation in the majority of the students. All the above observations were later on confirmed through the perception questionnaire. This was accompanied by frustration due to the lack of efficiency and correct operation of each option, followed by feelings of resignation, expressed by some pairs of users after unsuccessfully repeated attempts to return to the main menu.

Secondarily, some participants reflected anxious emotions about difficulties in finding the required information, or a certain level of distraction with some elements of the site (images, photographs), which eventually may have affected their attention to the required instructions. It drew attention the appearance of anxiety patterns in one of the pair of user; dynamics of asymmetric relationship occurred, when one of the members adopted a dominant attitude towards his partner getting to "take control", and directing the other one. In spite of his limited facial expression, possibly due to concentrating on having a good performance because of being the person "in charge", the user expressed his anxiety to quickly complete the requested tasks.

At last, frequent reactions of surprise were manifested by some users as new information and functions were discovered during the navigation through the website. In particular, this type of emotional response was evidenced in pairs with symmetrical relationship dynamics, with a climate of cooperation and sociability, which produced a sense of confidence for the members involved, to freely express their opinion.

5   Conclusions

Usability and especially UX are well established concepts, but still under review. There are well known and widely used usability evaluation methods, but UX evaluation is still a challenging task. There is an overwhelming amount of UX methods, and the list is still growing.

Virtual museums evolved from digital media in the pre-internet era, to on-line museums and immersive digital museums. Virtual museums' UX is a critical concern, and virtual museums' UX evaluation is a relevant topic.

Even if heuristic evaluation is a usability related method, it also offers valuable UX related information. Usability issues detected through a heuristic evaluation are sources of potential poor UX. General usability heuristics, such as Nielsen's, are hard to apply when evaluating virtual museums. We suggest the use of specific heuristics instead.

UX aspects beyond usability's dimensions should be evaluated using specific methods. Co-discovery offers valuable user thinking/thoughts insides. It offers a first-hand look on users' perception, reactions, responses and emotions. The co-discovery experiment on Pre-Colombian Museum highlighted severs usability issues. But more important, it provided valuable information on users' perception, thoughts and emotions.

As future work, we will extend our research to other case studies. The set of specific usability heuristics that we developed and the methodology of evaluating UX in virtual museums that we proposed require further validation.

References

1. ISO 9241-210: Ergonomics of human-system interaction—Part 210: human-centred design for interactive systems. International Organization for Standardization, Geneva (2010)
2. Rusu, C., Rusu, V., Roncagliolo, S., González, C.: Usability and user experience: what should we care about? Int. J. Inf. Technol. Syst. Approach **8**(2), 1–12 (2015)
3. Lewis, J.: Usability: lessons learned… and yet to be learned. Int. J. Hum.-Comput. Interact. **30**(9), 663–684 (2014)
4. Allaboutux.org: All About UX. www.allaboutux.org. Accessed 9 Jan 2017
5. Google Cultural Institute. www.google.com/culturalinstitute/. Accessed 9 Jan 2017
6. Pre-Columbian Museum. www.precolombino.cl. Accessed 9 Jan 2017
7. ISO 9241-11: Ergonomic requirements for office work with visual display terminals (VDTs) – Part 11: Guidance on usability. International Organization for Standardization, Geneva (1998)
8. Bevan, N., Carter, J., Harker, S.: ISO 9241-11 revised: what have we learnt about us-ability since 1998? In: Kurosu, M. (ed.) Human-Computer Interaction. LNCS, vol. 9169, pp. 143–151. Springer, Switzerland (2015)
9. Roto, V., Law, E., Vermeeren, A., Hoonhout, J.: User experience white paper. Bringing Clarity to the Concept of User Experience. http://www.allaboutux.org/uxwhitepaper. Accessed 9 Jan 2017
10. Dumas, J., Fox, J.: Usability testing: current practice and future directions. In: Sears, A., Jacko, J. (eds.) The Human – Computer Interaction Handbook: Fundamentals. Evolving Technologies and Emerging Applications, pp. 1129–1149. Taylor & Francis, New York (2008)

11. Cockton, G., Woolrych, A., Lavery, D.: Inspection – based evaluations. In: Sears, A., Jacko, J. (eds.) The Human – Computer Interaction Handbook: Fundamentals, Evolving Technologies and Emerging Applications, pp. 1171–1189. Taylor & Francis, New York (2008)
12. International Council of Museums. http://icom.museum/the-vision/museum-definition/. Accessed 9 Jan 2017
13. MacDonald, C.: Assessing the user experience (UX) of online museum collections: perspectives from design and museum professionals. MW2015: Museums and the Web 2015. http://mw2015.museumsandtheweb.com/paper/assessing-the-user-experience-ux-of-online-museum-collections-perspectives-from-design-and-museum-professionals/. Accessed 9 Jan 2017
14. Sylaiou, S., Liarokapis, F., Kotsakis, K., Patias, P.: Virtual museums, a survey and some issues for consideration. J. Cult. Heritage **10**, 520–528 (2009)
15. Haynes, J., Zambonini, D.: Why are they doing that!? How users interact with museum web sites. In: Trant, J., Bearman, D. (eds.). Museums and the Web 2007: Proceedings, Toronto. Archives & Museum Informatics. http://www.archimuse.com/mw2007/papers/haynes/haynes.html. Accessed 9 Jan 2017
16. Fantoni, S.F., Stein, R., Bowman, G.: Exploring the relationship between visitor motivation and engagement in online museum audiences. In: Trant, J., Bearman, D. (eds.). Museums and the Web 2012: Proceedings, Toronto: Archives & Museum Informatics. http://www.museumsandtheweb.com/mw2012/papers/exploring_the_relationship_between_visitor_mot. Accessed 9 Jan 2017
17. Rondanelli, N.: Necesidades de los usuarios de muesos virtuales. Pontificia Universidad Católica de Valparaíso, Chile (2015)
18. Aguirre, N.: Experiencia de usuario en museos virtuales. Pontificia Universidad Católica de Valparaíso, Chile (2015)
19. Muñoz, P.: Propuesta metodológica para evaluar la experiencia de usuario en museos virtuales. Pontificia Universidad Católica de Valparaíso, Chile (2015)
20. Nielsen, J., Mack, R.L.: Usability Inspection Methods. Wiley, New York (1994)
21. Rusu, C., Rusu, V., Roncagliolo, S., Quiñones, D., Rusu, V.Z., Fardoun, Habib M., Alghazzawi, Daniyal M., Collazos, César A.: Usability heuristics: reinventing the wheel? In: Meiselwitz, G. (ed.) SCSM 2016. LNCS, vol. 9742, pp. 59–70. Springer, Cham (2016). doi:10.1007/978-3-319-39910-2_6

Customer Behavior and Social Media

Why Social Media Is an Achilles Heel?
A Multi-dimensional Perspective on Engaged
Consumers and Entrepreneurs

Adela Coman[(⊠)], Ana-Maria Grigore,
and Oana Simona Caraman Hudea

University of Bucharest, Bucharest, Romania
{adela.coman,ana.grigore,oana.hudea}@faa.unibuc.ro

Abstract. The main goals of this paper are: to identify what drives consumers and businesses to use social media; to observe the main usage patterns in the case of Romanian graduate students from a multi-dimensional perspective: as consumers (the individual level); as entrepreneurs (the company level); and the sociological level (side effect felt due to interaction on social networks (SNSs). Our research is an exploratory one. We conducted interviews with 40 graduate students who are also entrepreneurs in small and medium-sized companies (SMEs), aged between 23 and 35 (Millennials) who usually spend more than two hours on SNSs. Questionnaires were built on three variables, namely, engagement, confidence and technological abilities of consumers/entrepreneurs. In this paper, we undertook to structure our quantitative analysis of qualitative data around several hypotheses, generating, for the validation/invalidation thereof, centralized frequency tables with associated, relevant graphs (for all hypotheses) and correlation-related issues, reflected by the use of the directional Spearman (rho) coefficient (for the last hypothesis considered). Such differentiated approach emerged from our intention to cover a wider range of procedures, while revealing the most interesting and suggestive results of our study, considering the limitations imposed as to the maximum size of articles. The results obtained show that, in general, the subjects' behavior is marked by a lack of trust, source of vulnerability, both for consumers and entrepreneurs. This vulnerability permeates all researched sections, with different intensity, which justifies the name we have chosen, the Achilles heel.

Keywords: Consumers · Entrepreneurs · Engagement · Trust · Power

1 Introduction

Network Readiness Index (2016) reveals us exactly where Romania is positioned in terms of *Internet access*. Thus, the Internet availability sub-index shows that Romania ranks 47 of 143 countries, with an average of 5.2 (index values are between 1 and 7). The degree of availability is calculated based on three parameters, namely: infrastructure, availability and Internet use skills, each of the three with a share of about one third of the index value. Romania ranks 52nd in infrastructure, 61st in availability and 66th in skills.

© Springer International Publishing AG 2017
G. Meiselwitz (Ed.): SCSM 2017, Part I, LNCS 10282, pp. 139–158, 2017.
DOI: 10.1007/978-3-319-58559-8_13

Surprisingly, the Internet use by individual consumers places Romania on the 61st place (the top half) with an average of 4.5. Companies are positioned worse than individual consumers, entrepreneurs ranking 76 (3.5 value), and the governmental structures are least involved in using the Internet, Romania being the 85th in the ranking (3.6 value).

Despite the fact that Romania is in a relatively favorable position in terms of Internet access (47th) and Internet use (66th), the *economic and social impact* of Internet use is still very low. Romania ranks 80th among 143 countries in terms of Internet use impact (average value - 3.5). The economic impact places us 85th (3.1), and the social impact 77th (4.0) in this ranking.

Internet development is favored by the growth of social networks (SNSs), the most active users of these are the youngsters in the Millennials generation, aged between 20 and 35 years old.

About the Millennials (people born after 1982) there are numerous studies (Oblinger and Oblinger 2005; Raines 2002; Veen 2004; Karpati 2002) that managed to shape a portrait of them. Among the many features identified for the Millennials are: they are good at technology; show preference for structure; are eager for entertainment and uniqueness, scanning abilities; multi-tasking; non-linear learning style; processing disrupted flows. The German report (Veen 2004) refers to the Millennials as Homo Zappiens, due of their ability to use technology.

In this context, our objective was to decode the youngsters' behavior on social networks, mainly of students, as they belong to the Millennials generation. Thus, we selected a total of 40 students of bachelor and masters studies in Romania who are also entrepreneurs. Our objective was to find out if there is a general pattern of network use. What is the extent of their engagement on SNSs, as consumers, on the one hand, and as entrepreneurs, on the other hand? To what extent they possess the necessary skills to impact social networks? What are the side effects (Achilles heel) that students, in their double role, claim as a result of SNSs interaction?

Our paper is organized as follows: in the first section we review the social media literature, in an attempt to define the basic concepts we operate with: social media, consumer, entrepreneur, motivation for using the social media, trust, power. In the second section we present the research methodology and then we discuss the results. Finally, we draw conclusions, discuss the limits of our study findings and indicate some directions to follow for future research.

2   Literature Review

Specialized literature defines, on one hand, the environment and, on the other hand, the user.

Boyd and Ellison (2007) define social media as web services allowing individuals to build a public or semi-public profile within a given system; to compile a list of users to connect with; see and follow their own connections, as well as others' within the system (Logan 2014).

According to The Interactive Advertising Bureau (IAB), social media comprises three elements, namely: social media websites (SNSs), blogs and mobile networks

(IAB 2009). In this paper we discuss about the behavior of users on social network websites/social networks (SNSs).

Carter (2016) shows that social network sites (SNSs) are communication websites where individuals express themselves and groups act; on the other side, these are meeting websites where business people use individual discourse to understand markets and make predictions.

From our point of view, social networks are *tools* that individuals use to shape their role through the activities and behaviors they adopt. Therefore, if the role played is that of a consumer, by the activities undertaken on SNSs, the individual tries to build a favorable profile and a positive image among friends and third parties, mainly because he/she desires to gain power and influence and thus, to increase his/her self-esteem (Baconschi 2015); if the role is that of an entrepreneur, through the actions started on SNSs, he/she seeks to obtain money, power and influence and thus, to develop his/her business (Ghenea 2011). In other words, the desire for power and influence motivates individuals to adopt specific behaviors, depending on their purposes.

According to the roles theory, the consumer's behavior looks a lot like actions in a play where every consumer has his/her own text, costume and props necessary to "stage the show" (Goffman 1959). Since they play numerous roles, consumers may choose to act differently, according to the "play" starring at that time. Therefore, they can play the role of the "chooser," communicator, researcher of their own identity, victim, activist, pleasure-seeker or influencer – one at a time – or sometimes – all at once (Gabriel and Lang 1995).

A very important role of the social networks is the extent to which these allow brands and consumers to connect, communicate and express engagement (Rohm et al. 2012). According to Burns (2006), *consumer's engagement* has been defined as the process to guide a potential consumer to an idea of brand enhanced by the context. Therefore, engagement is an important element in the consumer-brand relation (Haven 2007; Gambetti and Graffigna 2010).

In the online world, consumers seek to play an increasingly bigger *role* in the goods' purchasing and consumption process (Calder et al. 2009). A recent study (Parent et al. 2011) defines engagement in the brand-consumer relation on social networks as limited by the following actions: creating and posting online content relevant for consumers; exerting a certain degree of control on the content so that it can be shared with friends and even modified by them; creating a sense of community between consumers; facilitating dialogue between consumers, rather than communicating a direction of discussion. Lately, however, the consumer succeeded to tip the scale in his/her favor. Therefore, by *generating content, by an extremely careful selection of favorite brands* (taken actions), the consumer proves his/her choices can really be a source of power and economic and social benefits. This power comes from the demand for goods and services (the impact of the decision to buy), from information (sent and received), from the ability to adapt the content encountered on the SNSs to own needs and, finally, from the ability to mobilize and structure resources allowing a greater number of community members to benefit from such resources (Labrecque et al. 2013).

SNSs such as Facebook, Twitter and YouTube are widely adopted by *entrepreneurs* who try to use them for the benefit of their businesses. From the entrepreneurship perspective, SNSs are marketing tools. Little is known about how

SNSs influence entrepreneurs. And even less is known about the way in which network use facilitates behaviors and activities meant to help them develop, discover new markets and opportunities (Fischer and Reuber 2011). For entrepreneurs, power is generated by the easy access to *information,* as well as the speed with which this information is spread on the market (Labrecque et al. 2013). From this point of view, a greater use of networks by entrepreneurs may be a significant power indicator.

Burns (2011) has shown that when entrepreneurs start a business, they bring to it capital in a number of different forms such as: financial, human (that means previous managerial or field experience and training) and also social, derived from access to appropriate professional networks. Firkin (2003) states that more capital entrepreneurs bring to their businesses, particularly the one derived through networks, more likely they are to succeed. At the same time, Ghenea (2011) points out that information from the contact networks (generally social networks on the Internet, but without underestimating in any way the still valuable traditional social networks) is an extremely powerful weapon that entrepreneurs can use any time in the development of their business. Social capital in the form of networks of friends and commercial contacts is important because it can bring with it credibility, it can provide the first customer, or low-cost or free office-space (Burns, 2011). Or, the thousands of friends on Facebook and/or thousands followers on Twitter can validate (or invalidate, or correct) the idea in its path to a business opportunity (Ghenea 2011). On the other side, Di Fiore (2011) draws attention on the fact that social capital is consumed and professional networks essentially help you better manage your capital. The approach must be selected according to the importance of the request, for example when asking a favor on LinkedIn or Facebook you cannot endanger the friendship with that person; and this reduces pressure on both sides, the same author says.

Social capital is built on relations – relations are the core of the social life (develop relations with other individuals, as social beings), but also of the entrepreneurial approach to do business; relations with clients, suppliers, employees, banks and owners. All relationships are based on trust, self-interest and reputation (Dubini and Aldrich 1991). *Trust* is an important component of the social life (Christakis and Fowler 2015). It is obvious that it can be extremely risky to trust anyone. We are never more vulnerable than when we trust someone. Therefore, trust can be a source of risk and vulnerability.

The level of trust in social networks is different. In countries such as the USA, people feel comfortable to interact with strangers; no entrepreneur hesitates to share his/her business ideas with others and he/she does not fear his/her ideas could be stolen. In contrast, Hostiuc (2016) shows that Romanians hold everything well hidden, thinking they have the best idea in the world and they will become millionaires. Ghenea (2011) also draws attention on the fact that, for reasons difficult to identify, very few Romanian entrepreneurs at the beginning of their business really use information on social networks – for example, says Ghenea, many young entrepreneurs, that probably spend much more time on Facebook than watching TV, fail to take into consideration in their business analysis simple things such as checking an idea or a concept on the existing social networks.

Trust plays an important role in the consumer-SNSs relation. There are different definitions of trust based on terms such as: goodwill, integrity, ability, competence

(Gefen, 2002; Gefen et al. 2003). On these platforms, where consumers interact with one another, community members may get closer to one another, thereby providing a potential source of trust through exchange of information (about products and not only) (Lu et al. 2010). Finally, trust is the one that can influence the consumer's intention to buy (Lorenzo et al. 2007).

This confidence underlies the element that defines the model known in specialized literature as the technology acceptance model (TAM) (Davis 1989). Acceptance, by users, of the facilities offered by technology was the first step in building this theory (Davis et al. 1989). TAM states that the constituents of technologies play an important role in the acceptance of systems by users (Pavlou 2003). Initially, Davis (1989) defined the concept of perceived usefulness as the degree to which a person believes that using a particular system would enhance his/her job performance. It is one of the main reasons for which people are generally receptive to new technologies. Moreover, the way in which these technologies are used may predict, with relative accuracy, the user's behavior, including that of consumers and the entrepreneurs (Pavlou 2003).

The new generation of Romanians understands the need to open up, to share their ideas with others before going further, although this is a difficult process related to our history to "defend" against enemies and competition (Hostiuc, 2016). Over time, due to historical circumstances, the Romanians' main objective was survival. This determined Romanians to avoid uncertainty. Moreover, in Romania there is no culture for risk taking also because of the past regime, with the state as main decision-maker.

3 Methodology

Since our objective was to decode the youngsters' behavior on social networks, especially students (Millennials generation), we addressed, to a number of 40 students of bachelor and master's degree in Romania, two types of questionnaires – one with specific questions for students as consumers and the other for the same students as entrepreneurs. By doing so, we wanted to know if there is a general pattern for the use of social networks by students or, simply put, to find out what our students do on social networks.

Our specific questions were meant to: clarify the term engagement and the extent of it on SNSs, as consumers, on one hand, and as entrepreneurs, on the other hand; reveal the nature and size of the technological skills students hold as consumers or entrepreneurs in order to exert impact on networks; identify the side effects (Achilles heel) that students, in their double role, claim on SNSs. We consider that, in this way, we covered three levels, namely: the individual level (consumer); the organizational level (entrepreneur and company) and the social level/sociological dimension related to vulnerabilities, trust, influence and power mentioned in the specialized literature.

Our research is qualitative at the base. In order to outline the general pattern of using SNSs by students, we took into account three variables as theoretical background for our study: engagement, technological skills and trust in the students' relation with networks. We chose these variables as basis for our research as they are closely related to the specialized literature (Burns and Christiansen 2011; Drury 2008) and from a conceptual standpoint they are related. These combined variables show us that individuals seek to gain power within the networks, whether is it about power based on demand (influence others to buy); power based on information (circulation of information created or transmitted by the user); and community-based power (the power to mobilize and structure resources for the benefit of individuals and community) (Labreque et al. 2013).

Yet, the analysis of qualitative data, structured around several hypotheses, is quantitative, generating, for the validation/invalidation of the same, centralized frequency tables with associated, relevant graphs (for all hypotheses) and correlation-related issues, reflected by the use of the directional Spearman (rho) coefficient (for the last hypothesis considered). Such differentiated approach emerged from our intention to cover a wider range of procedures, while revealing the most interesting and suggestive results of our study, considering the length limitations imposed.

Knowing that the frequency tables, respectively the corresponding graphical representations speak by themselves, under the elaborated form rendered by the authors in the Results and Discussions section, not imposing any additional comments in terms of detailing the methodology used, we exclusively focus herein on the methodology relating to the Spearman (rho) coefficient. This coefficient is highly useful when dealing with ordinal data fit for a bi-varied correlation determination, such coefficient allowing for the transformation of the original inputs into ranks, without being influenced in any way by the average representativeness (Opariuc 2011).

The formula used in the context of this coefficient takes two forms, depending on the repetitiveness or non-repetitiveness of the established ranks (directly suggested in the following by the detailed presentation of the associated results):

$$\rho = 1 - \frac{6 \times \sum dif\_rank^2}{n \times (n^2 - 1)}$$

respectively, for identical ranks, as in our case:

$$\rho = 1 - \frac{n \times (\sum rank_1 \times rank_2) - \sum rank_1 \times \sum rank_2}{\sqrt{n \times \sum rank_1^2 - (\sum rank_1)^2} \times \sqrt{n \times \sum rank_2^2 - (\sum rank_2)^2}}$$

where *dif_rank* represents the difference between the ranks of the values of variables relating to each respondent, n, the sample size, namely the number of respondents, and *rank_1. rank_2*, the rank of the first, respectively of the second variable.

When coming to construe this coefficient, which is bidirectional, as above-mentioned, we have to consider two steps: the first step concerns the identification of the intensity of the correlation relationship, if any, this being directly related to the value obtained, belonging to the interval $[-1;1]$, an extreme value reflecting either a perfect negative correlation of variables (-1) or a perfect positive one (1), while the absolute lack of correlation of the same being indicated by their median value (0); the second step consists in determining the significance level of the result obtained or otherwise said, in revealing the precision of the same. This can be done by comparing the obtained value (for different sizes of errors: 1%, 5% or 10%) either with the ones provided by the Spearman coefficient significance level tables, or, if the number of entries exceeds 10 (as in our case), with the ones provided by the t-student test, considering $n - 2$ freedom degrees for the two variables used, by resorting to the formula:

$$t = \rho \times \sqrt{\frac{n - 2}{1 - \rho^2}}$$

4   Results and Discussions

In order to be as coherent as possible in revealing the results obtained, we decided to clearly structure them by hypotheses, thereby covering, step by step, our beliefs initially mentioned at pure theoretical level:

Hypothesis 1: Higher the students' involvement on social networks, greater their engagement:

  Hypothesis 1a. As consumers – to favorite brands;
  Hypothesis 1b. As entrepreneurs – to their own brand/product/service.

  To analyze the level of involvement of respondents as consumers, we considered the following elements: ads viewed and their impact on consumers; share of online shopping compared to total purchasing; benefits of network presence as consumers; effective promotion of favorite brands (undertaken actions).
  The ads viewed on social networks have an important role in the customer-brand relation. Thus, 55% of consumers say that ads viewed on social media have a high and very high impact on their decision to buy a product while only 20% say that ads viewed have no impact or a very low impact in deciding to buy products (Table 1).

Table 1. Consumer engagement perceived by the social media ads impact on the purchase decision

Respondents	Medium to very high impact on the purchase decision	Low to very low impact on the purchase decision
40	22	8
100%	55%	20%

  A proof that ads on social media have a strong influence on the purchasing behavior is the large number of consumers *buying online - 88%* - while 13% say they prefer to buy products predominantly from traditional stores (Table 2).

Table 2. Consumer engagement perceived by the online purchase of products

Respondents	Online purchase of products	Other forms of purchase of products
40	35	5
100%	88%	13%

The consumers' engagement depends on the extent to which the same relate social media to various *benefits* such as: promotion, diversity, novelty, commodity, opportunity and accessibility. As shown in Table 3, 75% of consumers associate social media to the above mentioned benefits while 25% do not perceive it as generating benefits.

Table 3. Consumer engagement perceived by the benefits provided by the same (promotion, diversity, novelty, comfort, opportunity, accessibility)

Respondents	Benefits brought by social media	No benefits generated by social media
40	30	10
100%	75%	25%

Connection to brands may be best analyzed if we consider the *actions undertaken* by consumers for their favorite brands.

As shown in Table 4, 38% of respondents (consumers) declare they advertise for their favorite brands, 30% say that after they see the products on networks they try to order them, and 23% create content about their favorite brands and share it. Therefore, we can identify a very strong link between consumers and their favorite brands.

Table 4. Consumer engagement perceived by their involvement in brand-related activities

Respondents	Seeing and trying to order fashioned products	Making publicity for preferred products	Creating and distributing interesting contents
40	12	15	9
100%	30%	38%	23%

In the case of respondents as *entrepreneurs*, engagement was analyzed considering the use of social networks for business purposes; the number of functions used on each network and the extent to which they promote their sales via social networks.

As shown in Table 5 above, 55% of entrepreneurs use 2 or more networks (Facebook and Twitter), 13% use only one network (usually Facebook). Other networks such as Instagram, Pinterest, LinkedIn and Yelp are less used for business. We can also notice that, surprisingly, 33% of entrepreneurs declare they do not use social media for their business (Table 5).

Table 5. Entrepreneur engagement perceived by the number of social media used

Respondents	Two or more types of social media used	One type of social media used	No social media used
40	22	5	13
100%	55%	13%	33%

Facebook is *the main social network* used by entrepreneurs to do *business*. Among Facebook users, 81% use 2 or more functions while 19% use one function (Table 6).

Table 6. Entrepreneur engagement perceived by the number of Facebook functions used

Respondents	Two or more Facebook functions used	One Facebook function used
26	21	5
100%	81%	19%

Among Twitter users, 73% declare they use 2 or more functions of the platform, and 27% say they use only one function (Table 7).

Table 7. Entrepreneur engagement perceived by the number of Twitter functions used

Respondents	Two or more Twitter functions used	One Twitter function used
11	8	3
100%	73%	27%

As for using networks to *promote sales*, out of the 27 respondents using social networks, 78% follow the sales growth/promotion, while 22% chose not to promote their sales through social media (Table 8).

Table 8. Entrepreneur engagement perceived by their intention to promote sales thereby

Respondents	Promoting sales via social media	Not promoting sales via social media
27	21	6
100%	78%	22%

We can conclude that the entrepreneurs' engagement on social media is high since they use two or more social networks; for each network they use at least 2 functions; and most of them use social networks to promote their sales.

In conclusion, hypothesis 1 regarding the engagement is validated, both in case of consumers (hypothesis 1a) and entrepreneurs (hypothesis 1b).

If the first 3 dependent variables taken into account related to *the consumers' engagement* to their favorite brands fit into the *general pattern* manifested by consumers on social media, according to the specialized literature (are influenced by the ads, buy online, and do this because they associate networks with certain benefits), the variable regarding *actions undertaken* to promote favorite brands (consumers advertise brands, are influenced by ads on SNSs and create and distribute content to promote favorite brands) tells us that consumers actively influence online demand. This type of influence turns into a *source of power* for consumers, as carriers of demand. This observation is in accordance with previous studies (Labrecque et al. 2013) that say that today's consumer is rather a super consumer; and the way this manifests in the digital environment reveals a form of power (Labrecque et al. 2013).

In the case of the *entrepreneurs' engagement* to own product/brand, the discussion is more complicated. Thus, the use of networks (two on average) and the number of functions (at least 2) show that entrepreneurs use *information* generated on networks mainly to promote their own brand/product to increase sales (general pattern). But the fact that 33% of entrepreneurs do not use networks for their own business suggests that the capability of those entrepreneurs to influence the markets is reduced, and the power – as access to new markets, consumers and opportunities – they have by means of networks is not sufficiently capitalized. From the specialized literature perspective, SNSs are more than a marketing tool for entrepreneurs (Fischer and Reuber 2011), because it provides access to new resources and broad communities. Thus, those who do not use the networks are working against themselves, by limiting their access to information, resources and opportunities (development). This increases the degree of vulnerability and risk exposure for the companies they lead.

Hypothesis 2: Lack of trust in social networks describes individual behavior, both as consumer and entrepreneur.

For consumers, lack of trust has been researched in terms of associations consumers make with social media, namely: promotion, manipulation, diversity, novelty, commodity, time saving, publicity, opportunity and accessibility.

Another important indicator to establish the level of trust in networks is represented by the *disadvantages* users perceive in relation to social media (waste of time; feeling of loneliness, frustration; promotion of negative behaviors, excessive publicity, social network addiction, contact with people one does not know and/or like). A third pillar was the extent to which consumers felt *influenced* (in buying a product) by social media.

As shown in Fig. 1, a quarter (25%) of consumers declared *they feel manipulated* by social networks. On the other hand, consumers relate networks to *benefits* such as: commodity, accessibility, publicity, diversity, promotion and novelty, opportunity and time saving in doing their shopping.

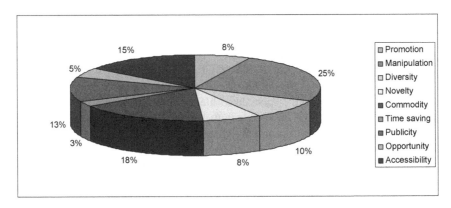

Fig. 1. What is social media for consumers?

In the same time, 23% of consumers mentioned that they experiment *negative emotions* when using social media. The great majority, however, declared that they did not experience such feelings related to social networks.

Trust relation may also be tested taking into account the disadvantages the consumers feel when using social networks (Shin 2010) Table 9 summarizes the main disadvantages experienced by the students-consumers.

Table 9. Consumer lack of trust in social media perceived by basic disadvantages caused by it.

Respondents	Wasting time	Creating the illusion of no loneliness	Promoting negative behavior models	Establishing contacts with unknown people you dislike	Seeing too many publicity	Creating dependency
40	4	7	9	2	5	13
100%	10%	18%	23%	5%	13%	33%

Felt disadvantages are: SNSs create addiction (33%); promote negative behaviors (23%); create the illusion of no loneliness (18%); too much publicity (13%; waste of time (10%) and establish contact with people you do not know and do not like (5%).

In the case of consumers, we can say that social networks are not based on unconditional trust because *25% of consumers said they feel manipulated* when using such networks. But, this has not prevented them from using social networks, out of commodity, accessibility, publicity, etc. On the other hand, lack of trust also comes from the disadvantages noticed by consumers, such as promotion of negative behaviors or addiction to social networks. Moreover, 23% of consumers declared they have negative emotions when using social networks.

Lack of trust has been researched, in the case of *entrepreneurs*, from the perspective of those who say *they do not use social media for their businesses*. We also wanted to observe the *reasons* for which they chose not to use SNSs for business.

We can notice that a number of 13 entrepreneurs (33%) – do not use social media for their businesses (Fig. 2).

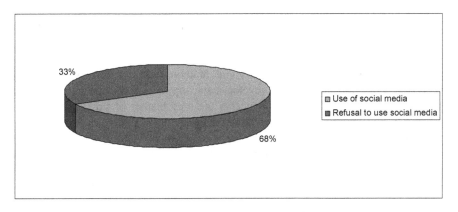

Fig. 2. Use of social media for business

When asked about the reasons why they do not use social media, most entrepreneurs (69%) declared that they see no benefit for the company, and 4 said they do not have the required skills.

Therefore, we can conclude that entrepreneurs that do not use social media justify this choice by lack of trust in the potential benefits they could obtain in using networks for their companies, and to a lesser extent by lack of skills.

Analyzing results both from consumer's (Hypothesis 2a), and the entrepreneur's (Hypothesis 2b) perspective, we notice that hypothesis H2 is validated: respondents generally lack trust in social networks.

In the specialized literature there are many references to the role of SNSs in building *social relationships* (Ba and Pavlou 2002; Cheema and Kaikati 2010). For example, showed how the dimension and features of a person's or company network matter for the *results* obtained, both by the *individual* and the *company*.

Specialized studies define addiction to SNSs as the compulsive use of SNSs manifesting in behavioral addiction symptoms. These symptoms often include conflict and frequent changes of mood.

The results of our research on trust, in this context, may be interpreted as follows: consumers consider aggressive/inappropriate manifestations as SNS disadvantages/ associated risks; 23% experience negative emotions due to SNS interactions; their mood changes frequently when individuals realize not being alone is more an illusion than a reality. However, *pre-eminence on the networks* is a necessity (Taylor et al. 2011). And it is exactly this need for pre-eminence in terms of asserting their identity on the networks that makes consumers be more and more present on the network and be tolerant to the manipulation feelings they frequently experience. The need for pre-eminence, on the one side, makes the consumer be active and committed on the networks; manipulation, on the other side, makes him/her rather critical and distrustful. This means that the consumer is *vulnerable* in the sense that the need for pre-eminence causes him/her to always be online. At the same time, his/her actions are undermined by the lack of trust generated by the effects of the multiple connections (not all desired) that individuals may have in the digital space. Otherwise said, vulnerability is the price paid by consumers, a result of the "always on" system.

In entrepreneurship, there is little literature about *social competence*, a concept that appears to affect the resources entrepreneurs are capable of accessing, as well as what they can effectively do (actions) in collaboration with those they interact with (Baron and Tang 2009). All these studies show how network features, specific relations or individual differences regarding social skills affect the companies' economic results.

In this regard, it must be kept in mind that our research targets the student-entrepreneur who generally tries to develop a start-up. It is common sense to believe that he/she does not have full confidence in the way his/her brand is positioned on social networks. The entrepreneur-student could use social networks to check and promote his/her idea/business, but he/she can also be worried that, given his/her lack of resources, someone else might steal his/her idea. The reluctance to access networks may suggest the entrepreneurs' low social skills, which make him/her vulnerable in business. But, unlike consumers who pay a price – vulnerability – because they are and have to be the wall, despite disadvantages and negative feelings – for entrepreneurs, the same type of vulnerability occurs because of their non-participation in the digital space.

Hypothesis 3: The technological skills of social network users are a source of power and economic benefits:

Hypothesis 3a. For consumers – they can buy anytime, anything, without effort and restrictions;
Hypothesis 3b. For entrepreneurs – increased sales and management of customer relations.

We analyzed the consumers' technological skills from two points of view, namely: the *time* spent on social networks and *the frequency of accessing social networks* from mobile phones for information and/or shopping.

We notice that most consumers (43%) spend more than two hours on social networks, either for information, shopping or for both (Table 10).

Table 10. Consumer technical abilities in using social media perceived by the knowledge accumulated by accessing the same several hours per day.

Respondents	Up to one hour per day	Between one and two hours per day	More than two hours per day
40	9	14	17
100%	23%	35%	43%

Consumers tend to access SNSs from their personal computer, but also from tablets or mobile phone. Generally, students have an increased propensity for using smartphones. As consumers, our respondents considered the phone as the main device/tool to access networks. This is the reason why we chose to test the consumer's technological skills in terms of the *frequency* with which they use *mobile phones* to collect information about products and services, or to access online stores for shopping.

In our case, all consumers use mobile phones to access networks, half of them (50%) indicating a very high degree of usage and 43% indicating a very high usage of smartphones for information and/or shopping.

In other words, the *technological skills* of respondents as consumers allow them to use mobile phones for information and consumption, 78% of them spending more than one hour daily on social networks (SNSs).

As for our respondents as *entrepreneurs*, we chose to test their technological skills in how they see themselves in using social networks (SNSs). Things become a little more complicated as most entrepreneurs see themselves as average (44%) or beginners (19%) in using networks. 37% of entrepreneurs perceive themselves as advanced.

Of all entrepreneurs, only 4 (10%) declare they have no skills to use social networks.

The observations that can be drawn from analyzing the entrepreneurs' skills in using social media are: most entrepreneurs see themselves as beginners or average in using networks; they spend, on average, between one and two hours, or more than two hours on networks via mobile phones.

However, 33% of entrepreneurs do no use social networks for their companies. Even if, in principle, most show the ability to use new technologies, 10% of those who do not use social media are not capable of doing it, because they lack the necessary skills.

In short, we can say that, in case of consumers, the ability to use networks actually helps them be active and manifest in this environment as consumers. On the other hand, individuals in their position of entrepreneurs are less ready, from the technological point of view, and less efficient in using networks for their businesses.

Therefore, hypothesis 3 regarding the technological skills of social network users is only partially confirmed, meaning that only consumers exploit social media as a source of power and economic benefits (Hypothesis 3a).

The results of our research on the users' ability to use SNSs may be interpreted as follows: Internet progress, the emergence of Web 2.0, together with the development of SNSs channeled power to users. In this regard, consumers apparently use the full network facilities. Through SNSs, consumers become informed and buy products and services, without effort and restrictions. This finding is consistent with the specialized studies which say that in the online space, users benefit from the so-called "disinhibition effect" that enables them to express freely in this environment. In the case of respondents-consumers, this disinhibition effect manifests through their *actions*, starting from the simple information to the actual purchase.

In the case of respondents-entrepreneurs, our findings are, again, a little more complicated: entrepreneurs see themselves as beginners or average in using SNSs. On the other side, 33% of them do not use SNSs, either because they do not see SNSs' benefits or because they do not possess the necessary skills. In other words, entrepreneurs do not have access to the power of networks, so they cannot capitalize the information available there, they cannot relate with people when they need help and they do not have access to the resources needed to develop their business. In short, they cannot develop the social competences necessary to become visible in the business world.

Reaching a quite different level of approach, the last generic hypothesis considered is rendered, in fact, by the union of two opposite hypotheses: H0 (the null hypothesis) and H1(the alternative hypothesis), being formulated based on the specific requirements relating to the correlation analysis specific context, namely the perception of benefits related to SNSs use by consumers and entrepreneurs. Is there or not a link on how respondents relate to the benefits of SNSs, as consumer and entrepreneurs at the same time?

H0: There is no correlation between the level of specific benefits brought by social media to consumers and the level of specific benefits brought by social media to entrepreneurs.

H1: There is a correlation between the level of specific benefits brought by social media to consumers and the level of specific benefits brought by social media to entrepreneurs.

The results rendered below are intended to reveal the acceptance or the rejection of the null hypothesis (H0), doubled by the related comments.

The results obtained are based on the association of the values, expressed both in absolute and relative values in Table 11, generated by the answers of respondents to two questions: Qa. *To what extent do you think that social media effectively help you in developing your business?* (for entrepreneurs) and Qb. *To what extent do you think that social media effectively help you in buying products?* (for consumers):

Table 11. Absolute and relative values associated with answers to Qa and Qb

Respondents		Very much (VN)	Much (M)	Medium (MD)	Little (L)	Very little (VL)	Not at all (NAA)
Entrepreneurs	40	8	12	4	3	0	13
	100%	20%	30%	10%	8%	0%	33%
Consumers	40	4	11	17	6	2	0
	100%	10%	28%	43%	15%	5%	0%

The preliminary processing of data for the application of the Spearman coefficient involves identifying the position of each element of the common range of answers for the two variables (Table 12) and the determination of the related ranks, as rendered in Table 13, presented in Appendix.

Table 14, also presented in Appendix, reveals all operations necessary, given the identified ranks, for getting the Spearman coefficient.

The next step consists in applying the Spearman coefficient formula specific for variables with identical ranks, this leading to:

$$\rho = 0.584101$$

This suggests, as expected, an existing positive correlation, medium in intensity, between the two variables had in view (the value ranging between 0 and 1), indicating that we should reject the null hypothesis stating that *there is no correlation between the level of specific benefits brought by social media to consumers and the level of specific benefits brought by social media to entrepreneurs*, therefore accepting H1.

As this affirmation should be analyzed in terms of correctness, we proceed with comparing such value with the ones encountered in the Spearman coefficient significance level table, ascertaining that it exceeds even the most restrictive value in terms of certitude ($p < 0.01$), thereby allowing us to accept the veracity of H1 with a level of trust of more than 99%.

$$0.584101 > 0.405000$$

The same is obtained while using the t-student test for determining the significance level, considering *38* freedom degrees:

$$t = 4.436028$$

$$4.436028 > 2.429000$$

confirming, with a sampling-related error of less than 1%, that the two variables considered are, indeed, correlated with one another.

5 Conclusions

Generally, respondents fall into the general pattern of SNSs use from the way they manifest their *engagement*: they are influenced by the ads on the networks, they shop online, and they do this because they associate networks with certain benefits: consumers advertise for their favorite brand and create and distribute content in order to promote their favorite brands. In the case of entrepreneurs, 67% of them fall into the general pattern in terms of engagement: they are present on at least two social networks, they use at least two functions of each network to promote their product. However, there are a significant number of respondents (13) who choose not to use social networks for their businesses, for various reasons. In their case, the lack of engagement on social networks for the benefit of their businesses translates into a source of *vulnerability*.

Regarding the *lack of trust* shown by respondents against social networks, we note that our study does not confirm the findings of specialized studies in the field that show that trust among users is generated, mainly, by the uncertainty regarding the protection of personal data or privacy (Markos et al. 2012). As consumers, our respondents feel manipulated (25%) and have negative feelings when using SNSs. Instead, for entrepreneurs, the lack of trust is evidenced by non-participation (33%) and their belief that presence on social networks cannot bring any benefit to them.

The dichotomous nature of human behavior is manifested in the *skill level* related to the use of SNSs. Thus, if respondents-consumers prove to have the technological skills to make their presence felt on the SNSs and take advantage of the benefits offered by them, as entrepreneurs, the same respondents see themselves as having moderate skills and some even no skills in using networks in the benefit of their businesses. From this point of view, we can say that those entrepreneurs deprive themselves from the access to resources and opportunities, although this behavior is somewhat justified if we take into account that these entrepreneurs are still in the start-up phase.

Moreover, we found that there is no correlation between the level of specific benefits brought by social media to consumers and the level of specific benefits brought by social media to entrepreneurs.

In this context, we can state that our students use social networks to express their assumed identities differently, each type of identity having certain features. However, regardless of their assumed identity, they are distrustful when using networks, reluctance we identified as lack of trust and designated as *Achilles heel*. If we remember the fight between David and Goliath (Gladwell 2013), we can say that the users' lack of trust is exactly what can "kill" the powerful Goliath – social networks in our case.

Our study's limitations are two, namely: (1) the small number of respondents we identified as suited for this type of research; (2) the fact that they belong to the same university, limitations that make impossible the generalization of results. As future research directions, we consider useful: (1) to structure subjects on type of consumers/businesses; (2) to launch comparative studies on two directions, namely: with consumers/entrepreneurs in the same age category, but without university education; or with other age categories.

Appendix

See Tables 12, 13 and 14.

Table 12. Identification of the position of each element of the range of answers

Range of outputs	Position
Not at all	NAA (1)
Very little	VL (2)
Little	L (3)
Medium	MD (4)
Much	M (5)
Very much	VM (6)

Table 13. Determination of the rank output elements

Entrepreneurs	Position	1	2	3	4	5	6
	Repetitive items	13	0	3	4	12	8
	Rank	**7**	**0**	**15**	**18.5**	**26.5**	**36.5**
Consumers	Position	1	2	3	4	5	6
	Repetitive items	0	2	6	17	11	4
	Rank	**0**	**1.5**	**5.5**	**17**	**31**	**38.5**

Table 14. Operations for determining the Spearman coefficient

$Rank_1$	$Rank_2$	$Rank_1*Rank_2$	$Rank_1^2$	$Rank_2^2$
36.5	17	620.5	1332.25	289
18.5	38.5	712.25	342.25	1482.25
7	17	119	49	289
18.5	5.5	101.75	342.25	30.25
7	31	217	49	961
18.5	17	314.5	342.25	289
7	17	119	49	289
36.5	17	620.5	1332.25	289
26.5	5.5	145.75	702.25	30.25
15	31	465	225	961
7	17	119	49	289
18.5	17	314.5	342.25	289
7	31	217	49	961
36.5	1.5	54.75	1332.25	2.25
15	38.5	577.5	225	1482.25
26.5	17	450.5	702.25	289
7	31	217	49	961
26.5	31	821.5	702.25	961
26.5	5.5	145.75	702.25	30.25
15	31	465	225	961
26.5	17	450.5	702.25	289
26.5	5.5	145.75	702.25	30.25
26.5	38.5	1020.25	702.25	1482.25
26.5	31	821.5	702.25	961
36.5	31	1131.5	1332.25	961
36.5	17	620.5	1332.25	289
26.5	17	450.5	702.25	289
26.5	17	450.5	702.25	289
36.5	17	620.5	1332.25	289
26.5	31	821.5	702.25	961
36.5	5.5	200.75	1332.25	30.25
26.5	5.5	145.75	702.25	30.25
36.5	17	620.5	1332.25	289
7	17	119	49	289
7	31	217	49	961
7	38.5	269.5	49	1482.25
7	17	119	49	289
7	17	119	49	289
7	1.5	10.5	49	2.25
7	31	217	49	961
Total **443.5**	**403**	**8571**	**12622.25**	**10463.5**

References

Ba, S., Pavlou, P.A.: Evidence of the effect of trust building technology in electronic markets: price premiums and buyer behavior. MIS Q. **26**(3), 243–268 (2002)

Baconschi, T.: Facebook: Fabrica de narcisism. Humanitas, Bucharest (2015)

Baron, R.A., Tang, J.: Entrepreneurs' social skills and new venture performance: mediating mechanisms and cultural generality. J. Manag. **35**(2), 282–306 (2009)

Boyd, D.M., Ellison, N.B.: Social network sites: definition, history and scholarship. J. Comput.-Mediated Commun. **13**(1), 210–230 (2007). doi:10.1111/j.1083-6101.2007.00393.x

Burns, G.N., Christiansen, N.D.: Methods of measuring faking behavior. Hum. Perform. **24**(4), 358–372 (2011). doi:10.1080/08959285.2011.597473

Burns, P.: Entrepreneurship and Small Business. Palgrave Macmillan, New York (2011)

Calder, B.J., Malthouse, E.C., Schadel, U.: An experimental study of the relationship between online engagement and advertising effectiveness. J. Interact. Mark. **23**(November), 321–331 (2009)

Carter, D.: Hustle and brand: the sociotechnical shaping of influence. Social Media + Society, 1–12 (2016). http://journals.sagepub.com/doi/abs/10.1177/2056305116666305

Cheema, A., Kaikaki, A.M.: The effect of need for uniqueness on word-of-mouth. J. Mark. Res. **47**(3), 353–363 (2010)

Christakis, N.A., Fowler, J.H.: Connected: The Surprising Power of Our Social Networks and How They Shape Our Lives. CurteaVeche Publishing, Bucharest (2015)

Davis, F.D.: Perceived usefulness, perceived ease of use and user acceptance of information technology. MIS Q. **13**(3), 319–340 (1989)

Davis, F.D., Bagozzi, R.P., Warshaw, P.R.: Use acceptance of computer technology: a comparison of two theoretical models. Manag. Sci. **4**(8), 982–1003 (1989)

Di Fiore, A.: Cum iti salveaza Linkedin relatiile de business. Rev. Cariere **1**, 42 (2011)

Drury, G.: Social media: should marketers engage and how can it be done effectively? J. Direct Data Digit. Mark. Pract. **9**(3), 274–277 (2008)

Dubini, P., Aldrich, H.: Personal and extended networks are central to the entrepreneurial process. J. Bus. Ventur. **6**(5), 305–313 (1991)

Firkin, P.: Entrepreneurial capital. In: Burns, P. (ed.) Entrepreneurship and Small Business. Palgrave Macmillan, New York (2003)

Gefen, D.: Reflections on the dimensions of trust and trustworthiness among online consumers. Database Adv. Inf. Syst. **33**(3), 38–53 (2002)

Gefen, D., Karahanna, E., Straub, D.W.: Trust and TAM in online shopping: an integrated model. MIS Q. **27**(1), 51–90 (2003)

Fischer, E., Reuber, A.R.: Social interaction via new social media: how can interactions on Twitter affect effectual thinking and behavior? J. Bus. Ventur. **26**, 1–18 (2011)

Gabriel, Y., Lang, T.: The Unmanageable Consumer. Sage, London (1995)

Goffman, E.: The Presentation of Self in Everyday Life. Anchor Books, Doubleday, New York (1959)

Haven, B.: Marketing's New Key Metric: Engagement. Forrester Research (2007). http://snproject.pbworks.com/f/NewMetric_Engagement.pdf

Gambetti, R.C., Graffigna, G.: The concept of engagement: a systematic analysis of the ongoing marketing debate. Int. J. Mark. Res. **52**(6), 801–826 (2010). doi:10.2501/S14707 85310201661

Ghenea, M.: Antreprenoriatul. Universul Juridic, Bucuresti (2011)

Gladwell, M.: David and Goliath: Underdogs, Misfits and The Art of Battling Giants. Little, Brown and Company, New York (2013)

Hostiuc, C.: Implicatiile unei lipse acute de incredere. Rev. Bus. Mag. **2**, 66 (2016)

Karpati, A.: Next Generation (2002). http://www.emile.eu.org/Papers11.htm

Labrecque, L.I., von demEsche, J., Mathwick, C., Novak, T.P., Hofacker, C.F.: Consumer power: evolution in the digital age. J. Interact. Mark. **27**, 257–269 (2013)

Lorenzo, C., Constantinides, E., Geurts, P., Gomez, M.: Impact of web experience on E-consumer response, E-commerce and web technologies. In: Psaila, G., Wagner, R. (eds.) E-Commerce and Web Technologies, pp. 191–200. Springer, Berlin/Heidelberg (2007)

Lu, Y., Zhao, L., Wang, B.: From virtual community members to C2C E-commerce buyers: trust in virtual communities and its effect on consumers' purchase intention. Electron. Commer. Res. Appl. **9**(4), 346–360 (2010)

Logan, K.: Why isn't everyone doing it? A comparison of antecedents to following brands on Twitter and Facebook. J. Interact. Advertising **14**(2), 60–72 (2014). doi:10.1080/15252019.2014.935536

Markos, E.C., Labrecque, L.I., Milne, G.L.: Web 2.0 and consumers' digital footprint: managing privacy and disclosures choices in social media. In: Close, A.G. (ed.) Online Consumer Behavior: Theory and Research in Social Media, Advertising and E-Tail. Routledge, New York (2012)

Network Readiness Index (2016). http://reports.weforum.org/global-information-technology-report-2016/networked-readiness-index/

Oblinger, D., Oblinger, J.: Educating the Next Generation. Educause, Boulder (2005). http://www.edu-cause.ed/ir/library/pdf/pub7101.pdf

Opariuc-Dan, C.: Applied Statistics in Social-human Sciences - Relations Analysis and Statistical Differences, 1st edn. Arhip-Art Sibiu, Publisher (2011)

Parent, M., Plangger, K., Bal, A.: The new WTP: willingness to participate. Bus. Horiz. **54**(219), 229 (2011)

Pavlou, P.A.: Consumer acceptance of electronic commerce: integrating trust and risk with the technology acceptance model. Int. J. Electron. Commer. **7**(3), 101–134 (2003)

Raines, C.: Generations at Work, Managing Millenials (2002). http://www.generationsatwork.com/articles/millenials.htm

Rohm, A.J., Milne, G.R., Kaltcheva, V.: The role of online social media in brand-consumer engagement: an exploratory study. In: Interactive Marketing Research Summit Proceedings, 31 August 2012. doi:10.1108/JRIM-01-2013-0009

Shin, D.-H.: The effects of trust, security and privacy in social networking: a security-based approach to understand the pattern of adoption. Interact. Comput. **22**(5), 428–438 (2010)

Taylor, D.G., Lewin, J.E., Strutton, D.: Friends, fans and followers: do ads work on social networks? J. Advertising Res. **51**(1), 258–275 (2011)

Veen, W.: A new force for change: homo zappiens. Learn. Citizen **7**, 5–7 (2004)

Interactive Advertising Bureau. http://www.iab.com/wp-content/uploads/2015/07/2009-iab-annual-report-final.pdf

The Influence of Privacy, Trust, and National Culture on Internet Transactions

Jon Heales[1(✉)], Sophie Cockcroft[1], and Van-Hau Trieu[2]

[1] University of Queensland, Brisbane, Australia
j.heales@uq.edu.au, s.cockcroft@business.uq.edu.au
[2] University of Melbourne, Melbourne, Australia
van-hau.trieu@unimelb.edu.au

Abstract. A privacy paradox still exists between consumers' willingness to transact online and their stated Information privacy concerns. MIS research has the capacity to contribute to societal research in this area (Dinev 2014) and cultural differences are one important area of investigation. The global nature of e-commerce makes cultural factors likely to have a significant impact on this concern. Building on work done in the area of culture and privacy, and also trust and privacy, we explore the three way relationship between culture, privacy and trust. Emerge. A key originality of this work is the use of the GLOBE variables to measure culture. These provide a more contemporary measure of culture and overcome some of the criticisms levelled at the much used Hofstede variables. Since the late 1990s scholars have been exploring ways of measuring Privacy. Whilst attitudinal measures around concern for information privacy are only one proxy for privacy itself, such measures have evolved in sophistication. Smith et al. developed the Global Information Privacy Scale which evolved into the 15 question parsimonious CFIP scale (Smith 1996) Leading on from this Malhotra developed the internet users information privacy concerns (IUIPC) which takes into account individuals differing perceptions of fairness and justice using social contract theory. We present the results of an exploratory empirical study that uses both GLOBE and IUIPC via a set of scenarios to determine the strength of national culture as an antecedent to IUIPC and the concomitant effect of IUIPC on trust and risk.

Keywords: Cross cultural IS research · GLOBE project · Privacy · Trust · Risk beliefs

1 Introduction

The concept of *privacy* can be used to describe many sociological, legal, philosophical, and philosophical aspects of modern life. In a 2011 interdisciplinary review of Information Privacy research [1] reviewed all these aspects in depth. The work developed here focuses primarily on Information Privacy. Recent advances in storage, collection and analysis of personal data, social networking and the ubiquitous nature of IT, together with increased government surveillance have produced heightened awareness of information privacy in the media and in the public conscience. However, Information Systems (IS) researchers continue to observe a mismatch between attitudes to information privacy

© Springer International Publishing AG 2017
G. Meiselwitz (Ed.): SCSM 2017, Part I, LNCS 10282, pp. 159–176, 2017.
DOI: 10.1007/978-3-319-58559-8_14

and actual outcomes and behaviours. Attitudes toward information privacy differ across the world. Previous studies have shown that there is a relationship between race and ethnic origin, and information privacy concern. Since Electronic Commerce (EC) is acknowledged to be a global activity, work should be undertaken develop models that test our understanding of the interplay between privacy policies, attitudes, trust and culture [2]. [1] put forward the acronym APCO (Antecedents -> Privacy Concerns -> Outcomes). To describe the common macro model in empirical privacy research [3] developed a full integrative framework analysing existing empirical research and its multiple antecedent and consequent factors. Our work is particularly concerned with the culture-privacy concern- trust-behaviour model. Literature relating to this is described in below.

2 Prior Research

2.1 Concern for Information Privacy: Existing Research and Measurement Scales

The notion of privacy is notoriously hard to describe. Since the advent of Information systems and more recently internet based commerce, information privacy has been seen as synonymous with privacy in general although there are distinct lines of research around privacy of the person privacy as a right, or as a commodity. The past fifteen years have seen a maturing in the measurement scales for information privacy in the 1990s researchers began to accept *privacy concern* as a measurable proxy for information privacy. Early studies attempted to measure individuals' attitudes to information privacy using a one dimensional scale [4]. This scale did not, however, capture the multidimensional nature of individuals privacy concerns. This was superseded by a 15 question instrument, developed by Smith et al. [5], which reflects four dimensions of information privacy concern (collection, errors, secondary use, and unauthorised access to information). These dimensions were later revalidated by Stewart and Segars [6]. This instrument known as the concern for Information privacy (CFIP) instrument, or adaptations thereof have been used in a number of studies [7–12]. These basic measures have formed an enduring basis for Information Privacy research. Sipior Ward and Conolly (2013) noted that even after the advent of the IUIPC [13] (Malhotra 2004) measurement scale researchers tended to use the earlier scale. The main point of the IUIPC scale was to adapt the earlier CFIP scale to encompass internet users concerns. It draws on social contract theory to streamline the concept of privacy in internet based environments to three factors, collection, control and awareness which go to make up the second order factor IUIPC.

We adapt the instrument used by Malhotra et al., because it captures a second order factor, Internet Users' Information Privacy Concern (IUIPC). This instrument retains the more general information privacy questions from earlier studies.

There have been five highly cited reviews of the privacy literature. These and their findings are summarized in Table 1. What has emerged over the past fifteen years or so is a privacy paradox namely that individuals' actions in protecting their own privacy or surrendering to the policies of government or organisations are quite different from their espoused privacy concerns. This paradox has led researchers down a number of interesting paths of enquiry. In particular, as described by Dinev (2014) beyond the definition and conceptualisation of privacy there are the anthropological and cultural angle of privacy. These aspects can be described as Macro Environmental factors and include culture and governmental regulations and are relevant to the present work.

Table 1. Key information privacy reviews

[3]	[3] focussed specifically on empirical studies at the individual level, Classifying them according to their antecedent and consequent factors and exploring *controversial* relationships. They define culture as a macro environmental factor and also make the distinction of organisational factors, socio relational factors such as social norms. Information contingencies referring to the type of information collected. They also make explicit the notion of general CFIP vs Specific CFIP where the concerns are linked to a particular IS instantiation such as a website. A key recommendation was that The causal relationships between information privacy concerns, trust belief, and risk belief need to be further verified
[1]	This review provides an interdisciplinary view, exploring the concept of Privacy itself. Smith et al. propose the APCO model (Antecedents -> Privacy concerns-> Outcomes). They propose that context is less important that producing studies that are comparable and repeatable and again call for research beyond the individual level
[14]	Critical analysis of IS literature classification by theoretical contribution, Characteristics (e.g. respondent type), respondent origin, level of analysis, tools, practices. The authors found that much research was carried out at the individual level (rarely multilevel (e.g. organizational or societal) and often only across one or two cultures. They suggested a need for more investigation into the differences between stated behaviour and actual action
[15]	Summarised and compared [1, 14] and synthesised their arguments. A common measure for information privacy was suggested and it was noted that more practical studies were required and in particular those focussed on actual outcomes
[16]	This review takes fifteen established theories in online information privacy research and develops an integrated framework for further research. The framework highlights the trade-off between expected benefits and privacy risks the trade-off between privacy risks and efficacy of coping mechanisms

Concern for information privacy has appeared in empirical studies as both the dependent and independent variable. When featured as a dependent variable the antecedents are often personal characteristics such as demographics, personality traits, knowledge and experience or Psychological or socio-psychological factors [17] many researchers have begun to explore psychological aspects of decision making on privacy e.g. computer anxiety [6], self-efficacy [18, 19]. Frequency of internet use has been associated with lower levels of privacy concern, and less experience with higher levels of anxiety [7] The effects of gender, age and personality type on attitudes to information privacy have been explored e.g. [18, 20, 21]. Further, there have been a number of empirical studies that focus on so-called privacy calculus whereby a value can be imputed for information privacy [22–27].

As an independent variable privacy is often explored in relation to its impact on trust, risk and behavioural intention. The role of CFIP and its more recent descendent, IUIPC in empirical models is explored at length in a review article by Li (2011). A quasi model has evolved in these studies APCO [1] which establishes the context that all or most privacy studies incorporate an antecedent to privacy concern, and a number of outcomes. Our particular interest is National Culture as an antecedent to Privacy Concern and we describe that factor in more detail in the next section. In 2004 Bellman noted that National culture has been incorporated as a demographic factor in many works, but has rarely been studied in isolation as an antecedent to privacy attitudes. This was echoed at that time by, Mahmood et al. [28]. Who noted that future researchers should focus specifically in the impact of culture. Since then there has been some development in the area of national culture and privacy.

2.2   National Culture

Table 2 gives a summary of research specifically focusing on Culture as an antecedent in every case the Hofstede and Hofstede [29] variables were used. For an explanation of the abbreviations of these variables see Sect. 3.

Table 2. Previous studies of national culture and privacy

Study	Hofstede variable	Hypothesis relating to attitude to information privacy	Supported
[30]	UA	High UA High Concern	No
	PD	High PD High Concern	No
	IND	High IND High Concern	No
[31]	PD	Low PDI High Concern	Yes (secondary use, more regulation)
	MAS	Low MAS High Concern	Yes (secondary use, online security)
	IND	Low IND High Concern	Yes (errors)
[18]	UA	High IND High Concern	Yes
	IND	Hi UA High Concern	No (HI UA Low concern)
[32] (cross cultural US and China)	MAS	High MAS High Concern	No effect
	UA	High UA High Concern	Yes
	PD	High PD High Concern	No (opposite)
	IND	High MAS High Concern	Yes
[33]	PD	High PD High Concern	Yes
	IND	High IND High Concern	Yes
	MAS	High MAS High Concern	Yes
	UI	High UI low concern	Yes
[34]	Hypothesis not specific to Hofstede variable	The effect of perceived enjoyment of IM on behavioral intention to use IM is higher for Chinese than for Americans	Yes individualism emphasizes the benefit or utilitarian outcome in their use of CMC more than collectivism
Dinev 2006	Hypothesis not specific to Hofstede variable	Individuals in Italy have lower Internet privacy concerns than individuals in the U.S.	Yes (suggested due to IND index)

Culture is an antecedent in this study and trust, risk and behavioral intention are consequent. We extend the work in these studies by using the GLOBE cultural dimensions. Each dimension was considered from the viewpoint of its effects on privacy concerns. A much cited paper on trust and culture Jarvenpaa et al. [35] notes the fact that *participants were not necessarily born in the country studied* as a limitation. Use of the GLOBE variables and judicious demographic questioning in this study addresses this shortcoming.

Culture as a demographic indicator has been used in a number of privacy studies. Most recently Bellman et al. [7] used national regulation as a means of revealing CFIP. They hypothesized three explanations for differences in privacy concerns: culture, internet experience and political desires using the Hofstede and Hofstede [29] dimensions to describe culture. Only culture and internet experience turned out to be significant. i.e., it is nature and experience rather than government intervention that determines an individual's attitude to information privacy.

However, the validity of National Culture measures to date has been criticized for accuracy and relevance, particularly with regard to cultural boundaries. These and other criticisms of the use of cultural factors by [36] have been largely overcome by the GLOBE project [37]. GLOBE re-examines national culture in a new way mitigating many of the concerns of earlier approaches. This study represents a move away from the Hofstede [38] national cultural dimensions in favor of those developed in the GLOBE project (many of which are developed from the foundations developed by Hofstede). These variables are presented with the proposed model. Heales et al. [39] and [40] provide a more extensive background on the development and use of the GLOBE cultural dimensions in an IS setting.

2.3   Trust and Behavioral Intention

Behavioral intention (BI) in EC has a strong relationship with trust. Although trust is difficult to define, Gefen et al. [41] conduct a rigorous review of the various dimensions of trust in an e-commerce setting.

Two early studies on trust specifically explored privacy concern more deeply; Malhotra et al. [13] drew on social contact theory to present a framework for users' privacy concerns and proposed and tested a causal model between IUIPC and BI. They identified three factors, trusting beliefs, risk beliefs and BI. Trust also featured as an antecedent to BI in the work of Liu et al. [42] who tested the model through a variety of questions concerning how the respondent felt about structural features of an internet site. Figure 1 provides a starting point for the work developed here.

Gefen and Heart [2] called for the inclusion of national culture in studies of e-commerce trust beliefs. In more recent years antecedents of privacy have more commonly included perceived information sensitivity [43]. How culture affects perceptions of risk and trust [44]. How culture affects willingness to disclose personal information in cross country studies [45, 46] and how privacy affects trust [47]. We look specifically at culture as an antecedent for Privacy and hypothesize the likely effect of cultural dimensions on IUIPC [48].

| -Notice
-Choice
-Awareness | Level or degree of trust | -Repeat Purchase
-Visit Again
-Recommend to friends |

Privacy ➡ Trust ➡ Behavioral intention

Fig. 1. Privacy-trust-behavioral intention model (adapted from Liu et al. [42])

3 Proposed Study and Model

Figure 2 details the research model. There are some points to note with reference to this model. In the IUIPC model collection measures the same concept as Smith's collection construct, and control and awareness together represent the other three CFIP dimensions of Improper use, secondary use and errors. An explanation of each of the remaining constructs in the model follows.

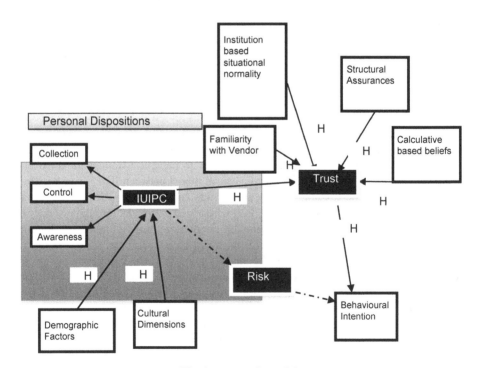

Fig. 2. Research model

3.1 Trust

Trust includes beliefs relating to integrity, benevolence, ability, and predictability. Familiarity reduces social complexity and uncertainty, thus is likely to enhance trust. The assessment that a new transaction will be a success based on how customary and familiar the situation appears (situational normality) also leads to trust. Trust can also be shaped by an assessment of the costs and benefits to the other party of cheating or cooperating, this is known as calculative based trust. Structural assurances such as policies or web seals are also likely to increase trust [49]. A full discussion of these antecedents is given in [41]. This leads us to hypothesize:

H1 Familiarity with a trustworthy e-vendor will positively affect trust in that e-vendor
H2 Perceptions of situational normality will positively affect trust in an e-vendor
H3 Calculative based beliefs will positively affect trust in an e-vendor

The structural assurance questions in the survey related to information assurance in the context of a commodity product (book) as opposed to look and feel product (e.g. clothes) Thus it would be expected that such seals would increase trust in a vendor and hence BI.

H4 Structural Assurances will positively affect trust in an e-vendor

Finally, based on prior work [41], trust allows the user to subjectively rule out undesirable behaviours by the vendor and hence heighten levels of intended use.

H5 Trust will positively affect BI

3.2 Risk

Many authors have used a trust-risk model to explain behaviours in the consumer-firm relationship (see for example [50]. In essence the model suggests that in a situation in which risks are present, trust plays an important role in determining one's risk taking behaviour [13]. Personal traits are known to influence both trusting beliefs and risk beliefs. A tendency to worry over information privacy will influence how a person perceives a given risk. If a user has a high degree of information privacy concern it is likely that they will also have highly developed risk beliefs. Risk beliefs refer to the expectation that loss will occur as a result of releasing personal information to an online firm. Risk was included in the model post-hoc and thus we did not set out to specifically test any hypotheses in this area, but have included it in the research model, see [51].

3.3 Demographic Factors

Internet use has widely been identified as a factor that reduced IUIPC [7]. It has been suggested that younger users have a greater degree of awareness about privacy and how to protect themselves and hence are less anxious about privacy, these results were borne out by Gauzente [52]. The original study by Milberg et al. [30] showed that females tend to be more concerned than males. This leads us to propose:

H6-1 Age will be negatively associated with IUIPC
H6-2 Internet experience is negatively associated with IUIPC
H6-3 Female users are likely to have a higher level of IUIPC

3.4   Cultural Dimensions

As noted above, we chose to use the GLOBE cultural dimensions. We present the hypotheses derived from the use of GLOBE cultural dimensions on IUIPC:

Power Distance

A culture of high PD is characterized by a hierarchy of authority and control, centralization of knowledge and responsibility, excessive rule and a more restricted exchange of knowledge [37]. The reverse is true of lower PD cultures that are characterized by less hierarchy, fewer rules, greater decentralization of knowledge and free flow of information. We suggest that cultures with low PD emphasize a flatter hierarchy and greater equality in relationships. Thus those with low PD would be more willing to share information, and have a more egalitarian view on privacy. The converse is true that high PD cultures would tend to want to control and guard information by adopting a high IUIPC stance. This argument leads to:

H7-1 PD scores will be positively associated with IUIPC scores.

Uncertainty Avoidance

UA is the extent to which a society relies on social norms and procedures to alleviate the unpredictability of future events. In high UA cultures, people would be expected to have high levels of CFIP because they would aim to reduce uncertainty by being cautious and careful about the information they divulged through the internet so that they would be more certain as to what was done with any information provided. On the other hand, people scoring low on UA are less interested in reducing uncertainty and would not be concerned about how information they provide is used. The ability to reduce uncertainty with a computer system is highly valued for high UA individuals [53]. Therefore, the relationship between UA and IUIPC exists, thus:

H7-2 High uncertainty avoidance will be associated high IUIPC

Institutional Collectivism

High values of IC encourage and reward collective distribution of resources and collective action. In such cultures cooperation is seen as more important than the individuals needs [54]. In such an environment attitudes toward privacy are likely to be more relaxed, leading to:

H7-3 IC will be negatively associated with values of IUIPC

Humane Orientation

HO targets the individual's focus on others' wellbeing, and people rather than task oriented approach. Paternalistic and patronage relationships are valued, and individuals value harmony [55]. It follows that individuals exhibiting high levels of HO would be concerned about privacy.

H7-4 HO will be positively associated with values of IUIPC

Performance Orientation

In cultures with the highest reported PO scores, training and development is highly valued. People believe in taking initiative and emphasize performance. It is likely that these people will be concerned about privacy and would strive to ensure that privacy issues are addressed, thus:

H7-5 PO will be positively associated with values of IUIPC

Future Orientation

Kluckhohn and Strodtbeck [56] first identified this phenomenon that represents a culture's focus on the past, present or future. A past-oriented culture might evaluate plans in terms of customs, traditions, or history, while a future-oriented culture would evaluate plans in terms of future benefits. People with high FO scores would be more concerned about privacy issues in the future and would likely have a high IUIPC score, thus:

H7-6 FO will be positively associated with values of IUIPC

Gender Egalitarianism

In societies where the differences in gender are high, gender inequality will be apparent. Men tend to focus on hierarchy and independence, while women focus on intimacy and solidarity, thus women would be more concerned over privacy issues.

H7-7 High GE will be associated with high IUIPC

Group Collectivism

This dimension refers to the extent to which members of a society take pride in membership in small groups such as their family and close circle of friends, and the organizations in which they are employed. In countries with high group collectivism scores, being a member of a family and of a close group of friends is important and there is an inclination to put friends and family before society's rules and procedures. This focus and tendency to share may lead people to be less concerned about privacy.

H7-8 High GC will be associated with low IUIPC

Assertiveness

In cultures where assertiveness, confrontational, and aggressive behavior is condoned, individuals are more likely to be concerned about information privacy because they focus on the right to control information about themselves [57]. These arguments lead us to hypothesise:

H7-9 ASS scores will be positively associated with IUIPC scores

3.5   Privacy

Consensus in the trust literature (Malhotra et al. [13]) implies:

H8 There is a negative relationship between IUIPC and the degree of trust an individual has when making an online transaction

4   Research Method

Using the a modified version of the Malhotra et al. [13] model and questionnaire, a web-based survey instrument was used to collect data from a cross-section of Internet users on the constructs in the model. The survey subjects varied in age from 15 to 73 and the gender balance was 55% female and 45% male. Table 3 illustrates the countries of birth of participants. There were 53 questions in the survey. Respondents were asked a series of demographic questions, including some based on culture related variables. They were then presented with two scenarios one of which involved a discount club that gave discounts on CDs Books and electronics in exchange for personal purchase preference information (such as favorite category, brand design etc.), the second was the same scenario only asking for personal financial information (such as income, mortgage payments, investments).

The data collected from the questionnaire were subject to analysis using structural equation modelling. First, the measurement model was tested to ensure that items loaded satisfactorily on to the constructs being measured. No significant departures from normality were detected in the data.

Table 3. Countries of birth of participants

Australia	48	England	6
China	54	India	4
Singapore	5	US	3
Thailand	3	Philippines	3
Hong Kong	2	Switzerland	1
Taiwan	10	Ireland	2
Indonesia	4	Malaysia	9
Italy	1	Total	155

The survey measured both Global information privacy concerns (GIPC) and the more contemporary Internet Users Information Privacy Concerns (IUIPC). We collected this data with a view to comparing the nature of the two constructs and help resolve the differences between them. We used PLS to test the structural integrity of the model, however individual relationships were tested using multiple regression. The results for the complete model are shown in Fig. 3.

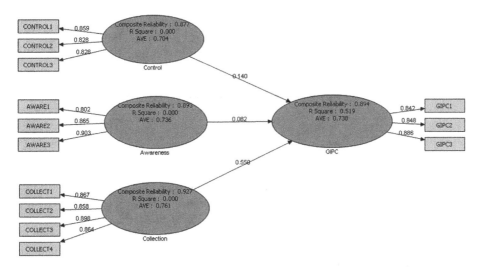

Fig. 3. Model of GIPC showing loadings of Control, Awareness and Collection

5   Results

First we examined the differences between GIPC and IUIPC before inclusion in the full research model. The survey measured both GIPC and IUIPC. We discuss our results with respect to both, then go on to test the full model.

5.1   Test of GIPC and IUIPC

As expected, IUIPC was significantly correlated with GIPC ($R = 0.675$, $p < 0.01$). The constructs contributing to GIPC and IUIPC were tested using both PLS and multiple regression. Collection contributed strongly to GIPC (loading of 0.55), and Control showed a weak contribution to GIPC (0.14). Overall, the model contributes to an R^2 of 0.519 for GIPC.

The regression testing of GIPC, *Control*, *Awareness*, and *Collection* variables were computed by averaging each construct's indicators, and regressing *Control Awareness* and *Collection* against GIPC (see Table 4 below). *Collection* contributed significantly at the $p < 0.01$ level, while weak association are shown with *Control* at the $p < 0.10$ level.

Table 4. Summary results for the stepwise regression of collect, control, and aware against GIPC

Variable	Mean Square	$F_{(3,163)}$	t	Sig.	Unstandardized Coefficients	Std. Err of Estimate	Adj. R Square
Model:							
Dependent Variable: GIPC	70.826	84.617		0.000			0.499
collect		6.962	.000		.864	.364	0.487
control		1.694	.092		.551	.079	0.021
aware		.247	.805		.202	.119	0.000

Testing of the full relationship between GIPC and *Collect*, *Control* and *Aware*, using PLS (see Fig. 3). The model resulted in an R^2 of 0.499 for GIPC. This test indicates the GIPC and IUIPC are not the same construct, and are significantly different. For example, IUIPC assumes that *Collect Control* and *Aware* contribute equally to its value, however *Collect* only contributes 43.5% of the value of GIPC. *Control* only has a loading of 0.140 on GIPC (significant at only $p < 0.05$), and the loading of *Aware* on GIPC is 0.082 (not significant). Therefore we conclude that GIPC should not be used to proxy for IUIPC.

Because we believe GIPC and IUIPC are different constructs, we use IUIPC in the full model. All testing therefore is undertaken using IUIPC.

5.2 Full Model

Figure 4 shows the full model with loadings between indicators and latent variables. The full model resulted in an R^2 of 0.438 for *Behavioral Intention*. *Demographic* factors and *Trust* contributed significantly to *Behavioral Intention*, while *Risk* was found to be a moderating factor between *Trust* and *Behavioral Intention* (see Fig. 4). Table 5 summarizes the results of the hypothesis testing.

IUIPC is a latent variable derived from *Collect, Control* and *Awareness*. We hypothesised that IUIPC would also be affected by *Demographic* and *Cultural* factors. *Demographic* factors were slightly significant at the $p < 0.10$ level (one tail).

Trust is a latent variable derived from IUIPC, *FamVend*, *StructAss*, and *CalcBel*. All variables contributed significantly to *Trust* at the $p < 0.01$ level (one tail) and *StructAss* at the $p < 0.05$ level (one tail).

Risk was found to contribute directly to *Behavioral Intention* (0.174, $p < 0.05$), and also acted as a moderating variable to the effect that *Trust* had on *Behavioral Intention* (0.21, $p < 0.05$).

As noted above, IUIPC and GIPC are not the same constructs. We substituted GIPC for IUIPC and obtained a similar R^2 for *Behavioral Intention* (0.402). However the

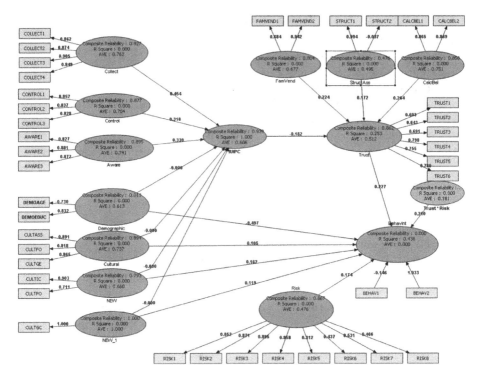

Fig. 4. Model of national culture, trust and internet privacy concerns

influence of demographic and cultural variables on GIPC was not significant, and bivariate correlations revealed no significant associations with the cultural dimensions. We conclude that demographic and cultural factors do not influence GIPC. Additional work is needed to investigate this issue further to determining the underlying reasons for this difference.

The demographic factors of *Age* and *Education* had a barely significant association with IUIPC (0.080, $p < .10$ one-tail). However the loading on *Behavioral Intention* was high at 0.497, $p < .01$, indicating older users' *Behavioral Intention* was to reveal more personal information, as were users with less *Education*.

6 Discussion

There has been little work exploring the role of culture in the relationship between privacy, trust, risk and behavioral intention in e-commerce. This work contributes to the body of knowledge in that area. It also confirms the validity of the second order factor IUIPC first put forward by [13] as being explained by first order factors; collection, control and awareness. An additional unexpected finding was the mediating role of risk in the relationship between IUIPC and behavioral intention.

Table 5. Summary of results

No.	Hypothesis	Effect	Comments
H1	Familiarity with a trustworthy e-vendor will positively affect trust in that e-vendor	+ve $p < 0.01$	
H2	Calculative based beliefs will positively affect trust in an e-vendor	+ve $p < 0.01$	
H3	Structural Assurances will positively affect trust in an e-vendor	+ve $p < 0.05$	
H4	Trust will positively affect BI	+ve $p < 0.01$	Confirmed by regression.
H5 -1	Age will be negatively associated with IUIPC	+ve $p < 0.1$	One-tail test
H5 -2	Female users are likely to have a higher level of IUIPC	Not Sig.	
H6- 1	PD scores will be positively associated with IUIPC scores	Not Sig.	
H6- 2	High UA will be associated high IUIPC	Not Sig.	
H6- 3	IC will be negatively associated with values of IUIPC	Not Sig.	Post hoc sig with BI, $p < 0.05$
H6- 4	HO will be positively associated with values of IUIPC	Not Sig.	
H6- 5	PO will be positively associated with values of IUIPC	Not Sig.	Post hoc sig with BI, $p < 0.05$
H6- 6	FO will be positively associated with values of IUIPC	Not Sig.	
H6- 7	High GE will be associated with high IUIPC	Not Sig.	
H6- 8	High GC will be associated with low IUIPC	Not Sig.	Post hoc sig with BI, $p < 0.05$
H6- 9	ASS scores will be positively associated with IUIPC scores	Not Sig.	
H7	There is a negative relationship between IUIPC and the degree of trust an individual has when making an online transaction	+ve $p < 0.05$	
	Risk – Post hoc testing	Sig	Risk sig with BI, $p < 0.05$ Risk found to moderate relation between Trust and BI, $p < 0.01$

Cultural variables load better on to BI than IUIPC. It is well known that there are cultural differences in shopping habits [58], and this may be independent of attitude to information privacy.

The encouraging results of this study suggest an extension of the research to additional country clusters. Such an extension will help ensure an appropriate cultural and demographic mix. We expect the hypotheses to continue being supported, and allow for further investigation into parts of this model that have not achieved significance.

Because of the lack of influence of privacy on behavioral intention (IUIPC on *Trust* and *Behavioral Intention*), this finding leads us to conclude that users are more influenced by trust and risk (risk also mitigating trust), not so much by privacy concerns. Practitioners should therefore focus on building trust, and reducing risk.

7   Limitation

The major limitation of this work is the small sample size.

8   Conclusions

This research has built on prior research to show how national cultural dimensions and privacy are important in developing trust in a web-based e-commerce environment. The research combines the work of Bellman et al. [2, 7], and Milberg et al. [33] with the Globe cultural dimensions to examine the influence that culture has on privacy concerns and trust. This further contributes to the cultural theoretical foundation called for by others [2, 7]. Preliminary findings indicate calculative beliefs and familiarity with the vendor (and to a lesser extent structural assurances) to be a key factors influencing trust and thus behavioural intention.

Age and educational level were found to directly influence behavioural intention, but not IUIPC or CFIP. Additional work is needed to tease out this issue.

Group collectivism emerges as significant within the sample, but a dichotomy of cultures may explain this. Work is progressing to expand the survey sample.

Finally, CFIP and IUIPC are not the same, although they are correlated. Again further work is needed to better understand the underlying differences.

To help improve the completion of internet transactions, Practitioners should focus on building trust and reducing risk. We found that cultural influences, age, and educational level directly influenced behavioural intention, so practitioners should focus on educating older, and less educated citizens to reduce their concerns about internet transaction completion.

Culture was found not to influence IUIPC, however it did have a direct influence on behavioural intention. Further work is needed to fully understand the basis of this behaviour. For example, one reason might be that some cultures do not care about privacy when considering divulging sensitive information, or they may feel that privacy is not an issue.

References

1. Smith, H.J., Dinev, T., Xu, H.: Information privacy research: an interdisciplinary review. Mis Q. **35**(4), 989–1015 (2011)
2. Gefen, D., Heart, T.: On the need to include national culture as a central issue in e-commerce trust beliefs. J. Glob. Inf. Manag. **14**(4), 1 (2006)
3. Li, Y.: Empirical studies on online information privacy concerns: literature review and an integrative framework. Commun. Assoc. Inf. Syst. **28**(1), 453–496 (2011)
4. Culnan, M.J.: How did they get my name?: an exploratory investigation of consumer attitudes toward secondary information use. Mis Q. 341–363 (1993)
5. Smith, H.J., Milberg, S.J., Burke, S.J.: Information privacy: measuring individuals' concerns about organizational practices. Mis Q. 167–196 (1996)
6. Stewart, K.A., Segars, A.H.: An empirical examination of the concern for information privacy instrument. Inf. Syst. Res. **13**(1), 36–49 (2002)
7. Bellman, S., et al.: International differences in information privacy concerns: a global survey of consumers. Inf. Soc. **20**(5), 313–324 (2004)
8. Liu, C., et al.: Beyond concern—a privacy-trust-behavioral intention model of electronic commerce. Inf. Manag. **42**(2), 289–304 (2005)
9. Earp, J.B., Payton, F.C.: Information privacy in the service sector: an exploratory study of health care and banking professionals. J. Organ. Comput. Electron. Commer. **16**(2), 105–122 (2006)
10. Lin, Y., Wu, H.-Y.: Information privacy concerns, government involvement, and corporate policies in the customer relationship management context. J. Glob. Bus. Technol. **4**(1), 79 (2008)
11. Rose, E.A.: An examination of the concern for information privacy in the New Zealand regulatory context. Inf. Manag. **43**(3), 322–335 (2006)
12. Fodor, M., Brem, A.: Do privacy concerns matter for Millennials? Results from an empirical analysis of location-based services adoption in Germany. Comput. Hum. Behav. **53**, 344–353 (2015)
13. Malhotra, N.K., Kim, S.S., Agarwal, J.: Internet users' information privacy concerns (IUIPC): the construct, the scale, and a causal model. Inf. Syst. Res. **15**(4), 336–355 (2004)
14. Belanger, F., Crossler, R.E.: Privacy in the digital age: a review of information privacy research in information systems. Mis Q. **35**(4), 1017–1041 (2011)
15. Pavlou, P.A.: State of the information privacy literature: where are we now and where should we go? Mis Q. **35**(4), 977–988 (2011)
16. Li, Y.: Theories in online information privacy research: a critical review and an integrated framework. Decis. Support Syst. **54**(1), 471–481 (2012)
17. Li, Y.: A multi-level model of individual information privacy beliefs. Electron. Commer. Res. Appl. **13**(1), 32–44 (2014)
18. Cho, H., Rivera-Sanchez, M., Lim, S.S.: A multinational study on online privacy: global concerns and local responses. New Media Soc. **11**(3), 395–416 (2009)
19. Osatuyi, B.: Personality traits and information privacy concern on social media platforms. J. Comput. Inf. Syst. **55**(4), 11–19 (2015)
20. Vance, D.A.: On the effects of exogenous and endogenous variables on information privacy concerns: a preliminary comparative study. In: Proceedings of the 2000 Information Resources Management Association International Conference on Challenges of Information Technology Management in the 21st Century. IGI Global (2000)
21. Bansal, G., Zahedi, F.M., Gefen, D.: Do context and personality matter? Trust and privacy concerns in disclosing private information online. Inf. Manag. **53**(1), 1–21 (2016)

22. Dinev, T., et al.: Privacy calculus model in e-commerce–a study of Italy and the United States. Eur. J. Inf. Syst. **15**(4), 389–402 (2006)
23. Dinev, T., Hart, P.: An extended privacy calculus model for e-commerce transactions. Inf. Syst. Res. **17**(1), 61–80 (2006)
24. Dinev, T., et al.: Information privacy and correlates: an empirical attempt to bridge and distinguish privacy-related concepts. Eur. J. Inf. Syst. **22**(3), 295–316 (2013)
25. Morosan, C., DeFranco, A.: Disclosing personal information via hotel apps: a privacy calculus perspective. Int. J. Hospitality Manag. **47**, 120–130 (2015)
26. Xu, F., Michael, K., Chen, X.: Factors affecting privacy disclosure on social network sites: an integrated model. Electron. Commer. Res. **13**(2), 151–168 (2013)
27. Xu, H., et al.: The role of push-pull technology in privacy calculus: the case of location-based services. J. Manag. Inf. Syst. **26**(3), 135–173 (2009)
28. Mahmood, M.A., Bagchi, K., Ford, T.C.: On-line shopping behavior: cross-country empirical research. Int. J. Electron. Commer. **9**(1), 9–30 (2004)
29. Hofstede, G.H., Hofstede, G.: Culture's Consequences: Comparing Values, Behaviors, Institutions and Organizations Across Nations. Sage, Thousand Oaks (2001)
30. Milberg, S.J., et al.: Values, personal information privacy, and regulatory approaches. Commun. ACM **38**(12), 65–74 (1995)
31. Bellman, S., et al.: International differences in information privacy concern: implications for the globalization of electronic commerce. In: Advances in Consumer Research, vol. XXXi, pp. 362–363 (2004)
32. Lowry, P.B., Cao, J.W., Everard, A.: Privacy concerns versus desire for interpersonal awareness in driving the use of self-disclosure technologies: the case of instant messaging in two cultures. J. Manag. Inf. Syst. **27**(4), 163–200 (2011)
33. Milberg, S.J., Smith, H.J., Burke, S.J.: Information privacy: corporate management and national regulation. Organ. Sci. **11**(1), 35–57 (2000)
34. Li, D., Chau, P.Y., Van Slyke, C.: A comparative study of individual acceptance of instant messaging in the US and China: a structural equation modeling approach. Commun. Assoc. Inf. Syst. **26**(1), 5 (2010)
35. Jarvenpaa, S.L., Tractinsky, N., Saarinen, L.: Consumer trust in an internet store: a cross-cultural validation. J. Comput.-Mediated Commun. **5**(2), 0 (1999)
36. Myers, M.D., Tan, F.B.: Beyond models of national culture in information systems research. Adv. Topics Glob. Inf. Manag. **2**, 14–29 (2003)
37. House, R.J., et al.: Culture, Leadership, and Organizations: The GLOBE Study of 62 Societies. Sage Publications, Thousand Oaks (2004)
38. Hofstede, G.: Culture's Consequences: Comparing Values, Behaviors, Institutions, and Organizations Across Nations, 2nd edn. Sage Publications Inc., Thousand Oaks (2001)
39. Heales, J., Cockcroft, S., Raduescu, C.: The influence of national culture on the level and outcome of IS development decisions. J. Glob. Inf. Technol. Manag. **7**(4), 3–28 (2004)
40. Cockcroft, S., Rekker, S.: The relationship between culture and information privacy policy. Electron. Mark. **26**(1), 55–72 (2016)
41. Gefen, D., Karahanna, E., Straub, D.W.: Inexperience and experience with online stores: the importance of TAM and trust. IEEE Trans. Eng. Manag. **50**(3), 307–321 (2003)
42. Liu, C., et al.: Beyond concern: a privacy-trust-behavioral intention model of electronic commerce. Inf. Manag. **42**(1), 127–142 (2004)
43. Bansal, G., Zahedi, F.M., Gefen, D.: The impact of personal dispositions on information sensitivity, privacy concern and trust in disclosing health information online. Decis. Support Syst. **49**(2), 138–150 (2010)
44. Greenberg, R., Wong-On-Wing, B., Lui, G.: Culture and consumer trust in online businesses. J. Glob. Inf. Manag. **16**(3), 26–44 (2008)

45. Gupta, B., Iyer, L.S., Weisskirch, R.S.: Facilitating global e-commerce: a comparison of consumers' willingness to disclose personal information online in the U.S. and in India. J. Electron. Commer. Res. **11**(1), 41–52 (2010)
46. Treiblmaier, H., Chong, S.: Trust and perceived risk of personal information as antecedents of online information disclosure: results from three countries. J. Glob. Inf. Manag. **19**(4), 76–94 (2011)
47. McCole, P., Ramsey, E., Williams, J.: Trust considerations on attitudes towards online purchasing: the moderating effect of privacy and security concerns. J. Bus. Res. **63**(9), 1018–1024 (2010)
48. Van Slyke, C., et al.: Concern for information privacy and online consumer purchasing. J. Assoc. Inf. Syst. **7**(1), 16 (2006)
49. Zhang, X.N., Prybutok, V.R.: A consumer perspective of e-service quality. IEEE Trans. Eng. Manag. **52**(4), 461–477 (2005)
50. Van Slyke, C., et al.: Concern for information privacy and online consumer purchasing. J. Assoc. Inf. Syst. **7**(6), 415–444 (2006)
51. Sharma, S., Crossler, R.E.: Disclosing too much? Situational factors affecting information disclosure in social commerce environment. Electron. Commer. Res. Appl. **13**(5), 305–319 (2014)
52. Gauzente, C.: Web merchants' privacy and security statements: how reassuring are they for consumers? A two-sided approach. J. Electron. Commer. Res. **5**(3), 181–198 (2004)
53. Hofstede, G.: Culture's recent consequences: using dimension scores in theory and research. Int. J. Cross Cultural Manag. **1**(1), 11–17 (2001)
54. Wagner, J.A.: Studies of individualism-collectivism: effects on cooperation in groups. Acad. Manag. J. **38**(1), 152–173 (1995)
55. Dhillon, G.: Violation of safeguards by trusted personnel and understanding related information security concerns. Comput. Secur. **20**(2), 165–172 (2001)
56. Kluckhohn, F.R., Strodtbeck, F.L.: Variations in value orientations (1961)
57. Kinicki, A., Kreitner, R.: Organizational Behavior: Key Concepts Skills Best Practices. McGraw-Hill, Irwin (2003)
58. Kacen, J.J., Lee, J.A.: The influence of culture on consumer impulsive buying behavior. J. Consum. Psychol. **12**(2), 163–176 (2002)

Analysis of Trade Area for Retail Industry Store Using Consumer Purchase Record

Sachiko Iwasaki[1]([envelope]), Ko Hashimoto[2], Kohei Otake[1],
and Takashi Namatame[1]

[1] Chuo University, Bunkyo-ku, Tokyo, Japan
sachikoi@namalab.org,
{otake,namatame}@indsys.chuo-u.ac.jp
[2] Graduate School of Chuo University, Bunkyo-ku, Tokyo, Japan
a12.w6dw@g.chuo-u.ac.jp

Abstract. For retail industry such as supermarket and convenience store, it is important to understand customers. In marketing perspective, to match marketing activity to customer needs is one of the most important strategy for retail industry. In this study, we focus on trade area of retail store. If we can grasp the trade size of a store, manager can plan optimal strategy, e.g. how to spend for advertise activity and where we should open a new store. In this study, we use ID-POS data which is the purchase record with customer identification data of a super market chain and calculate the trade area radius, then we show the cause and effect model to estimate trade area size using store causal data. Moreover, we evaluate our model and discuss how to be decided the trade area size.

Keywords: Trade area · ID-POS data · Consumer purchase behavior

1 Introduction

Consumer purchase behavior is one of the main research areas of marketing. In recent years, many kind of consumer behavior or activity data in the field of marketing can be obtained, i.e. ID-POS data which is purchase record for each customer in a store or customer attributes. Hence, many stores or retail company want to utilize these data for more effective and efficient for marketing activities.

For retail store, it is an important to grasp the trade area, because if the store can grasp his/her trade area, then he/she can advertise efficiently in the trade area or grasp the needs of main trade area. Especially for Japanese retail store, e.g. supermarket and department store, folding flyer in newspaper is very popular advertising tool, thus to grasp the trade area is very important. Moreover, when manager plan to open a new store, to analyze the potential selling intense is very important issue. As shown these topics, the trade area is one of important factor for store managing.

In this study, we analyze trade areas of stores of a supermarket chain in Japan. Based on the purchase record of each store, we calculate a radius of trade area, and analyze some variables which effects on the size of trade area.

© Springer International Publishing AG 2017
G. Meiselwitz (Ed.): SCSM 2017, Part I, LNCS 10282, pp. 177–189, 2017.
DOI: 10.1007/978-3-319-58559-8_15

2   Related Studies and Objective of Our Study

One of the most famous trade area analyzing model is Huff model (Huff 1963). Huff model is a probabilistic choice model based on attraction of store and distance from customer address to the store. The parameter for distance shows the intention to disturb to access to store. Huff model was used in various scenes to analyze trade area or store power.

However, Huff model needs not only own store data but also competitive store around the store. Thus, when the manager of a chain wants to calculate his trade area, Huff model cannot utilize to this objective. Many of the other attraction models like MLN or MCI model are needed competitive stores' data. However, in real business situation, it is very difficult to obtain these other stores' data. Thus, it is an important issue to analyze the trade area or selling power of own store using only already getting data.

Yamazaki (1996) analyzed trade area using transaction data of a sport club. The result was displayed on geographic information system. The manager could grasp the trade area of the club by observing the display and plan an effective advertising like folding flyer of newspaper.

Yokoyama et al. (1996) showed trade area and purchase model to predict the amount of sales with consumers' preference based on Huff model. They used conjoint analysis to analyze consumer's preference, then regression model are utilized to predict the amount of sales. From the result of analysis, they pointed out that accessibility is one of the most attractive factor for choosing store.

In this study, we use the POS data with customer identifying data of the supermarket chain (i.e. ID-POS data) and some opened statistical data or GIS (geometrical information data) like Google map. The stores of the chain are located at the area of a Japanese regional urban area, and there are over 50 stores which are located in near prefecture. Some of them are located on plain but the others are located in mountainous area. The number of residence and competitive store around each store is not same, thus the competitive situation is not same, too. Then we need to consider these specific conditions to estimate the trade area.

3   Data

3.1   About Supermarket Chain

In this study, we focus on a Japanese supermarket chain. This chain have over 53 stores in a same region. We name each store from S1 to S53. Some of them are located on urban or suburbs, however the other is located on country area. The size of the largest store is about 2,000 m^2 however the smallest store is only 300 m^2. These stores treat all categories of food mainly.

3.2   Data Summary

This chain introduce member card system (frequent shoppers program: FSP) and POS (point of sales) system. ID-POS (POS data with customer Identification number) contains purchase date, time, receipt number, purchase items, the number of purchase and price with customer ID. Thus, the manager can obtain detail purchase record of each customer. We use 3 months records (04/2015–06/2015), the summary statistics is shown in Table 1.

Table 1. Chain summary

Term	From 01/04/2015 to 30/06/2015
No. of store	53 (located on 2 prefectures)
No. of member card holder	About 650 thousand
No. of purchase items	About 8.9 million items
Purchase amount	About 17.5 billion JPY

The store size and location cluster are shown in Tables 2 and 3, respectively.

Table 2. Store size categories

Size	Store
Small (<1,000 m²)	S1, S2, S3, S4, S7, S9, S10, S11, S14, S15, S16, S20, S33, S34, S42, S45, S46, S53
Medium (other)	S5, S6, S8, S12, S17, S18, S19, S21, S22, S23, S25, S26, S27, S28, S29, S31, S32, S36, S37, S38, S43, S44, S47, S48, S49, S50, S51, S52
Large (>1,500 m²)	S13, S24, S30, S35, S39, S40, S41

Table 3. Location categories

Area	Store
Urban	S1, S5, S9, S10, S19, S22, S25, S30, S35, S36, S39, S45, S51
Suburbs	S2, S3, S4, S11, S12, S13, S14, S15, S16, S18, S20, S21, S23, S28, S31, S32, S33, S34, S37, S38, S40, S41, S42, S43, S44, S46, S47, S48, S49, S50, S52, S53
Local	S6, S7, S8, S17, S24, S26, S27, S29

Figure 1 shows the sales transition in analyzing term. As shown in Fig. 1, sales amount of almost weekend are higher than weekday, however especially Monday and Friday are typical lower. However, in early in May, it was continuing high amount due to long holiday (in Japan, it is calls Golden Week from late April to early May).

When we focus on each store, the amount of sales of each store must not have this common rule. Figure 2 shows the transition of sales amount of a store (S1). This store is small and located on urban area. We can guess that many of customers are office worker and residents near store, thus the sales is not high on weekend. Actually, this

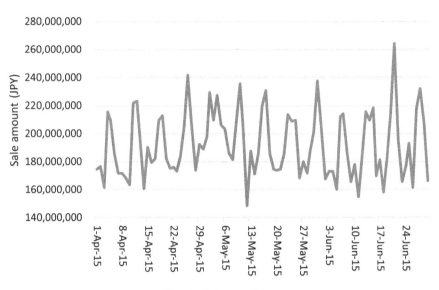

Fig. 1. Sales transition

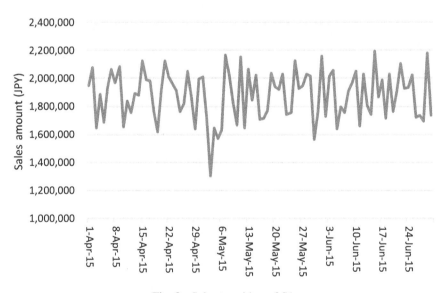

Fig. 2. Sales transition of S1

store emphasizes lunch box or side dishes on assortment rather than fresh items such as vegetables, meats or fishes. As shown in this example, the sales is not same among the stores.

Figure 3 shows scatter plots of the number of visit, number of purchase item and purchase amount for each customer and each store. The correlation between the

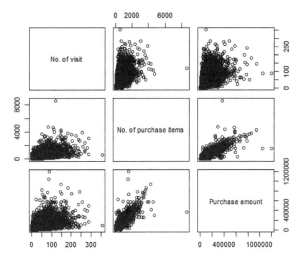

Fig. 3. Scatter plot of purchase data

number of purchase item and purchase amount is high, however the correlation between the number of visit to store and the other variables are not high. It may show that usage of store is not same with respect to each store.

4   Analysis and Discussions

The outline of our analysis is shown in Fig. 4. First we aggregate the purchase data with respect to each customer and each store, second calculate the radius of some percentile distance for each store, and third investigate the cause of effect to decide the radius.

The detail of our model is explained from the next subsection.

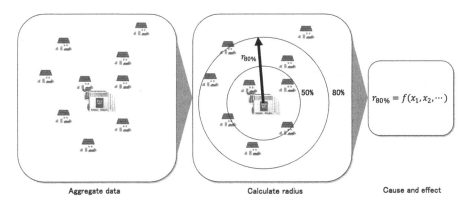

Fig. 4. Outline of our analysis

4.1   Distance Between Customer and Store Address

To calculate the distance between each customer's address and store address, first, we give longitude and latitude to all addresses using google geocoding. Next, the distance is calculated using Hubeny's formula, which considers the curve of the earth in order to determine the distance between two coordination. The equation is given as follows,

$$d = \sqrt{(d_y R)^2 + (d_x N \cos \mu_y)^2} \tag{1}$$

where d_y is the latitude difference between two points, d_x is the longitude difference, μ_y is the average latitude of the two positions, R is the radius of curvature of the meridian, and N is the transverse radius of curvature. The data were projected on the WGS84 datum. Thus, the following ellipsoid parameters were obtained: 6,378,137 m for the semi-major a and 6,5356,752 m for the minor b. Moreover, R and N are defined as follows.

$$R = \frac{a(1 - e^2)}{W^3} \tag{2}$$

$$N = \frac{a}{W} \tag{3}$$

$$W = \sqrt{1 - e^2 \sin^2 \mu_y} \tag{4}$$

$$e = \sqrt{\frac{a^2 - b^2}{a^2}} \tag{5}$$

R and e is called "meridian radius of curvature" and "major eccentricity", respectively.

4.2   Calculate Radius of Trade Area

Next, we calculate the radius of trade area of each store.

To achieve this, first, we gather the purchase data of each store from database. Second, the number of visiting, the number of purchase item are summed up with respect to customer, then we put it in order by the distance from the store. Third, we find the distances of some cumulative probability. Table 4 shows an example. The 1st column is the distance from a store to customer's home address, and it is arranged by distance. From the 2nd to 4th columns are Number of visiting the store, the number of purchase items and purchase amount. Moreover, from the 5th to 7th of the table is cumulative ratios for each variable. As shown this table, we found 5 for 50 percentile distance (radius) according to the number of visiting. Thus we can interpret 50% of customer are into circle whose center are store with radius 5. Furthermore, we found 4 and 3 of distance for the number of purchase and purchase amount, respectively.

Table 4. An example to calculate radius

Distance	No. of visit	No. of purchase	Purchase amount	Cum. no. of visit	Cum. no. of purchase	Cum. purchase amount
1	4	65	1200	4.0%	6.5%	10.0%
2	14	100	2000	18.0%	16.5%	26.7%
3	20	210	2800	38.0%	37.5%	**50.0%**
4	4	125	1300	42.0%	**50.0%**	60.8%
5	8	75	1200	**50.0%**	57.5%	70.8%
6	9	125	900	59.0%	70.0%	78.3%
7	10	80	400	69.0%	78.0%	81.7%
8	4	70	500	73.0%	85.0%	85.8%
9	15	50	200	88.0%	90.0%	87.5%
10	12	100	1500	100.0%	100.0%	100.0%
Total	100	1000	12000			

4.3 Result of Analysis

Using the method in the previous subsection, we can calculate the radius for each cumulative ratio. Table 5 shows the summary statistics of radius for some percentiles.

Table 5. Summary statistics of radius (meter)

Percentile		25%	50%	70%	80%	90%
No. of visiting	min.	82.7	299.9	547.4	773.8	1161.1
	average	522.3	1143.5	2196.3	3277.6	5577.7
	median	381.9	766.5	1430.3	2282.2	4364.3
	max.	1690.0	3952.8	10027.4	10938.2	17934.7
	st. dev.	383.5	877.1	2075.3	2761.3	3988.4
Number of purchase items	min.	82.7	299.9	565.2	773.8	1116.6
	average	571.6	1169.8	2201.6	3268.7	5271.2
	median	409.4	788.6	1393.9	2282.2	4191.9
	max.	1933.0	3952.8	10088.3	10938.2	17410.6
	st. dev.	429.5	909.3	2149.1	2854.7	3999.5
Purchase amount	min.	94.8	299.9	598.0	773.8	1116.6
	average	582.6	1233.6	2244.8	3299.1	5346.9
	median	473.6	788.6	1430.3	2340.7	4204.8
	max.	1933.0	4834.8	10088.3	11647.6	18102.6
	st. dev.	423.8	1028.7	2214.1	2902.2	4081.7

As shown in Table 5, for example, the number of purchase items of 50% have various values, the minimum is about 300 m but the maximum is about 4,000 m. Figure 5 shows the histograms of 80% of the number of visiting. The radius of each store is not similar, because the location situation and customer are not same.

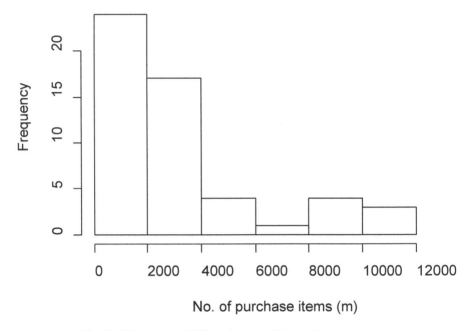

Fig. 5. Histogram of 80% trade area of the number of purchase

For the next analysis, we analyze the effect of various causes for trade area size. To do this, we use multiplicative regression analysis, the equation is shown in Eq. (6).

$$y_i = \beta_0 \prod_{j=1}^{p} \beta_j^{x_{ij}} \varepsilon_j \qquad (6)$$

where $\beta_0, \beta_1, \ldots, \beta_p$ are the interrupt and slope parameters and ε_j is the residual. Taking the logarithm of y_i, Eq. (6) can be treat as linear model which can be used the ordinal least square method. The reasons why multiplicative model is adapted is the distance is not negative value and effects of some variables seem exponentially, when we use multiplicative model, we obtain only positive predicted values. In addition, the variables vary broadly, thus if we use a linear model, the residual may not distribute homogeneously.

In this study, we use "No. of parking," "square root of parking," "cube root of parking," "sales area," "location," "No. of items" "population around store (in 1 km radius of store address)," "No. of household (in 1 km radius of store address)" and "No. of household size" for explanatory variables of our regression model. The reason why we set 3 kinds of parking lot is the effectiveness of the number of parking does not seem linear, thus the combination of these variables may express non-linear effect. The variable "location" has 3 factors; urban, suburb or country, and the other variables are continuous. In analysis, we omit "urban" level. The variables according with household are gotten from jSTAT MAP supported by National Statistics Center[1].

The response variable is 80% cumulative ratio of "No. of visiting," "No. of purchase items" and "purchase amount."

When we analyze regression model, we adopt variable selection to choose significant variable statistically[2]. Table 6 shows the selected variables and the value of parameters for 3 kinds of 80% radius model. All results of our models are summarized in the tables of appendix.

Table 6. Result of multiplicative regression model (The value is displayed by exponential form, so for example E−01 means 10^{-1}).

Explanatory variables	No. of visiting	No. of purchase items	Purchase amount
Intercept	8.39E+00	7.90E+00	7.81E+00
No. of parking	−1.16E−02	−1.11E−02	−1.08E−02
Square root of parking	9.78E−01	8.71E−01	8.39E−01
Cube root of parking	−2.02E+00	−1.68E+00	−1.60E+00
Location (suburb)	3.31E−01	3.05E−01	3.04E−01
Location3 (country)	1.21E+00	1.18E+00	1.18E+00
Population	−2.15E−05	−2.07E−05	−2.09E−05
No. of household	3.67E−05	3.35E−05	3.38E−05

All 3 models of Table 6 selected common variables. When population is lower then the trade area is larger. We can interpret the result that a store located on country need customers who live far from the store, thus as a result, the trade area becomes wider.

The value of multiplicative correlation coefficients are about 0.870 for all models. Figure 6 shows the scatter plot of actual versus predicted value of trade area for the number of purchase items. Some points are not close to 45o line, thus we may need some further analysis. However, almost stores are well predicted, thus the results are generally appropriate. All scatter plots are shown in appendix in calse of higher percentage, the multiple corelation coefficient value are higher, thus outliers are fewer and the prediction is achieved appropriately. However about especially larger distance, the other variables may be needed additionaly.

About percentiles, models of higher percentile are better predicted. Especially, 25% cumulative probability model are not well-predicted. One of the reasons obtained these results, we may point out the core customer of store are not 25% region, but broader area. Moreover about the larger radius, the fitting of predicted value are not well. Almost of these store are located on country, thus the number of population around store is not many thus the stores must consider the wider area, thus the various noise (e.g. the number of competitive store or difference of lifestyle of residences) may be ignoring in our models. However, our model are well-predicted on the whole.

---

[1] https://jstatmap.e-stat.go.jp/gis/nstac/.

[2] We used "lm" and "step" function of R language in analyses. So the variable selection is based on AIC.

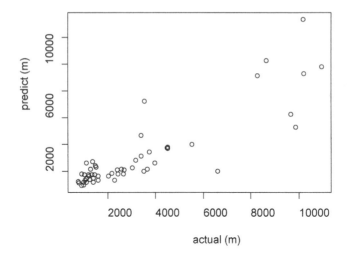

Fig. 6. Actual vs. predict (No. of purchase items)

5 Concluding Remarks

In this study, we focus on consumer behavior, especially selecting store behavior. From the viewpoint of store or store manager, we analyzed the range of consumer for the store that is trade area, using ID-POS data. Then we analyzed the trade area radius using regression model. From out result, we could estimate well prediction for trade area radius. Our model can be utilized to optimize area marketing strategy or open a new store, because the trade area can be estimated.

In this study, we only calculate the radius for each store, however, we did not consider items which is assortment in store. To match the needs of customer of each store, we need to know the true needs of core customer or heavy user. In future work, we will consider the needs of items and gather our analysis. In addition, we did not consider the competitive store around each store. When the number of competitor are larger, than the competition are severer, thus it may be effected on the change of trade area radius. Moreover, the coexistence of plural stores of same chain were not considered. Some customer may use properly some stores, for example, lunch box is purchased near office, however almost of foodstuff are purchased near home. These are also our future works.

Appendix

In this appendix, we show the result of our multiplicative regression models. From Tables 7, 8 and 9 show the coefficient value of each data. Figure 7 shows scatter plots of actual versus predicted value obtained our regression analyses.

Table 7. Coefficient values of multiplicative regression model (No. of visiting)

Variables	25%	50%	70%	80%	90%
Intercept	4.44E+00	5.89E+00	7.76E+00	8.39E+00	9.35E+00
No. of parking	−3.77E−03	−1.93E−03	−8.99E−03	−1.16E−02	−1.15E−02
Sq root of No. of parking	1.47E−01	9.23E−02	8.18E−01	9.78E−01	1.02E+00
Cube root of No. of parking			−1.74E+00	−2.02E+00	2.19E+00
Sales area					
Location (suburb)		3.17E−01	4.21E−01	3.31E−01	3.21E−01
Location (country)		1.07E+00	1.45E+00	1.21E+00	1.08E+00
No. of items	3.10E−05	−2.39E−06			−2.23E−05
Population			−1.54E−05	−2.15E−05	4.04E−05
No. of household			2.81E−05	3.67E−05	
No. of person per household	−7.52E−06				
Multiple correlation coefficient	0.499	0.764	0.890	0.867	0.855

Table 8. Coefficient values of multiplicative regression model (No. of purchase items)

Variables	25%	50%	70%	80%	90%
Intercept	3.47E+00	5.81E+00	7.19E+00	7.90E+00	9.12E+00
No. of parking		−2.33E−03	−7.04E−03	−1.11E−02	−1.24E−02
Sq root of No. of parking	4.77E−02	1.09E−01	5.87E−01	8.71E−01	1.06E+00
Cube root of No. of parking			1.13E+00	−1.68E+00	−2.23E+00
Sales area					
Location (suburb)		3.07E−01	2.09E−01	3.05E−01	3.37E−01
Location (country)		1.10E+00	1.32E+00	1.18E+00	1.14E+00
No. of items	5.13E−05				−2.03E−05
Population	−2.56E−06	−2.91E−06	−2.11E−06	−2.07E−05	3.51E−05
No. of household				3.35E−05	
No. of person per household	4.40E−01				
Multiple correlation coefficient	0.670	0.805	0.899	0.870	0.878

Table 9. Coefficient values of multiplicative regression model (Purchase amount)

Variables	25%	50%	70%	80%	90%
Intercept	3.99E+00	5.81E+00	7.17E+00	9.12E+00	9.11E+00
No. of parking		−2.33E−03	−7.03E−03	−1.24E−02	−1.24E−02
Sq root of No. of parking	3.99E−02	1.09E−01	5.77E−01	1.06E+00	1.06E+00
Cube root of No. of parking			−1.09E+00	−2.23E+00	−2.22E+00
Sales area	6.23E−04				
Location (suburb)		3.07E−01	1.96E−01	3.37E−01	3.39E−01
Location (country)		1.10E+00	1.30E+00	1.14E+00	1.12E+00
No. of items					
Population	−3.40E−06	−2.91E−06	−2.43E−06	−2.03E−05	−2.11E−05
No. of household				3.51E−05	3.65E−05
No. of person per household	5.31E−01				
Multiple correlation coefficient	0.687	0.825	0.892	0.878	0.878

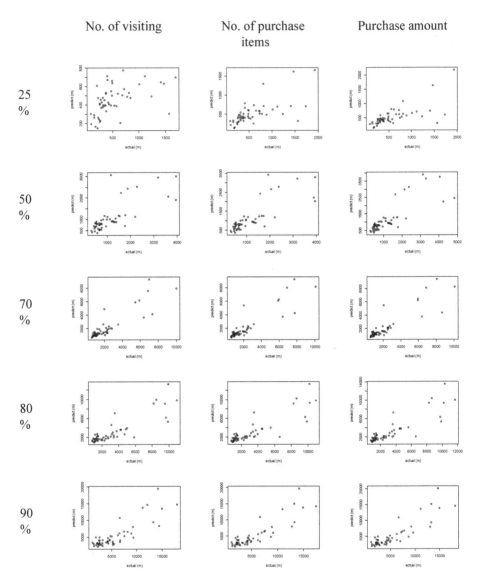

Fig. 7. Scatter plot of actual vs. predicted radius (horizontal axis = actual, vertical axis = predicted)

References

Huff, D.L.: A probabilistic analysis of shopping center trade areas. Land Econ. **39**, 81–90 (1963)

Hubeny, K.: Weiterentwicklung der Gauss'schen Mittelbreitenformeln. Z. Vermess **84**, 159–163 (1959)

Lilien, G.L., Rangaswamy, A., De Bruyn, A.: Principles of Marketing Engineering. 2nd edn. DecisionPro (2012)

Sato, E.: Present and tasks of trade area analysis. Commun. Oper. Res. Soc. Jpn. **42**(3), 137–142 (1997). (in Japanese)

Yamazaki, T.: An application of geographic information system to the trade area analysis for commercialized sports clubs. J. Jpn. Soc. Sports Indus. **6**(2), 15–23 (1996). (in Japanese)

Yokoyama, S., Okanda, H., Ishikawa, K.: Market area analysis in new general merchandise store advancement project. J. Soc. Proj. **2**(2), 19–26 (1996)

From Bowling to Pinball: Understanding How Social Media Changes the Generation of Value for Consumers and Companies

Marc Oliver Opresnik$^{(\boxtimes)}$

Luebeck University of Applied Sciences, Public Corporation,
Mönkhofer Weg 239, 23562 Lübeck, Germany
opresnik@fh-luebeck.de

Abstract. The traditional communications paradigm, which relied on the classic promotional mix to craft Integrated marketing communications (IMC) strategies, must give way to a new paradigm that includes all forms of social media as potential tools in designing and implementing IMC strategies. Consequently, there needs to be a transition of market communication from 'Bowling' to 'Pinball' and a new model of marketing communication in the social media environment which is the 6C model of marketing communication.

Keywords: Social media marketing · Marketing communication · Marketing management · Web 2.0 · Marketing 4.0 · Integrated marketing communication · Social computing · Social media

1 Introduction

'The world is flat' is the title of a book written by Pulitzer prize winner Friedman in 2005 [1]. According to Friedman, the beginning of the twenty-first century will be remembered not for military conflicts or political events, but for a whole new age of globalization – a 'flattening' of the world.

Fiedman was right: The rapid explosion of advanced technologies now means that all out of a sudden knowledge pools and resources have connected all over the planet, levelling the playing field as never before, so that each business and entrepreneur is potentially a customer and at the same time an equal competitor of the other. The rules of the game have changed forever –and these do account for all business sectors and functions alike. Companies, organizations and entrepreneurs all have to run faster in order to stay in the same place.

Against this background, marketing communication is also undergoing rapid development as the way of communicating has changed forever. The increasing popularity of blogging, pod-casting, and social networks enable the modern world customers to broadcast their views about a product or service to a potential audience of billions, and the proliferation of Internet access to even the poorest communities gives everyone who wants to the tools to address issues with products and companies. Consequently, advertising does not work anymore, at least not like it used to do in the past. In former times, marketers used to be able to buy some advertising time on TV or

© Springer International Publishing AG 2017
G. Meiselwitz (Ed.): SCSM 2017, Part I, LNCS 10282, pp. 190–199, 2017.
DOI: 10.1007/978-3-319-58559-8_16

a paper ad, but nowadays more and more customers are using Video on Demand and get their news online. The conversations that took place under industrial broadcast media about products happened in rather small groups, and their influence and impact disappeared as soon as they were spoken. Nowadays, the conversations happen in real time and in front of potentially billions of people, and they are archived for decades to come.

Of course, there are ample opportunities as well: Small companies do not have to outspend the biggest companies anymore; now they can outsmart them with sophisticated social media marketing strategies. They do not have to spend thousands on focus groups or marketing research projects as they potentially have their market's pulse at their fingertips with online searches.

Against this background, media planning is undergoing a dramatic change from traditional ATL communication tools such as newspapers and magazines to non-traditional BTL tools such as mobile and Internet marketing [2–4]. Figure 1 displays that mobile and desktop Internet adspend is already accounting for nearly 1/3 of the Global adspend market in 2016 [5].

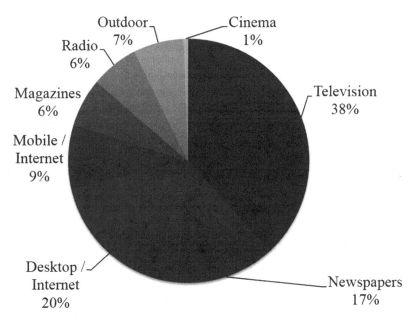

Fig. 1. Global shares of total adspend by medium in % 2016 (Source: Based on ZenithOptimedia research, www.zenithoptimedia, accessed 20th April 2017)

According to ebizmba.com the world's largest social networking site is Facebook, which was initially founded by Mark Zuckerberg in order to stay in touch with his fellow students from Harvard University. In January 2017, the ten most popular social websites (tracked by number of unique visitors worldwide per month) were [6]:

1. Facebook (US)	1,100 million
2. YouTube (Google) (US)	1,000 million
3. QZone (Tencent QQ) (China)	750 million
4. WeChat (China)	700 million
5. Twitter (US)	310 million
6. Sina Weibo (China)	300 million
7. LinkedIn (US)	255 million
8. Pinterest (US)	250 million
9. Google Plus+ (US)	120 million
10. Tumblr (Yahoo!) (US)	110 million

The Chinese social media sites are mainly active in their home country. In the West, it is possible to get away with a two-way platform strategy consisting of Facebook and Google (owner of YouTube). However in China, there are not only social media platforms that do not exist elsewhere in the world, but there are also multiple overlapping platforms and ecosystems that are in constant movement. For example, WeChat is the go-to platform not only for chatting and e-commerce transactions, but also for P2P transfer, bill payment and even mutual fund investment. For an outsider, an environment like this requires persistent monitoring in order to understand, plan and execute for maximum impact of the Chinese customers.

Social media are Internet-based technologies that facilitate online conversations and encompass a wide range of online, word-of-mouth forums including social networking websites, blogs, company sponsored discussion boards and chat rooms, consumer-to-consumer e-mail, consumer product or service ratings websites and forums, Internet discussion boards and forums, and sites containing digital audio, images, movies, or photographs, to name a few [7]. Since 2009, the official company and brand web sites have typically been losing audience. This decline is believed to be due to the emergence of social media marketing by the brands themselves, an increasingly pervasive marketing practice [8].

2 'Pinball' Instead of 'Bowling' as the New Marketing Communication Paradigm

Integrated marketing communications (IMC) have traditionally been considered to be largely one-way in nature ('Bowling' – see below Fig. 2). In the old paradigm, the corporation and its agents developed the message and transmitted it to potential consumers, who may or may not have been willing participants in the communication process. The control over the dissemination of information was in the hands of the firm's marketing organization. The traditional elements of the promotion mix (advertising, personal selling, public relations and publicity, direct marketing and sales promotion) were the tools through which control was asserted [5].

The twenty-first century is witnessing an explosion of Internet-based messages transmitted through these media. They have become a major factor in influencing various aspects of consumer behaviour including awareness, information acquisition,

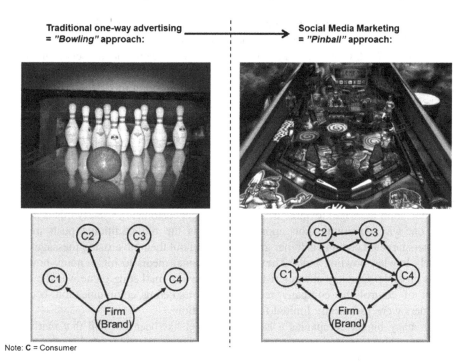

Fig. 2. The bowling to pinball model: transition of market communication from 'Bowling' to 'Pinball' (Source: Hollensen and Opresnik, 2015)

opinions, attitudes, purchase behaviour and post-purchase communication and evaluation [9]. Unfortunately, the popular business press and academic literature offers marketing managers very little guidance for incorporating social media into their IMC strategies.

Social networking as communication tools has two interrelated promotional roles.

Social networking should be consistent with the use of traditional IMC tools
That is, companies should use social media to talk to their customers through such platforms as blogs, as well as Facebook and Twitter groups. These media may either be company-sponsored or sponsored by other individuals or organizations.

Social networking is enabling customers to talk to one another
This is an extension of traditional word-of-mouth communication. While companies cannot directly control such consumer-to-consumer (C2C) messages, they do have the ability to influence the conversations that consumers have with one another. However, consumers' ability to communicate with one another limits the amount of control companies have over the content and dissemination of information. Consumers are in control; they have greater access to information and greater command over media consumption than ever before.

Marketing managers are seeking ways to incorporate social media into their IMC strategies. The traditional communications paradigm, which relied on the classic promotional mix to craft IMC strategies, must give way to a new paradigm that includes all forms of social media as potential tools in designing and implementing IMC strategies [10]. Contemporary marketers cannot ignore the phenomenon of social media, where available market information is based on the experiences of individual consumers and is channeled through the traditional promotion mix. However, various social media platforms, many of which are completely independent of the producing/ sponsoring organization or its agents, enhance consumers' ability to communicate with one another [11].

Although a little oversimplified, marketing in the pre-social media era was comparable to "Bowling" another [5].

A game of bowling shows how you may have traditionally communicated with your consumers, with the firm and the brand (the bowler) rolling a ball (the brand communication message) towards the pins (our target customers). Clearly this is a very direct one-way communication approach. This is the old traditional push model. Marketers targeted certain customer groups and sent out their advertising messages like precisely bowled bowling balls. They used traditional media to hit as many bowling pins as possible. One key characteristic of this bowling marketing game was the large amount of control the company retained over marketing communication because consumers were given only limited freedom of action.

For many bigger companies a large TV-budget has been the ball that marketers rolled down the lane, trying to hit as many the pins as possible. Marketers were in control, happily counting how many "pins" they had hit, and how often. Success in this game was clear-cut, and the metrics clear [12].

In a social media marketing world, the bowling metaphor does not fit anymore. On this arena marketing can be better described as playing "Pinball": Companies serve up a "marketing ball" (brands and brand-building messages) into a dynamic and chaotic market environment [13]. The "marketing ball" is then diverted and often accelerated by social media "bumpers", which change the ball's course in chaotic ways. After the marketing ball is in play, marketing managers may continue to guide it with agile use of the "flippers" but the ball does not always go where it is intended to.

Consequently, in the "pinball" world, you cannot know outcomes in advance. Instead, marketers have to be prepared to respond in real time to the spin put on the ball by consumers. When mastered well, the pinball game can deliver big point multipliers, and if the company is very good, even more balls can be shot into the game. A reason for this may be that today consumers have a large audience to bring up new topics on the communication agenda. In the ideal situation, you are reaching networked influencers, advocates, and other high-value consumers, who may sustain and spread positive conversations about the brand across multiple channels.

Occasionally, the marketing ball will come back to the company. At this point, the firm (brand) has to use the flippers to interact and throw it back into the social media sphere. If the company or the brand do not feed the social marketing media sphere by flipping communications back, the ball will finally drop through the flippers and on longer term, the two way relationship between consumers and the firm (brand) will die [5].

3 6C Model of Social Media Marketing Communication

In the Fig. 3 below the 'Bowling to Pinball' model is further elaborated into an extended model of interactive market communication [5].

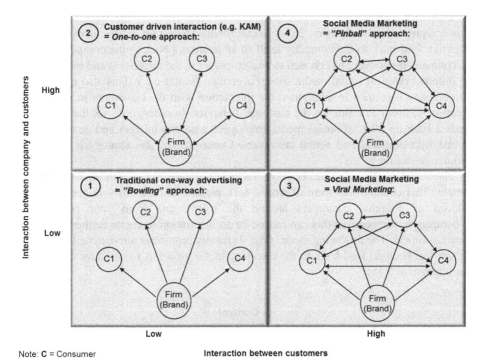

Fig. 3. The extended interactive market communication model according to Hollensen/Opresnik (Source: Hollensen and Opresnik, 2015)

The four different communication styles, represented in Fig. 3 are, shall be briefly described here.

The Traditional One-Way Advertising (Mass Media Advertising Like Television Advertising, Newspaper/Magazine Advertising Etc.)
This strategy represents the "Bowling" approach where the firm attempts to "hit" as many customers with "shotgun" mass media methods. Normally this approach is a one-way communication type.

Customer-Driven Interaction
This approach represents a higher degree of interaction between the company and its different key customers. Often the company finds some Key Account managers, who have the responsibility of taking care of the one-to-one interaction between the firm and its key accounts (customers).

Viral Marketing
This is representing the version 1.0 of Social Media Marketing, where the company e.g. uses an untraditional YouTube video to get attention and awareness about its brand. The interaction between the potential 'customers' is quite high (blogging sites etc.), but the feed-back to the company is relatively low (no double arrows back to the company).

Social Media Marketing
This is representing the version 2.0 of Social Media Marketing, where there is also an extensive feed-back to the company itself (double arrows back to the company). Here the company proactively has chosen to be a co-player in the discussion and blogging on the different relevant social media sites (Facebook, Twitter etc.). This also means that the company here tries to strengthen the interaction with the customers in a positive direction, in order to influence the customer behavior. In order to do so, the company needs a back-up team of social media employees who can interact and communicate on-line with potential and actual customers. Consequently, this strategy is also very resource demanding.

The social media (e.g. Facebook or Twitter) are essentially vehicles for carrying content. This content – in form of words, text, pictures and videos – is generated by millions of potential customers around the world, and from your perspective (= company's perspective) this can indeed be an inspiration to create further value for these customers. The following model (Fig. 4) mainly represents alternative 4 in Fig. 3. If there had been no feed-back to the company in the model, it would have been more like alternative 3 [5].

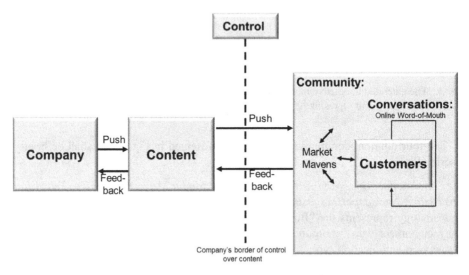

Fig. 4. The 6C model of social media marketing communication according to Hollensen/Opresnik (Source: Hollensen and Opresnik, 2015)

Figure 4 defines six distinct, interrelated elements (Cs) that explain the creation and retention of consumer engagement, seen from a company perspective. However the user-generated contents still plays an important role in the model.

Company and Contents

The 6C model begins with the company and the content it creates. Basically, the Internet remains a 'pull' medium, in the way that firms seek to pull viewers to its content, and finally to the company itself. However, before any 'pull' can happen, the content has to be pushed (seeded) forward in the chain. Content can take the form of e.g. a Facebook product or brand page, and/or a YouTube video pushed out to viewers. Consequently, content pushed into the social media sphere by a company acts as a catalyst for our model of engagement or participation.

Control

The dashed line denoting control in the 6C model (Fig. 3) is intended to represent a wall beyond which the company let over control of its brand to the online community and the customers. In order to accelerate the viral uptake of its brand messaging, the company sometimes gives up the digital rights and blocks in order to encourage online community members to copy, modify, re-post, and forward the content. The content is intended to be copied and/or embedded into people's websites, blogs, and on Facebook walls. The key point to this stage in the process is that the company (the content creator) must be willing, and even embrace, the fact that they no longer have full control over the content: it is free to be taken, modified, commented on, and otherwise appropriated by the community of interest. This may challenge the conventional 'brand management' wisdom stating that managers must keep control of brand image and messaging.

Community

The company creates content and pushes it over the symbolic border of control to the other side, where a community of interested consumers now takes it up. At this point, communication becomes bidirectional. The use of arrows in Fig. 3 for push and pull, attempts to reflect the 'give-and-take' that goes on between a community and the company, represented by the content creators. In its simplest form, it is reflected in the art of commenting: posting reactions, on Facebook or YouTube, to the content. In some cases the company can even lean about 'customer behaviour' in the market by following these online community discussions. In an ideal world, a series of reflexive conversations take place in the community, independent of any action by the company, which will often have a passive role as an observer. When transferring the 'content' into the online community, the company and the content providers often try to target the 'Market Mavens', which are defined as individuals who have access to a large amount of marketplace information, and proactively engage in discussions with other online community members and customers to diffuse and spread this content. Market mavens are typically the first to receive the message and transmit it to their immediate social networks. They function as connectors or bridges between different subcultures and their network of social hubs can facilitate immediate transmission of the content to thousands of online community members.

Customers and Conversations

The ultimate expression of engagement occurs when a multitude of online conversations circle around the phenomenon and content, as illustrated above and in Fig. 4. The 6C model distinguishes between the online community and potential customers, as the latter are usually a subset of the former. The online community may also include people who have heard of the Web-based initiative but not directly participated in it. In general, there seems to be a growing escalation in participation on the part of customers; a willingness to engage with a brand that extends beyond just purchase decisions at the point of sale.

According to the 6C model, Social media further extend the conversations between marketers and consumers through a feedback loop, which might happen after some on-line conversation (blogging etc.) in the community. After some time of online conversation the company may have chats with the online community in hopes of influencing purchase decisions. Moreover, social media initiatives provide marketers a glimpse into the world of customer-to-customer communication, which represents a significant extension of the more traditional advertising and word-of-mouth communication.

Furthermore, social media provide insights into the behavior of non-customers. Most social media marketers try to trigger buzz among prospective customers. This has led to social sharing whereby online community member broadcast their thoughts and activities to strangers all over the world. This social sharing has opened the lives of individual consumers that companies can then exploit to tailor their offerings to better match preferences.

4   Conclusion

In summary, the traditional one-way advertising (mass media advertising like television advertising, newspaper/magazine advertising etc.) represents the "Bowling" approach where the firm attempts to "hit" as many customers with "shotgun" mass media methods. Normally this approach is a one-way communication type. This is no longer feasible in an environment where customers have become prosumers and where is also an extensive feed-back to the company itself. Consequently, social media marketing like in the pinball model has to strengthen the inter-action with the customers in a positive direction, in order to influence the customer behaviour and build profitable relationships.

References

1. Friedman, T.L.: The World is Flat: The Globalized World in the Twenty-First Century. London (2007)
2. Samanta, I.: The effect of social media in firms' marketing strategy. J. Mark. Oper. Manag. Res. 2(3), 163–173 (2012)
3. Tiago, M.T., Veríssimo, J.M.: Digital marketing and social media: why bother? Bus. Horiz. 57(6), 703–708 (2014)
4. Mangold, W.G., Faulds, D.J.: Social media: the new hybrid element of the promotion mix. Bus. Horiz. 52(4), 357–365 (2009)
5. Hollensen, S., Opresnik, M.: Marketing – A Relationship Perspective, 2nd edn. München (2015)

6. Top 15 Most Popular Social Networking Sites in January 2017 (2017). http://www.ebizmba. com/articles/social-networking-websites. Accessed 1 Feb 2017
7. Lacho, K., Marinello, C.: How small business owners can use social networking to promote their business. Entrep. Exec. **15**, 127–134 (2010)
8. Brodie, R.J., Coviello, N.E., Brookes, R.W., Little, V.: Towards a paradigm shift in marketing: an examination of current marketing practices. J. Mark. Manag. **13**(5), 367–382 (1997)
9. Chaston, I.: Evolving "new marketing" philosophies by merging existing concepts: application of process within small high-technology firms. J. Mark. Manag. **14**, 273–291 (1998)
10. Doyle, P.: Marketing in the new millennium. Eur. J. Mark. **29**(12), 23–41 (1995)
11. Kotler, P.: Method for the millennium. Mark. Bus. (February), 26–27 (1997)
12. Kotler, P., Armstrong, G., Opresnik, M.: Marketing: An Introduction, 13th edn. New Jersey (2016)
13. Tuten, T., Solomon, M.R.: Social Media Marketing. New York (2013)

Online Travel Agencies as Social Media: Analyzing Customers' Opinions

Virginica Rusu[1], Cristian Rusu[2], Daniel Guzmán[2],
Silvana Roncagliolo[2], and Daniela Quiñones[2(✉)]

[1] Universidad de Playa Ancha de Ciencias de la Educación, Valparaíso, Chile
virginica.rusu@upla.cl
[2] Pontificia Universidad Católica de Valparaíso, Valparaíso, Chile
{cristian.rusu,silvana.roncagliolo}@pucv.cl,
daniel.e.guzman.s@gmail.com,danielacqo@gmail.com

Abstract. Online travel agencies generate online communities. Travelers share their opinions, comment on their experiences, and quantitatively evaluate services. Their quantitative and qualitative reviews offer valuable information for other potential travelers. The paper analyzes customers' (quantitative) opinions extracted from www.hotelclub.com in February 2016, before the website was closed. Data relationships and trends are identified and interpreted as Customer eXperience outcomes.

Keywords: Online travel agencies · Customer eXperience · User eXperience

1 Introduction

Online travel agencies generate online communities. Travelers share their opinions, comment on their experiences, and quantitatively evaluate services. Their quantitative and qualitative reviews offer valuable information for other potential travelers. Their opinions also express their experiences as customers.

Usability is a basic concept in Human – Computer Interaction. A well-known definition is the one provided by the ISO 9241-210: "the extent to which a system, product or service can be used by specified users to achieve specified goals with effectiveness, efficiency and satisfaction in a specified context of use" [1].

User eXperience (UX) extends the usability concept beyond effectiveness, efficiency and satisfaction. The ISO 9241-210 standard defines UX as a "person's perceptions and responses resulting from the use and/or anticipated use of a product, system or service" [1]. As usability, UX applies to software systems, but also to products and services.

Customer eXperience (CX) is a broader concept. As Lewis highlights, it addresses the growing emphasis on service design and the Service Science as discipline [2]. Service Science is an interdisciplinary area of study focused on systematic innovation in service. A compelling CX leads to enhanced customer attraction and retention.

As UX extends the usability concept, CX extends the UX concept. Service Science and CX may benefit from the adoption of lessons learned in usability engineering and

© Springer International Publishing AG 2017
G. Meiselwitz (Ed.): SCSM 2017, Part I, LNCS 10282, pp. 200–209, 2017.
DOI: 10.1007/978-3-319-58559-8_17

UX design. However, the obvious link between Human – Computer Interaction and Service Science was not yet properly attended.

The paper analyzes customers' (quantitative) opinions extracted from www. hotelclub.com in February 2016, before the website was closed; HotelClub is now part of Hoteles.com. Section 2 briefly describes the concepts of UX and CX, and their evaluation. Section 3 analyzes the HotelClub case study. Section 4 highlights conclusions and future work.

2 eXperiences and Evaluations

A well-known usability definition was proposed by the ISO 9241 standard back in 1998 [3]. The ISO 9241 standard was updated in 2010 [1]. Yet a new revision started briefly after, in 2011 [4]. It proves the evolving nature of the usability concept.

UX extends the usability concept beyond effectiveness, efficiency and satisfaction, dimensions recurrently referred in most of usability's definitions. As usability, UX does not limit to software systems; it also applies to products and services. UX is usually considered as an extension of the usability concept [5]. The "User Experience White Paper" aims to "bring clarity to the UX concept" [6]. But instead of giving a unique UX definition, the document mentions the wide collection of definitions available at www. allaboutux.org [7].

As Joshi highlights, the concept of CX is increasingly discussed, but is rarely defined [8]. Laming and Mason consider CX as: "the physical and emotional experiences occurring through the interactions with the product and/or service offering of a brand from point of first direct, conscious contact, through the total journey to the post-consumption stage" [9]. Gentile, Spiller and Noci identify several CX dimensions: sensorial, emotional, cognitive, pragmatic, lifestyle, and relational [10]. Nambisan and Watt also identify CX dimensions: pragmatic, hedonic, sociability, and usability [11]. They explicitly relate CX to usability.

There are well established usability evaluation methods. If we consider UX as usability's extension, all these methods may be used in assessing part of the UX dimensions. But evaluating all UX aspects is much more challenging. Allaboutux.org refers to almost 90 UX methods [7]. The amount of methods that are proposed is overwhelming especially for novice UX evaluators/designers.

If we consider CX as an extension of UX, that means UX and usability evaluation methods are also able to evaluate some CX aspects. But evaluating other CX aspects requires specific methods.

CX is developed through a sequence of interactions between the customer and the company (or companies) that offer the product and/or service, called customer "touch-points". CX should be assessed at least at each touch-point, and CX evaluation methods should address the specificity of each interaction/touch-point. Applying a single evaluation method offers a limited perspective and results. If time and resources are available, several quantitative and qualitative methods should be used.

Our research work first focused on transactional websites' usability; most of the case studies were online travel agencies. We proposed a methodology to evaluate transactional websites [12]; we also developed a set of usability heuristics for transactional web applications [13]. Later on we extended our research to UX, and recently to CX.

Researches usually focus on qualitative travelers' comments, but we decided to take an alternative approach, focusing on quantitative data. In a previous study we analyzed quantitative data on travelers' opinion, freely available at two online travel agencies' websites: www.tripadvisor.cl and www.hotelclub.com [14]. Data relationships and trends were identified. The study was limited to quantitative data on hotels located in Viña del Mar, one of the most popular tourist destinations in Chile, and focused on www.tripadvisor.cl, as very few reviews were available on www.hotelclub.com.

3   Case Study: www.hotelclub.com

HotelClub was an online travel agency oriented to hotels/accommodations. Its website (www.hotelclub.com) was closed in February 2016. HotelClub is now part of Hoteles.com.

We analyzed almost 4700 travelers' quantitative reviews on hotels from major Latin American cities: Bogota, Buenos Aires, Ciudad de Mexico, Lima, Montevideo, Panama, Quito, Rio de Janeiro and Santiago de Chile. We also analyzed almost 7700 travelers' quantitative reviews on hotels from Sydney.

Travelers' reviews freely available at www.hotelclub.com were both qualitative (comments) and quantitative (numeric evaluation). Quantitative evaluations were made using a 5 points scale, from 1 (worst) to 5 (best), on the following dimensions: D0 – *Overall rating*, D1 – *Amenities*, D2 – *Cleanliness*, D3 – *Hotel staff*, D4 – *Comfort*, D5 – *Location*, D6 – *Value*. Travelers were classified by HotelClub in 6 types: *Business*, *Single*, *Family*, *Friends*, *Couple*, *LGBT*.

As observations' scale is ordinal, and no assumption of normality could be made, data were analyzed using nonparametric statistics tests. We used p-value ≤ 0.05 as decision rule.

We performed Spearman ρ tests to check the hypothesis:

- H_0: $\rho = 0$, the dimensions Dm and Dn are independent,
- H_1: $\rho \neq 0$, the dimensions Dm and Dn are dependent.

We performed Kruskal–Wallis H tests to check the hypothesis:

- H_0: there are no significant differences between the opinions of different type of travelers,
- H_1: there are significant differences between the opinions of different type of travelers.

3.1   Bogota

We analyzed 202 reviews of travelers to Bogota. They identified themselves as Business (57), Single (42), Family (25), Friends (21), and Couple (51). 6 travelers did not specify the group they belong to.

Spearman ρ test results are shown in Table 1. There are significant correlations between all dimensions. Most of the correlations are strong or moderate. Dimension D5 – *Location* is weakly correlated to dimension D3 – *Hotel staff*.

Table 1. Spearman ρ test for Bogota

	D0 – Overall rating	D1 – Amenities	D2 – Cleanliness	D3 – Hotel staff	D4 – Comfort	D5 – Location	D6 – Value
D0	1	0.749	0.629	0.610	0.676	0.595	0.598
D1		1	0.571	0.481	0.621	0.557	0.604
D2			1	0.559	0.690	0.409	0.463
D3				1	0.555	**0.397**	0.531
D4					1	0.460	0.577
D5						1	0.425
D6							1

3.2 Buenos Aires

We analyzed 326 reviews of travelers to Buenos Aires. They identified themselves as Business (33), Single (27), Family (44), Friends (58), Couple (145), and LGBT (1). 18 travelers did not specify the group they belong to.

Spearman ρ test results are shown in Table 2. There are significant correlations between all dimensions. Most of the correlations are moderate. There are only few strong and few weak correlations.

Table 2. Spearman ρ test for Buenos aires

	D0 – Overall rating	D1 – Amenities	D2 – Cleanliness	D3 – Hotel staff	D4 – Comfort	D5 – Location	D6 – Value
D0	1	0.666	0.569	0.599	0.642	0.419	0.572
D1		1	0.443	**0.392**	0.519	0.372	0.422
D2			1	0.526	0.609	0.409	0.489
D3				1	0.473	**0.385**	0.461
D4					1	**0.314**	0.532
D5						1	**0.371**
D6							1

3.3 Ciudad de Mexico

We analyzed 1428 reviews of travelers to Ciudad de Mexico. They identified themselves as Business (448), Single (224), Family (199), Friends (117), Couple (382), and LGBT (11). 47 travelers did not specify the group they belong to.

Spearman ρ test results are shown in Table 3. There are significant correlations between all dimensions. Most of the correlations are strong or moderate. Dimension D5 – *Location* is weakly correlated to dimension D4 – *Comfort*.

Table 3. Spearman ρ test for Ciudad de Mexico

	D0 – Overall rating	D1 – Amenities	D2 – Cleanliness	D3 – Hotel staff	D4 – Comfort	D5 – Location	D6 – Value
D0	1	0.685	0.607	0.640	0.654	0.426	0.613
D1		1	0.552	0.567	0.631	0.357	0.505
D2			1	0.554	0.656	0.475	0.521
D3				1	0.545	0.450	0.575
D4					1	**0.391**	0.509
D5						1	0.430
D6							1

3.4   Lima

We analyzed 393 reviews of travelers to Lima. They identified themselves as Business (78), Single (63), Family (67), Friends (38), Couple (134), and LGBT (1). 3 travelers did not specify the group they belong to.

Spearman ρ test results are shown in Table 4. There are significant correlations between all dimensions. Most of the correlations are strong or moderate. Dimension D5 – *Location* is weakly correlated to dimensions D3 – *Hotel staff*, D4 – *Comfort*, and D6 – *Value*.

Table 4. Spearman ρ test for Lima

	D0 – Overall rating	D1 – Amenities	D2 – Cleanliness	D3 – Hotel staff	D4 – Comfort	D5 – Location	D6 – Value
D0	1	0.692	0.608	0.536	0.616	0.534	0.543
D1		1	0.580	0.465	0.564	0.414	0.451
D2			1	0.579	0.715	0.432	0.512
D3				1	0.497	**0.341**	0.533
D4					1	**0.390**	0.463
D5						1	**0.375**
D6							1

3.5   Montevideo

We analyzed 69 reviews of travelers to Montevideo. They identified themselves as Business (15), Single (14), Family (5), Friends (5), Couple (29), and LGBT (1).

Spearman ρ test results are shown in Table 5. There are significant correlations between all dimensions. Most of the correlations are strong or moderate. Dimension

D5 – *Location* is weakly correlated to dimensions D1 – *Amenities*, D2 – *Cleanliness*, D3 – *Hotel staff*, and D4 – *Comfort*.

Table 5. Spearman ρ test for Montevideo

	D0 – Overall rating	D1 – Amenities	D2 – Cleanliness	D3 – Hotel staff	D4 – Comfort	D5 – Location	D6 – Value
D0	1	0.714	0.569	0.645	0.666	0.405	0.696
D1		1	0.547	0.569	0.681	**0.321**	0.689
D2			1	0.489	0.722	**0.298**	0.687
D3				1	0.618	**0.267**	0.591
D4					1	**0.340**	0.788
D5						1	0.444
D6							1

3.6 Panama

We analyzed 1116 reviews of travelers to Panama. They identified themselves as Business (188), Single (210), Family (192), Friends (121), Couple (392), and LGBT (9). 4 travelers did not specify the group they belong to.

Spearman ρ test results are shown in Table 6. There are significant correlations between all dimensions. Most of the correlations are strong. A few correlations are moderate.

Table 6. Spearman ρ test for Panama

	D0 – Overall rating	D1 – Amenities	D2 – Cleanliness	D3 – Hotel staff	D4 – Comfort	D5 – Location	D6 – Value
D0	1	0.764	0.704	0.712	0.775	0.516	0.745
D1		1	0.671	0.626	0.717	0.511	0.654
D2			1	0.645	0.783	0.451	0.619
D3				1	0.654	0.454	0.629
D4					1	0.462	0.673
D5						1	0.453
D6							1

3.7 Quito

We analyzed 137 reviews of travelers to Quito. They identified themselves as Business (18), Single (36), Family (18), Friends (10), Couple (50), and LGBT (2). 3 travelers did not specify the group they belong to.

Spearman ρ test results are shown in Table 7. There are significant correlations between all dimensions. Most of the correlations are strong or moderate. Dimension D5 – *Location* is weakly correlated to dimensions D2 – *Cleanliness*, and D3 – *Hotel staff*.

Table 7. Spearman ρ test for Quito

	D0 – Overall rating	D1 – Amenities	D2 – Cleanliness	D3 – Hotel staff	D4 – Comfort	D5 – Location	D6 – Value
D0	1	0.753	0.570	0.633	0.603	0.546	0.671
D1		1	0.563	0.542	0.600	0.495	0.494
D2			1	0.580	0.678	**0.346**	0.484
D3				1	0.523	**0.397**	0.564
D4					1	0.456	0.578
D5						1	0.583
D6							1

3.8   Rio de Janeiro

We analyzed 722 reviews of travelers to Rio de Janeiro. They identified themselves as Business (97), Single (109), Family (76), Friends (92), Couple (304), and LGBT (9). 35 travelers did not specify the group they belong to.

Spearman ρ test results are shown in Table 8. There are significant correlations between all dimensions. Most of the correlations are strong or moderate. Dimension D5 – *Location* is weakly correlated to dimensions D1 – *Amenities*, and D4 – *Comfort*.

Table 8. Spearman ρ test for Rio de Janeiro

	D0 – Overall rating	D1 – Amenities	D2 – Cleanliness	D3 – Hotel staff	D4 – Comfort	D5 – Location	D6 – Value
D0	1	0.720	0.665	0.647	0.653	0.500	0.642
D1		1	0.636	0.567	0.610	**0.378**	0.537
D2			1	0.586	0.660	0.412	0.526
D3				1	0.534	0.431	0.526
D4					1	**0.322**	0.552
D5						1	0.427
D6							1

3.9   Santiago de Chile

We analyzed 294 reviews of travelers to Santiago de Chile. They identified themselves as Business (77), Single (35), Family (21), Friends (27), Couple (123), and LGBT (2). 9 travelers did not specify the group they belong to.

Spearman ρ test results are shown in Table 9. There are significant correlations between all dimensions. Most of the correlations are strong or moderate. The only dimension weakly correlated to all others is D5 – *Location*.

Table 9. Spearman ρ test for Santiago de Chile

	D0 – Overall rating	D1 – Amenities	D2 – Cleanliness	D3 – Hotel staff	D4 – Comfort	D5 – Location	D6 – Value
D0	1	0.688	0.621	0.593	0.593	**0.387**	0.625
D1		1	0.566	0.480	0.567	**0.299**	0.507
D2			1	0.577	0.632	**0.319**	0.514
D3				1	0.493	**0.383**	0.590
D4					1	**0.295**	0.534
D5						1	**0.363**
D6							1

3.10 Sydney

We analyzed 7659 reviews of travelers to Sydney. They identified themselves as Business (662), Single (540), Family (859), Friends (462), Couple (2095), and LGBT (43). 9 travelers did not specify the group they belong to.

Spearman ρ test results are shown in Table 10. There are significant correlations between all dimensions. Most of the correlations are strong or moderate. Dimension D5 – *Location* is weakly correlated to dimensions D0 – *Overall rating*, D1 – *Amenities*, and D2 – *Cleanliness*.

Table 10. Spearman ρ test for Sydney

	D0 – Overall rating	D1 – Amenities	D2 – Cleanliness	D3 – Hotel staff	D4 – Comfort	D5 – Location	D6 – Value
D0	1	0.680	0.546	0.525	0.580	**0.329**	0.512
D1		1	0.549	0.542	0.572	**0.366**	0.497
D2			1	0.527	0.597	**0.391**	0.421
D3				1	0.520	0.401	0.480
D4					1	0.425	0.531
D5						1	0.423
D6							1

3.11 Kruskal–Wallis H Tests Results

The Kruskal–Wallis H test results (p-values) for all locations are shown in Table 11.

In general, most of the time there are no significant differences between the opinions of different type of travelers. Significant differences occur once for Bogota (dimension D1 – *Amenities*), twice for Rio de Janeiro (dimensions D2 – *Cleanliness*

Table 11. Kruskal–Wallis H test results (p-values)

	D0 – Overall rating	D1 – Amenities	D2 – Cleanliness	D3 – Hotel staff	D4 – Comfort	D5 – Location	D6 – Value
Bogota	0.030	**0.012**	0.161	0.094	0.264	0.285	0.097
Buenos Aires	0.658	0.075	0.651	0.633	0.584	0.881	0.893
Ciudad de Mexico	**0.000**	0.078	**0.017**	0.069	0.173	**0.018**	**0.000**
Lima	0.505	0.520	0.226	0.414	0.772	0.082	0.905
Montevideo	0.918	0.151	0.325	0.815	0.628	0.242	0.679
Panama							
Quito	0.967	0.874	0.067	0.148	0.257	0.680	0.412
Rio de Janeiro	0.054	0.074	**0.007**	0.538	0.225	**0.020**	0.250
Santiago de Chile	0.740	0.459	0.990	0.550	0.819	0.977	0.362
Sydney	**0.000**	**0.000**	**0.000**	**0.000**	**0.000**	**0.000**	**0.000**

and D5 – *Location*), and four times for Ciudad de Mexico (dimensions D0 – *Overall rating*, D2 – *Cleanliness*, D5 – *Location*, and D6 – *Value*). Sydney is an exception: significant differences occur for all dimensions.

4 Conclusions

Online travel agencies generate online communities. Quantitative and qualitative reviews offer valuable information for other potential travelers. Travelers' opinions also express their experiences as customers.

Assessing CX is more challenging than assessing UX and usability. We took a quantitative approach, analyzing travelers' opinion, freely available at www.hotelclub. com until February 2016. We analyzed almost 4700 travelers' quantitative reviews on hotels from major Latin American cities, but also almost 7700 reviews on hotels from Sydney. In general, most of the time there are no significant differences between the opinions of different type of travelers. Only in the case of Sydney significant differences occur for all dimensions.

In all cases, there are significant correlations between all surveyed dimensions. Most of the correlations are strong or moderate. Some weak correlations are usually related to dimension D5 – *Location*. That is probably because all other dimensions are intrinsically related to the hotels, but location is mainly related to the environment.

As future work, we will extend our research to other case studies. We intend to check if the preliminary conclusions are valid in new contexts.

References

1. ISO 9241-210: Ergonomics of human-system interaction — Part 210: Human-centred design for interactive systems. International Organization for Standardization, Geneva (2010)

2. Lewis, J.: Usability: lessons learned... and yet to be learned. Int. J. Hum.-Comput. Interact. **30**(9), 663–684 (2014)
3. ISO 9241-11: Ergonomic requirements for office work with visual display terminals (VDTs) – Part 11: Guidance on usability. International Organization for Standardization, Geneva (1998)
4. Bevan, N., Carter, J., Harker, S.: ISO 9241-11 revised: what have we learnt about usability since 1998? In: Kurosu, M. (ed.) HCI 2015. LNCS, vol. 9169, pp. 143–151. Springer, Cham (2015). doi:10.1007/978-3-319-20901-2_13
5. Rusu, C., Rusu, V., Roncagliolo, S., González, C.: Usability and user experience: what should we care about? Int. J. Inf. Technol. Syst. Approach **8**(2), 1–12 (2015)
6. Roto, V., Law, E., Vermeeren, A., Hoonhout, J.: User Experience White Paper. Bringing Clarity to the Concept of User Experience. http://www.allaboutux.org/uxwhitepaper. Accessed 9 Jan 2017
7. Allaboutux.org: All About UX. www.allaboutux.org. Accessed 9 Jan 2017
8. Joshi, S.: Customer experience management: an exploratory study on the parameters affecting customer experience for cellular mobile services of a telecom company. Procedia – Soc. Behav. Sci. **133**, 392–399 (2014)
9. Laming, C., Mason, K.: Customer experience – an analysis of the concept and its performance in airline brands. Res. Transp. Bus. Manag. **10**, 15–25 (2014)
10. Gentile, C., Spiller, N., Noci, G.: How to sustain the customer experience: an overview of experience components that co-create value with the customer. Eur. Manag. J. **25**(5), 395–410 (2007)
11. Nambisan, P., Watt, J.H.: Managing customer experiences in online product communities. J. Bus. Res. **64**, 889–895 (2011)
12. Otaiza, R., Rusu, C., Roncagliolo, S.: Evaluating the usability of transactional web sites. In: Advances in Computer-Human Interaction (ACHI 2010), pp. 32–37. IEEE Computer Society Press (2010)
13. Quiñones, D., Rusu, C., Roncagliolo, S.: Redefining usability heuristics for transactional web applications. In: 11th International Conference on Information Technology: New Generations (ITNG 2014), pp. 260–265. IEEE Computer Society Press (2014)
14. Rusu, V., Rusu, C., Guzmán, D., Espinoza, D., Rojas, D., Roncagliolo, S., Quiñones, D.: Assessing the customer eXperience based on quantitative data: virtual travel agencies. In: Marcus, A. (ed.) DUXU 2016. LNCS, vol. 9746, pp. 499–508. Springer, Cham (2016). doi:10.1007/978-3-319-40409-7_47

Analysis of Cancellation Factors Based on the Characteristics of Golf Courses in Reservation Sites

Naoya Saijo[1]([✉]), Kohei Otake[2], and Takashi Namatame[2]

[1] Graduate School of Science and Engineering, Chuo University, 1-13-27, Kasuga, Bunkyo-ku, Tokyo 112-8551, Japan
al3.rx7m@g.chuo-u.ac.jp
[2] Faculty of Science and Engineering, Chuo University, 1-13-27, Kasuga, Bunkyo-ku, Tokyo 112-8551, Japan
{otake,nama}@indsys.chuo-u.ac.jp

Abstract. In this study, we analyze cancellation factors based on the characteristics of golf courses in reservation sites. Firstly, we classify each golf course using causal data such as price range, course type and capacity and review data using k-means clustering. As a result, golf courses were classified into four clusters and we analyzed characteristics of golf courses each cluster. Secondly, in order to identify factor of cancellation each characteristic of golf courses, we performed logistic regression analysis targeting on each cluster using golf course reservation data and user attribute data. From the result of these analysis, we identified same common cancellation factors and different cancellation factors by characteristics of each golf course.

Keywords: Consumer behavior · Cancellation factor · K-means clustering · Logistic regression analysis

1 Introduction

Recently, electronic commerce (EC) market extends drastically by spread of Internet. Purchasing on Internet has been expanding year after year on facility reservation products, but the risk of cancellation is also increasing. While EC site establish as a purchase channels, it is important matter that the reduction of the opportunity loss by the cancellation of user in an reservation sites of the hospitality industry such as hotel and golf courses. Under such situation, there are many studies purposing on the reducing cancellation [1, 2]. However, these studies did not focus on characteristics of cancellation targets, it is not satisfying that the study of the cancellation factor to focus on action at the time of the cancellation of user.

2 Purpose of This Study

The study purposes to identify cancellation factors based on the characteristics of golf courses in reservation sites.

© Springer International Publishing AG 2017
G. Meiselwitz (Ed.): SCSM 2017, Part I, LNCS 10282, pp. 210–222, 2017.
DOI: 10.1007/978-3-319-58559-8_18

This study uses the data provided by a golf courses reservation site. Specifically, this study uses reservation data, user data, causal data, and review data. Reservation data contains some information of golf courses such as play date and play fee. User data contains user attribute such as gender and generation. Causal data is consisted on golf course attribute such as price range, course type and capacity. Review data contains review of golf course such as review score. In this study, we use only data which have following conditions.

- Reservation data
    - Play date on April 1, 2014–March 31, 2015
    - Play start at 7:00–11:00
- User data
    - Age between 20–79
- Causal data
    - Located in Kanto district
- Review data
    - Golf courses existing play data in the term of reservation data

3   Analysis of Cancellation Factors

3.1   Flow of Analysis

We show the outline of analysis in Fig. 1.

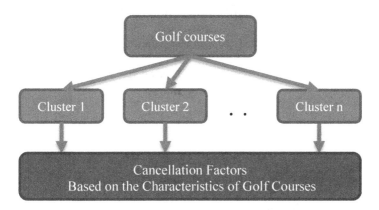

Fig. 1. Outline of analysis

Firstly, we classify golf courses using causal data such as price range, course type and capacity, and review data such as review score on the basis of the thought that it is difference that action at the time of the cancellation of user by characteristics of golf courses. Moreover, we defined the characteristics of each cluster. Secondly, to identify factors of cancellation of golf courses, we perform logistic regression analysis targeting on each cluster using reservation data such as play date and play price and user data such as gender and generation.

3.2   K-means Clustering

We classify golf courses using causal and review data on the basis of the thought that it is difference that action at the time of the cancellation of user by characteristics of golf courses. We use k-means clustering to classify golf courses. d is defined as formula (1).

$$d = \sum_{x_j \in X} \min_{i \in k} \|x_i - c_i\|^2 \tag{1}$$

$x_j (j = 1, \ldots, n)$ is the value for j, and n is the number of cases. Also c_i is the center of cluster $i (i = 1, \ldots, k)$ [3, 4]. We classify golf courses into four clusters from the viewpoint of easy to interpret.

3.3   Logistic Regression Analysis

In order to identify factors of cancellation each characteristics of golf courses, we try to perform logistic regression analysis targeting on each cluster using reservation and user data. When regression coefficient is defined as β_k and explanatory variable is defined as x_k, probability of occurring cancellation p is shown as formula (2) [5].

$$p = \frac{\exp\{\beta_0 + \beta_1 x_1 + \cdots + \beta_k x_k\}}{1 + \exp\{\beta_0 + \beta_1 x_1 + \cdots + \beta_k x_k\}} \tag{2}$$

Where p of (2) defines below, and we estimate parameter β_k.

$$p = \begin{cases} 1 & \cdots & \text{Cancelled} \\ 0 & \cdots & \text{played} \end{cases}$$

4   Results

4.1   Classification of Golf Courses by the Characteristics

Firstly, we classify golf courses using causal and review data on the basis of the thought that it is difference that action at the time of the cancellation of user by characteristics of golf courses. We use k-means clustering to classify golf courses. Variables used by k-means clustering are shown below (Table 1).

Standardized variables of Table 1 are used by k-means clustering. Also, the number of cluster was tried from three to six. Based on the interpret Table 4 cluster model own supported. Basic aggregation of quantitative data is shown in Table 2.

In each cluster contain 25 to 36 golf courses. Secondly, Following characteristic, we show the component ratios of variable in Figs. 2, 3, 4 and 5.

Table 1. Variable used by k-means clustering

Variable attribute	Variable	Explanation
Qualitative data	Price range	1: Low price 2: Medium price 3: High price (lower 25% of average price per year is defined as low price, and top 25% of average price per year is defined as high price)
	Price change	1: Small price change 2: Medium price change 3: Large price change (lower 25% of price variance per year is defined as small price change, and top 25% of price variance per year is defined as large price change)
	Course type	Hill, Mountain, Forest, Riverbed
	Self-play	1: Only self-play 0: Not only self-play
	Practice area	1: Yes, 0: No
	Hotel	1: Yes, 0: No
Quantitative data	Capacity	Capacity par day
	Number of golf course	Number of golf courses in the same city
	Review score	Min:1–Max:5 (average)
	Number of review	Number of review

Table 2. Summary statistics of quantitative data of k-meams clustering

	Cluster 1	Cluster 2	Cluster 3	Cluster 4
Aggregate of golf courses	32	25	33	36
Capacity (mean)	21.813	41.040	33.758	35.250
Number of golf course (mean)	5.176	3.742	4.095	3.639
Review score (mean)	3.716	3.742	4.095	3.660
Review score (variance)	0.201	0.168	0.122	0.117
Number of review (mean)	36.781	40.800	55.545	56.833

- Figure 2 shows rate of price range. Cluster 2 and cluster 4 include many low price and cluster 3 includes many high price.
- Figure 3 shows rate of course type. Only cluster 1 includes mountain, forest, and riverbed.
- Figure 4 shows rate of self-play. Only cluster 3 does not include self-play.
- Figure 5 shows rate of the presence in a hotel. Only cluster 2, all golf courses have a hotel. Moreover only cluster 4, all golf courses do not have a hotel.

The features of classified four clusters were shown in Table 3.

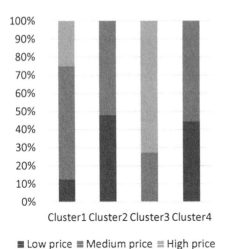

Fig. 2. Component ratio of price range

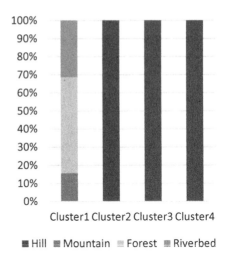

Fig. 3. Component ratio of course type

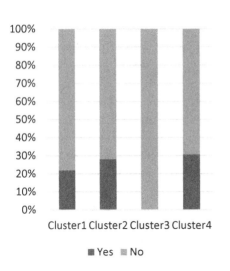

Fig. 4. Component ratio of self-play

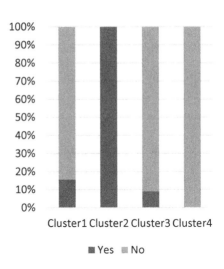

Fig. 5. Component ratio of hotel

There are several features each cluster. The variables affecting classification are price range, course type, self-play, hotel, capacity, review score and number of review. From the features of golf courses (Table 3), we defined the characteristics of each cluster as Table 4.

Table 3. The features of each cluster

	Aggregate of golf courses	The features of golf courses
Cluster 1	32	Small capacity Not hill course Large dispersion of review score
Cluster 2	25	Large capacity Low price With hotel in golf courses
Cluster 3	33	High price Not self-play Large review score
Cluster 4	36	Low price Many review Without hotel in golf courses

Table 4. The characteristics of each cluster

	The characteristic of golf courses
Cluster 1	Unique courses
Cluster 2	Public courses being able to stay
Cluster 3	High class and popular courses
Cluster 4	Public courses being unable to stay

4.2 Identification of Cancellation Factors Each Characteristic of Golf Courses

Secondly, we performed logistic regression analysis with respect to each cluster using reservation and user data for identifying factor of cancellation each characteristic of golf courses. Data used by logistic regression analysis is shown below (Table 5).

It can be found that there is almost same in cancellation rate for each cluster. The variable of logistic regression analysis are shown below (Table 6).

We select variables by stepwise method for each model. Moreover, we checked accuracy by 10-fold cross-validation. The results of logistic regression analysis are shown in Tables 7, 8, 9 and 10 and Figs. 6, 7, 8 and 9. The asterisks *, **, *** and period · indicate that the coefficients are statistically different from zero at the 0.1, 1, 5, 10 percent level in Tables 7, 8, 9 and 10.

Cluster 1: Unique Courses

Table 7 shows the result, and Fig. 6 shows the value of parameter β_k of cluster 1. Seven variables are selected by stepwise method in R language. Main variables affecting cancellation are Play, Reservation, Holiday, Score and Start_8. As the result of 10-fold cross-validation, accuracy is 61.5%.

Cluster 2: Public Courses Being Able to Stay

Table 8 shows the result, and Fig. 7 shows the value of parameter β_k of cluster 2. Eight variables are selected by stepwise method in R language. Main variables affecting cancellation are Generation_70, Reservation, Play, Holiday, Mail and Registration. As the result of 10-fold cross-validation, accuracy is 63.2%.

Table 5. Data used by logistic regression analysis

	Number of reservation	Number of cancellation	Cancellation rate
Cluster1	8698	3777	0.434
Cluster2	6132	2506	0.409
Cluster3	14085	5965	0.424
Cluster4	13172	7586	0.424

Table 6. Variables used by logistic regression analysis

Variable attribute		Variable	Explanation
Response variable		Cancel	1: Cancel, 0: Not cancel
Explanatory variable	User attribute	Gender	1: Male, 0: Female
		Generation	20 s–70 s (factor)
		Residence	1: Kanto district 0: Other district
		Mail	1: Wish direct mail 0: Not wish direct mail
		Score	Number of used score management service (standardization)
		Registration	Number of days from registration date to March 31, 2015 (integer)
		Play	Number of play per year (standardization)
	Reservation attribute	Start	Play start time at 7 o'clock–10 o'clock (factor)
		Player	Number of player per reservation (standardization)
		Price	Price per player (standardization)
		Reservation	Number of days from reservation date to play date (standardization)
		Holiday	1: Holiday, 0: Weekday
		Season	1: High season 0: Not high season (High season: March–June, September–November)

Cluster 3: High Class and Popular Courses

Table 9 shows the result, and Fig. 8 shows the value of parameter β_k of cluster 3. Seven variables are selected by stepwise method in R language. Main variables affecting cancellation are Reservation, Play, Gender, Season and Holiday. As the result of 10-fold cross-validation, accuracy is 61.9%.

Cluster 4: Public Courses Being Unable to Stay

Table 10 shows the result, and Fig. 9 shows the value of parameter β_k of cluster 4. Eight variables are selected by stepwise method in R language. Principal variables affecting cancellation are Reservation, Play, Price, Gender and Season. As the result of 10-fold cross-validation, accuracy is 63.8%.

Table 7. Result of logistic regression analysis (cluster 1)

Explanatory variable	Parameter β_k
(intercept)	−0.554**
Generation_30	−0.054
Generation_40	0.218
Generation_50	0.043
Generation_60	−0.036
Generation_70	0.154
Score	−0.089***
Registration	0.077**
Play	0.448***
Start_8	0.112˙
Start_9	−0.091
Start_10	−0.047
Reservation	0.036***
Holiday	0.276***

***: 0.001, **: 0.01, *: 0.05, ˙: 0.1

Table 8. Result of logistic regression analysis (cluster 2)

Explanatory variable	Parameter β_k
(intercept)	−0.345
Generation_30	0.135
Generation_40	0.227
Generation_50	0.022
Generation_60	−0.221
Generation_70	−0.715*
Mail	−0.168*
Registration	0.141***
Play	0.411***
Price	0.105**
Reservation	0.458***
Hoilday	0.186*
Season	−0.091

***: 0.001, **: 0.01, *: 0.05, ˙: 0.1

The characteristic variables of each models is shown below (Table 11). Also, (+) show plus regression coefficient, and (−) show minus regression coefficient.

The accuracy of each model is shown in Table 12.

Table 9. Result of logistic regression analysis (cluster 3)

Explanatory variable	Parameter β_k
(intercept)	0.088
Gender	−0.425***
Play	0.426***
Player	0.063**
Price	0.080***
Reservation	0.437***
Hoilday	0.129**
Season	−0.148***

***: 0.001, **: 0.01, *: 0.05, ˙: 0.1

Table 10. Result of logistic regression analysis (cluster 4)

Explanatory variable	Parameter β_k
(intercept)	0.193˙
Gender	−0.295**
Mail	−0.075
Score	−0.047*
Registration	0.090***
Play	0.455***
Price	0.274***
Reservation	0.520***
Season	−0.114**

***: 0.001, **: 0.01, *: 0.05, ˙: 0.1

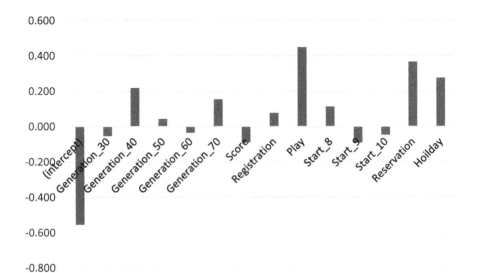

Fig. 6. Parameter β_k of logistic regression analysis (cluster 1)

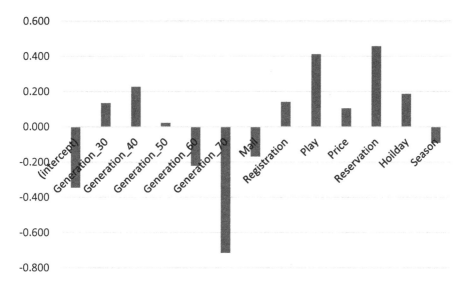

Fig. 7. Parameter β_k of logistic regression analysis (cluster 2)

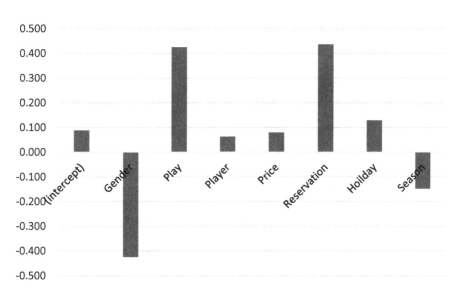

Fig. 8. Parameter β_k of logistic regression analysis (cluster 3)

5   Discussions

The common cancellation factors of all clusters are the users who reserved frequently and reserved early. It is thought that the users who is used to use reservation sites decrease resistance to cancellation. Also, for the users reserving early is the largest

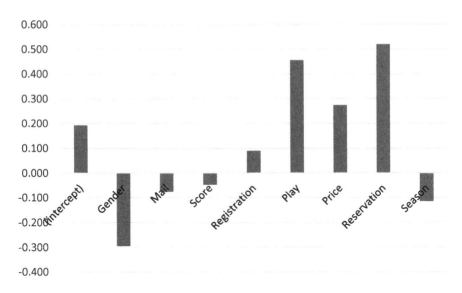

Fig. 9. Parameter β_k of logistic regression analysis (cluster 4)

Table 11. The characteristic variables of each model

	Characteristic of golf courses	Characteristic variables
All cluster	–	Play (+) Reservation (+)
Cluster1	Unique courses	Score (−) Start_8 (+) Holiday (+)
Cluster2	Public courses being able to stay	Age_70 (−) Holiday (+) Mail (−) Registration (+)
Cluster3	High class and popular courses	Season (−) Gender (−) Holiday (+)
Cluster4	Public courses being unable to stay	Price (+) Gender (−) Season (−)

Table 12. The accuracy of each model

	Accuracy (%)
Cluster1	61.5
Cluster2	63.2
Cluster3	61.9
Cluster4	63.8

cancellation factor, it is thought that carrying out the policy which not canceled by them is connected with decreasing cancellation.

The cancellation factors of cluster 1 (unique courses) are the users who do not use score management service, and the reservation that start time is early. Cluster 1 contains golf courses with small capacity and course type is other than hills. Moreover, because of Large Dispersion of review score, many of them may be golf courses where user preference is divided. For unique courses, it is thought that the users who consider that condition such as start time is more important than course condition tend to cancel.

The cancellation factor of cluster 2 (public courses being able to stay) is young users. Cluster 2 contains golf courses with large capacity and hotel facility. Moreover, because of low price, many of them may be a golf course of public course. For Public courses being able to stay, it is thought that young users who tend to enter schedule such as business tend to cancel more than the old users who do not tend to enter schedule such as business.

The cancellation factors of cluster 3 (High class and popular courses) are female users and the reservation that is not high season. Cluster 3 contains golf courses with high price and not self-play without caddy service. Moreover, because of large review score, many of them may be is a golf course of popular course. For popular courses, it is thought that the reservation that is high season do not tend to cancel because of tending to fill up the reservation.

The cancellation factors of cluster 4 (Public courses being unable to stay) is the reservation that play price is high. Cluster 4 contains golf courses with many review and without hotel in golf course. Moreover, because of low price, many of them may be a golf course of public course. For public courses being unable to stay, it is thought that many users think that play price want to keep low.

6 Conclusion

In this study, we considered to identify the cancellation factors based on the characteristics of golf courses in reservation sites. Firstly, we classified golf courses using causal and review data on the basis of the thought that it is difference that action at the time of the cancellation of user by characteristics of golf courses. As the result, golf courses were classified into four clusters, and we defined characteristics of golf courses each cluster. Secondly, in order to identify factor of cancellation each characteristic of golf courses, we performed logistic regression analysis each cluster using reservation data and user data. Through these analyses, we could identify same common cancellation factors and different cancellation factors each characteristic of golf courses.

However, accuracy of each model was not high. Accordingly, it is a future work that constructing better models. For example, devising explanatory variable, and performing other analysis are considered.

Acknowledgment. We are deeply grateful Kazuhiro Fukunaga, Katsuyuki Mitsuyama and Golf Digest Online Inc. for providing datasets and useful comments.

References

1. Kato, Y., Namateme, T.: Reservation behavior analysis on EC site -Discriminant Model of Cancel Behavior of Golf Course Reservation. In: National Conference of the Japan Society for Management Information 2015 Autumn of Japan, pp. 113–116 (2015). (in Japanese)
2. Matsushima, K., Kobayashi, K., Oro, T.: Individual reservation behavior under uncertainty. Infrastruct. Plan. Rev. Jpn. **17**, 655–666 (2000). (in Japanese)
3. Onoda, T., Sakai, M., Yamada, S.: Experimental comparison of clustering results for k-means by using different seeding methods. In: Conference of the Japanese Society for Artificial Intelligence of Japan, vol. 25, pp. 1–4 (2011). (in Japanese)
4. Kato, N., Hamuro, Y., Yada, K.: Data Mining its Application. Asakura Publishing Co. Ltd., Shinjuku-ku (2008). (in Japanese)
5. Tango, T., Yamaoka, K., Takagi, H.: logistic Regression Analysis. Asakura Publishing Co. Ltd., Shinjuku-ku (1996). (in Japanese)

Analysis of the Characteristics of Repeat Customer in a Golf EC Site

Yusuke Sato[1(✉)], Kohei Otake[2], and Takashi Namatame[2]

[1] Graduate School of Science and Engineering, Chuo University, 1-13-27
Kasuga, Bunkyo-ku, Tokyo 112-8551, Japan
a13.bthf@g.chuo-u.ac.jp
[2] Faculty of Science and Engineering, Chuo University, 1-13-27 Kasuga,
Bunkyo-ku, Tokyo 112-8551, Japan
{otake,nama}@indsys.chuo-u.ac.jp

Abstract. In recent years, acquisition of repeat customers is emphasized for EC sites. On the other hand, the defection rate from the first purchase to the second purchase is the highest. There are much attention to acquire the repeat customers in the EC sites in this situation. The purpose of this study is to clarify factors necessary for acquiring repeat customers. Especially, we construct models that predict whether or not to repurchase within a certain period using membership information variables, purchase behavior variables and web browsing behavior variables. Using these models, we extract characteristics relate to presence or absence of repurchase and propose marketing measures to promote to repurchase.

Keywords: Consumer behavior · Repeat customer · Logistic regression

1 Introduction

Due to recent advances in the current internet environment, the market size of EC (Electronic Commerce) market that trades products on the internet is in rapid expansion. In addition, competition for customer acquisition is occurring and acquisition cost of new customers is rising in this market. Therefore, acquisition of repeat customers who use the EC site continually is regarded as important. In the EC site market, there is a feature customer defection rate from the first purchase to the second purchase is the highest, and the subsequent rate customers who have purchased for the second time decreases [1]. Therefore, when considering acquisition of repeat customers, it is important to prevent separation from first purchase to second purchase. The transition of customer defection rate from the first purchase to the multiple purchases is shown below (Fig. 1) [2].

Hence, it is important to understand the behavior of repeat customers, and it allows decreasing of defection customers [3–6]. Especially, the target EC site of this study provides the system of make reservations for golf courses in addition to purchasing golf supplies. So, customer retention on the EC site without limiting total number and purchase price of items purchased at second purchase brings sales increase as a whole.

© Springer International Publishing AG 2017
G. Meiselwitz (Ed.): SCSM 2017, Part I, LNCS 10282, pp. 223–233, 2017.
DOI: 10.1007/978-3-319-58559-8_19

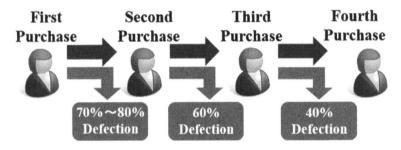

Fig. 1. Transition of customer defection rate

The purpose of this study is to clarify the factors specific to customers who repurchase through the analysis of behavior at the first purchase at the EC site.

Using the result of the analysis, we also propose marketing policy for the time of first purchase to encourage repurchase.

2 Data Sets

In this study, we target on the general EC site relating to golf. The EC site provides some services such as EC of golf equipment, reservations for golf courses, manage golf score, etc. In this study, we used following data.

- Customer information data (age, sex, registration date, etc.)
- Purchase data (category of purchase items, purchase date, whether purchased item is used item or not, etc.)
- Access history data (login date and time, URL of access page, URL of referrer page, etc.)
  * Period for each data: 8 months from January to August, 2014.

The category name of the product included in the purchase data is shown in Table 1.

The landing route and browsing page name included in the access log data is shown in Tables 2 and 3.

In this study, we analyzed the bellow customer. The reason for this is that we defined the first three months of the data period as the first purchase period and the six months from the first purchase month as the repurchase period.

Table 1. Category name of item

Category	Item
Men's wear	Tops for men, pants for men, etc.
Lady's wear	Tops for women, pants for women, etc.
Golf club	Putter, iron, etc.
Accessory	Golf ball, golf glove, etc.
Other	Calendar etc.

Table 2. Browsing page name

Browsing page name	Golf beginner page
Golf course reservation page	Golf style page
Golf news page	Golf trip page
Golf lesson page	Golf community page
Golf score management page	Golf event page
Golf movie page	Golf school page

Table 3. Landing route name

Landing route name
Landing from search engine
Landing from mail magazine
Landing from news site
Landing from Facebook
Landing from bookmark
Landing from golf information site
Landing from other EC site
Landing from golf brand site
Landing from Amazon
Landing from Yahoo! shopping
Landing from price comparison site
Landing from internet auction site of Yahoo!
Session disconnection or simultaneously starting a plurality of windows

[Customers]

- Customers who bought for the first time between January and March 2014
  * We exclude the customer who has passed for more than 2 years from registration.

So, the number of analyzed customers was 8,181, of which 3,228 customers repurchased within 6 months.

In this study, the purpose was to predict the presence or absence of repurchase within a certain period from the first purchase. When the objective variable to be predicted is binary, binomial logistic regression models are often used [7].

The Binomial logistic regression model is a type of classifier that performs class discrimination. By interpreting significant explanatory variables in the constructed model, it is possible to clarify the characteristics that affect the presence or absence of repurchase. In the binomial logistic regression analysis, the customer's repurchase probability p_i is expressed by the following equation [8].

$$p_i = \frac{\exp\{\sum_{j=0}^{m} \beta_j X_{ij}\}}{1 + \exp\{\sum_{j=0}^{m} \beta_j X_{ij}\}} \tag{1}$$

X_{ij}: Factors affecting repurchase ($X_{i0} = 1$)

β_j: Parameters for each explanatory variable (β_0 is Intercept).

As an explanatory variable used in the model construction, we created three variables from membership information data, nine variables from purchasing behavior at first purchase, and 27 Web-browsing behaviors at the first purchase date. Details of the explanatory variables are shown in Tables 4 and 5.

Table 4. Dmographic variables and purchasing behavior variables used in the model construction

Type of variable		Variable name	Data type
Objective variable		Whether customer repurchase within 6 months from first purchase or not	0 or 1
Explanatory variable	Demographic variables	Age	Integer
		Number of days from membership registration to first purchase	Integer
		Whether customer is an mail magazine subscriber or not	Integer
	Purchasing behavior variables	Total amount at first purchase	Integer
		Total number of items purchased at first purchase	Integer
		Whether customer purchased men's wear item at the first purchase or not	0 or 1
		Whether customer purchased lady's wear item at the first purchase or not	0 or 1
		Whether customer purchased golf club item at the first purchase or not	0 or 1
		Whether customer purchased accessory item at the first purchase or not	0 or 1
		Whether customer purchased other item at the first purchase or not	0 or 1
		Whether customer purchased used item at the first purchase or not	0 or 1
		Whether customer purchased sale item at the first purchase or not	0 or 1

* Demographic Variables was created by membership information data
Purchasing Behavior Variables was created by purchase data
Access History Variables was created by Web browsing data.

Although the number of target customers in this research was 8,181, at the time of model construction, we randomly sampled the number of non-repurchased customers by setting the number equal to the number of repurchased customers.

Furthermore, in order to verify the prediction accuracy of the model, we set 70% of the data as training data and 30% as the test data, for each non-repurchased customer

Table 5. Access history variables used in the model construction

Type of variable		Variable name	Data type
Explanatory variable	Access history variables	Browsing frequency of golf course reservation page	Integer
		Browsing frequency of golf news page	Integer
		Browsing frequency of golf lesson page	Integer
		Browsing frequency of management golf score page	Integer
		Browsing frequency of golf movie page	Integer
		Browsing frequency of golf beginner page	Integer
		Browsing frequency of golf style page	Integer
		Browsing frequency of golf trip page	Integer
		Browsing frequency of golf community page	Integer
		Browsing frequency of golf event page	Integer
		Browsing frequency of golf school page	Integer
		Whether landing from search engine or not	0 or 1
		Whether landing from mail magazine or not	0 or 1
		Whether landing from news site or not	0 or 1
		Whether landing from Facebook or not	0 or 1
		Whether landing from bookmark or not	0 or 1
		Whether landing from golf information site or not	0 or 1
		Whether landing from other EC site or not	0 or 1
		Whether landing from golf brand site or not	0 or 1
		Whether landing from Amazon or not	0 or 1
		Whether landing from Yahoo! Shopping or not	0 or 1
		Whether landing from price comparison site or not	0 or 1
		Whether landing from internet auction site of Yahoo!	0 or 1
		Session disconnection or simultaneously starting a plurality of windows	0 or 1
		Average number of page view at first purchase date	Integer
		Average login time of all session at first purchase date	Integer
		Number of login at first purchase date	Integer

and each repurchased customer. As a result, the datasets used in the model construction was split as follows (Table 6).

In addition, in order to grasp the characteristics of repurchased customers more precisely, we constructed repurchase prediction model for each purchase item category

Table 6. Datasets used in the model construction

	Training data	Test data	Total
Non repurchased customers	2260	968	3228
Repurchased customers	2260	968	3228
Total	4520	1936	6456

such as wear item, golf club item and accessory item at first purchase. This is because the behavior at the first purchase is considered different depending on the purchase category. Purchasing behavior variables and number of datasets (training data and test data) used in these model construction are shown in Tables 7 and 8.

Table 7. Purchasing behavior variables used in model construction for each purchase category

Variables	Wear model	Club model	Accessory model
Total purchase amount of each item at first purchase	O	O	O
Total number of items at first purchase	O	O	O
Whether customer purchased wear item at the first purchase or not	×	O	O
Whether customer purchased golf club item at the first purchase or not	O	×	O
Whether customer purchased accessory item at the first purchase or not	O	O	×
Whether customer purchased other item at the first purchase or not	O	O	O
Whether customer purchased used item of each item at the first purchase or not	O	O	O
Whether customer purchased sale item of each item at the first purchase or not	O	O	O

Table 8. Datasets used in repurchase prediction model for each purchase category

	Training data	Test data	Total
Wear item model	1608	690	2298
Club item model	1356	580	1936
Accessory item model	1948	834	2782

In order to confirm the prediction accuracy of the constructed model, we performed hold-out validation by using the training data and test data. Specifically, we created a confusion matrix like a following table and we calculated prediction accuracy of the constructed model by using following equations (Table 9).

Accuracy (ACC): Percentage of the total number correctly predicted among the total number predicted.

Table 9. Confusion matrix

		Predicted class	
		Positive	Negative
Actual class	Positive	True Positive (TP)	True Negative (TN)
	Negative	False Negative (FN)	False Negative (FN)

$$ACC = \frac{TP + TN}{FP + FN + TP + TN}$$

Precision (PRE): Percentage of the total number that is a positive class actually among the total number predicted positive class.

$$PRE = \frac{TP}{TP + FP}$$

Recall (REC): Percentage of the total number predicted positive class among the total number that is a positive class actually

$$REC = \frac{TP}{FN + TP}$$

F-measure: harmonic mean of PRE and REC

$$F\text{-measure} = 2 \times \frac{PRE \times REC}{PRE + REC}$$

3 Analysis of Repeat Customer

We built a model that predicts repurchase for the entire customer using binomial logistic regression analysis with stepwise selection method. We selected explanatory variables of coefficient of significant probability less than 0.05.

From Table 10, we can see that variables created from Web browsing data are selected much. In addition, the confusion matrix for the test data of this model and the evaluation indicator for confirming the prediction accuracy are shown in Tables 11 and 12.

Subsequently, we built discriminate model focusing only customer who purchased each product category such as wear item, golf club item and accessory item at the time of first purchasing. Table 13 shows the explanatory variables that selected by the model construction for each purchase category.

From Table 13, in all three models, variables of whether landing from bookmark or not, average number of page view at first purchase date and number of login at first purchase date are selected commonly. In addition, the confusion matrix for the test data of these three models and the evaluation indicator for confirming the prediction accuracy are shown in Tables 14, 15 and 16.

Table 10. Estimated value of selected partial regression coefficient

Explanatory variables	Partial regression coefficient
(Intercept)	−0.023
Age	0.082
Number of days from membership registration to first purchase	−0.076
Mail magazine registration	0.087
Total amount at first purchase	0.137
Whether customer purchased used item at the first purchase or not	−0.120
Browsing frequency of golf course reservation page	0.085
Browsing frequency of golf community page	0.089
Whether landing from news site or not	0.060
Whether landing from bookmark or not	0.284
Whether landing from other EC site or not	−0.098
Average number of page view at first purchase date	0.129
Number of login at first purchase date	0.243

Table 11. Confusion matrix of model for entire customer

		Predicted class	
		Positive	Negative
Actual class	Positive	626	342
	Negative	372	596

Table 12. Evaluation indicator of model for entire customer (%)

ACC	PRE	REC	F-measure
63.1	51.2	64.7	57.2

In comparison with accuracy of model for entire customer, it can be seen that there is no difference in accuracy of model between any models (Table 17).

4 Discussions

First, we consider the model predicting repurchase for entire customers. We could see that customers who purchased for the first time immediately after membership registration are leading to repurchase. It is considered important for acquiring repeat customers to promote golf equipment early after membership registration and to shorten the number of days until initial purchase. Moreover, since the partial regression coefficient of purchase of used items is negative, it seems that it is possible to encourage repurchase by recommending new item at the first purchase. Furthermore, since the partial regression coefficients of the e-mail magazine registration, browsing frequency of page other than shopping page and the landing from the news site are

Table 13. Estimated value of selected partial regression coefficient for each purchase category

Explanatory variables	Partial regression coefficient		
	Wear model	Club model	Accessory model
Intercept	−0.010	−0.043	−0.017
Age	0.227	–	–
Number of days from membership registration to first purchase	–	–	−0.098
Total purchase amount of each item at first purchase	–	0.128	–
Total number of items at first purchase	–	0.186	–
Whether customer purchased used item of each item at the first purchase or not	–	−0.256	–
Whether customer purchased sale item of wear item at the first purchase or not	0.132	–	–
Browsing frequency of golf course reservation page	–	–	0.110
Browsing frequency of management golf score page	0.151	–	0.133
Browsing frequency of golf style page	–	–	0.187
Browsing frequency of golf community page	–	–	0.207
Whether landing from bookmark or not	0.255	0.185	0.246
Whether landing from Amazon.com or not	−0.128	–	–
Whether landing from Yahoo! Shopping or not	–	–	−0.164
Average number of page view at first purchase date	0.133	0.128	0.233
Number of login at first purchase date	0.343	0.258	0.262

Table 14. Confusion matrix of model for customers who purchased wear item

		Predicted class	
		Positive	Negative
Actual class	Positive	226	119
	Negative	119	226

Table 15. Confusion matrix of model for customers who purchased golf club item

		Predicted class	
		Positive	Negative
Actual class	Positive	187	103
	Negative	113	187

Table 16. Confusion matrix of model for customers who purchased accessory item

		Predicted class	
		Positive	Negative
Actual class	Positive	226	191
	Negative	131	286

Table 17. Evaluation indicator of model for customers who purchased each category (%)

	Wear item model	Club item model	Accessory item model
ACC	65.5	62.8	61.4
PRE	50.0	51.4	44.1
REC	65.5	64.5	54.2
F-measure	56.7	57.2	48.7

positive, it can be said the customer who is highly interested in golf on a daily basis repurchased. From this, it seems that continuing attraction of customers' interests by periodically distributing e-magazines and news related to golf after membership registration will lead to a reduction of defection rate. Regarding that the estimated value of the partial regression coefficient of the whether landing from other EC site or not is negative and that the partial regression coefficient of whether landing from bookmark is positive, it is inferred that the customer is not using other EC site and uses only this EC site. It seems that these customers already settle in the EC site for purposes other than purchasing.

Second, we consider the model constructed using only customers who purchased wear items. Since partial regression coefficient of whether customer purchase discount items is positive, it is considered effective as measure to encourage repurchase recommending discount items of wear items at the first purchase. Regarding that the partial regression coefficient of the browsing frequency of management golf score page at the first purchase date is positive, it is inferred that customer using the score management function of the EC site during the period until the first purchase or is interested in the score management function repurchased. Considering that the EC site provides score management app, it seems that concentrating on product recommendation in the app will lead to a reduction of defection rate.

Third, we consider the model constructed using only customers who purchased club items. It seems that the customer purchased high price club or didn't purchase used clubs repurchased. In other words, with respect to purchasing of clubs, a reduction of defection rate is expected by recommending without limiting price.

Finally, we consider the model constructed using only customers who purchased accessory items. We can observe that customers who purchased for the first time immediately after membership registration are leading to repurchase. From this result, in the purchasing accessory items whose average price is inexpensive compared to other item categories, it is considered as effective measure for reduction of defection rate that to urge early purchase after membership registration. In addition, since the partial regression coefficient of the browsing frequency of golf course reservation page is positive, the customer purchases inexpensive accessories items on the way to reserve a golf course repurchased. In other words, by recommending expendable items such as golf balls to the customer who is likely to reserve a golf course, customer retention can be expected. Moreover, since customers who browse pages other than shopping page much repurchased, it can be inferred that customers who purchased on impulse when visiting the EC site for purposes other than purchasing repurchased. Therefore, considering the low price of the accessory item, it seems that prompting unplanned purchasing promotes the acquisition of repeat customers.

In addition, since partial regression coefficient of average number of page view at first purchase date is positive in all of the four models constructed, it seems that repurchase is promoted by implementing measures to make customer stay at the EC site as long as possible. Since partial regression coefficient of the number of login on the first purchase date is positive as well, we considered that customers who took a long time to purchase repurchased. From this, it seems that recommendations of similar items promote repurchase.

5   Conclusion

In this study, we extracted the characteristic of customers who repurchase and tried to propose marketing measures. Especially, we built model that predict repurchase within a certain period by binomial logistic regression analysis. As a result of model, we could clarified the characteristics related to repurchase. Moreover, we built models predicting repurchase focusing only customer who purchased each product category such as wear item, golf club item and accessory item at the time of first purchasing. As a result of these model, it was found that characteristic of customers who repurchase are different for each category and we could propose marketing measures to promote to repurchase in detail. However, the prediction accuracy of the constructed model in this research is not sufficient and there is room for improvement. We think that we can build a more precise prediction repurchase model by incorporating variables of behavior before and after the first purchase into the model.

Acknowledgment. We thank Golf Digest Online Inc. for permission to use valuable datasets and Mr. Kazuhiro Fukunaga and Mr. Katsuyuki Mitsuyama for their useful comments.

References

1. DIAMOND. http://diamond.jp/articles/-/36261
2. LTV-Lab. https://wakuten.net/
3. van den Poel, D., Wouter, B.: Predicting online-purchasing behavior. Eur. J. Oper. Res. **166**(2), 557–575 (2005)
4. Blanca, H., Julio, J., Martín, M.J.: Customer behavior in electronic commerce: the moderating effect of e-purchasing experience. J. Bus. Res. **63**(9–10), 964–971 (2010)
5. Yamashita, H., Suzuki, H.: Analysis of purchasing behavior of customers focusing on sale items: logistic regression analysis with consideration of clustering of binary data. J. Oper. Res. Soc. Jpn. **60**(2), 81–88 (2013). (in Japanese)
6. Hamuro, Y., Nakanishi, M., Yamamoto, S.: Analysis of web access log data by the classification by aggregating integrated emerging pattern. J. Oper. Res. Soc. Jpn. **53**(2), 75–84 (2008). (in Japanese)
7. Hisamatsu, T., Togawa, T., Asahi, Y., Namatame, T.: Proposal of finding purchase sign model in an EC site. J. Oper. Res. Soc. Jpn. **58**(2), 94–100 (2013). (in Japanese)
8. Toshiro, T., Kazue, Y., Haruyoshi, T.: Logistic Regression Analysis: Practice of Statistical Analysis Using the SAS (Statistical Analysis System). Asakura Publishing, Shinjuku-ku (1998). (in Japanese)

Video Blogs: A Qualitative and Quantitative Inquiry of Recall and Willingness to Share

Purvi Shah, Eleanor T. Loiacono(✉), and Huimin Ren

Worcester Polytechnic Institute, Worcester, MA, USA
{pshah, eloiacon, hren}@wpi.edu

Abstract. In the last few years, user-generated video blogs (vlogs) have become very popular on video sharing communities and websites such as YouTube. Unboxing and Haul are a genre of video blogs on YouTube where consumers unbox a new product or display their new haul of clothes, to inform other consumers about latest product trends and fashion. Despite the increased viewership of the unboxing and haul vlogs, there is a void in understanding how much information do viewers retain from these vlogs and why and how viewers decide to share these vlogs in their social network. Our research examines how unboxing and haul vlogs influence viewers' recall and their willingness to share these vlogs in their social network, revealing that vlogs' usefulness, humor and involvement have a positive impact on viewers' willingness to share. However, we did not find any relationship between willingness to share and recall. Furthermore, we qualitatively analyzed the content of viewers' recall and the main reason of willingness to share, finding that female haul vlog viewers recall more brand names than male haul vlog viewers do and female unboxing vlog viewers pay more attention to vloggers than product information.

Keywords: Unboxing · Haul · Video blogs · User generated content · Willingness to share · Recall

1 Introduction

User-generated video blogs (vlogs) have become popular on video sharing communities and websites. Recently two of the most popular online vlogs are unboxing (a video in which a person captures the process of unpacking a new product purchased by him/her) and haul (a video in which a person displays items recently purchased, including product details and price) Vlogs. Currently, there are over 1.1 billion searches on YouTube for the term "unboxing" [1] and over 1.1 billion search results for the term "haul" [2]. These videos provide information about new products, their features and benefits, and latest fashion trends. At the same time, it is a useful interactive tool for companies to advertise their products and brands because these videos are user generated content which consumers find more credible than information broadcast by companies directly [3].

In such research area, video blogs have a significant influence on consumers' purchasing behavior [4–7]. According to a survey, 57% of Consumer Electronics shoppers watch Unboxing videos before purchasing [8], and 40% of Haul video viewers will visit

© Springer International Publishing AG 2017
G. Meiselwitz (Ed.): SCSM 2017, Part I, LNCS 10282, pp. 234–243, 2017.
DOI: 10.1007/978-3-319-58559-8_20

the stores mentioned in the videos [9]. 66% of recent purchasers agree that "YouTube is one of the best sites to help me visualize how different products fit into my lifestyle" [10]. Despite the importance of video blogs, there is little research explaining the influence of vlog characteristics on viewers' behaviors. The purpose of this research is to examine how unboxing and haul vlogs influence the viewers' willingness to share and recall behavior.

Humor, usefulness and involvement are three main factors found to influence a consumer behavior in our vlog study. The goal is to examine the impact of these three factors on viewers' recall and willingness to share vlogs in their social networks. In addition, we explore what kind of content viewers would recall when they watched different types of vlogs based on vlogger's gender, such as male haul (MH), male unboxing (MU), female haul (FH), and female unboxing (FU) vlogs. The purpose of this research is to compare the differences in viewers of different types of vlogs, indicating whether vlog type and vlogger's gender will influence viewers' recall and willingness to share.

The remainder of our paper is organized as follows. The literature and hypotheses are presented in Sect. 2. Section 3 describes the research model and method. Section 4 discusses the results. Finally, Sect. 5 concludes the paper with implications and directions for future research.

2   Literature Review and Hypotheses

Recall is a critical part of a consumer's purchase decision-making process [11]. Similarly, the willingness of a consumer to share information about a product with a friend is related to their level of satisfaction with the product [12]. This satisfaction with the Vlog is likely to increase the ability to recall the product (See Fig. 1). It is, therefore, expected that,

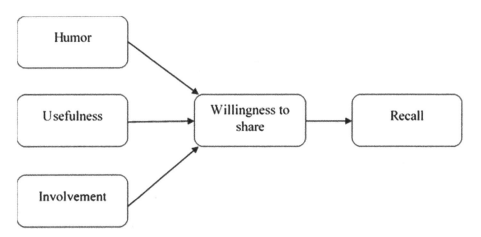

Fig. 1. A conceptual framework of factors influencing vlog viewers' recall and willingness to share the vlog

H1: A consumer's willingness to share will have a positive impact on his or her recall

Many types of user-generated content (UGC) are focused on providing entertainment through humor [13, 14]. Further, people are drawn to humorous videos [15] because they are emotionally arousing. This increased arousal facilitates their desire to share the content with others [16]. Thus,

H2: A humorous Vlog will have a positive impact on a consumer's willingness to share

Usefulness has been defined broadly as the degree to which a person believes that using a system will improve his/her performance [17]. Specifically, in this research it is operationalized as the overall usefulness of the information contained in the Vlog. Just as the usefulness of online reviews is thought to increase the attitude of toward the UGC [18], usefulness is thought to enhance the willingness of someone to share the Vlog with others.

H3: A useful Vlog will have a positive impact on a consumer's willingness to share

Consumer involvement is "the level of perceived personal importance, interest or relevance evoked by a stimulus or stimuli, which are linked by the consumer to enduring, situation-specific goals" [19]. Consumer involvement with the product is dependent on the extent of a consumer's decision process and his/her search for information [20]. Level of interest (involvement) in a product has been shown to increase a consumer's willingness to share information about the product [21]. Based on this research, it is hypothesized that,

H4: Involved consumers will be more willing to share a Vlog

Each of the variables of interest were measured using existing multi-item 5 point Likert scales using a web survey. Based on the above framework, two models were tested to quantitatively to address our research questions. Model 1 examined the impact of Humor, Usefulness and Involvement on the willingness to share through a linear regression.

$$Sharing = \beta_0 + \beta_1 Humor + \beta_2 Usefulness + \beta_3 Involvement \tag{1}$$

In model 2, a logistic regression tested the relationship between recall and willingness to share.

$$Recall = \beta_0 + \beta_1 Sharing \tag{2}$$

3   Method

An online survey was designed through which viewers were randomly assigned to one of the four conditions (2 types of blogs × 2 types of Vlogger's gender = 4 conditions) in which they were asked to view a vlog. The vlog for each product was a real world UGC found on the Internet and all the vlogs were further edited to be approximately two and a half minutes.

After watching the video, viewers were asked to answer several questions about the video including top 5 recall items, willingness to share, whether the video is humorous or not and why, whether the video was useful or not and why, and their involvement with the product(s) showcased in the vlogs. In addition, their demographic information, such as gender, age, education, and occupation was also asked (See Fig. 2).

Fig. 2. Data collection and analysis process

Data was collected through a Qualtrics survey link posted on Amazon's Mechanical Turk panel, a consumer panel, which has been considered a valuable and effective means of data collection [22, 23].

Of the total sample of 1575 respondents, 41 responses with incomplete data and/or incorrect responses to an attention filter question were removed resulting in a usable sample of 1534. Table 1 shows the sample description of the survey. All participants were adults (over the age of 18) with the average age of 35.44 years old in the United States (See Fig. 3). The sample comprised of 62% females.

Table 1. Results for model 1 and model 2

Variables	Coefficients	Std. error	Sig. (p-val)
H → W	0.304***	0.097	0.002
U → W	0.777***	0.081	0.000
I → W	0.409***	0.121	0.001
W → R	−0.090	0.080	0.262

Note: H = Humor; U = Useful; I = Involvement; W = Willingness to Share; R = Recall

Finally, the data was analyzed qualitatively through content analysis using a software called NVivo 11 Pro and quantitatively through regression analysis using a statistical tool, SPSS 23.

4   Results

4.1   Quantitative Data

In order to understand the influence of vlogs, data was quantitatively examined to ascertain how unboxing and haul vlogs affected viewers' recall and willingness to share these vlogs in their social networks. Table 1 shows the results of regression analysis. The results indicate that humor, usefulness, and involvement have a positive impact on

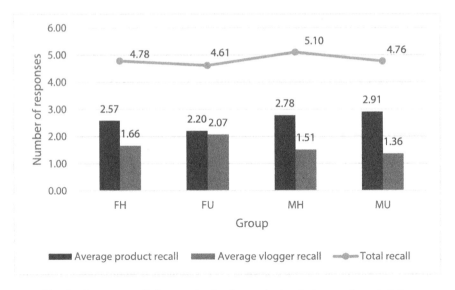

Fig. 3. Average recall from each vlog by product and vlogger characteristics

viewers' willingness to share. Amongst these three variables, usefulness of the vlog has the maximum impact. The viewers' willingness to share has no significant impact on recall. Recall was calculated by a count of the correct responses that viewers remembered about the products, vloggers, and other vlog features. Our results reveal that viewers would share the vlog with their social networks when they perceived it as humorous and useful. In addition, when they were involved with the products showcased in the vlog, they had a high willingness to share the vlog. However, it was interesting to find that there is no significant relationship between willingness to share and recall.

Furthermore, the data was qualitatively analyzed to explicate the main reasons of viewers' willingness to share and to highlight the main items recalled from the vlogs. Figure 3 shows the average recall from each vlog by product and vlogger characteristics. First, we found that viewers recall more about the product features than vlogger features in every vlog, indicating that viewers pay more attention to the products when they watched the video blog. However, there is a difference between female unboxing and male unboxing vlogs. Female unboxing vlog viewers recalled more about the vlogger as compared to product information, whereas male unboxing vlog viewers recalled more product information than vlogger characteristics. Viewers of the male haul vlog had the highest overall recall and viewers of female unboxing vlog had the lowest overall recall.

4.2   Qualitative Data

To answer the second research question, what kind of content would viewers recall after watching different types of vlogs, we analyzed the word frequency in the four types of vlogs by product and vlogger characteristics. The word clouds in Figs. 4 and 5 show the difference between top 20 recall product terms from female haul and male haul video. We found that female haul vlog viewers recalled more brand names than viewers of male haul vlog did. For instance, viewers recalled Aeropostale, American Eagle, Nordstrom, and Marshalls in the female haul vlog, while they recalled only Hollister and Abercrombie in the male haul vlog, although both of them mentioned at least four brand names in the video. Furthermore, male haul vlog viewers recalled more details about the products than viewers of female haul vlog did. It can be explained by the example that viewers remembered detailed features of clothes such as elbow, sleeves, double pockets, patches from the male haul vlog, while they recalled only apparel types, such as rompers, dress, and jeans from the female haul vlog.

Fig. 4. Top 20 recall product terms from female haul vlog

Fig. 5. Top 20 recall product terms from male haul vlog

Figures 6 and 7 present the top recall terms from viewers of female unboxing and male unboxing vlogs. Unboxing vlog viewers recalled more personal factors about the female vloggers than did those viewing male vloggers. Though the product and packaging received the most mentions, numerous viewers recalled aspects of the female vlogger's physical appearance and actions, such as her pants, her blond hair, and "crazy" ways. However, for those viewing male vloggers, the majority of items recalled were about the product features in the vlog, such as gaming, ps4, controller, and consoles. They did not have anything to do with the vlogger's personal appearance.

Finally, the motivation behind viewers' willingness to share these vlogs was qualitatively analyzed. Since, more than 85% of viewers were not willing to share the Vlog in their social networks (See Fig. 8), it was important to understand the reason for

Fig. 6. Top 20 recall terms from female unboxing vlog

Fig. 7. Top 20 recall terms from male unboxing vlog

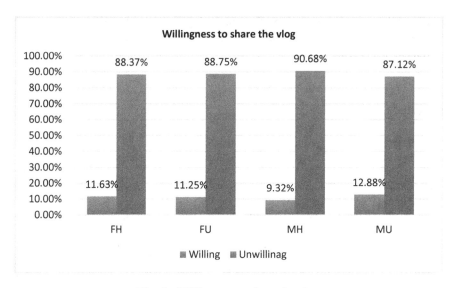

Fig. 8. Willingness to share the vlog

this unwillingness. Participants repeatedly stated that they were not willing to share the Vlog because they generally did not share such vlogs or were not in the habit of sharing them on social media, although they searched and watched the vlogs quite often. In addition, around 13% of respondents explained that their social network friends were not interested in the products showcased in the vlogs, so they were not willing to share the vlogs.

5   Conclusion, Implications and Future Work

Vlogs are gaining popularity in both academic research and industry. This research, based on quantitative and qualitative analyses, found that usefulness, humor, and involvement have a positive impact on viewers' willingness to share these vlogs in their social networks. However, there was no significant relationship between viewers' willingness to share and recall. As seen in the data analysis, male haul viewers had the highest overall recall among the viewers of the four vlogs. In addition, female unboxing viewers had the highest recall count of vlogger characteristics and male unboxing viewers had the highest recall count of product characteristics.

This research aids both researchers and practitioners looking to understand how consumer decision-making is influenced in the context of UGC and particularly vlogs. These findings not only facilitate pre-purchase information search for consumers, but also encourage companies to engage vloggers with unique personas to test and endorse their products and brands. Theoretically, it lends insight and opens avenues for future research in this new and upcoming field.

Steps for future research include investigating the influence of the viewer gender on recall and willingness to share, examining the moderating effects of viewer gender, vlogger gender, vlog type, and product and vlogger characteristics, and testing if willingness to share mediates the relationships between humor, usefulness, and involvement with recall.

References

1. YouTube Data: U.S. Classification as a "haul" video was based on public data such as headlines, tags, etc., and may not for every "haul" video available on YouTube (2015)
2. Google Data: Indexed views on YouTube (2014)
3. Berthon, P., Pitt, L., Campbell, C.: Ad Lib: when customers create the Ad. Calif. Manag. Rev. **50**, 6–30 (2008)
4. Kim, H.-W., Gupta, S., Koh, J.: Investigating the intention to purchase digital items in social networking communities: a customer value perspective. Inf. Manag. **48**, 228–234 (2011)
5. Loiacono, E.T., Watson, R.T., Goodhue, D.L.: WebQual: an instrument for consumer evaluation of web sites. Int. J. Electron. Commer. **11**, 51–87 (2007)
6. Shah, P., Loiacono, E.: Information search in an era of connected consumers. In: Obal, M. W., Krey, N., Bushardt, C. (eds.) Let's Get Engaged! Crossing the Threshold of Marketing's Engagement Era. DMSPAMS, pp. 243–244. Springer, Cham (2016). doi:10.1007/978-3-319-11815-4_78
7. Shah, P., Loiacono, E.T.: The effect of source, medium, and audience characteristics in the context of vlogs. In: 2016 American Marketing Association's Winter Educators' Conference Poster (2016)
8. Google Millward Brown CE Study, n = 1,529 CE shoppers (2015)
9. Buck, L.: Why retailers should embrace haul videos (2014)
10. U.S. Statistics: Google Consumer Surveys, Surveyed: YouTube, Hulu (2014). ESPN.com
11. Keller, K.: Conceptualizing, measuring, and managing customer-based brand equity. J. Mark. **57**, 1–22 (1993)
12. Farris, P.W., Bendle, N.T., Pfeifer, P.E., Reibstein, D.J.: Marketing Metrics: The Definitive Guide to Measuring Marketing Performance. Pearson Education Inc., Upper Saddle River (2010)
13. Verna, P.: User-generated content: will Web 2.0 pay its way? eMarketer 1–31 (2007)
14. Art, M.M.: Marketing to generation Y: messages that get their attention. LIMRA' s MarketFacts Q. **28**, 16–23 (2009)
15. Purcell, K.: The state of the online video (2010). Downloaded on 4 April 12. http://pewinternet.org/Reports/2010/State-of-Online-Video.aspx
16. Berger, J.A., Milkman, K.L.: Social transmission, emotion, and the virality of online content (2009). Unpublished manuscript downloaded on 14 June 2010. http://marketing.wharton.upenn.edu/documents/research/virality.pdf
17. Davis, F.D.: Perceived usefulness, perceived ease of use, and user acceptance of information technology. MIS Qual. **13**, 319–340 (1989)
18. Bahtar, A.Z., Muda, M.: The impact of user-generated content (UGC) on product reviews towards online purchasing – a conceptual framework. Procedia Econ. Financ. **37**, 337–342 (2016)
19. Verbeke, W., Vackier, I.: Profile and effects of consumer involvement in fresh meat. Meat Sci. **67**, 159–168 (2004)
20. Laurent, G., Kapferer, J.-N.: Measuring consumer involvement profiles. J. Mark. Res. **22**, 41–53 (1985)

21. Taylor, D.G., Levin, M.: Predicting mobile app usage for purchasing and information-sharing. Int. J. Retail Distrib. Manag. **42**(8), 759–774 (2014)
22. Bates, J.A., Lanza, B.A.: Conducting psychology student research via the Mechanical Turk crowdsourcing service. N. Am. J. Psychol. **15**, 385–394 (2013)
23. Buhrmester, M., Kwang, T., Gosling, S.D.: Amazon's Mechanical Turk a new source of inexpensive, yet high-quality, data? Perspect. Psychol. Sci. **6**, 3–5 (2011)

Valuation of Customer and Purchase Behavior of a Supermarket Chain Using ID-POS and Store Causal Data

Syun Usami[1(✉)], Kohei Otake[2], and Takashi Namatame[2]

[1] Graduate School of Science and Engineering, Chuo University,
Hachioji, Japan
a13.nnma@g.chuo-u.ac.jp
[2] Faculty of Science and Engineering, Chuo University, Hachioji, Japan
{otake,nama}@indsys.chuo-u.ac.jp

Abstract. Along with the growth of internet market a shopping, retailers such as supermarket chains need a strategy corresponding to customers in each store. The purpose of this research using ID-POS data of supermarket chain is to clarify customer characteristics and purchase behavior for each store. First of all, we categorize stores based on causal data concerning each store such as sales floor area and peripheral population. Second, we analyze customer's purchasing behavior using ID-POS data for each class that we tried to classify above, and extract characteristic purchasing behavior. Finely we evaluate these results together and clarify customer characteristics and purchasing behavior for each store causal.

Keywords: POS · Store causal data · Association analysis · Decile analysis · Hierarchical cluster analysis

1 Introduction

Recently, EC (Electronic Commerce) sites that are online stores to purchase variety of products through internet getting popular (Fig. 1). Under such situation, in real-world retailing such as supermarket industry, are required improvement of sales by unique service.

In order to propose some new unique services, analyst must know the characteristics of customers and tendency of purchasing behavior. Moreover, characteristics of each store are equally important to consider because the characteristics of store such as floor layout, competitor of the area and population of the market area, are very different. However, previous analyses of real-world retailing performed only purchasing history. It is necessary analyze using store causal data to improve the sales because customers are different depending on the surrounding environment.

© Springer International Publishing AG 2017
G. Meiselwitz (Ed.): SCSM 2017, Part I, LNCS 10282, pp. 244–255, 2017.
DOI: 10.1007/978-3-319-58559-8_21

Fig. 1. Global online retail sales have increased 17% yearly since 2007 [1]

2 Purpose of This Study

In this study, we aim to clarify customer characteristics and purchasing behavior using store causal data. It can provide useful suggestion for proposing sales strategies such as shelf allocation within stores and types of products to be stocked compared to analysis using only sales history. In addition, analysis of the relationship between product sales histories, will lead to improvement in store sales and satisfaction.

3 Analytical Procedure

We use ID-POS (point of sales with customer ID number) data of 53 store at a supermarket chains from March 2015 to February 2016 excluding nonmember data. Figures 2 and 3 the summarizing own data.

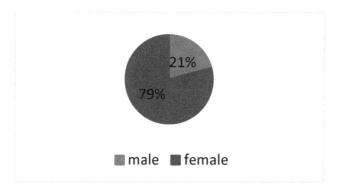

Fig. 2. Male-female ratio of all customers

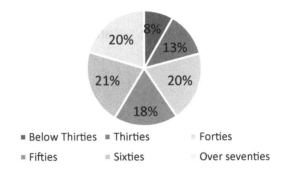

Fig. 3. Compared ratio of age

Figure 4 shows the outline of analytical procedure. First, we classify stores by cluster analysis using store causal data. Second, focusing on each classified cluster, we aggregate customer characteristics such as age structure and household composition and classify customers. Second, we perform association analysis on purchasing behaviors and clarify concurrent selling commodities for each cluster. Finally, we clarify customer characteristics and purchasing behavior for each store causal from these analysis results.

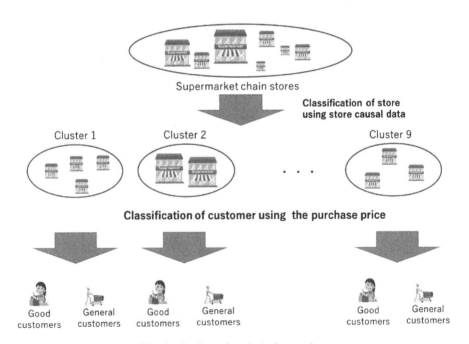

Fig. 4. Outline of analytical procedure

4 Analysis Method

4.1 Hierarchical Clustering Analysis

Hierarchical cluster analysis is a method of classifying objects by creating collections of objects similar to each other from a group in which objects of different properties are mixed based on the distance between objects.

In this study, 53 stores were classified into nine clusters by using store causal data, in order to clarify the relationship between the characteristics owned by the store and the customer characteristic and purchasing behavior.

The cosine distance was used as the distance between objects used for classification, and the Ward method [2] was adopted to merge cluster (Table 1).

Table 1. Variables used for hierarchical clustering

Variable name	Summary
The maximum parking number	The maximum number of parking lots of each stores
Sales floor space	Sales floor space of each stores
City center	Based on the address of the store, three dummy variables were created from the
Suburbs	surrounding information on the map
Mountainous areas	Apply: 1 Not apply: 0
The number of items	POS data with ID of each stores
The population in commerce areas	A circle with the diameter of the cube root of the maximum parking number centering on the store was set as a set trade area, and the population of the market area was totalized

4.2 Decile Analysis

Decile analysis is an analytical method for calculating the sales composition ratio of each rank by ranking the purchase price of all customers, based on purchase history data.

Generally, decile analysis is conducted to clarify customers with high purchase price per cluster and to evaluate differences in purchase behavior with other customers.

In this study, we performed decile analysis for each cluster that classified by hierarchical cluster analysis, and we defined that Decile rank 1 to 8 customers as "general customers" and 9 to 10 customers as "good customers".

4.3 Association Analysis

Association analysis or market basket analysis in marketing is used to extract meaningful relevance between products from enormous log data. In order to pick up concurrent selling relationship and to obtain suggestions leading to sales measures such as display and sales floor placement, association analysis was conducted.

In this analysis, association analysis is performed for "good customer" and "general customer" set for each cluster, we used the basket ID assigned to the shopping cart as a key for making concurrent selling relationship.

5 Results of Analysis

5.1 Store Classification

The results of the hierarchical cluster analysis are shown in Tables 2 and 3.

Table 2. Result of hierarchical cluster analysis (1)

Cluster	Number of stores	Average parking number	Average sales floor space	Average number of items	Average population in commerce areas
1	6	49.5	852.5	21794.7	56798.7
2	5	76.2	958.1	23726.8	69637.0
3	9	68.3	734.7	19412.3	33160.4
4	3	733.3	1524.6	28499.7	11721.0
5	5	131.8	1137.3	25644.8	14143.8
6	10	148.6	1346.5	27322.7	51253.8
7	6	170.0	1377.6	26993.8	107992.8
8	5	141.2	1569.1	29773.2	123128.0
9	4	387.8	854.5	17575.3	176676.0

Table 3. Result of hierarchical cluster analysis (2)

Cluster	Percentage of city center stores	Percentage of suburban stores	Percentage of mountainous areas stores
1	100%	0%	0%
2	0%	100%	0%
3	0%	100%	0%
4	0%	0%	100%
5	0%	0%	100%
6	0%	100%	0%
7	0%	100%	0%
8	100%	0%	0%
9	50%	50%	0%

- Clusters 1 and 8
  They composed only of city center stores.
- Clusters 2, 3, 6 and 7
  They composed only of suburban stores, clusters 4 and 5 are clusters constituted only of mountainous stores.
- Cluster 9
  It composed of city center stores and suburban stores.

In order to extract customer features for each cluster, we compiled the ratio of male and female (Fig. 5), the ratio of age, the ratio of unmarried and married (Fig. 6), and the ratio of the number of household members.

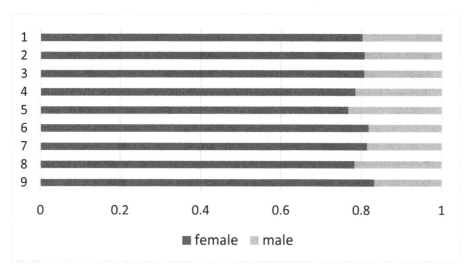

Fig. 5. Ratio of male and female per cluster

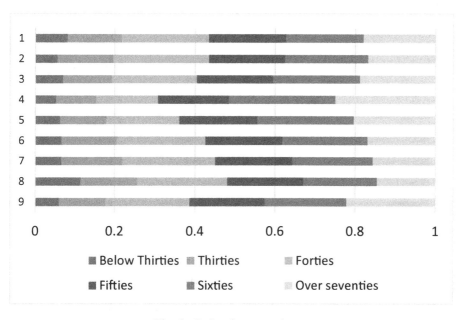

Fig. 6. Ratio of age per cluster

From the Fig. 8 in the ratio of male to female, the cluster with the lowest female ratio is cluster 1, the highest cluster is cluster 9. In the ratio of unmarried and married, the cluster with the lowest marriage ratio is cluster 1, the highest cluster is cluster 2, 7. However, there was not much difference between the clusters in either case.

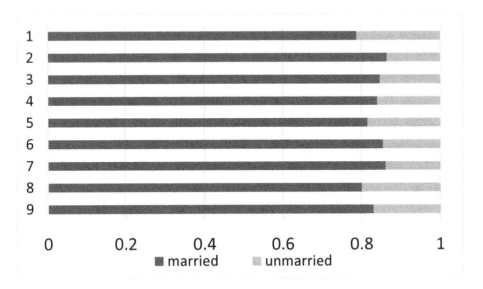

Fig. 7. Ratio of unmarried and married per cluster

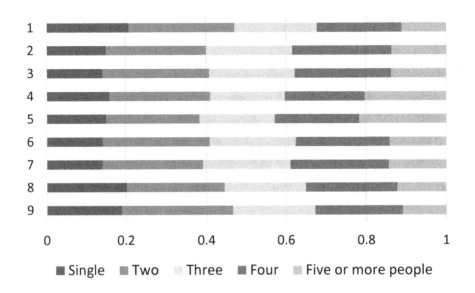

Fig. 8. Ratio of the number of household members per cluster

On the other hand, the number of households and age differed among the clusters. In the ratio of the number of household members, the proportion of "1 person" in clusters 1, 8, 9 is high, while in the clusters 4, 5, the ratio of "5 or more people" is high.

In this way, it was found that there is a difference in characteristics of customers for each cluster (Fig. 7).

5.2   Classification of Customers and Evaluation of Purchasing Behavior

We performed a decile analysis for each cluster and classified our customers as "general customers" and "good customers."

Then, we analyzed purchasing behavior such as aggregation of product categories with high purchase price.

Table 4 shows the number of goods per purchasing opportunity for general customers and good customers is described for each cluster.

Table 4. Number of items per purchase average

Cluster	General customers	Good customers
1	7.0	10.0
2	7.6	10.9
3	6.9	9.7
4	9.0	12.8
5	9.4	12.5
6	8.4	11.8
7	8.2	10.9
8	7.7	11.5
9	5.9	9.0

From Tables 5, 6, 7 and 8 show the top five items of the item category with high purchase price are listed. In this paper, we described only the results of cluster 1 and cluster 4.

The number of items per purchase is higher for good customers than for general customers. Also, it can be seen that there is a difference in the number of items per purchasing opportunity for each cluster.

Table 5. Top 5 items of category in cluster 1 (general customers)

Category name	Total purchase price (ten thousand yen)
Frozen boiled rice	2,029
Sushi	1,833
Brand pork	1,714
Yogurt	1,547
Milk	1,417

Table 6. Top 5 items of category in cluster 1 (good customers)

Category name	Total purchase price (ten thousand yen)
Brand pork	7,602
Japanese beef	7,288
Frozen boiled rice	5,289
Yogurt	5,190
Sushi	4,718

Table 7. Top 5 items of category in cluster 4 (general customers)

Category name	Total purchase price (ten thousand yen)
Sushi	1,998
Japanese beef	1,543
Brand pork	1,005
Frozen chicken	931
Bread	916

Table 8. Top 5 items of category in cluster 4 (good customers)

Category name	Total purchase price (ten thousand yen)
Special Japanese beef	6,735
Brand pork	4,829
Sushi	4,409
Frozen chicken	4,047
Pork	3,472

- Cluster 1

For general customers, merchandise categories that do not require cooking such as ready to eat sushi and frozen boiled rice are higher in purchase price, whereas good customers are higher price of merchandise category requiring cooking such as brand pork and Japanese beef.

  Although not listed in the table, beer and the third beer (malt-free beer like alcoholic beverage) were included at the top of purchase price for both general customers and good customers.

- Cluster 4

There was almost no difference between categories where ordinary customers' purchase price was high and categories with high purchase price of superior customers.

5.3   Association Analysis

Using the purchase history from 2015/03/01 to 2016/02/29, we conducted association analysis with basket ID as the key for general customers and good customers in all clusters.

At this time, we extracted the association rule with support: greater than or equal 0.1%, Lift: greater than or equal 1%, rule length: 2 as each threshold (Table 9).

Table 9. Top 5 items of category in cluster 4 (general customers)

Cluster	General customers	Good customers
1	52	272
2	72	458
3	52	270
4	128	792
5	164	658
6	108	564
7	90	558
8	90	430
9	8	170

There were many association rules are extracted for general customers, even for good customers. The clusters with number of rules to be extracted are clusters 4, 5 and 6, and clusters with few rules to be extracted are clusters 1, 3 and 9.

Tables 10, 11, 12 and 13 describe characteristic rules from the extracted association rules. In this study, we described only the results of cluster 1 and cluster 4.

It can be seen that there is a difference between general customers and good customers, we did not find much difference between clusters.

Table 10. The extracted association rule in cluster 1 (general customers)

Antecedent	Consequent	Confidence	Support	Lift
Japanese style confectionery bread	Western style confectionery bread	35.4	2.1	3.3
Banana	Yogurt	20.6	1.2	2.0
Fermented soybeans	Yogurt	20.1	1.3	1.9
Chocolate	Packaged snack	18.0	1.0	2.8
Western style confectionery bread	Yogurt	13.1	1.4	1.3

Table 11. The extracted association rule in cluster 1 (good customers)

Antecedent	Consequent	Confidence	Support	Lift
Chinese cabbage	Tofu	36.9	1.3	2.5
Enoki mushroom	Tofu	36.5	1.6	2.5
Potato	Onion	35.2	1.6	5.8
Frying	Tofu	34.8	1.4	2.4
Carrot	Onion	29.2	1.5	4.8

Table 12. The extracted association rule in cluster 4 (general customers)

Antecedent	Consequent	Confidence	Support	Lift
Japanese style confectionery bread	Western style confectionery bread	35.9	2.4	3.7
Enoki mushroom	Blunder	32.6	1.3	5.8
Chinese noodle	Bean sprouts	30.1	1.3	4.4
Tempura	Tofu	28.6	1.3	2.2
Deep-fried chicken	Salad	18.7	1.2	2.9

Table 13. The extracted association rule in cluster 4 (good customers)

Antecedent	Consequent	Confidence	Support	Lift
Frying	Tofu	51.1	3.8	2.3
Enoki mushroom	Tofu	47.2	2.9	2.2
Chinese cabbage	Tofu	46.2	1.1	2.1
Blunder	Tofu	44.3	4.4	2.0
Fermented soybeans	Tofu	43.6	4.0	2.0

6 Discussions

As the customer characteristic of Clusters 1 and 8, the number of households is one person, the unmarried rate is slightly high, and the proportion of elderly people is low. Clusters 1 and 8 are considered to be clusters where single households in 30 s to 40 s are more than other clusters. On the other hand, as a feature of purchasing behavior, cluster 1 includes beer and third beer in upper category of purchase price. It seems that this is because customers of single households are using stores in Cluster 1, which is centered on small stores, to buy alcoholic drink.

As the customer characteristic of suburban stores in clusters 2, 3, 6 and 7, the ratio of 2 to 4 people in household composition ratio is 70%, that are higher than other clusters, while the ratio of one or five people is low. From these facts, it is speculated that customers are mainly housewives of nuclear families living in the suburbs.

As a characteristic of purchasing behavior, clusters 2, 6, and 7 are such that the number of purchased goods per purchasing opportunity is large and the number of extracted association rules is also large. In Cluster 3, the number of products purchased per purchasing opportunity is small, but this is probably because the average store area is small and the number of products is small. As association rule, typical characteristic was not found. In the clusters 4 and 5 in the mountainous area, the number of households was 5 or more, and the ratio of households in the 60 s and over 70 s was higher in the ages. From these facts, clusters 4 and 5 are considered to be clusters of elderly people couple families who live in mountainous areas compared with other clusters.

The characteristic of purchasing behavior is that the purchase price of sushi is high, the number of purchased goods per purchasing opportunity is large, and the number of extracted association rules is large.

Also, since it is a cluster with an average parking number of 100 or more, it is thought that there are many customers who visit by car and buy many items at a time.

As a feature of purchasing behavior common to all clusters, general customers have higher product categories that do not require cooking, whereas good customers tend to have higher-ranking product categories requiring cooking. In addition, as a result of association analysis, rules such as "chocolate - snack" and "banana - yogurt" are found for general customers, and rules such as "potatoes - onions" and "wooden mushrooms - tofu" are found for good customers.

For this reason, we think that there are differences in the purpose of using supermarkets for general customers and good customers, and it is necessary to propose appropriate measures for each.

7 Conclusion and Future Works

Study, first, we classified stores by cluster analysis using store causal data. Second, focusing on each classified cluster, we aggregate customer characteristics such as age structure and household composition and classified customers. In addition, we performed association analysis on purchasing behaviors and clarified concurrent selling commodities for each cluster. Finally, we clarified customer characteristics and purchasing behavior for each store causal from these analysis results.

Own analysis revealed that there are differences in customer characteristics and purchasing behavior depending on the characteristics of each store, such as the sales floor area and the population within the trading area. By using this result, it is possible to propose marketing measures unique to that store according to the surrounding environment, store size, etc., which were not taken into account in analysis using only the purchase history. In order to classify the stores more accurately, it is necessary to consider a method for the commercial areas of each store, taking into account competing stores and the like. In addition, it is thought that more useful suggestions can be obtained by looking at changes in purchasing trends such as the seasons of each cluster and considering customers using many stores.

References

1. ATKearney. https://www.atkearney.com/consumer-products-retail/ideas-insights/featured-art icle/-/asset_publisher/KQNW4F0xInID/content/online-retail-is-front-and-center-in-the-quest-for-growth/10192
2. Romesburg, C.: Cluster Analysis for Researchers, pp. 133–135. Lulu.com
3. Decile Analysis. http://www.totalcustomeranalytics.com/decile_analysis.htm
4. Nagasawa, T., Yamagishi, A., Yokoyama, S.: Analysis of consumer purchase behavior using supermarket sales data and regional information. Commun. Jpn. Ind. Manag. Assoc. **25**(3), 158–163 (2015)
5. Namatame, T., Suyama, N.: Weather effects on consumer behavior in retailing - an analysis by using a supermarket's POS data. Bull. Inst. Commer. **41**(8), 1–29 (2010)
6. Sato, M., Kato, E., Matsuda, Y.: Research of FSP analysis in food supermarket. UNISYS Technol. Rev. **25**(3), 330–338 (2005)
7. Annie, L.C., Kumar, A.: Market basket analysis for a supermarket based on frequent itemset mining. Int. J. Comput. Sci. **9**(5), 257–264 (2012)

Promoting Technological Innovations: Towards an Integration of Traditional and Social Media Communication Channels

Timm F. Wagner[✉]

School of Business and Economics,
Friedrich-Alexander-Universität Erlangen-Nürnberg, Nuremberg, Germany
timm.wagner@fau.de

Abstract. The aim of this study is to examine how the mechanisms of consumer adoption of technological innovations have been affected by the advent of social media. For this purpose, a list of major adoption determinants is derived from previous research, including theories such as innovation diffusion theory, the technology acceptance model, and the unified theory of acceptance and use of technology. Findings from empirical research are used to show which adoption determinants can be influenced through firms' communication efforts and how this can be done. After outlining how social media jumbles the established routines and mechanisms of marketing communications, this article explains how these new circumstances in the social media landscape can assist firms to facilitate innovation adoption. The main contribution of this article is to connect the established research field of technology and innovation adoption with the new and emerging field of social media research.

Keywords: Technological innovation · Innovation diffusion theory · Technology acceptance model · UTAUT2 · Marketing communications · Social media

1 Introduction

In the past there was a general consensus, particularly among technology firms, that market success would come automatically if companies could develop products that were superior to existing solutions. However, countless examples of failed technology products clearly demonstrate that firms still struggle to establish their innovations in the market [1, 2]. In this regard, one major challenge is that companies and consumers differ significantly in their perceptions of products. On the one hand, companies are often convinced about the performance of their own product, they undervalue substituting solutions, and they overestimate the demand for their product in the market. On the other hand, consumers are often uncertain whether the innovation works as promised, they are skeptical about its usefulness, or they are simply satisfied with the existing solution and do not see the need to change [3]. An important reason for these two distinct perspectives is that consumers' product evaluations are based on individual perceptions rather than on 'the facts'. Consequently, companies should acknowledge consumer perceptions as a pivotal success factor for the adoption of innovations [4].

© Springer International Publishing AG 2017
G. Meiselwitz (Ed.): SCSM 2017, Part I, LNCS 10282, pp. 256–273, 2017.
DOI: 10.1007/978-3-319-58559-8_22

The antecedents of consumer adoption on an individual level have already been investigated by researchers from various fields, including marketing [e.g., 5], innovation management [e.g., 6], and information systems [e.g., 4]. This large body of literature has yielded a variety of theories on the underlying adoption mechanisms.

Since consumers' perceptions of a new product or technology are essential in regard to its market success, it is crucial for companies to determine what these perceptions are and, based on this understanding, to influence them in a positive way [3]. Given the complexity and newness of many technological innovations, the effective use of reasoned marketing communication activities is critical in this regard [7–12]. It is not surprising, therefore, that various studies have been published about how to design these communications [e.g., 13–18].

Although these research efforts have generated a large number of valuable insights regarding the promotion of technological innovations, the recent and ongoing rise of (online) social media confuses these findings because long-established communication mechanisms are changed through social media [e.g., 19–21]. In particular, social media has greatly improved the extent of consumer-consumer interactions, implying a significant loss of information sovereignty from a company perspective [22]. Moreover, firm-consumer interactions have developed from being a one-sided communication flow (through mass media) towards being a two-way communication flow [23, 24].

These changed communication mechanisms represent a major challenge for companies, who need to understand what these changes imply for their communication activities. Although there have been studies that specifically address the interplay between traditional and new media communication channels [e.g., 25, 26], it is not clear how these changed circumstances affect the current understanding of how the adoption of technological innovations can effectively be promoted. This study seeks to address this research gap. In particular, it is the aim of this article to integrate the research fields of innovation adoption and social media by examining how distinct determinants of innovation adoption are affected by the changed communication mechanisms of social media.

2   Technological Innovations and Barriers to Adoption

Before this article takes a closer look at the adoption of technological innovations, it is necessary to elaborate on the nature of technology products. First of all, common terms such as 'technological innovation', 'technology product', or 'high-tech product' are mostly used interchangeably. Although various definitions of 'high-technology' exist in the literature [e.g., 27 (p. 79), 28 (p. 10), 29 (p. 146)], most share a common understanding about the characteristics of high-tech markets. In contrast to low-tech product environments, high-tech product environments include a greater degree of market turbulence, shorter product life cycles, higher consumer involvement during purchase decisions, rapid technological changes, and a higher level of uncertainty [28, 30]. Garcia et al. [31] distinguish between receptive and resistant innovations. While receptive innovations are welcomed by consumers because the degree of necessary behavioral change and uncertainty is low, resistant innovations are – regardless of their potential benefits – initially refused by consumers.

The main cause of this innovation resistance is related to the nature of technological innovations. First, the newness of many technological innovations increases the uncertainty, because consumers are uncertain about the innovation's potential uses, its benefits, its risks and whether it works as promised [32]. The higher the degree of newness of an innovation as perceived by consumers, the greater the effort that is necessary to promote its adoption [33]. Innovations can be new to consumers, to a company, or to an industry [29 (p. 373), 34]. Newness can concern the whole product, or only single components of a product. Moreover, the degree of newness can range from incremental to radical [35]. Secondly, perceived (technological) complexity is a further determinant of innovation resistance [36] because it also increases uncertainty from a consumer standpoint [16]. Thirdly, technological innovations often require consumers to change their behavior, including their beliefs, attitudes, traditions, or routines [37, 38]. When behavioral changes are necessary for the adoption of a technology product, negative attitudes toward the product may occur, resulting in innovation resistance [37, 39, 40].

3   Determinants of Innovation Adoption

a. Innovation Diffusion Theory

Various theoretical models have been developed and tested to explain the determinants of innovation adoption [for overviews of the relevant studies, see e.g., 41–43]. The main goal of this section is to identify the most important and frequently discussed determinants of innovation adoption, rather than portraying all the determinants of innovation adoption that have been examined in the literature. Thus, three major theoretical concepts are presented and then complemented by two further important adoption determinants.

First of all, innovation diffusion theory (IDT) is grounded in social psychology, and since the 1960s, it has been widely discussed and used to study the adoption of technological innovations [12, 44]. IDT proposes five innovation attributes based on consumers' perceptions and argues that these influence the adoption of an innovation [12]. First, *relative advantage* is the degree to which an innovation is perceived as superior to existing solutions. The greater the perceived relative advantage of an innovation, the higher will be adoption intentions and adoption behavior [3]. Second, *compatibility* describes the degree to which an innovation is consistent with consumers' existing values, beliefs, and needs, which, in turn, positively affects innovation adoption. Third, *complexity* refers to the degree to which consumers perceive an innovation to be difficult to understand or use. Perceived complexity is negatively related to innovation adoption. Fourth, *trialability* reflects whether it is possible for users to try out an innovation, and it is suggested that this is positively related to innovation adoption. Fifth, *observability* describes the degree to which an innovation and its effects are visible to others. When observability is high, it is easy to explain an innovation to other consumers, which has a positive influence on adoption [12].

b. **Technology Acceptance Model**

As well as IDT, the technology acceptance model (TAM) has been widely used to predict technology adoption. TAM employs theories from social psychology, particularly the theory of reasoned action [45] and the theory of planned behavior [46]. It suggests that the intention and behavior of users in relation to the adoption of technology is primarily dependent on the technology's *perceived usefulness* and *perceived ease of use* [47]. Perceived usefulness refers to the extent to which individuals believe that a particular technology would increase their productivity [48]. Perceived ease of use reflects the degree to which individuals assume that using a particular technology would be free of effort [47]. Perceived usefulness refers to the same adoption determinant as relative advantage in IDT, and perceived ease of use inversely addresses the same determinant as complexity in IDT [49].

TAM was originally developed to study the adoption of information technology in an organizational setting, but since then it has been applied to a myriad of different technological innovations, including studies outside the field of information systems as well as research in both organizational and consumer use settings [for a review, see e.g., 42, 43].

c. **Unified Theory of Acceptance and Use of Technology**

Although TAM is still (frequently) used to study technology acceptance in a variety of contexts, the theory has been refined by incorporating further aspects with the aim of enhancing its predictive power. This effort has led to the unified theory of acceptance and use of technology (UTAUT), which also focuses primarily on organizational contexts [43].

Four constructs have been included in UTAUT to represent the direct determinants of technology acceptance and usage behavior. The first two constructs are the equivalents of the two adoption determinants in TAM. *Performance expectancy* is the equivalent of perceived usefulness. *Effort expectancy* refers to perceived ease of use. The third construct, *social influence*, addresses the extent to which individuals believe that important others (e.g., friends and family) think that they should use the new technology. Fourth, the construct *facilitating conditions* reflects the degree to which individuals believe that there are organizational and technical resources to support their usage of the new technology [43]. The positive effects of performance expectancy and effort expectancy have been already validated in the large number of TAM studies (under the headings of perceived usefulness and ease of use). In addition, a significant amount of research exists that has validated the important role of social influence and facilitating conditions on innovation adoption [e.g., 6, 50, 51].

To provide a better prediction of technology adoption in the context of consumer use, UTAUT was adapted by adding three more adoption determinants, resulting in UTAUT2 [4]. The additional constructs are *hedonic motivation*, *price value*, and *habit*.

First, hedonic motivation concerns people's perception of fun or pleasure during technology usage. The significant impact of affect on innovation adoption is supported by various studies. Demangeot and Broderick [52], for example, reveal that *pleasure* and *arousal* are important adoption determinants. Whereas pleasure refers to positive emotions such as happiness and enjoyment, a key emotion related to arousal is *excitement* [53]. This notion is further strengthened by the work of Beaudry and Pinsonneault [54], who show that happiness and excitement have a positive impact on technology usage. Moreover, Turel et al. [55] find that *playfulness value*, which is positively influenced by *enjoyment*, has a positive impact on behavioral intentions regarding the adoption of technological innovations.

Price value, the second additional determinant in UTAUT2, addresses the cost of a technology, which – in contrast to the case in the organizational context – is an important determinant of individual adoption in a consumer use setting [4].

Third, habit refers to consumers' habitual technology usage and is defined as the degree to which individuals tend to behave automatically because of training [56]. Whereas Venkatesh et al. [4] demonstrate a direct positive impact of habit on individual technology use, Limayem et al. [56] show that habit has a moderating effect on the relationship between adoption intention and behavior.

d. **Further Determinants: Perceived Trust and Opinion Leadership**

With regard to the adoption of technological innovations, *perceived trust* and *opinion leadership* are further important aspects. Although they are not contained in the core models of the theories above, they are frequently discussed in the context of innovation adoption. First of all, research has shown that perceived trust in a technology or innovation can be a critical factor in explaining individual adoption [57–60]. Since technology environments are characterized by a high level of uncertainty perceived by consumers [28], trust can be an important counterweight to this uncertainty [e.g., 57]. In general, trust is defined as "the willingness of a party to be vulnerable to the actions of another party based on the expectation that the other party will perform a particular action important to the trustor, irrespective of the ability to monitor or control that other party" [61 (p. 712)]. In the context of this article, trust implies that consumers believe that their expectations of a technological innovation will be met, although they are not able to control this by themselves [for a review of trust conceptualizations, see e.g., 62]. As a consequence, when consumers have trust in a technological innovation, their perceived uncertainty decreases, which has a positive influence on innovation adoption [57, 60].

The second further determinant that is important to consider in relation to innovation adoption is the concept of opinion leadership. The two-step flow of communication suggests that information (e.g., information about a new product) first reaches opinion leaders. Then, in the second step, the information is spread by the opinion leaders to their social groups in an influential way [63, 64]. The important role of opinion leaders is based on the understanding that consumers are much more influenced in their decision-making by their personal networks than by, for instance, mass media communication efforts, such as TV advertising [65].

Opinion leaders can influence their followers in an informational or in a normative way [66]. Informational social influence means that followers receive information (e.g. direct advice) from an opinion leader and perceive this information as "evidence about reality" [66 (p. 629)]. Normative social influence, on the other hand, implies that an opinion leader indirectly exerts social pressure. Because people desire to conform to the expectations of their social group [67], they tend to imitate the behavior of their opinion leaders, including the adoption of certain products [68]. This notion is supported by social learning theory [69]. It suggests that individuals learn from their observations of others in their social group, and that non-verbal communication is also important for behavioral changes. Normative social influence is also partly contained in UTAUT and UTAUT2, where it is represented through the social influence construct [43].

4 The Role of Communication Activities in Promoting Adoption

In the following section, this article elaborates on the impact of communication activities on innovation adoption. The previous section has outlined various adoption determinants derived from different theoretical perspectives. Most of the determinants presented above have in common that they can be affected by companies through communication efforts, since their evaluation is mostly based on consumers' perceptions.

Several studies suggest that certain concrete communication efforts make innovation adoption more likely. Based on their empirical study, Heidenreich and Kraemer [40] argue that it is a promising approach to design advertisements that compare the product benefits of new and existing products (*relative advantage, perceived usefulness*). They also recommend the use of mental simulation, which means showing consumers concrete situations in which the technology is used, with the goal of enhancing *perceived usefulness*. To increase the *perceived compatibility* of an innovation, the authors suggest that it should be specifically emphasized that the innovation does not conflict with existing behaviors or routines. Zhao et al. [70] further investigate the use of mental simulation and find that focusing on the *outcome* of the use of a product is more effective if the consumers are working in a cognitive information processing mode (*perceived usefulness*). In contrast, they show that focusing on the *process* of using a product is a more promising communication strategy if the consumers are likely to be working in an affective information processing mode (*perceived ease of use, hedonic motivation*). In their analysis of automobile print advertisements, Baccarella et al. [71] reveal that car brands most frequently highlight value and experience cues in their advertisements, to enhance *perceived usefulness, price value*, and *perceived trust*. Ram and Sheth [10] recommend that product trial is facilitated (*trialability*), with the aim of reducing consumers' perception of risk (*complexity, perceived ease of use*). Moreover, they suggest that barriers created by consumers' established traditions (which conflict with *compatibility*) are overcome by designing communication activities that educate consumers about the innovation's functionality (*perceived usefulness, perceived ease of use, complexity, compatibility*). El Houssi et al. [14] demonstrate that using analogies is an effective means of communicating an innovation's distinctive benefits to consumers (*perceived usefulness*). Moreover, Feiereisen et al. [15] reveal the effectiveness of including visuals in advertisements that stimulate mental imagery by presenting a scenario with the innovation in use, to enhance product comprehension (*perceived usefulness, perceived ease of use, complexity, compatibility*). Talke and Snelders [18] demonstrate that communication efforts for new high-tech consumer products are most effective in regard to adoption when they contain messages on the product's personal and social consequences for the owner (*hedonic motivation*). Furthermore, these authors find that there is a positive impact on adoption when technical and financial information is conveyed in a concrete and specific format (*compatibility, complexity, perceived usefulness, perceived ease of use*).

As mentioned above, some adoption determinants cannot be influenced in the same way by communication activities. First, the *observability* (IDT) of an innovation depends on the innovation itself, rather than being susceptible to the influence of communication activities [12]. Second, *trialability* (IDT) directly affects consumer perceptions of an innovation, but cannot be influenced by communication activities [12]. Third, *price value* (UTAUT2) addresses the cost of an innovation and does not dependent on perceptions (note that the value of an innovation is primarily represented by perceived usefulness). Fourth, *habit* (UTAUT2) is based on the amount of innovation usage and hence cannot be influenced by communication activities [4]. Table 1

Table 1. Determinants of innovation adoption that can be influenced by communication activities

The probability of innovation adoption increases when consumers…		Corresponding construct names derived from the literature[*]
1.	…perceive an innovation to be useful (in general, but also in comparison with existing solutions)	Perceived usefulness (also relative advantage; performance expectancy)
2.	…assume that it will be easy for them to use an innovation. This includes the effort of learning how to use an innovation	Perceived ease of use (also complexity; effort expectancy)
3.	…assume that they do not have to change their existing behavior, beliefs, or values	Compatibility
4.	…face social pressure to adopt an innovation. This pressure can be *active* when consumers believe that important others (e.g. friends, family) think they should use the innovation, and can also be *passive* when consumers see opinion leaders who use the innovation and strive to conform to opinion leaders' behavior	Normative social influence
5.	…receive positive/useful information (e.g. direct advice) in regard to an innovation from an opinion leader	Informational social influence
6.	…believe that there are resources (e.g. technical support) to support their innovation usage	Facilitating conditions
7.	…perceive fun, pleasure or excitement in regard to an innovation	Hedonic motivation
8.	…believe that their expectations in an innovation will be met, although they are not able to control this directly by themselves	Perceived trust

[*]Adoption determinants have been validated in empirical studies; most of them are collected from IDT [12], TAM [47], UTUAT [43], and UTAUT2 [4]. Further explanations are presented in Sect. 3 of this article.

summarizes those adoption determinants that can be directly influenced by communication activities. This article will discuss these later in relation to social media.

5 Social Media: A Game Changer in Marketing Communications

In recent years, a dramatic change in the media landscape has significantly upset the established mechanisms of marketing communications [20]. The number of active social media users has continuously increased, and people's engagement with social media has expanded tremendously. Companies have responded to the growing number of active social media users by increasing their spending on social media activities, such as producing firm-generated content and advertising on social media sites [72]. Between 2013 and 2014, for example, worldwide social network advertising spending increased from $11.36 billion to $17.74 billion, a rise of 56.2% [73]. Forecasts for 2017 predict that worldwide social network advertising spending will surpass $40 billion [74]. These numbers show vividly that companies have embraced social media as an important (new) element of their promotion mix [75]. Although skeptics originally questioned the overall impact of social media efforts on firm performance (e.g., sales and stock price), various studies have dispelled these doubts and have shown the positive influence of *online* social media marketing activities on *offline* performance measures [e.g., 72, 76–78].

From the perspective of marketing communications, there are important changes through social media. First of all, social media enables communication between consumers in a way that was previously impossible. Before the emergence of the internet, consumer-consumer interaction – so-called 'word-of-mouth' (WOM) – had already been identified as a great influence on consumers' buying decisions [79]. The extent of WOM, however, has increased tremendously through the advent of the internet, and especially through the emergence of social media platforms, because communication possibilities between consumers have been radically simplified [24]. This increased influence of WOM has made its role in new product success even more important, resulting in a variety of research in the field of 'electronic word-of-mouth' (eWOM) [e.g., 80–83].

Another outcome of simplified consumer-consumer interactions through social media is that companies have lost their traditional information sovereignty: eWOM implies that consumers actively share information about (new) products. This is especially important because information from social media is perceived as more trustworthy than messages from traditional channels of marketing communication [84]. This notion is supported by Akdeniz et al. [85], who found that third-party signals are perceived as more credible because they are less likely to be perceived as marketing signals.

Besides the facilitation of consumer-consumer interactions, social media has changed the traditional one-sided communication between consumers and firms into a two-way information flow [23, 24]. Previously, companies mainly used traditional channels, such as the mass media, to communicate with consumers, and consumers did not have a chance to respond in a substantive way. Today, consumers can use social media platforms to contact firms directly through their social media presence. Since communications from consumers to firms on social media are usually public, firms face higher pressure than before to respond in an adequate way [23]. When consumers are dissatisfied, there is an inherent risk that other consumers will join the consumer-firm interaction with further complaints, and this can (in extreme cases) lead to online firestorms that involve an extensive and uncontrolled spread of negative eWOM [86].

The changes arising from the use of social media are challenging for marketing departments, but social media also brings clear advantages. First, consumer-firm interactions can be used by companies to build trusting relationships with customers, which can lead to positive outcomes, such as repeat purchases or positive eWOM [24]. Second, companies can monitor consumers' social media activities and gain important insights [87]. These consumer insights can be used not only to create meaningful social media messages, but also to develop new products and services, as they give a deep understanding of consumer needs. Third, companies have the opportunity to measure the effectiveness of their messages directly, because most social media platforms offer various metrics. On Facebook, for example, the administrators of brand pages can see several page and post metrics, including the number of 'likes', the reach on Facebook, and user engagement. These insights help with a continuous improvement in message effectiveness. Fourth, social media can be used to identify specific consumer groups, including innovators and early adopters. For example, there are specific social media groups (e.g., certain forums) where these consumers share information about new technology products. Also, opinion leaders are much easier to identify in social media than in an offline environment, because they are likely to manage their own social media channels, for example on Twitter or YouTube, to share their experiences or give advice to their audiences [80].

Furthermore, if the aim is to design convincing messages on social media, it is important to understand users' motivations for engaging on social media. De Vries and Carlson [88] have summarized the existing findings in this regard and have suggested distinct needs that are gratified with social media usage. First, consumers use social media to access information and, in particular, helpful, functional and useful content [89–92]. Second, consumers' motivation to use social media is based on the gratification of social interaction needs [93]. For example, social media sites such as Instagram, Snapchat, Pinterest, or Tumblr enable users to communicate with others and/or to share ideas and content [94, 95].

6 The Influence of Social Media on Innovation Adoption

This section explains what the new circumstances in the social media landscape can offer with regard to firms' communication activities as the firms seek to enhance consumer perceptions of adoption determinants. It is important to mention here that social media channels should always be understood as an *expansion* of traditional communication channels and not as a *replacement* [75]. As shown in Fig. 1, it is proposed that companies need to use both traditional and social media communication channels to influence consumers' perceptions of technological innovations. The following section elaborates on the suggested aspects in detail.

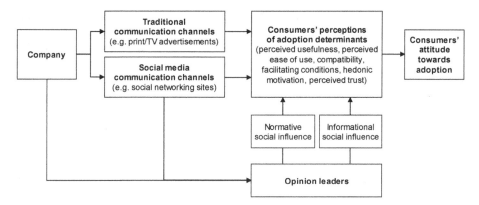

Fig. 1. How companies can influence adoption determinants through communication

Perceived Usefulness. Social media platforms are generally very suitable for explaining the usefulness of technological innovations to consumers. For example, on social networking sites such as Facebook or Instagram, brands can vividly tell stories about various usage situations by uploading pictures and videos [96]. On video sharing platforms such as YouTube, publishing videos with testimonials explaining the advantages of an innovation over existing solutions is another option for enhancing perceived usefulness. Moreover, since social media is very fast in terms of content creation and consumption, it is possible for brands to tell many more stories about the usefulness of their innovations than they can using other media outlets. Another important advantage of social media is that brands can have discussions with consumers about certain characteristics of an innovation. This helps to resolve potential misunderstandings in terms of the usefulness of the innovation. With regard to opinion leadership, social media platforms offer opinion leaders the opportunity to reach a much larger audience than in the 'offline world'. It is therefore more important than ever to convince opinion leaders to reach out to their social media followers in order to tell those followers about the benefits of an innovation. It is not surprising, therefore, that aiming to reach opinion leaders on social media sites such as Instagram, Snapchat, YouTube, and Facebook is already an important part of everyday practice in industries such as fashion or beauty products [97–100].

Perceived Ease of Use. To improve consumer perceptions of an innovation's ease of use, it is necessary to communicate the *process* of product usage [70]. For this, social media offers a variety of opportunities. As suggested above in relation to perceived usefulness, videos can be placed on different platforms so that users can experience how easy and effortless it is to use a particular innovation. Brands might produce these videos themselves or, which can be even more convincing, might motivate other users (including opinion leaders) to talk about the ease of use of an innovation with members of their social media community. In fact, a myriad of videos of this kind already exists. For example, in so-called 'unboxing videos', users record themselves during the unpacking of a new product. In the context of high-tech consumer products in particular, this kind of user-generated content is extremely welcome to the online community. For example, an Apple iPhone 7 unboxing video by the YouTuber Marques Brownlee was viewed more than eight million times in only three months [101]. The important role of consumers' initial product reviews has been emphasized by recent research [102–108]. Against this background, companies should try to engage actively in this field, with the aim of generating positive eWOM. Of course, product reviews –whether they are published in a written or a video-based format – can not only affect perceived ease of use; consumer product reviews are also able to address the usefulness of an innovation and also other adoption determinants, including perceived compatibility.

Compatibility. Consumers judge an innovation to be compatible when they think that they do not have to change their existing behavior, beliefs, or values significantly. Potential worries in this regard can easily be detected on social media platforms. A brief look into a product-related forum (e.g. on Reddit, or CNET forums) or in certain user groups on social networking sites illustrates that users very commonly discuss their concerns on social media. Thus, consumer insights systematically generated through social media monitoring can help companies to understand these concerns and to avoid misunderstandings or fears at an early stage.

Normative Social Influence. When people recognize that important others use an innovation, they tend to conform to this behavior. Also, the chances of innovation adoption increase when people believe that important others want them to use an innovation. These two mechanisms of normative social influence are both enabled through the advent of social media. In fact, social media users usually have many more interactions with many more people than consumers in the 'offline world'. During these interactions, social media users learn more about the attitudes and behavior of others, since consumers on social networking sites share this information with their online network. Therefore, the role of normative social influence has significantly increased. This is the reason why it is much more important today for companies to persuade opinion leaders to use and promote their products (as mentioned above).

Informational Social Influence. The same logic applies to informational social influence. As social media has given opinion leaders great power by providing them with easy and free tools to communicate with their audiences, their direct influence has increased and should therefore be the focus of companies who want to promote the adoption of their innovations. Moreover, social media has made it easier for companies to identify opinion leaders, because they can obtain public social media metrics such as the number of followers a user has on a social media platform.

Facilitating Conditions. Social media platforms offer excellent opportunities to enhance consumer perceptions of facilitating conditions. Today, when consumers face a problem that they do not know how to solve, they can access a variety of online tutorials on social media sites. For example, there is a YouTube tutorial where users can learn "10 of the most common must-know features in Microsoft Excel 2010", and this has now two and a half million views [109]. Similarly, there is a YouTube video of 'Eli the Computer Guy' explaining how to repair a laptop, and this video has already been viewed by over 630,000 people [110]. Although there are tutorials produced by companies on how to use technological innovations and how to solve potential problems, there is a myriad of user-generated tutorials available on social media. This huge amount of (free) support on almost every product and almost every problem radically changes consumers' perceptions of facilitating conditions in regard to any technological innovation. That consumers use social media to access helpful content has also been confirmed by previous research [89, 111].

Hedonic Motivation. Innovation adoption is facilitated when consumers perceive that emotions such as fun, pleasure or excitement are connected with using an innovation. Until now, it was companies that were faced with the challenge of transmitting these emotions using traditional communication channels. However, social media can take on this role because seeking entertainment has been found to be one of the most important gratifications to which people aspire through social media usage [e.g., 91, 104, 112]. Therefore, companies might frame their messages in regard to certain appeals, including fun or excitement, which can positively influence innovation adoption.

Perceived Trust. Trust can be directed both towards a brand (e.g. 'I trust this brand') [113] and towards a product or technology (e.g. 'I trust an autonomous vehicle') [57, 62, 114]. Although trust is a complex construct and its determinants require further research, social media offers opportunities to influence consumers' trust. Since social media represents a way to enhance social relationships between users, it can also be used to build trusting relationships between consumers and brands [24]. There are already various examples of firms presenting themselves on social media in a more personal manner than they used to. For example, companies employ social media managers who engage in discussions with users and humanize the firm from a con-sumer perspective. These consumer-firm interactions can lead to positive relationships, ultimately enhancing consumers' trust in the firm.

7 Conclusion

Technology firms face a recurring challenge of promoting the consumer adoption of their innovations. To meet this challenge successfully, this article has shown that it is promising to expand traditional communication channels with the new opportunities offered by social media. In sum, this study offers four main contributions. First, it illustrates which determinants of innovation adoption can be generally influenced by communication efforts, and how this can be done. Second, it helps us to understand how the changed communication mechanisms of social media can be used to promote the adoption of technological innovations. Third, it contributes to the growing body of literature in social media research, by transferring established theories of technology and innovation adoption to the field of social media, with the aim of clarifying the usefulness of social media from a marketing perspective. Fourth, the findings of this study help practitioners who focus on marketing technological innovations to review their communication approaches with regard to the optimal use of traditional and social media communication channels.

In spite of its contributions, the article clearly illustrates that future research is needed to enhance the understanding of how to promote technological innovations. On the one hand, further research should focus on how messages can be designed to shape consumer perceptions in an optimal way, regardless of the communication channel. For example, because of the complexity of technological innovations, there needs to be research that examines what level of technical complexity in a message is most effective under what circumstances. On the other hand, further research should investigate how companies should use social media to promote their innovations. For example, studies could examine which brand post appeals are best suited to affect consumer attitudes in the context of technological innovations. Against this background, the present article should be understood as opening the door to future research in the interesting field of innovation adoption and social media.

References

1. Castellion, G., Markham, S.K.: Perspective: new product failure rates: Influence of Argumentum ad populum and self-interest. J. Prod. Innov. Manag. **30**, 976–979 (2013)
2. van der Panne, G., van Beers, C., Kleinknecht, A.: Success and failure of innovation: a literature review. Int. J. Innov. Manag. **7**, 309–338 (2003)
3. Gourville, J.T.: Eager sellers stony buyers: understanding the psychology of new-product adoption. Harvard Bus. Rev. **84**, 98–106 (2006)
4. Venkatesh, V., Thong, J.Y.L., Xu, X.: Consumer acceptance and use of information technology: extending the unified theory. MIS Q. **36**, 157–178 (2012)
5. Srinivasan, R., Lilien, G.L., Rangaswamy, A.: Technological opportunism and radical technology adoption: an application to e-business. J. Mark. **66**, 47–60 (2002)
6. Delre, S.A., Jager, W., Bijmolt, T.H.A., Janssen, M.A.: Will it spread or not? The effects of social influences and network topology on innovation diffusion. J. Prod. Innov. Manag. **27**, 267–282 (2010)
7. Midgley, D.F.: Innovation and New Product Marketing. Croom Helm, London (1977)
8. Mohr, J.J., Sarin, S.: Drucker's insights on market orientation and innovation: Implications for emerging areas in high-technology marketing. J. Acad. Mark. Sci. **37**, 85–96 (2009)
9. Slater, S.F., Mohr, J.J., Sengupta, S.: Radical product innovation capability: literature review, synthesis, and illustrative research propositions. J. Prod. Innov. Manag. **31**, 552–566 (2014)
10. Ram, S., Sheth, J.N.: Consumer resistance to innovations: the marketing problem and its solutions. J. Consum. Mark. **6**, 5–14 (1989)
11. Risselada, H., Verhoef, P.C., Bijmolt, T.H.A.: Dynamic effects of social influence and direct marketing on the adoption of high-technology products. J. Mark. **78**, 52–68 (2014)
12. Rogers, E.M.: Diffusion of Innovations, 5th edn. The Free Press, New York (2003)
13. Baccarella, C.V., Scheiner, C.W., Trefzger, T.F., Voigt, K.-I.: Communicating high-tech products – a comparison between print advertisements of automotive premium and standard brands. Int. J. Technol. Mark. **11**, 24–38 (2016)
14. El Houssi, A.A., Morel, K.P.N., Hultink, E.J.: Effectively communicating new product benefits to consumers: the use of analogy versus literal similarity. Adv. Consum. Res. **32**, 554–559 (2005)
15. Feiereisen, S., Wong, V., Broderick, A.J.: Analogies and mental simulations in learning for really new products: the role of visual attention. J. Prod. Innov. Manag. **25**, 593–607 (2008)
16. Higgins, S.H., Shanklin, W.L.: Seeking mass market acceptance for high-technology consumer products. J. Consum. Mark. **9**, 5–14 (1992)

17. Prins, R., Verhoef, P.C.: Marketing communication drivers of adoption timing of a new e-service. J. Mark. **71**, 169–183 (2007)
18. Talke, K., Snelders, D.: Information in launch messages: stimulating the adoption of new high-tech consumer products. J. Prod. Innov. Manag. **30**, 732–749 (2013)
19. Eismann, T.T., Wagner, T.F., Baccarella, C.V., Voigt, K.-I.: Untangling social media excellence: five typical patterns of super successful posts. In: Proceedings of the 16th International Marketing Trends Conference, pp. 727–735 (2017)
20. Kohli, C., Suri, R., Kapoor, A.: Will social media kill branding? Bus. Horiz. **58**, 35–44 (2015)
21. Trefzger, T.F., Baccarella, C.V., Scheiner, C.W., Voigt, K.-I.: Hold the line! The challenge of being a premium brand in the social media era. In: Meiselwitz, G. (ed.) SCSM 2016. LNCS, vol. 9742, pp. 461–471. Springer, Cham (2016). doi:10.1007/978-3-319-39910-2_43
22. Patterson, A.: Social-networkers of the world, unite and take over: a meta-introspective perspective on the Facebook brand. J. Bus. Res. **65**, 527–534 (2012)
23. Einwiller, S.A., Steilen, S.: Handling complaints on social network sites - an analysis of complaints and complaint responses on Facebook and Twitter pages of large US companies. Publ. Relat. Rev. **41**, 195–204 (2015)
24. Hennig-Thurau, T., Malthouse, E.C., Friege, C., Gensler, S., Lobschat, L., Rangaswamy, A., et al.: The impact of new media on customer relationships. J. Serv. Res. **13**, 311–330 (2010)
25. Bruhn, M., Schoenmueller, V., Schäfer, D.B.: Are social media replacing traditional media in terms of brand equity creation? Manag. Res. Rev. **35**, 770–790 (2012)
26. Kane, G., Labianca, G., Borgatti, S.P.: What's different about social media networks? A framework and research agenda. MIS Q. **38**, 275–304 (2014)
27. John, G., Weiss, A.M., Dutta, S.: Marketing in technology-intensive markets: toward a conceptual framework. J. Mark. **63**, 78–91 (1999)
28. Moriarty, R.T., Kosnik, T.J.: High-tech-marketing: concepts, continuity, and change. Sloan Manag. Rev. **30**, 7–17 (1989)
29. Voigt, K.-I.: Industrielles Management - Industriebetriebslehre aus prozessorientierter Sicht. Springer, Berlin (2008)
30. Gardner, D.M., Johnson, F., Lee, M., Wilkinson, I.: A contingency approach to marketing high technology products. Eur. J. Mark. **34**, 1053–1077 (2000)
31. Garcia, R., Bardhi, F., Friedrich, C.: Overcoming consumer resistance to innovation. MIT Sloan Manag. Rev. **48**, 82–88 (2007)
32. Moriarty, R.T., Kosnik, T.J.: High-Tech vs. Low Tech Marketing: Where's the Beef?. Harvard Business School Publish, Boston (1987)
33. Hoeffler, S.: Measuring preferences for really new products. J. Mark. Res. **40**, 406–420 (2003)
34. Garcia, R., Calantone, R.: A critical look at technological innovation typology and innovativeness terminology: a literature review. J. Prod. Innov. Manag. **19**, 110–132 (2002)
35. Dewar, R.D., Dutton, J.E.: The adoption of radical and incremental innovations: an empirical analysis. Manag. Sci. **32**, 1422–1433 (1986)
36. Hirunyawipada, T., Paswan, A.K.: Consumer innovativeness and perceived risk: implications for high technology product adoption. J. Consum. Mark. **23**, 182–198 (2006)
37. Ellen, P., Bearden, W., Sharma, S.: Resistance to technological innovations: an examination of the role of self-efficacy and performance satisfaction. J. Acad. Mark. Sci. **19**, 297–307 (1991)
38. Ram, S.: A model of innovation resistance. Adv. Consum. Res. **14**, 208–212 (1987)
39. Bagozzi, R.P., Lee, K.-H.: Consumer resistance to, and acceptance of, innovations. Adv. Consum. Res. **26**, 218–225 (1999)

40. Heidenreich, S., Kraemer, T.: Innovations - doomed to fail? Investigating strategies to overcome passive innovation resistance. J. Prod. Innov. Manag. **33**, 277–297 (2016)

41. Hoehle, H., Scornavacca, E., Huff, S.: Three decades of research on consumer adoption and utilization of electronic banking channels: a literature analysis. Decis. Support Syst. **54**, 122–132 (2012)

42. Schepers, J., Wetzels, M.: A meta-analysis of the technology acceptance model: investigating subjective norm and moderation effects. Inf. Manag. **44**, 90–103 (2007)

43. Venkatesh, V., Morris, M.G., Davis, G.B., Davis, F.D.: User acceptance of information technology: toward a unified view. MIS Q. **27**, 425–478 (2003)

44. Rogers, E.M.: Diffusion of Innovations, 1st edn. The Free Press, New York (1962)

45. Fishbein, M., Ajzen, I.: Belief, Attitude, Intention, and Behavior: An Introduction to Theory and Research. Addison-Wesley, Reading (1975)

46. Ajzen, I.: The theory of planned behavior. Organ. Behav. Hum. Decis. Process. **50**, 179–211 (1991)

47. Venkatesh, V., Davis, F.D.: A theoretical extension of the technology acceptance model: four longitudinal field studies. Manag. Sci. **46**, 186–204 (2000)

48. Davis, F.D.: Perceived usefulness, perceived ease of use, and user acceptance of information technology. MIS Q. **13**, 319–339 (1989)

49. Karahanna, E., Agarwal, R., Angst, C.M.: Reconceptualizing compatibility beliefs in technology acceptance research. MIS Q. **30**, 781–804 (2006)

50. Kulviwat, S., Bruner, G.C., Al-Shuridah, O.: The role of social influence on adoption of high tech innovations: the moderating effect of public/private consumption. J. Bus. Res. **62**, 706–712 (2009)

51. Sun, H.: A longitudinal study of herd behavior in the adoption and continued use of technology. MIS Q. **37**, 1013–1041 (2013)

52. Demangeot, C., Broderick, A.J.: Consumer perceptions of online shopping environments. J. Bus. Res. **30**, 461–469 (2010)

53. Mehrabian, A., Russel, J.A.: An Approach to Environmental Psychology. MIT Press, Cambridge (1974)

54. Beaudry, A., Pinsonneault, A.: The other side of acceptance: studying the direct and indirect effects of emotions on information technology use. MIS Q. **34**, 689–710 (2010)

55. Turel, O., Serenko, A., Bontis, N.: User acceptance of hedonic digital artifacts: a theory of consumption values perspective. Inf. Manag. **47**, 53–59 (2010)

56. Limayem, M., Hirt, S.G., Cheung, C.M.K.: How habit limits the predictive power of intention: the case of information systems continuance. MIS Q. **31**, 705–737 (2007)

57. Choi, J.K., Ji, Y.G.: Investigating the importance of trust on adopting an autonomous vehicle. Int. J. Hum.-Comput. Interact. **31**, 692–702 (2015)

58. Lippert, S.K., Davis, M.: A conceptual model integrating trust into planned change activities to enhance technology adoption behavior. J. Inf. Sci. **32**, 434–448 (2006)

59. Miltgen, C.L., Popovič, A., Oliveira, T.: Determinants of end-user acceptance of biometrics: integrating the "big 3" of technology acceptance with privacy context. Decis. Support Syst. **56**, 103–114 (2013)

60. Wu, K., Zhao, Y., Zhu, Q., Tan, X., Zheng, H.: A meta-analysis of the impact of trust on technology acceptance model: investigation of moderating influence of subject and context type. Int. J. Inf. Manag. **31**, 572–581 (2011)

61. Mayer, R.C., Davis, J.H., Schoorman, F.D.: An integrative model of organizational trust. Acad. Manag. Rev. **20**, 709–734 (1995)

62. Gefen, D., Karahanna, E., Straub, D.W.: Trust and TAM in online shopping: an integrated model. MIS Q. **27**, 51–90 (2003)

63. Arndt, J.: A test of the two-step flow in diffusion of a new product. Journal. Mass Commun. Q. **45**, 457–465 (1968)
64. Lazarsfeld, P.E., Berelson, B., Gaudet, H.: The People's Choice, 2nd edn. Columbia University Press, New York (1948)
65. Lazarsfeld, P.E., Menzel, H.: Mass media and personal influence. In: Schramm, W. (ed.) The Science of Human Communication. Basic Books, New York (1963)
66. Deutsch, M., Gerard, H.B.: A study of normative and informational social influences upon individual judgement. J. Abnorm. Soc. Psychol. **51**, 629–636 (1955)
67. Burnkrant, R.E., Cousineau, A.: Informational and normative social influence in buyer behavior. J. Consum. Res. **2**, 206–215 (1975)
68. Cialdini, R.B., Goldstein, N.J.: Social influence: compliance and conformity. Annu. Rev. Psychol. **55**, 591–621 (2004)
69. Bandura, A.: Social Learning Theory. Prentice-Hall, Englewood Cliffs (1977)
70. Zhao, M., Hoeffler, S., Zauberman, G.: Mental simulation and product evaluation: the affective and cognitive dimensions of process versus outcome simulation. J. Mark. Res. **48**, 827–839 (2011)
71. Baccarella, C.V., Scheiner, C.W., Trefzger, T.F., Voigt, K.-I.: High-tech marketing communication in the automotive industry: a content analysis of print advertisements. Int. J. Bus. Environ. **6**, 395–410 (2014)
72. Kumar, A., Bezawada, R., Rishika, R., Janakiraman, R., Kannan, P.K.: From social to sale: the effects of firm generated content in social media on customer behavior. J. Mark. **80**, 7–25 (2016)
73. eMarketer. Social Network Ad Spending Worldwide (2015). https://www.emarketer.com/Article/Social-Network-Ad-Spending-Hit-2368-Billion-Worldwide-2015/1012357. Accessed 5 Jan 2017
74. Statista. Social network advertising revenue from 2014 to 2017 (2017). https://www.statista.com/statistics/271406/advertising-revenue-of-social-networks-worldwide/. Accessed 5 Jan 2017
75. Mangold, W.G., Faulds, D.J.: Social media: the new hybrid element of the promotion mix. Bus. Horiz. **52**, 357–365 (2009)
76. Naylor, R.W., Lamberton, C.P., West, P.M.: Beyond the "like" button: the impact of mere virtual presence on brand evaluations and purchase intentions in social media settings. J. Mark. **76**, 105–120 (2012)
77. Stephen, A.T., Galak, J.: The effects of traditional and social earned media on sales: a study of a microlending marketplace. J. Mark. Res. **49**, 624–639 (2012)
78. Tirunillai, S., Tellis, G.J.: Does chatter really matter? Dynamics of user-generated content and stock performance. Mark. Sci. **31**, 198–215 (2012)
79. Richins, M.L., Root-Schaffer, T.: The role of involvement and opinion leadership in consumer word-of-mouth: an implicit model made explicit. Adv. Consum. Res. **15**, 32–36 (1988)
80. Cheung, C., Lee, M.K.O.: What drives consumers to spread electronic word of mouth in online consumer-opinion platforms. Decis. Support Syst. **53**, 218–225 (2012)
81. Hennig-Thurau, T., Gwinner, K.P., Walsh, G.: Electronic word-of-mouth via consumer-opinion platforms: what motivates consumers to articulate themselves on the internet? J. Interact. Mark. **18**, 38–52 (2004)
82. Trusov, M., Bucklin, R.E., Pauwels, K.: Effects of word-of-mouth versus traditional marketing: findings from an internet social networking site. J. Mark. **73**, 90–102 (2009)
83. You, Y., Vadakkepatt, G.G., Joshi, A.M.: A meta-analysis of electronic word-of-mouth elasticity. J. Mark. **79**, 19–39 (2015)

84. Foux, G.: Consumer-generated media: get your customers involved. Brand Strategy **8**, 38–39 (2006)

85. Akdeniz, M.B., Calantone, R.J., Voorhees, C.M.: Signaling quality: an examination of the effects of marketing- and nonmarketing-controlled signals on perceptions of automotive brand quality. J. Prod. Innov. Manag. **31**, 728–743 (2014)

86. Pfeffer, J., Zorbach, T., Carley, K.M.: Understanding online firestorms: negative word-of-mouth dynamics in social media networks. J. Mark. Commun. **20**, 117–128 (2014)

87. Schweidel, D.A., Moe, W.W.: Listening in on social media: a joint model of sentiment and venue format choice. J. Mark. Res. **51**, 387–402 (2014)

88. de Vries, N.J., Carlson, J.: Examining the drivers and brand performance implications of customer engagement with brands in the social media environment. J. Brand Manag. **21**, 495–515 (2014)

89. de Vries, L., Gensler, S., Leeflang, P.S.H.: Popularity of brand posts on brand fan pages: an investigation of the effects of social media marketing. J. Interact. Mark. **26**, 83–91 (2012)

90. Cvijikj, P.I., Michahelles, F.: Online engagement factors on Facebook brand pages. Soc. Netw. Anal. Min. **3**, 843–861 (2013)

91. Jahn, B., Kunz, W.: How to transform consumers into fans of your brand. J. Serv. Manag. **19**, 482–492 (2012)

92. Madupu, V., Cooley, D.O.: Antecedents and consequences of online brand community participation: a conceptual framework. J. Internet Commer. **9**, 127–147 (2010)

93. Park, N., Kee, K.F., Valenzuela, S.: Being immersed in social networking environment: Facebook groups, uses and gratifications, and social outcomes. CyberPsychology Behav. **12**, 729–733 (2009)

94. Gordon, R.: Creating community-connection experiences. In: Peck, A., Malthouse, E. (eds.) Medill on Media Engagement. Hampton Press, Cresskill (2010)

95. Libai, B., Bolton, R., Bugel, M.S., de Ruyter, K., Gotz, O., Risselada, H., et al.: Customer-to-customer interactions: broadening the scope of word of mouth research. J. Serv. Res. **13**, 267–282 (2010)

96. Trefzger, T.F., Baccarella, C.V., Voigt, K.-I.: Antecedents of brand post popularity in Facebook: the influence of images, videos, and text. In: Proceedings of the 15th International Marketing Trends Conference, pp. 1–8 (2016)

97. Booth, N., Matic, J.A.: Mapping and leveraging influencers in social media to shape corporate brand perceptions. Corp. Commun.: Int. J. **16**, 184–191 (2011)

98. Halvorsen, K., Hoffmann, J., Coste-Manière, I., Stankeviciute, R.: Can fashion blogs function as a marketing tool to influence consumer behavior? Evidence from Norway. J. Glob. Fashion Mark. **4**, 211–224 (2013)

99. Katona, Z.: How to Identify Influence Leaders in Social Media (2012). https://www.bloomberg.com/view/articles/2012-02-27/how-to-identify-influence-leaders-in-social-media-zsolt-katona. Accessed 22 Jan 2017

100. Kretz, G., de Valck, K.: "Pixelize me!": digital storytelling and the creation of archetypal myths through explicit and implicit self-brand association in fashion and luxury blogs. In: Belk, R.W. (ed.) Research in Consumer Behavior, pp. 313–329. Emerald Group Publishing Limited, Bingley (2010)

101. YouTube. iPhone 7 Unboxing: Jet Black vs Matte Black! (Video by Marques Brownlee) (2017). https://www.youtube.com/watch?v=J5HtSy5bATk. Accessed 13 Jan 2017

102. Chevalier, J.A., Mayzlin, D.: The effect of word of mouth on sales: online book reviews. J. Mark. Res. **43**, 345–354 (2006)

103. Chintagunta, P.K., Gopinath, S., Venkataraman, S.: The effects of online user reviews on movie box office performance: accounting for sequential rollout and aggregation across local markets. Mark. Sci. **29**, 944–957 (2010)

104. Cui, G., Lui, H.-K., Guo, X.: The effect of online consumer reviews on new product sales. Int. J. Electron. Commer. **17**, 39–57 (2012)
105. Floyd, K., Freling, R., Alhoqail, S., Cho, H.Y., Freling, T.: How online product reviews affect retail sales: a meta-analysis. J. Retail. **90**, 217–232 (2014)
106. Forman, C., Ghose, A., Wiesenfeld, B.: Examining the relationship between reviews and sales: the role of reviewer identity disclosure in electronic markets. Inf. Syst. Res. **19**, 291–313 (2008)
107. Ho-Dac, N.N., Carson, S.J., Moore, W.L.: The effects of positive and negative online customer reviews: do brand strength and category maturity matter? J. Mark. **77**, 37–53 (2013)
108. Marchand, A., Hennig-Thurau, T., Wiertz, C.: Not all digital word of mouth is created equal: understanding the respective impact of consumer reviews and microblogs on new product success. Int. J. Res. Mark. **34** (2017, forthcoming)
109. YouTube. Tutorial - Excel 2010 - 10 Things you must know (Video by Ilan Patao) (2017). https://www.youtube.com/watch?v=-SnBlC_1tSk. Accessed 13 Jan 2017
110. YouTube. Laptop Hardware Repair (Video by Eli the Computer Guy) (2017). https://www.youtube.com/watch?v=UKMEzrP14W4. Accessed 13 Jan 2017
111. Luo, M.M., Chea, S., Chen, J.S.: Web-based information service adoption: a comparison of the motivational model and the uses and gratifications theory. Decis. Support Syst. **51**, 21–30 (2011)
112. Ha, S., Stoel, L.: Consumer e-shopping acceptance: antecedents in a technology acceptance model. J. Bus. Res. **62**, 565–571 (2009)
113. Chaudhuri, A., Hoibrook, M.B.: The chain of effects from brand trust and brand affect to brand performance: the role of brand loyalty. J. Mark. **65**, 81–93 (2001)
114. Pavlou, P.A.: Consumer acceptance of electronic commerce: integrating trust and risk with the technology acceptance model. Int. J. Electron. Commer. **7**, 101–134 (2003)

Understanding the Gift-Sending Interaction on Live-Streaming Video Websites

Zhenhui Zhu[✉], Zhi Yang, and Yafei Dai

Institute of Network Computing and Information Systems,
Peking University, Beijing, China
zhenhui_zhu@pku.edu.cn, {yangzhi,dyf}@net.pku.edu.cn

Abstract. A new format of online videos called live-streaming videos gains its popularity day by day. The idea of watching what a streamer is doing and interacting with him/her attracts a lot of users and leads to the boom of live-streaming websites in the world. This study investigates the live-streaming website and the gift-sending interaction on it, using data crawled from one of the biggest live-streaming websites in China-Douyu.com. Our result shows the distributions of gifts and senders are very skewed, most gifts are bought by a small number of viewers and most gifts are received by a small number of channels. Meanwhile, more viewers and more time spent on a channel usually leads to more profit. Seeing others sending gifts also makes one viewer more likely send gifts. Some future research aspects are discussed.

Keywords: Live-streaming website · Channels · Streams · Gift-sending interaction · Power-law

1 Introduction

Watching online videos is a big entertainment in people's lives these days. The huge success of YouTube and some other online video websites shows people have great interest in watching these fun, UGC videos. A number of online video websites are founded during the last decade, and to attract viewers and seek success, new features are introduced.

In 2007, Justin Kan founded Justin.tv. He first broadcasted his life 24/7 in this website, which led to the success of Justin.tv and even popularized the term lifecasting [1]. Since then, live-streaming websites arose all around the world and gained their popularity day by day.

Twitch.tv, which is an online video website focuses on live-streaming game videos also founded by Justin Kan, now ranks 77th popular among all websites worldwide by Alexa.

In China, hundreds to thousands new live-streaming websites and applications emerged in the last two to three years, making year 2016 "the Year of live-streaming" in China. Any events from the streamer's life to outdoor activities to commercial events can be broadcasted. Right after the 2016 summer Olympics in Brazil, the famous Chinese swimming athlete Yuanhui Fu's live-streaming attracted over ten million viewers online.

G. Meiselwitz (Ed.): SCSM 2017, Part I, LNCS 10282, pp. 274–285, 2017.
DOI: 10.1007/978-3-319-58559-8_23

Seeing the heat of live-streaming websites, the academic world is interested in this phenomenon and many studies are done to seek the understanding of the user behavior, the feeling and benefits of watching these videos.

Kaytoue et al. [2] did a study on video game live streaming on Twitch.tv. He researched the audience, stream and streamer characteristics and studied how to predict the popularity of streams. Deng et al. [3] made a detailed research on the games played on Twitch, their features, channel and viewer distribution among different games and the impact of tournaments. Pires and Simon [4] compared the stream features of Twitch and YouTube. Hamilton [5] investigated how live streaming fosters participation and community. Nascimento et al. [6] and Edge [7] studied the community of live-streaming websites.

Though live-streaming websites are new, virtual gifts already exist for some time. Goode et al. [8] studied the virtual gifts in virtual world and concluded sending gifts enhances users' social status. Yang et al. [9] researched the connection between virtual gifts and interpersonal influence. Greenberg [10] put forward a possible technique for introducing virtual gift sending interaction into online live car racing games.

Despite the fact there are lots of research on the above topics, as far as we know, little has been done on the gift-sending interaction on live-streaming websites. Tough in fact virtual gifts have been the top earner in Chinese live-streaming markets [11].

In this paper, we present our findings on the website and the gift-sending interaction, an activity viewers interact with streamers and a way these websites earn profits. We did our experiment using the data of one of the most popular live-streaming websites in China-Douyu.com.

The rest of the paper is organized as follow. In Sect. 2, we introduce the background of Douyu.com, the origin of gift-sending interaction and the dataset we use. We get some basic information of Douyu.com in Sect. 3 and investigate gift-sending interaction in Sect. 4. In Sect. 5, we discuss future research aspects. The conclusion is in Sect. 6.

2   Background and Research Data

Founded in 2014, Douyu.com is now one of the biggest online live-streaming websites in China, ranks 288th popular in the world and 42nd popular in China by Alexa rank. It has on average over 7 million UV and over 66 million PV a day. It is a comprehensive live-streaming website, the broadcasted content includes computer games, outdoor activities, people's daily lives, singing and dancing, popular stars and commercial events. Among them computer games occupy a very big proportion.

People who broadcast are called streamers or broadcasters, every streamer has a single web page in this website named channel, those who watch these channels are viewers.

A typical page of a channel on Douyu.com is shown in Fig. 1. This page has the streamer's information, the content he is broadcasting, and gifts viewers can buy. The right side text part is viewers' chat messages. Most live-streaming websites' channel pages are alike. For those websites do not have gift functions like Twitch, the only difference is Twitch pages do not have the bottom gifts options and thus do not have gifts information on the screen.

Screen   Gifts Chat messages

Fig. 1. A typical channel page in Douyu.com

Now it naturally comes to the question: How does gift-sending interaction originate?

Virtual gifts are used by some live-streaming websites to gain profit. When a gift is bought and sent, the streamer and the website share its profit. Gifts all have their prices, usually ranging from 0.1 RMB to 500 RMB (we leave out gifts which users can get for free and the money unit in this paper is RMB).

Virtual gifts are extension to chat messages in live-streaming websites. When a gift is sent, the system lists this gift's information on the right text part of the channel. All viewers in this channel can see this. If the gift has a high value, for example, 100 RMB or higher, the system even projects the gift's icon directly on the left screen part. The higher the gift value, the more complex and vivid the icon.

This gives viewers a new way they interact with streamers. In traditional live-streaming websites like Twitch, there are few ways to distinguish viewers. But with these gifts, rich viewers accumulate their "fame" and level in this channel. The system lists top gift senders' information in the text part and welcomes them when they enter the channel, which makes them outstands, both in the streamer's eyes and other viewers' eyes.

Dataset. We crawled data of Douyu.com from 2016 Dec.17 to Dec.30. The dataset contains two kinds of data. One is about the global information of this website. We crawled the whole website's opening channels' data, including channel number, viewer number and channel type, every 10 min for a 14-day period. The other is one hundred popular channels' detail data for 14 days. In every channel, every gift type id, the sender's id, the timestamp (detail to minute) are recorded.

3   Basic Information About Douyu.com

We decide to get some basic information about Douyu.com before digging into the gift-sending interaction on it. In this section, we use the dataset of a fourteen-day continuous data of all the channels' information on Douyu.com to do the study.

The Channel Number. Here we conclude some basic information of the channel number in this website in Table 1.

Table 1. Channel number information

Mean channel number in a day	35989
Mean channel number in a snapshot	5984
Minimum channel number in a snapshot	1939
Maximum channel number in a snapshot	11538
Unique channels in the dataset	149424

Though on average there are 35989 unique opening channels in a day on Douyu. com, the opening channel number in any snapshot is not that high. It varies between 1939 and 11538. On average about 5984 channels are open in the same time.

Opening Pattern. In Fig. 2, we show the relation about channels' opening pattern. We see about 63% of 149424 channels open no more than one day a week on average, only 14% channels open at least half the days in dataset. Most channels do not broadcast streams frequently. But there are about 4% of them open every day.

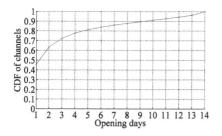

Fig. 2. CDF of channels by opening days   **Fig. 3.** CDF of streams by duration

Duration of Streams. In this part, we focus on the streams in the channels, instead of channels themselves. If a channel opens a piece of continuous time then stops, for example an hour, we call it a stream or a session. A single channel can have several streams in a single day as long as the streamer takes break during these streams. Using streams here is better than channel itself because we can observe how streamers choose to open and stop their live-streaming videos.

The distribution of stream duration is in Fig. 3. There are 686086 streams in the two-week dataset. Since our snapshot is every 10 min, whenever we see a channel in the dataset, we take it as having been opened for 10 min.

From Fig. 3 we can see the median of stream duration is 90 min. It is longer than the 45 min median time of stream in Twitch [2]. That's because unlike Twitch which focuses on games, Douyu.com is a more comprehensive website. Many channels broadcast already-made videos or big events, that raises the duration of streams.

Besides the 45 min median, over 70% streams are shorter than 200 min. The lasting time of most streams is no longer than 4 h, because the streamers need rest.

Changing Pattern of Channel and Viewer Number During a Day. From Table 1 we learn the channel number in Douyu.com varies during the time. So here we plot channel number and viewer number[1] to see this pattern. Fourteen-day data is averaged into 24 h in Fig. 4.

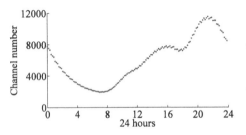
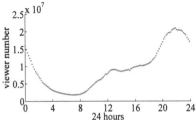

Fig. 4. Channel number changing pattern   **Fig. 5.** Viewer number changing pattern

The opening channel number shows a clear varying pattern in Fig. 4. It becomes lowest in early morning around 7 am, then gets higher. There is a small peak in around 16 pm in the afternoon, a small drop follows this peak during dinner time then the number becomes higher again, reaching the peak in 9–10 pm. The total viewer number information is in Fig. 5. It is in consistence with this varying pattern, the only difference is the small peak in the afternoon is a little earlier than streamers do.

Kaytoue et al. [2] also found the viewer count in a day on Twitch has two peaks. He owed these two peaks to different users from Europe and America. We agree with his findings on Twitch since its two peaks are more alike. But considering Douyu.com's viewers are mainly from mainland China and the two peaks are not quite the same in quantity, we think the two peaks in Douyu.com maybe just because many people have free time in the afternoon in China.

Channel Types, Viewer Types and Their Proportions. Douyu.com labels different channels according to their contents. There are five big categories defined by Douyu.

---

[1] To show the heat of a channel and attract viewers, Douyu.com sometimes exaggerates the viewer number by a multiplier. So the exact viewer number we crawled may not be precise, see the changing trend instead of exact number.

com: PC Games, Mobile Games, Entertainment & Activities (including sing, dancing, music, outdoor activities, comics and so on), Technology and Art & Sports (including educational videos, old movies, sports and so on).

These five categories occupy about 80% of the total videos in Douyu.com. Their proportion is in Table 2. Under these categories, there are smaller types of channels, like League of legends or DOTA2 in PC Games, music or fashion in Entertainment & Activities. We also list top 10 popular types and their proportions in Table 3.

In Table 2, PC Game channels do occupy a big proportion in this website, over 50%. This is one big feature how Douyu.com earns its original fame. Now many other contents like Entertainment & Activities and Art & Sports have their cakes too.

Table 2. Channel categories and proportion

PC Game	51.25%
Art & Sports	11.62%
Entertainment & Activities	11.44%
Mobile Game	6.06%
Technology	2.57%
Others	17.06%

Table 3. Top 10 channel Types (*means game)

By channel number		By viewer number	
League of Legends*	22.15%	League of Legends*	29.95%
Movie & TV	7.98%	Single Player Games*	7.30%
Single Player Games*	7.48%	Hearthstone*	4.84%
War of Warcraft*	3.74%	DOTA2*	4.22%
Overwatch*	3.66%	Movie & TV	3.90%
Beauties	3.56%	Outdoor Activities	3.82%
DNF*	2.69%	Beauties	3.63%
Sports	2.30%	Overwatch*	3.53%
Glory of the king*	1.98%	Onmyoji*	3.42%
Old games*	1.90%	Glory of the king*	3.00%

In the top 10 channel types by channel number, seven of them are games, among them Glory of the king is a mobile game. Movie & TV and Sports are from Art & Sports. Beauties is from Entertainment & Activities. This definitely shows Douyu.com is a comprehensive live-streaming website.

In Table 3 we also show the top 10 channel types that attract the most viewers. Six of them are in the top 10 channel types by channel number. Despite the fact the channel numbers of Outdoor Activities, DOTA2 and Hearthstone rank 11th, 12th, 13th, their viewer numbers are in the top 10. Mobile game Onmyoji is a new game released on 2016 September. It doesn't have many channels, only ranked 26th, but have a big number of viewers because of its popularity.

4 Gift-Sending Interaction Study

Unlike Twitch, which uses subscription, stickers and advertisements to help streamers and website earn money, gifts are widely used in many Chinese live-streaming websites to gain profit. In 2016, Greenberg [10] proposed a technique that viewers can send gifts as a game resource in online car racing games. This proposed technique has some similarity, but not quite the same as the widely used gift service in Chinese live-streaming websites. Up to now, little experiment about virtual gifts is done in real live-streaming websites.

In this part, we study the gift-sending interaction in Douyu.com. We propose several research questions, demonstrate their research methods and results in this section.

Q1: How do viewers choose between different gifts?
In Sect. 2 we have described the origin and price features of gifts. Virtual gifts are used by live-streaming websites to gain profit. When a virtual gift is bought and sent to a channel, its value is shared by the website and the streamer.

Here we want to answer the question about how do people choose between cheap or expensive gifts? What is the consumed amount of each gift type? What is the total value of these gifts?

To answer that, we listed some basic information of gifts in Table 4. Douyu.com has a number of gift types[2], some are available for all channels and some are special designed for typical channel types. Here for simplicity we only listed five specific gifts that are common for all channels, since they occupied 97.2% of the total gift value in the dataset.

From Table 4 we can observe the distributions of gifts and senders are very skewed, even severer than the well-known "80/20" rule. The consumed number of high-value gifts is much smaller than that for cheap-value gifts, but they occupy a high

Table 4. Gifts and their purchase details

Gift name	Price (RMB)	Consumed number	Accumulative unique senders (proportion)	Total gift value	Gift value proportion (accumulative)
Rocket	500	286	152 (0.5%)	143000	51.5% (51.5%)
Plane	100	749	510 (1.8%)	74900	27.0% (78.4%)
666	6	823	760 (2.7%)	4938	1.8% (80.2%)
Weak	0.2	118153	15669 (56.2%)	23630.6	8.5% (88.7%)
Like	0.1	236721	26641 (95.5%)	23672.1	8.5% (97.2%)
Others	N/A	N/A	27887 (100%)	7758.4	2.8% (100%)
Summary	N/A	N/A	27887 (100%)	277899.1	100%

---

[2] During festivals like Christmas when we crawled the data, douyu.com also changed the gift pictures and names to celebrate festival (like "rocket" to "Christmas rocket"). Since gifts' prices and functions are same, we treated them equally as normal times.

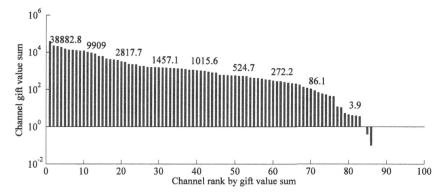

Fig. 6. 100 channels' gift value sum

proportion of the total gift value. And it is noteworthy about 80.2% of the total gift value are generated by only 2.7% of the total consumers. When sending gifts, the majority viewers only buy cheap gifts while the majority profit comes from minority viewers.

Q2: How does the gift-sending interaction look like on a high level for channels?
After studying gifts on a viewer level, now we want to find out the high-level result of gift-sending interaction.

In the dataset we have 100 channels randomly chosen from top 1000 channels. We count their gift value sum to see this high level pattern. Result is in Fig. 6.

The Y-axis in Fig. 6 is the gift value sum of each channel and the X-axis is channels' rank by money. Only 86 channels get gifts out of the chosen 100. We also wrote the 1st, 11th, 21st, 31st...81st channel's gift value sum in Fig. 6. A power-law exists, indicating several most popular channels have the most valuable gifts, others share little.

Q3: What's the relationship between viewer number and gift value sum of a channel?
It is easy to think that both viewer number and the time they spend on a channel may have impacts on the final value of gifts they buy. So here we use "viewer appearance number" instead of average viewer number. All the viewer number of a channel in every 10-min snapshot are summed as the final viewer appearance number of a channel.

We plot gift value sum and viewer appearance number of every channel in Fig. 7. The 14 channels whose total gift value is 0 are removed and 86 channel's data are left.

It is easy to observe that though the absolute relation is volatile, in general gift value sum has increasing nature with the increment of the viewer appearance number.

We do a linear regression of log10(gift value sum) on log10(viewer appearance number) and the result is in Table 5. The coefficient is 0.6421, $p < 0.001$, generally speaking, the logarithmic value of gift value sum is positively correlated with the logarithmic value of viewer appearance number, so is their original value.

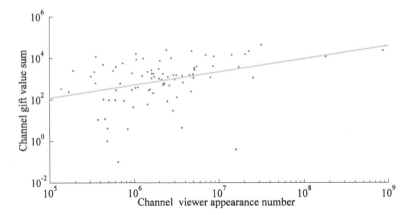

Fig. 7. Channel gift value sum and viewer appearance number

Generally speaking, if a channel attracts more viewers and let them spend more time on itself, it gets more gifts and earns more. Popularity is important for a streamer like any other industry. More fans, more benefits.

Table 5. Regression information of log10(gift value sum) on log10(viewer appearance number)

Coefficient	Intercept	P
0.6421	−1.1684	0.0006

Q4: Will other viewers' gift-sending behavior in the same channel stimulate viewers to send gifts?

We compute probability and conditional probability to study viewers' behavior in the 100 channels. The time unit is one minute. The probability for a viewer v_i sending gifts in a channel c is:

$$P(v_{i,c}) = \frac{n^c_{i,send}}{n^c_{open}} \tag{1}$$

where n^c_{open} is the total number of minutes channel c opens and $n^c_{i,send}$ is the total number of minutes viewer v_i sends at least one gift in channel c. Conditional probability for a viewer v_i sending gifts in a channel c is:

$$P\left(v_{i,c} \mid v_{j \neq i,c}\right) = \frac{n^c_{i,send'}}{n^c_{j,send}} \tag{2}$$

where $n^c_{j,send}$ is the total number of minutes having other viewers $v_{j,j \neq i}$ sending gifts, and $n^c_{i,send'}$ is the total number of minutes viewer v_i sends at least one gift in this minute later than other viewers do.

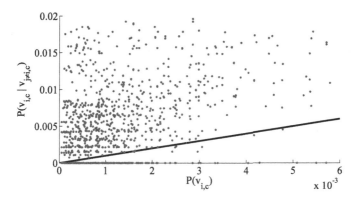

Fig. 8. Probability for sending gifts

We then plot each viewer's data in Fig. 8 where x-axis is $P(v_{i,c})$ and y-axis is $P(v_{i,c}|v_{j\neq i,c})$. We draw a point only when this viewer has sent a gift in this channel. 71.8% (20449 out of 28499) points are in the upper left part of Fig. 8, above y = x line, which indicates people's motivation for sending gifts is positively correlated with others' behavior. When seeing others sending gifts, they are more likely to do the same thing.

5   Discussion and Future Work

In this paper, we did research on live-streaming websites and the gift-sending interaction on it. Despite the fact we have a basic understanding of viewers and streamers' behavior in this website now, there are some parts that worth discussion.

First, our dataset only contains two weeks' data. This can give us a basic understanding about how viewers send gifts. But for more detailed research, a longer dataset period is better.

Second, live-streaming websites support Danmaku function, a function that projects users' comment directly and synchronously on the play screen. Danmaku function is studied in traditional video websites [12, 13], but not in live-streaming websites as far as we know. This can be a future study focus too.

Third, in the gift-sending interaction, we do experiments about what facts will stimulate viewers to send gifts, we think there may be other facts that worth future work. For example, in every channel, a viewer can accumulate "fame" and their user levels when buying and sending gifts, the streamers usually orally thank these viewers to show their gratification. Will this oral interaction satisfy users and stimulate them into sending gifts? Will the accumulated "fame" encourage them sending more gifts in the future? Will viewers behave differently in different types of channels? We think these all need future work.

Another aspect we think need more future research is the topology of the user following pattern. Most live-streaming websites have following systems, through which a user can follow other viewers to get their information. We are interested in this following system and crawled about thirty million users' following relationship data from Twich.tv in 2016 July. To our disappointment, the data shows the present relationship doesn't show much bi-directional interaction in it. The bi-link proportion is very low, roughly 1.09%, comparted to twitter's 22.1% [14]. Users in live-streaming websites like Twitch do not become friends. They just follow famous people. We think this topology phenomenon worth more research in the future.

6 Conclusion

In this paper, we present a study of live-streaming website and the gift-sending interaction in one famous website Douyu.com in China. To the best of our known, it is the first research that focuses on gift-sending interaction between streamers and viewers in real live-streaming website.

Our findings show the distributions of gifts and senders are very skewed in gift-sending phenomenon. Over 80% value of gifts are consumed by only 2.7% of viewers. And Several most popular channels get most gifts, others share little. Meanwhile, many facts have relations with the gift value sum. In general, if a channel attracts more viewers and let them spend more time on itself, it gets more gifts and earns more. Also, 71.8% viewers are likely to send gifts when they see others do, which shows stimulation is useful here.

References

1. Wikipedia page of Justin.tv. https://en.wikipedia.org/wiki/Justin.tv
2. Kaytoue, M., Silva, A., Cerf, L., Meira, W., Raïssi, C.: Watch me playing, I am a professional: a first study on video game live streaming. In: Proceedings of the 21st International Conference Companion on World Wide Web, pp. 1181–1188 (2012). doi:10.1145/2187980.2188259
3. Deng, J., Cuadrado, F., Tyson, G., Uhlig, S.: Behind the game: exploring the twitch streaming platform. In: Proceedings of the 2015 International Workshop on Network and Systems Support for Games (2015). doi:10.1109/NetGames.2015.7382994
4. Pires, K., Simon, G.: YouTube live and twitch: a tour of user-generated live streaming systems. In: Proceedings of the 6th ACM Multimedia Systems Conference, pp. 225–230 (2015). doi:10.1145/2713168.2713195
5. Hamilton, W.A., Garretson, O., Kerne, A.: Streaming on twitch: fostering participatory communities of play within live mixed media. In: Proceedings of the SIGCHI Conference on Human Factors in Computing Systems, pp. 1315–1324 (2014). doi:10.1145/2556288.2557048
6. Nascimento, G., Ribeiro, M., Cerf, L., Cesario, N., Kaytoue, M., Raissi, C., et al.: Modeling and analyzing the video game live-streaming community. In: Proceedings of the 2014 9th Latin American Web Congress, pp. 1–9 (2014). doi:10.1109/LAWeb.2014.9
7. Edge, N.: Evolution of the gaming experience: live video streaming and the emergence of a new web community. Elon J. Undergraduate Res. Commun. (2013)
8. Goode, S., Shailer, G., Wilson, M., Jankowski, J.: Gifting and status in virtual worlds. J. Manag. Inf. Syst (2014). doi:10.2753/MIS0742-1222310207

9. Yang, J., Ackerman, M.S., Adamic, L.A.: Virtual gifts and guanxi: supporting social exchange in a Chinese online community. In: Proceedings of the ACM 2011 Conference on Computer Supported Cooperative Work, pp. 45–54 (2011). doi:10.1145/1958824.1958832

10. Greenberg, J.: Interaction between audience and game players during live streaming of games. Technical Disclosure Commons (2016)

11. News about Virtual gifts in Chinese live-streaming markets. http://technode.com/2016/05/05/virtual-gifts-are-still-the-top-earner-in-chinas-live-video-streaming-market/

12. Chen, Y., Gao, Q., Rau, P.-L.P.: Understanding gratifications of watching danmaku videos – videos with overlaid comments. In: Rau, P.L.P. (ed.) CCD 2015. LNCS, vol. 9180, pp. 153–163. Springer, Cham (2015). doi:10.1007/978-3-319-20907-4_14

13. Liu, L., Suh, A., Wagner, C.: Investigating communal interactive video viewing experiences online. In: Kurosu, M. (ed.) HCI 2016. LNCS, vol. 9733, pp. 538–548. Springer, Cham (2016). doi:10.1007/978-3-319-39513-5_50

14. Kwak, H., Lee, C., Park, H., Moon, S.: What is Twitter, a social network or a news media? In: Proceedings of the 19th International Conference on World Wide Web, pp. 591–600 (2010). doi:10.1145/1772690.1772751

Social Issues in Social Media

Creating and Supporting Virtual Communities

A City that Happens on a Facebook Group

Andre O. Bueno$^{(\boxtimes)}$ and Junia C. Anacleto

Federal University of Sao Carlos, Sao Carlos, SP, Brazil
{andre.obueno,junia}@dc.ufscar.br

Abstract. During the last years, the number of Online Social Networks (OSNs) users has been growing in a fast pace. In this context, it is common for people to be part of virtual communities, which may range from neighbourhood communities to communities of an artist's fans. However, creating and managing successful municipal virtual communities remains a challenge. In this paper, we describe a five years experiment encompassing the creation and management of a virtual community of a Brazilian town with 21,400 inhabitants using the Facebook Groups Tool. Currently, the group has 14,132 members, which corresponds to 66% of the population. Since the beginning, we follow Scott Peck's theory of community building. As a result, we describe a number of strategies involving the creation and management of municipal virtual communities. Besides, we list some difficulties we faced because of the lack of support from Facebook Groups tool for this type of communities.

Keywords: Virtual community · Community · Online Social Network · Virtual community management · Municipal virtual community

1 Introduction

The number of social network users has been growing in a fast pace in the past years. Today, more than 31% of the world's population are social media active users [9]. By breaking geographical barriers through the use of the Internet, we are now talking more with people from other places and, hence, we talk less with people from our neighbourhood. Microsoft points out we are facing a growth of hyper-connectivity, i.e., we have never been so connected with each other as we are now [8]. However, being connected, being able to talk to other people does not mean that we are fulfilling our social needs as human beings. One can talk to many people on social networks, but that does not mean he is part of a group, of a community.

According to Clark [2], "communities have two fundamental communal elements of any social system that are a sense of solidarity and a sense of significance". In other words, a member of a community needs to feel something to the other members of the community and, at the same time, s/he needs to feel that s/he has a role to play on that community, s/he needs to feel that s/he belongs

© Springer International Publishing AG 2017
G. Meiselwitz (Ed.): SCSM 2017, Part I, LNCS 10282, pp. 289–306, 2017.
DOI: 10.1007/978-3-319-58559-8_24

and s/he is needed on it. However, creating and maintaining virtual communities remain a challenge among the researchers of the field.

Back in 1993, at the beginning of the Internet era, the United States' vice-president, Gore [7] said the following sentence in one of his speech: "Our new ways of communicating will entertain as well as inform. More importantly, they will educate, promote democracy, and save lives. And in the process they will also create a lot of new jobs. In fact, they're already doing it". Today, more than 20 years later, we are still trying to understand how to create and manage effective virtual communities, especially now with the popularization of the Online Social Networks (OSNs) [9].

Kim [10] states that "communities are ultimately based on timeless social dynamics that transcend the medium of connection. In other words, people are people, even in cyberspace". Nevertheless, in the virtual world, the way people interact to each other is different than when people meet face-to-face [23]. In this context, it is necessary to study how these interactions happen and, more importantly, formalize the process of dealing with them. That way, others may replicate such actions in order to create successful virtual communities.

In this paper, we present a number of strategies involving the process of creating and managing virtual communities. However, since there are different types of virtual communities, in this project, we focus on virtual communities that are extensions of communities that already exist in the physical world. In our case, virtual communities of cities.

Our strategies follow Scott peck's theory of community building [18], which is divided in four steps: pseudocommunity, chaos, emptiness and true community. According to him, every community needs to follow these steps sequentially in order to become a true community.

Our experiment started in 2011 when we created a virtual community for a small city in Brazil using the Facebook Groups tool. Now, five years later, we present what we have learned during all these years.

First, we present the community concept and we also describe Peck's theory of community building. Next, we introduce the Facebook Group of the city that we created in order to perform this experiment. Then, we describe our strategies to create and support this virtual group based on Peck's theory steps. To conclude, we present some implications and further investigations that we will do in order to extract more information from this virtual community.

2   Background and Related Work

2.1 Community Building

Community is a very complex concept that still remains without a single definition accepted by the researchers of the field. The history of trying to define the concept is long. Back in 1973, Clark [2] performed a re-examination of the community concept in order to formalize the current definitions for the concept. In the end, he concluded that even though there are many definitions for the concept, "communities have two fundamental communal elements of any social system that are a sense of solidarity and a sense of significance". According to him, the sense of solidarity encompasses all those sentiments that bring people together, like sympathy, gratitude, trust, and so on. We can also relate it to the sense of belonging presented by Maslow [11] on his pyramid of the human needs. Unfortunately, by trying to achieve the sense of solidarity, it becomes harder to achieve the second element: the sense of significance. The sense of significance is that feeling that members of a community have that they have a certain role to play on the community, i.e., each member thinks s/he has a function to fulfill. Both elements are closely linked and, in order to feel the sense of belonging, one must also have a sense of significance. Therefore, the ideal is to achieve a balance between both elements in order to have a community. Nevertheless, building a community in which its members achieve both senses is not a trivial task.

In this context, there are different theories involving the creation of communities [6,10,18]. After years dealing with the creation and management of online communities, Kim [10] said that he always found himself facing the same basic issues, like: persistent identity, newcomer confusion, etiquette standards, leadership roles and group dynamics. In his book, he presents 9 design strategies to build online communities which he called "Social Scaffolding". His strategies cover a big range of issues related to online communities. They range from reinforcing the importance of clarifying the purpose of the group to defining etiquette rules for it. The aim of his design strategies is to address general issues of online different types of communities. However, it does not provide more specific strategies to deal with specific types of communities.

Gardner [6] recommends 10 ingredients for building a community, which are:

1. wholeness incorporating diversity
2. a reasonable base of shared values
3. caring, trust, and teamwork
4. effective internal communication
5. participation
6. affirmation
7. links beyond the community
8. development of young people
9. a forward view
10. institutional arrangements for community maintenance.

In his book "Building Community" [6], he suggests a number of steps for the development of each one of these elements. However, many of these steps can be integrated into a virtual community environment, where these elements can be reinforced both by the members themselves and/or by the community manager. When talking about a Facebook Group, the group administrator can work in order to help the community at achieving them, which may result in a more connected community.

Both Gardner [6] and Kim [10] provide a list of elements that a community needs to have. However, they do not talk about the process of creating a community per se. In this context, the American psychiatrist Scott Peck wrote a book directly addressing the task of building a community and explaining the stages it goes through doing its creation. This book is called "The Different Drum: Community Making and Peace" [18]. In his book, he stages that community building goes through four steps, which are:

1. **Pseudocommunity:** in this first stage, people tend to be more friendly and sociable. They usually do not try to impose their opinions on subjects, neither discuss them too deeply, being more tolerant and open to accept divergences among other opinions. People try to maintain a happy mood during the interactions;
2. **Chaos:** here, interactions start to become more intense and deeper. People start to share problems, complaints and, more importantly, they start to disagree with each other, trying to convince them that their opinion about a certain subject is the right one;
3. **Emptiness:** in this stage, members empty their emotional and mental distortions that reduce their ability to really share, listen and help each other without a judge look. This is the hardest stage, because members need to put aside patterns they have been developing through their lives in order to maintain self-worth and positive emotion;
4. **True community:** in this stage, members become able to relate to each other's feelings. The discussions, even though some times may heat up, they never get sour. The mood is once more happier. Even when there is friction among the members in some discussions, they know that that is for a positive change. Finally, this is the stage in which one can say a true community exists, one where members can feel the sense of solidarity and the sense of significance (Fig. 1).

Fig. 1. The four stages of building a community proposed by Peck [18]

According to him, every community starts in the Pseudocommunity stage and, if it carries on, it will go until the last stage, which is the True community. Then, that can be seen as a community.

2.2   Virtual Communities

At the begin of the 90's, with the crescent adoption of the Internet, people have also started interacting with each other on the virtual world. Then, in 1993, Rheingold defined a new type of communities, which he called Virtual Communities [22]. He defined them as a community of people who interacts in the virtual world through the use of technology. Virtual communities have the potential of facilitating the communication among its members by compressing or expanding space-time. As a result, this may contributes to making online interaction more appealing to people [21].

Although virtual communities (also known as online communities or digital communities) can be classified as a type of community, they are in a different level of abstraction when compared to the other types of communities. Apart from them, virtual communities cannot happen by themselves. Every virtual community is also a geographic community, a community of interest or other type of community, i.e., virtual communities are always attached to some other type of community. This happens because the main characteristic of a virtual community is related to the way that interaction among its members happens, and not on its member's characteristics, as in other cases. Therefore, in this study, we are interested in a group of virtual communities that emerges from communities that already exist in the physical world, e.g., a community of a neighborhood, a street, a city, etc.

In this context, back in 1972, Etziori [4] developed the MINERVA (Multiple Input Network for Evaluating Reactions, Votes and Attitudes) project, which consists of a mass dialogue and response system. The purpose of MINERVA was to provide means for inhabitants of a city to communicate with each other, including city administrators authorities, such as councilmen, mayors, etc. According to him, "whether informed and active citizens generate more conflict or more consensus, have greater feelings of alienation or of involvement, will depend on the way the system for mass participation is used". He named such virtual communities of "Electronic Town Halls". Nevertheless, back then, there was no Internet to support the MINERVA project. Thus, users should use radio, TV, telephone and have some face-to-face meetings in order to communicate to each other, since there was no Internet. Therefore, the project died.

Nowadays, using Online Social Networks (OSNs) is already a common habit among many of us. According to the global agency We Are Social [9], by January of 2016, we were 7.395 billion people on Earth, whose 3.419 billion are active Internet users and 2.307 billion are active social media users. This significantly affects the way communication and connection occurs between friends and family [19]. Nowadays, using the Internet to communicate is the same as using the phone to chat was in the past [20].

As a consequence of this new reality, it is becoming common to see communities trying to expand their communication to the virtual world by using tools such as the Facebook Groups platform. By adopting this strategy, the community is able to cut geographical and temporal barriers at the same time.

3 The City and the Facebook Group

The city being studied in this project is situated in the Southeast of Brazil (400 km away from Sao Paulo). It has $1,064.790\,km^2$ and 21,400 inhabitants. Local economy is driven by agriculture, tourism e handicraft (Fig. 2).

Fig. 2. The city being studied in this project

According to the global agency We Are Social, in Brazil 50% of the population use Facebook [9]. In this context, Facebook groups are something quite popular among Brazilians. Therefore, once half of Brazil's population uses Facebook, i.e., they are already familiar with it, combined with its large scale adoption, made us choose it in our experiment.

On Dec. 26, 2011, we created a Facebook group for the city in order to perform our observations. Our main goal with this study is to understand how to manage a virtual community of a community that already exists in the physical world. Further, our goal for the group is to leverage the members' engagement with city management, i.e., make the citizens that are member of the group more concerned about how their city is being administrated.

Since the beginning, we adopted a strategy to have only one administrator for the group, which is one of the authors of this paper. Even though during the years a number of members had volunteered to become administrators or moderators of the group, all the volunteers were rejected. Differently from a community in the physical world, in a virtual community, the administrator of the community plays a very important role. The administrator is the only member who has more "power" than the others, because he has access to some features in the group that normal members don't have. Therefore, this strategy of having only one administrator was adopted because we wanted to be sure that we were going to be the only ones intervening on the group. Thereby, we avoided interference on our experiment, such as other group administrator removing posts or members without us knowing about such actions, etc.

In the next section, we describe the strategies we adopted based on the knowledge we have acquired over the years by performing this experiment. Besides, we also present some problems with the Facebook Groups tool to support municipal communities like ours. To finish, we describe the strategies we adopted to overcome such problems in order to have a true community.

4   Creating and Supporting the Virtual Community

As already mentioned, we have been performing this experiment for more than five years, which aims at creating and supporting a virtual community of a city in a Facebook group by following Peck's building community strategy [18].

In order to collect data from the group we adopted the cyber-ethnography approach [25], i.e., we have a profile that is a member of the group. By doing that, we are able to see the group the same way as other members and, as a result, we can better understand their behaviour and collect data. Over the years we have been trying different actions in order to advance the stages proposed by Peck to get to the true community stage.

Next we describe the path of the group through all the four stages proposed by Peck's theory.

4.1   The Pseudocommunity Stage

At the beginning, since the group had only a few members, the activity on it was small. However, the bigger it gets, the bigger is the number of activity on it, as we can see in Fig. 3.

Every day there are new people requesting to join the group. On average, 10 new members join the group. However, since September 2016, this average grew to 29 new members added per day. This change still needs more investigation of the researcher's team in order to understand the cause of it.

During all these years, there have been many peaks in the number of new members being added to the group, which usually occur based on situations that happen in the city. As an example, when there is an accident involving people from the city, or a big discussion about something related to the city administration, or politics, this number tends to grow, because people in the physical world (the city) are talking about this subject on the streets and, when

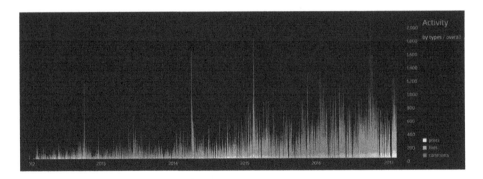

Fig. 3. Activity on the group over the years of its existence

they discover that the subject is also being discussed on the group, they want to be a part of it. Then, when situations like these happen, many citizens discover the group and send a request to join the group. By talking to people in such situation, we learned that they request to join the group because they want to know more about the subject being discussed. Other situation is when a person becomes a member of the group by a friend's invitation and, after trying it out, they start inviting many of his/her own friends to also become part of it, which sometimes may involve the insertion of dozens of new members in a day.

As already explained, in this step, members of a community tend to be more kind to each other and the conversation is more superficial, because everyone wants to cause a good impression. Then, in order to help the group at growing, we were always trying to incentive members to talk, by liking, commenting on posts and doing posts ourselves using our profile in the group. Generally, these posts were about random things involving the city, such as posts asking for some information, posts offering some product, someone sharing a picture of the city, and so on.

By doing that, we were aiming at leveraging members sense of solidarity, which could result in leveraging their activity in the group. According to Weil [26], "a central element of community building is shared tasks; when people invest in their community, their bond is strengthened". In other words, by encouraging members to interact in the group, they become more active on it, because they feel that they have a role to play in there, that people expect something from them. This is the sense of significance explained by Clark [2] as one of the most important parts of a community.

The group started with a few members but it has always been growing since then. Figure 4 shows the growing curve of the number of members in the group for the last three years.

In a Facebook Group, in order to join the group, a person needs to send a join request using his/her Facebook profile. Then, a member of the group needs to accept his/her request. In this context, we observed that it is very important to accept all the join requests as soon as possible, because, if a person requests

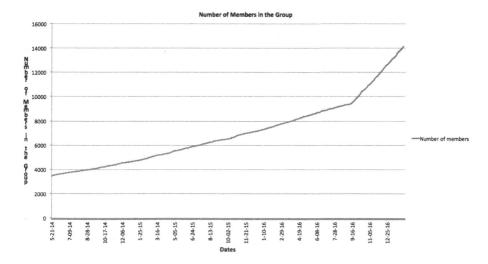

Fig. 4. Total number of members in the group for the last three years

to join the groups, but his/her request is ignored, this person may feel excluded. As a consequence, this person might create a bad first impression of the group, which may lead to him/her not feeling that him/her belong to the group, even though s/he is a member of the community in the physical world.

However, as the group started to grow, the number of discussions grew as well. Then, the group advanced to the second stage of Peck's theory, the Chaos stage.

4.2   The Chaos Stage

During this experiment, there was a situation that pushed the group even faster to the chaos stage. In this case, a councilman of the city joined the group and he started sharing his actions as a councilman in there. Then, members started interacting in his posts, some congratulating him, others complaining and discussing the subject with him and with other members.

The group that once had been used to ask for information about something in the city, to sell products and to talk about superficial things, after that situation, it included discussions about politics on its range of discussed subjects.

At that point, people in the city started to talk about the discussions that were happening in the group and they started sending requests to join the group in order to participate as well. As a consequence, the group started to increase its social capital [3] among the city's inhabitants.

In this stage, as previously described, members of the community start to explicit their opinions about subjects, even though others might not agree with them. Thus, many debates started to happen in the group, where the majority of the were about politics. However, at that time, the group also started to be used with other purpose, which is: a place to complain to the politicians about some problem in the city related to the city's administration. Then, politicians started to get involved on the discussions as well. As a result, some of these complaints made in the group started to get solved, what increased even more the social capital of the group.

However, with the popularity, the group started to face a new problem, which was the increasing of the number of members with unidentified profiles. Such profiles started to use the anonymity as a shield to hide while discussing in the group, without concerning about what they were saying, because they would not have to answer for it, once no one could know who they were behind those profiles. Then, the group started to lose credibility and members started to complain and ask the group administration for a solution. So, administration created a rule that prohibits unidentified profiles to have opinion in the group, i.e., they can participate, see posts, like them, even comment, however, they cannot have opinion in discussions. As a result, members who were leaving the group started to come back and the number of discussions that were decreasing went back to normal.

During the five years of the group's existence, on average, 11 people sent requests to join the group every day. From these 11 requests, on average, 10 became members. This one person per day that was not accepted represents unidentified profiles - profiles without identification, or someone or something that is not what it appears to be – which are not allowed in the group. However, over the years, the number of unidentified profiles requesting to join the group has been decreasing.

We believe this is happening because the population started to realize the importance and the impact of the group. At the begin, many tried to join using unidentified profiles to see how the group works and, also, to use it anonymously behind an unidentified profile. However, after seeing that the group administration was removing them and do not allowing new ones to join in, the number of requests started to decrease.

Another thing that became common in the group it was posts of members asking for help. Once members started to see the group a community in which they belonged, they started to open themselves in there. Since then, from time to time, people ask for help and, in many times, their requests are attended. Some examples of these posts are: people asking money to buy some medicine, stating that they do not have money to buy it; single pregnant moms asking for baby clothes and diapers; a father from a poor family asking for a Christmas toy to his son; etc. In most of the times, all the requests are attended.

By looking at these posts, we realized that the group had once more moved to the next stage of Peck's theory of community building [18], "Emptiness". Members of the group started to open themselves, both to discuss or to ask for help. The group was not a simple virtual community anymore, it became an extension of the city in the virtual world (Fig. 5).

Fig. 5. The Facebook group became an extension of the city in the virtual world

4.3 Emptiness Stage

In this stage, members empty their emotional and mental distortions that reduce their ability to really share, listen and help each other without a judge look. This is the hardest stage for the members, because they need to put aside patterns they have been developing through their lives in order to maintain self-worth and positive emotion. Now, members open themselves to the group and they start being themselves in there, without the need of hiding their true self.

At this point, the group is very active with dozens of posts everyday, ranging from posts selling products to discussions about politics, city problems, someone asking for some help, among others.

However, once members started to see the group as a place filled with friends, some of them started to use the group to post everything they thought it was interesting to share with others, even gossips. Then, a new problem emerged, which was the fact that some members were removing their posts after realizing that its content was not true, as they thought. The problem about that is that the members who only saw the post, but not the comments on it explaining the truth, would keep thinking that the post content was true. Here is an example: once, a member did a post telling that an employee of the city's municipal hospital had done a procedure in a wrong way while attending his son. Then, members started to comment on the post explaining to him that was the correct procedure. Thus, after realizing it, he removed the post. However, members who only saw his post kept thinking that the employee was wrong, because since the post had been removed, they could not read the truth in the comments.

In order to solve this problem, a new rule was created for the group, which says that it is prohibited to remove posts, i.e., if a member removes his/her post, s/he is remover from the group. As a result, members started to help at policing to see if any post had been removed. Every time they realized that a post had been removed, they would tell to the group administrator and send him a screenshot of the removed post, in order to prove that the post had indeed being removed. Besides, members also started to report unidentified profiles when they found one. In other words, members started to help at managing the group and caring about it. At the same time, now that members were more open to discuss any type of subject in the group, discussions about politics and city problems started to become the most common type of discussions in the group. In other words, members were starting to be more concerned about the city, i.e., the group was helping at leveraging their civic engagement.

Obar [15] defines Civic Engagement as "the process that involves moving an individual away from disinterest, distraction, ignorance, and apathy and towards education, understanding, motivation, and action". However, in order to do that, members need to open themselves while discussing in the group, by presenting their true opinion, even that results in others disagreeing with them.

As already mentioned, the goal of the group is to leverage member's engagement with the city's management. Therefore, by seeing the continuously growing number of members in the group, the behavior of the members in the group, which were opening themselves to ask for help and/or to help other members, we were sure that the group had achieved the last stage of Peck's theory of community building [18], which is the "True Community".

4.4 True Community Stage

According to the results provided by the Sociograph.io [24] tool (Fig. 3), over its existence, the group had 45.996 posts from 4.344 different authors. In total, there have been 313.000 likes, 18.000 shares and 119.000 comments. It is also possible to see that the member's activities in the group (posts, likes and comments) have been increasing over time.

At the moment this paper is being written, the group has 14,132 members, which corresponds to 66% of the city population (21,400). For us, we believe this percentage is already very impressive as it includes a large fraction of all the citizens, but if we remove from it the people who do not use Facebook, this percentage gets even higher.

We believe that the combination of the growing number of members together with the growing number of member's activities in the group over the years can be seen as indicators of the effectiveness of the group. More than that, we believe that this supports the claim that the city has indeed adopted the Facebook group as an extension of the physical community in the virtual world.

Besides, now, members of the group are able to relate to each other's feelings, which shows that they have a sense of solidarity among them. The discussions, even though some times may heat up, members understand that they disagree about that subject, however, in one next occasion, they are discussing again without getting sour because of the disagreement between them. This cases show how the group has really evolved to a true community, because, at the beginning of the group, it was common for a member to leave the group after a heat discussion, since they did not have a deep relationship with each other. Nowadays, even when there is friction among the members in some discussions, they know that is for a positive change.

Finally, according to Peck [18], this is the stage in which one can say a true community exists, one where members can feel the sense of solidarity and the sense of significance described by clark [2] as the main components of a community. So, we can affirm that this Facebook Group of this city became indeed a true community.

5   The Social Capital of a Virtual Community

As already mentioned, there are different types of communities, as presented by Clark in his review of the community concept [2]. In our case, we are working with virtual communities created from communities that already exist in the physical world, i.e., neighborhoods, cities, etc.

During the five years that we have been performing this experiment, we believe that credibility is the most important characteristic to define the success of a virtual community. Credibility can be seen as an important part of the social capital [3] of a community. Coleman [3] says "just as physical capital and human capital facilitate productive activity, social capital does as well". He also affirms that a group of people in which there is trustworthiness is able to accomplish much more than a group without that. In other words, a virtual community where its members have trust on it, tends to succeed more than one without it.

In this context, impartiality is a principle that is crucial to the managers of the virtual community. When dealing with any type of situation that occurs in the virtual community, managers need to be impartial and take the same actions towards every member of the community, basing their decisions on objective criteria, without providing any privilege to anyone. On a virtual community this is very important, because managers of the community has the power to perform some actions that normal members are not allowed to do. Then, managers need to be very careful when acting.

During his studies about Third places, Oldenburg [16] describes one of the features of a Third place as being the "Leveler". According to him, a place for socialization (like a virtual community) can not take into consideration the individual's status in the society. The economic and/or social status of a member have no impact in there, which leads to a sense of commonality among the members. As a result, this may increase the member's sense of significance [2] in the community, because they know that they have a role to play in there and that their social status does not interfere on that. While in there, they have the same "power" as other members, aside of the positions in the society.

Moreover, the Leveler feature also says that every person is allowed to become a member of that community, regardless of that social status. When talking about a virtual community, this principle also needs to be followed, i.e., every person in the community in the physical world is welcome to become a member of the virtual community, without exceptions. Once more, managers need to guarantee such thing to happen, otherwise, the virtual community will lose credibility among the city's inhabitants. Consequently, the virtual community's social capital will also decrease.

Then, if the group's administrators are impartial or act differently towards the members of the group, members realize that and the group's credibility decreases. As a result, they start complaining about it and their activity decreases. We had seen that happen in other groups of the city with the same purpose of ours. In these cases, the groups still exist, however, the activity on them (posts, comments, likes, etc.) decreased significantly.

6   Strategies for Creating and Supporting a Municipal Facebook Group

When looking in the literature for research about measuring and evaluating virtual community tools, it is common to find a number of works about how to measure usability [19] and some about measuring sociability on them [20]. However, besides evaluating what is already implemented in the tool, we believe that is also necessary to understand the behavior of the members of the community in order to see what they need that is not yet implemented. Moreover, by understanding their behavior, it also becomes possible to help at providing technological feedback for the designers, once members are not always familiar with the technological tools development. That way, the feedback to the Virtual Community tools' developers can be even more complete.

Thinking about that, after five years observing the behavior of the members of this virtual community following a cyber-ethnography approach [25], we were able to develop 14 strategies that we have been using in order to support this group. These strategies are based on the Peck's stages for building communities [18].

Here follow the list with the 14 strategies:

1. *The Group Administrator (GA) cannot be an employee (paid administrator) of the city hall, because s/he could/would tend to be impartial. The question is, who is paying his salary? S/He will most likely perform according to his employer's will;*

2. *The GA has to be impartial and trustworthy all the time, regardless of the subject and the members involved in any situation that s/he has to address. As a consequence, members will feel more free to share anything in the group without fearing repression by the group's administrator;*

3. *The GA needs to accept people's join requests as fast as possible. If a request is left unattended, that person might have a bad first impression about the group and dislike it before even becoming a member. That may result in an unsatisfied member, who does not feel like s/he belongs to the group;*

4. *Fake profiles cannot be allowed in the group. However, unidentified profiles (a store profile, etc.) can join with the condition of not being able to have opinion in posts or comments. Every time a situation involving an unidentified profile occurs, it's the GA's job to analyse it and take an impartial action;*

5. *The GA needs to help at creating rules about what can be posted in the group and what cannot. One way to do that is by creating pools where the group's members can vote and discuss which rules should be applied. That way, members feel they belong to the group and, more than that, they feel their voices are also heard, which may impact in the way they see the group. That way, their sense of significance is increased;*

6. *The GA needs to put the group rules on a visible place where every member can find it easily, specially the ones who recently became members of the group. As a suggestion, the group description would be a good place to put it;*

7. *The GA needs to answer all the members messages in order to show them s/he cares about the group and the about the members. The faster, the better;*

8. *The GA must remove all posts that are not related to the topic of the group. Even though there are numerous important subjects, the group needs to be strict to only its subject, which is the city. Otherwise, people interested in the group's subject (the city) will not be able to find the posts about it among many posts of topics that are not related to the group;*

9. *The GA needs to clear repeated posts, which sometimes may be a user error when using the Facebook Groups tool;*

10. *The GA needs to look at the posts and remove the ones that are not allowed in the group, according to the rules. S/he needs to do that daily (if possible, more than one time per day). That way, members will know that the group is not abandoned, which may increase the group's credibility among the members;*

11. *The GA needs to send direct messages to members if they are repeatedly posting the same thing. In this case, it is important to have a template of the message in order to treat all the members equally. Otherwise, this can lead to bad situations where a user feels inferior to another, because they were treated differently by the group's administrator. One example of this situation is when a new member of the groups is an entrepreneur and starts posting a photo for each one of his/her products on the group. Then, the GA needs to remove the posts (leaving only one) and to send this pre defined message to him/her;*

12. *The GA needs to remove members from the group whenever they break any of the group rules;*

13. *The GA needs to be alert to the group in order to see important posts that should be pinned to the group. This feature of the Facebook Groups tool allows a post to be pinned on the top of the group, allowing everyone to see it. However, the GA needs to be very careful when choosing which post to pin, always remembering of being impartial;*
14. *The GA can/should use the group's cover picture as a dynamic place where s/he can share news about the city management, advertise meetings of the chamber of councilors in order to motivate members to attend them, advertise philanthropy posts about parties, workshops, talks, etc., in order to help at advertising them. In order to do that, s/he needs to see the posts of the group and, every time s/he sees a post that s/he thinks it should be posted in the cover of the group, s/he needs to send a private message to the author of the post and ask to him/her if s/he can put that on the group's cover;*

We believe these strategies can help others at creating and supporting virtual communities that are really embraced by the community (the city), as ours.

7 Conclusion

After observing this Facebook group for more than five years, we found out that the group administrator (GA) has a very important role to play in such environment. The GA has to perform a number of actions in order to help a virtual community goes through all the stages of a community building proposed by Peck's theory [18].

Besides, it is very important to observe the members' behavior and, based on that, develop new strategies to deal with problems that might appear during the existence of the virtual community. When talking about these strategies, some of them are related to the features of the virtual community tool, but others are not. In order to keep the group working, the GA needs to develop perform some actions that goes beyond the support provided by the virtual community tool. During our study, we developed 14 strategies.

Finally, as a lesson learned, we believe the most important thing when dealing with a virtual community is credibility, i.e., the way members see the virtual community. In other words, how strong is the social capital of the virtual community among its members. In this case, the most important thing in order to increase the social capital of a virtual community is to have an impartial GA, especially if it is a virtual community of a community that already exists in the physical world. Regardless of the social status of a member in the society, all the members of the virtual community need to be treated equally in every situation. By doing that, the credibility of the group increases in the member's eyes and, as a consequence, their sense of significance in the group, because they know they are treated equally in there, that they are needed in there.

We expect that the strategies we developed during this study help others in the process of creating and supporting virtual communities for other cities. Then, other people will also increase their civic engagement and, as a result, they will also enjoy the benefits of having an extension of their city in the virtual world, as the inhabitants of the city being studied in this project.

Acknowledgments. We want to thank everyone who helped us during this project, specially the team of researchers from LIA, the members of the Facebook group studied in this project and CAPES for the financial support.

References

1. Angrosino, M.: Doing Ethnographic and Observational Research. Sage, Thousand Oaks (2007)
2. Clark, D.B.: The concept of community: a re-examination. Sociol. Rev. **21**(3), 397–416 (1973). doi:10.1111/j.1467-954X.1973.tb00230.x
3. Coleman, J.S.: Social capital in the creation of human capital. Am. J. Sociol. **94**, S95–S120 (1988)
4. Etzioni, A.: MINERVA: an electronic town hall. Policy Sci. **3**(4), 457–474 (1972). doi:10.1007/BF01405348
5. Etzioni, A.E.O.: Face-to-face and computer-mediated communities, a comparative analysis. Inf. Soc. **15**(4), 241–248 (1999). doi:10.1080/019722499128402
6. Gardner, J.W.: Building Community. Independent Sector, Washington, DC (1991)
7. Gore, Al.: Speech at the Superhighway Summit Royce Hall. UCLA, Los Angeles, 11 January 1993. http://www.ibiblio.org/icky/speech2.html. Accessed 4 Dec 2016
8. Harper, E.R., Rodden, T., Rogers, Y., Sellen, A., Human, B.: Human-Computer Interaction in the Year 2020 (2008). OAI: 10.1.1.153.4252
9. Kemp, S.: We are Social. Special Reports: Digital in 2016. http://wearesocial.com/uk/special-reports/digital-in-2016. Accessed 1 Dec 2016
10. Kim, A.J.: Community Building on the Web: Secret Strategies for Successful Online Communities. Addison-Wesley Longman Publishing Co., Inc., Boston (2000)
11. Maslow, A.H.: A theory of human motivation. Psychol. Rev. **50**(4), 370 (1943). doi:10.1037/h0054346
12. McKenna, K.Y., Bargh, J.A.: Plan 9 from cyberspace: the implications of the Internet for personality and social psychology. Pers. Soc. Psychol. Rev. **4**(1), 57–75 (2000). doi:10.1207/S15327957PSPR0401_6
13. Memarovic, N., Langheinrich, M., Cheverst, K., Taylor, N., Alt, F.: P-layers-a layered framework addressing the multifaceted issues facing community-supporting public display deployments. ACM Trans. Comput.-Hum. Interact. (TOCHI) **20**(3), 17 (2013). doi:10.1145/2491500.2491505
14. Monbiot, G.: The Age of Loneliness is Killing Us. Guardian (2014)
15. Obar, J.A., Zube, P., Lampe, C.: Advocacy 2.0: an analysis of how advocacy groups in the United States perceive and use social media as tools for facilitating civic engagement and collective action. J. Inf. Policy **2**, 1–25 (2012)
16. Oldenburg, R.: The Great Good Place: Café, Coffee Shops, Community Centers, Beauty Parlors, General Stores, Bars, Hangouts, and how They Get You Through the Day. Paragon House Publishers, Vadnais Heights (1989)
17. Palmer, P.J., Marty, M.E.: The Company of Strangers: Christians and the Renewal of America's Public Life. Crossroad, New York (1981)
18. Peck, M.S.: The Different Drum: Community Making and Peace. Simon and Schuster, New York (2010)
19. Phillips, D., Athwal, B., Robinson, D., Harrison, M.: Towards intercultural engagement: building shared visions of neighbourhood and community in an era of new migration. J. Ethn. Migr. Stud. **40**(1), 42–59 (2014). doi:10.1080/1369183X.2013.782146

20. Preece, J.: Sociability and usability in online communities: determining and measuring success. Behav. Inf. Technol. **20**(5), 347–356 (2001). doi:10.1080/01449290110084683

21. Renninger, K.A., Shumar, W.: Building Virtual Communities: Learning and Change in Cyberspace. Cambridge University Press, Cambridge (2002)

22. Rheingold, H.: The Virtual Community: Finding Commection in a Computerized World. Addison-Wesley Longman Publishing Co., Inc., Boston (1993)

23. Smith, M.A., Kollock, P.: Communities in Cyberspace. Psychology Press, Park Drive (1999)

24. Sociograph.io.: Analytics for Facebook Groups and Pages. http://sociograph.io/my.html. Accessed 7 Jan 2017

25. Ward, K.J.: Cyber-ethnography and the emergence of the virtually new community. J. Inf. Technol. **14**(1), 95–105 (1999). doi:10.1080/026839699344773

26. Weil, M.O.: Community building: building community practice. Soc. Work **41**(5), 481–499 (1996). doi:10.1093/sw/41.5.481

Examining the Legal Consequences of Improper Use of Social Media Sites in the Workplace

Alfreda Dudley[(✉)] and Davian Johnson

Department of Computer and Information Sciences,
Towson University, 8000 York Rd., Towson, MD, USA
adudley@towson.edu, sjohns48@students.towson.edu

Abstract. Social media has made radical and revolutionary changes; from the previous evolution of email and instant messaging to newer forms of communications (i.e., Facebook, LinkedIn, Twitter, etc.). These changes have had a tremendous amount of influence on the way people function and behave. The advanced elements contained within social media have expanded the social constructs of society (i.e., businesses, etc.) in virtual horizons. Boyd and Ellison define a web-based social networking site as a service that allows users to: "(1) Construct a public or semi-public profile with a bounded system; (2) articulate a list of other users with whom they share a connection; and, (3) view and traverse their list of connections and those made by others within the system" [3, p. 211]. This paper will examine the legal consequences on the impact of social networking technologies use in employment. Focusing primarily on the following question: Are there any legal recourses from an employer/employee perspective if they are victims of improper or inappropriate use of social media sites?

Keywords: Social media · Legal consequences · Employment

1 Introduction

Social media systems have created a new platform that allows everyone to engage in several forms of online communications. Facebook, Twitter, Instagram, blogs, wikis are more, have become popular online tools used for web based communications. These forms of interactions are not limited in private contexts only; these types of communications are also very prevalent in public and professional forums. "Nearly two-thirds of American adults (79%) use social networking sites (i.e. Facebook), up from 7% when Pew Research Center began systematically tracking social media usage in 2005" [16]. Social media in general has effected not just communication, but work, politics, sources for news, politics and even stress [16].

Social media has immense possibilities because it serves as many tools at once, but these multifaceted features are also the reason why it poses many problems. Boyd and Ellison define a web-based social networking site as a service that allows users to: "(1) Construct a public or semi-public profile with a bounded system; (2) articulate a list of other users with whom they share a connection; and, (3) view and traverse their

G. Meiselwitz (Ed.): SCSM 2017, Part I, LNCS 10282, pp. 307–316, 2017.
DOI: 10.1007/978-3-319-58559-8_25

list of connections and those made by others within the system" [3, p. 211]. The connectivity and social aspect of these tools allowing one to connect and interact with others encourages connecting with and "friending" other users. Social media tools allow for one to post many types of content such as text, images, video, hyperlinks while allowing other user's to interact and view content (depending on the site and profile settings). There are some concerns however about the posting of such content and its availability when it is consumed out of context or by unintended users. Other concerns related to privacy and security of access and availability of content or certain posts. One also needs to examine privacy settings in relation to shared content with "friended" users. Whether it's sending a get-well message to a friend or using social media for a more serious purpose, users must remember that in the legal sphere, social messaging is still an unchartered territory [8]. This paper will examine some of the legal consequences on the impact of social networking technologies, focusing on its use in employment. Focusing primarily on the following question: Are there any legal recourses from an employer/employee perspective if they are victims of improper or inappropriate use of social media sites?

2   The Impact of Social Media Sites in Employment

Smartphones and other portable devices such as iPads, tablets, and even internet hot-spots integrated into motor vehicles, have encouraged the blurring of work and personal time; almost manacling people to their devices. It is becoming difficult to differentiate then the work day starts and ends or when one's personal time begins. According to a recent survey, one-third of the workforce in the United States uses social media for at least an hour a day at work, and one-quarter of American workers would not take a job if their access to social media at work was cut off [8]. It some instances social media use is encouraged while at work to help engage with customers, promote materials and disseminate news and other resources. Although there are many noted benefits for its use in organizations, the overall implications are not fully understood. As noted by Treem and Leonardi, "Scholars have suggested that social media adoption in organizations is outpacing empirical understanding of the use of these technologies" [15]. Social media sites have become channels for public discourse about almost any issue, including complaints related to the workplace. Justifiably, employers are concerned about preventing negative posts, which have led to the development of social media policies to manage employees' online activities. The central focus of these policies define how employees should identify their affiliation with the organization, the tone of language they should use, and margin on the type of information an employee may share [8, 10]. Creating effective policies intended to control employees' online activities require an understanding of the current laws regarding social media and the knowledge of responsibilities associated with both employees and employers.

First, an employer has the legal recourse to reprimand employees for improper online behavior during working hours; as long there are stated policies in place that are clearly defined and communicated. Moreover, employers have a right and responsibility to monitor how employees are using social media during the work period. If employers ignore their employee's social media activity, they may end up facing any number of serious problems (i.e., tension, morale problems and complaints within the organization), both internally and externally (i.e., lawsuits or regulatory action). However, some critics point out that most of what people post on social networks is private and perfectly harmless, and has no bearing on their work [11].

Second, an employer can, and must, intervene when an employee's online actions are placing the employer at legal risk, such as betraying confidential information, or infringement of the Federal Trade Commission's rules on endorsements of the company's products, or threatening or harassing a co-worker. The employee's misconduct would not have been discovered had the employer not conducted a thorough investigation. However, employers must be mindful to investigate responsibly.

There are instances when an employer cannot terminate an employee for expression of opinion, particularly regarding engagement in outside recreational activities. This is dependent however on jurisdiction and context. If engaging in social media is considered "off-duty" and conducted outside of the scope of one's employment as recreation, this may raise questions on how social media use is classified. For example, in the New York Labor Law § 201-d there are protections concerning the discrimination against engagement in certain activities. In summary, it is stated:

> "Unless otherwise provided by law, it shall be unlawful for any employer or employment agency to refuse to hire, employ or license, or to discharge from employment or otherwise discriminate against an individual in compensation, promotion or terms, conditions or privileges of employment because of" ....

> "c. an individual's legal recreational activities outside work hours, off of the employer's premises and without use of the employer's equipment or other property" [14].

Aside from job dismissal, social media posts can also result in lost employment opportunities. Employers can access additional information about applicants via their social media page. An example, CNNMoney.com reported the following incident: Connor Riley was offered a job at CISCO. After the offer, he sent the following tweet: *"Cisco offered me a job! Now I have to weigh the utility of a fatty paycheck against commute to San Jose and hating the work."* A CISCO employee, Tim Levad, saw the post and responded with his own tweet: *"Who is the hiring manager? I'm sure they would love to know that you will hate the work. We here at Cisco are versed in the Web."* [17] Mr. Riley's employment offer was rescinded.

The First Amendment of the U.S. Constitution affords that every citizen has a right to freedom of speech. However, this right is not absolute and does not negate recourses. In a related legal case: Immunomedics, Inc. v. Does (2001), the plaintiff, Jean Doe aka moonshine posted a message in Yahoo! The message board was dedicated to postings regarding, Immunomedics, a publicly-held biopharmaceutical firm. Jean Doe stated in her postings that she was an employee and expressed her concerns about her employer. Immunomedics sued Jane Doe (moonshine), statin violation of confidentiality. In addition, Immunomedics served a subpoena on Yahoo! (to disclose the identity of moonshine). Yahoo responded by moving to stop the subpoena on the basis that moonshine has a First Amendment right of free speech and anonymous speech. The trial judge ruled in favor Immunomedics. The Appeals Court supported the trail judge's ruling [7].

2.1 The National Labor Relations Board (NLRB) and Social Network Systems

The NLRB is the federal agency that enforces the statutory rights of all employees covered by the NLRA (National Labor Relations Act). The NLRA covers prosecution of companies with policies that unduly interfere with employee communications about work matters such as wages, hours, and working conditions, even on social media [12]. "The NLRB is a unique agency that make critical decisions determined by five members that establish rules through mediation rather than rule making, offer answers too many pressing workplace questions arising from technological and legal advances" [6]. The case in the next section represents the legal repercussions from impropriate usages and access of social media sites technology in the workplace.

NLRB v. American Medical Response of Connecticut (AMR). The National Labor Relations Board (NLRB) filed suit against an employer, American Medical Response of Connecticut (AMR), for the suspension and firing of an employee who posted negative comments about her supervisor on her Facebook page. NLRB alleged that the employer retaliated against the terminated employee for her postings and for requesting the presence of her union representative at an investigatory interview that led to discipline. Most importantly, NLRB maintained that the employer's rules on blogging and internet posting, which included social media use, standards of conduct relating to discussing co-workers and superiors, and solicitation and distribution, were overbroad, interfering with employees' right to engage in concerted activities for mutual aid and protection under section 7 of the National Labor Relations Act [12].

Soon after the suit was filed by the NLRB, AMR agreed to concede with NLRB, to modify its policies. The company settlement promised to grant employees' requests for Union representation, and to revise its Internet and social media policies. In this case, the NLRB simply clarified that these generally permissible policies regulating free speech are not permissible if they interfere with employees' rights to organize labor unions and engage in concerted activities [12].

2.2 The Federal Stored Communications Act and Social Network Systems

The Federal Stored Communications Act law, noted as, 18 U.S.C. Chapter 12 §§ 2701–2712, was enacted to broaden the scope of the Fourth Amendment. The Fourth Amendment did not include language to cover the protection of privacy regarding online content. This act defined, in conjunction, with online/electronic communications, in the following areas: (a) Offense, where it is basically defined as access without authorization of a facility; (b) Punishment, where it defines the penalties associated with said offense; and (c) Exceptions, which basically states that this act does not apply to suppliers of online/electronic communications found under Sects. 2703, 2704 or 2518.

The following cases represent the legal repercussions and application(s) of the Federal Store Communications Act showing impropriate access of social media technology in the workplace.

Pietrylo v. Hillstone Restaurant Group. In a case settled in 2009, two restaurant workers sued their employer in federal court in New Jersey after they were fired for violating the company's core values. According to court documents, their supervisors gained access to postings on a password-protected MySpace page meant for employees but not managers. The jury found that the employer, Hillstone Restaurant Group, had violated the Federal Stored Communications Act and the equivalent New Jersey law, and awarded the employees $3,403 in back pay and $13,600 in punitive damages. The restaurant company appealed before the two parties reached an undisclosed settlement, said Fred J. Pisani, the workers' attorney. Hillstone said, "We're pleased that the matter was resolved and the plaintiffs have gone their separate way [2]."

Ashley Payne v. Barrow County School District. In August 2009, the Barrow County School District allegedly forced Apalachee High School English teacher to resign, after receiving an anonymous tip about photos posted on her personal Facebook page. In these photos, the teacher was shown holding alcoholic beverages. The school found the photos from teacher's vacation to Europe showing her holding wine and beer, as well as, a posting indicating that she was "headed out to play Crazy Bitch Bingo" at a local bar. The school stated that it was acting in response to a complaint from a parent but, according to the teacher, her Facebook page was private and she hadn't "friended" any of her students. The teacher subsequently sued the school district, alleging violations of state labor law [4, 10, 17].

In the lawsuit, Payne accused the school system of unlawful termination, and a Piedmont Circuit judge David Motes issued a summary judgment in April that the Barrow County School System had not acted illegally, and he couldn't force the school district to give Payne her job back. It should be noted that the State of Georgia does not required websites or state portals to incorporate privacy policies. Therefore, Borrow County did not have a social medial policy in place for their employees. Payne's lawyers filed a notice of appeal with the Georgia Court of Appeals.

2.3   International Case Involving Social Media Sites and Employment

Legal issues involving Social media posts and work place information, not only affects employees and employers in the U.S; but, in other countries as well. For example, in a related case in Ireland, an exam supervisor was terminated after he was found to have sent "tweets" from his phone while overseeing the Leaving Cert English. Supervisors are expected to give their entire attention during the examination. Another example in Hungary, a Vodafone employee in Hungary was also terminated after he made comments towards T-Mobile, a competing firm which was having network trouble. According to Vodafone, the employee's online behavior was anti-competitive [10].

2.4   The Importance of Social Media Policy in Employment

Depending on the context of social media use, having policies in place can serve as helpful guidelines in establishing expectations, particularly in an employment setting. Employees should be made aware of policies that may impact their employment status.

If an employer is expecting its employees to act in accordance to particular policies, then this must be made clear. There are certain guidelines that can be helpful when creating guidelines, and should establish behaviors for interacting with the content of others and for posting all types of content (i.e., pictures, comments, videos, links and more). The following items are addressed when creating a social media policy:

1. It creates a safe space for employees to share their concerns before going online.
2. It outlines what's considered confidential information.
3. It is clear about the consequences of your employees' actions online.
4. It designates a company spokesperson responsible for answering questions about your company on social media.
5. It discusses the proper way to engage with others online.
6. It discusses what's considered illegal.
7. It reflects the company's culture.
8. It educates employees. [1]

Keep in mind that some content is clearly allowed to be discussed and shared online, but establishing clear boundaries can protect both employer and employee. For instance in regarding confidential information, employees should not discuss private business matters, customer information and other nonpublic data in a public social media forum. Even in the case where the information is assumed to be private, safeguards on social media may not prevent that information from being unintentionally disseminated more publicly. As an example, examining the social media policy for the large electronic corporation, BestBuy they have included the following as part of their social media policy [2]:

What You Should Do:

- Disclose your Affiliation: If you talk about work related matters that are within your area of job responsibility you must disclose your affiliation with Best Buy.
- State That It's YOUR Opinion: When commenting on the business. Unless authorized to speak on behalf of Best Buy, you must state that the views expressed are your own. Hourly employees should not speak on behalf of Best Buy when they are off the clock.
- Protect Yourself: Be careful about what personal information you share online.
- Act responsibly and ethically: When participating in online communities, do not misrepresent yourself. If you are not a vice president, don't say you are.
- Honor Our Differences: Live the values. Best Buy will not tolerate discrimination (including age, sex, race, color, creed, religion, ethnicity, sexual orientation, gender identity, national origin, citizenship, disability, or marital status or any other legally recognized protected basis under federal, state, or local laws, regulations or ordinances).
- Offers and Contests: Follow the normal legal review process. If you are in the store, offers must be approved through the retail marketing toolkit.

Although these guidelines are specific to Best Buy, they serve to illustrate some very important guidelines.

3 Discussion on the Cases

Among the three cases involving social media and employment, it seems that all the employees suffered punitive repercussions from the employers for the misuses or violations of policies. It can be stated, based on the legal outcomes of the cases, that the employers and employees were not aware of the following: (1) Employers – Communicating their policies and procedures on the use of social media sites to their employees; and, (2) Employees – Not aware of or understanding existing social media site policies. There are other legal considerations that employers must be aware of in addition to the misuse social media policies and procedures. Along with various suits that have grabbed media attention, the potential for further litigation is broad, lawyers' caution. For example, a worker could file a sexual-harassment suit after a manager repeatedly tries to "friend" her on Facebook. Or an applicant might accuse a hiring manager of reneging on a job offer after learning the candidate's religious affiliation on Twitter [2].

In evaluation, there are those who believe that "social media is about communicating all the no-nos of office life, such as political views", says Shanti Atkins. Shanti Atkins is an attorney who is chief executive of ELT Inc., a San Francisco firm selling online training services in workplace-compliance areas such as social media. While others believe as Philip L. Gordon, the Denver-based chairman of the privacy and data-protection practice group at law firm Littler Mendelson PC believes that "the intersection of social media and the office is a potential minefield." Even when a company prevails in such legal actions, "there are reputational risks," Mr. Gordon added. "The company can become a poster child for a particular type of employment claims" [2].

Every employee needs to be informed that whatever they post on social media is bound to be seen by their employers or even prospective employers. Social media post are loaded with personal information that gives insight to their character, behavior and attitude of the social media account. Experts say an employer's best defense against legal action is to establish a social-media policy that outlines what is and isn't appropriate in social media, and then educate employees about the policy. Brian D. Hall, an employment-law partner at Porter Wright Morris & Arthur LLP in Columbus, Ohio, estimates that fewer than half of U.S. companies have a social-media policy. Mr. Hall and others say the amount of legal action resulting from employer missteps in social media is likely to rise at least until more case law is established [8].

4 Conclusion

Posting to social media sites can raise numerous legal challenges and is subject to vast potential liability. Social media sites are no different in this capacity than any other communications technologies (i.e., phone). As these sites continue to gain popularity; they will continually to evolve and create moving targets that can be difficult to control and monitor. Despite the risks, organizations and individuals will continue to use social media. It would be beneficial to organizations to train their managers to navigate social media issues just as they train managers to use other tools. To understand both views of employee and as an employer there are several questions to consider:

- Is the facility mentioned by name?
- Can the employer otherwise be identified?
- Does the post violate the organization's social media policy?
- Is the post offensive? Is it insubordinate?
- Should the organization respond to the post? If so, how and who should respond?
- Should the manager act against the employee? If so, what action is appropriate?
- Is the employee's speech protected?
- Can the poster claim other legal protections?
- What, if anything, should be done about the employees who liked the post?

These are just a few questions that should be considered when an organization is drafting a policy or is made aware of posts by employees.

Much has been written about what motivates people to post information about their employers online. Although some discussions focus on attention- seeking, a large section of the literature focuses on the frustration felt by staff members when they believe they have no other way to express their grievances to their employers. A communication strategy that actively seeks input of and feedback from employees may be the most effective strategy in the prevention of negative postings. A well-drafted social media strategy and policy supported by a culture that values open communication about issues concerning employees cannot be overemphasized as an effective approach for minimizing the risk of employees posting negative comments. But if an organization finds itself the subject of such postings, a response plan should be in place.

It seems when it comes to social media, the best defense is still a good offense. So if an organization does not have a policy in place or one that is concerned about blocking social media in the workplace, now is the time to create such a social media policy. There is always help to address the legal issues regarding the relationships between employers and employees. With the help of the NLRB, companies can prepare their staff for training in legal issues, because they offer answers to many pressing workplace questions arising from technological and legal advances.

It's not complicated to initiate social media policies for the workplace. Employers and employees benefit from education, communication, and expectation of policies. These policies can be implemented by incorporating several different methods and venues. Those assigned to drafting policies should research and use resources that are appropriate for their specific organizational culture. Moreover, employers should also look at how often their organization's policies are reviewed. For example, many hospitals review policies on a 3-year rotation (Mayo Clinic Center for Social Media, n. d.). Given the fluidity with which the landscape changes, social media policies should be reviewed at least annually [9, 16].

5 Future Work

When considering the area of social media, there are many variables involved. This paper mainly looked at the policies of these technologies. As part of our future work, the authors will continue to study the impacts of social media in the workplace. We also are interested in analyzing a large number of social media policies implemented by large corporations, small businesses, educational, governmental institutions and non-profits for an in-depth comparison. In addition, we want to study how social media policies impact other groups/segments of society (i.e., students, age, income, etc.). The authors feel that it would be beneficial to expand this study by including a quantitative/qualitative component to further investigate the perceptions of social media policies in employment. These future studies will also include investigating the legal and ethical impacts of these policies.

References

1. Akitunde, A.: Employees Gone Wild: 8 Reasons you need a social media policy today. Hiring and HR - American Express Open Forum (2013)
2. Best Buy. Best Buy Social Media Policy (2016). http://forums.bestbuy.com/t5/Welcome-News/Best-Buy-Social-Media-Policy/td-p/20492
3. Borzo, J.: Employers Tread a Minefield - Wall Street Journal, Eastern Edition, p. B6, 21 January 2011. Academic Search Complete, Web (2016)
4. Boyd, D., Ellison, N.: Social network sites: definition, history, and scholarship. J. Comput.-Mediat. Commun. **13**, 210–230 (2008)
5. Fillmore, C.C.: RIDING THE WAVE: social media in local government. New Hampshire Bar J. **52**(4), 16–23 (2012). Academic Search Complete
6. Green, M.Z.: Symposium panel Iii: opportunities for improvement in changing times: the NLRB as an uberagency for the evolving workplace. Emory Law J. **64** (2015)
7. Immunomedics, Inc. v. Doe – A.2d – (2001 WL 770389, Superior Ct. App. Div., N.J., 2001)
8. Kierkegaard, S.: Twitter thou doeth? Comput. Law Secur. Rev. **26**(6), 577–594 (2010)
9. Liebler, R.: Here we are now, entertain us: defining the line between personal and professional context on social media. Pace Law Rev. **35** (2014)
10. Merabet, S.M.: The sword and shield of social networking: harming employers' goodwill through concerted Facebook activity. Suffolk Univ. Law Rev. **46** (2013)
11. Melick, G.: Top 10 Do's and Don'ts for Managing Employee Social Media Use. Association of Corporate Counsel. Meritas Law Firm Worldwide (2014)
12. O'Brien, C.N.: The first Facebook firing case under section 7 of the national la labor relations act: exploring the limits of labor law protection for concerted communication on social media. Suffolk Univ. Law Rev. **45** (2011)
13. Perrin, A.: Social Media Usage: 2005–2015. Pew Research Center (2015). http://www.pewinternet.org/2015/10/08/social-networking-usage-2005-2015/
14. Thomson Reuters. New York Labor Law § 201-d. Discrimination against the engagement in certain activities. http://codes.findlaw.com/ny/labor-law/lab-sect-20d.html#sthash.8XQbHRT0.v8isw02s.dpuf (n.d.)
15. Treem, J., Leonardi, P.: Social media use in organizations: exploring the affordances of visibility, editability, persistence, and association. Commun. Yearb. **36**, 143–189 (2012)

16. Walden, J.A.: Integrating social media into the workplace: a study of shifting technology use repertoires. J. Broadcast. Electron. Media **60**(2), 347–363 (2016). Communication & Mass Media Complete

17. Wise, P.A.: Tweet, tweet, you're fired. Employ. Labor Relat. Law **7**(4), 7–12 (2009). Academic Search Complete

Inter-country Differences in Breaking News Coverage via Microblogging: Reporting on Terrorist Attacks in Europe from the USA, Germany and UK

Kaja J. Fietkiewicz[(⊠)] and Aylin Ilhan

Department of Information Science,
Heinrich Heine University, Düsseldorf, Germany
{Kaja.Fietkiewicz,Aylin.Ilhan}@uni-duesseldorf.de

Abstract. The micro-blogging service Twitter proved to be a suitable social media platform for (breaking) news dissemination and commentary. Its immediate penetration and strong ability to spread such news was already investigated by several researchers. Breaking news themselves play an important role in the "24-hour news culture" we live in today. In less than two years several terrorist attacks stroke Europe. Twitter was one of the live reporting tools that kept people from all over the world in the loop on the attacks as well as on the proceeding investigations. Did news agencies from three different countries report in a similar manner on all these attacks? Did their follower disseminate the breaking news through re-tweets on the same scale? Are tweets on terrorist attacks more likely to be retweeted?

Keywords: Twitter · Breaking news · Terror attacks · News dissemination · Inter-country comparison · News services · Retweetability

1 Introduction

In less than two years, several terrorist attacks stroke the European society. Each time Twitter was one of the live reporting tools that kept the public in loop. How did news agencies from different countries report on these breaking events on Twitter? How did users react to such news?

Twitter is a micro-blogging service that allows its users to share tweets, messages of no more than 140 characters, with each other. After its launch on July 13, 2006, Twitter quickly became popular worldwide [1], also among older social media users [2]. The messages (tweets) are available to the public and are included in the tweet lists of the followers, who have subscribed to someone's Twitter stream [3–5]. With time, Twitter has become an instrument for dissemination and subsequent debate on news stories [6] as well as one of the top services used by semantic web researchers to spread information [7]. Bruns and Burgees [6] emphasize the dual nature of Twitter as a social networking site and an "ambient information stream."

Twitter's development from everyday communication and life-sharing towards a news dissemination and commentary tool is similar to the one of older social media

© Springer International Publishing AG 2017
G. Meiselwitz (Ed.): SCSM 2017, Part I, LNCS 10282, pp. 317–336, 2017.
DOI: 10.1007/978-3-319-58559-8_26

platforms like, e.g. blogs, which has been established as first-hand reporting and follow-on commentary or discussion platforms [6, 8]. Now, they are widely applied for journalistic and quasi-journalistic activities [6, 9, 10] as well as follow-on discussion and, according to Bruns [11], the "gatewatching." Gatewatching is the "highlighting, sharing and evaluating relevant material released by other sources in order to develop a more comprehensive understanding" [6]. The "sharing" occurs through tweeting links to further sources or retweeting posts of other users. Ettema [12] identified Twitter and blogging as journalistic tools for the 21st century.

Twitter can be also considered as an awareness system, "intended to help people construct and maintain awareness of each other's activities, context or status, even when the participants are not co-located" [13, 14]. Twitter became "part of an ambient media system where users receive a flow of information from both established media and from each other" [13]. This "ambient" function of Twitter [13, 15] is best recognizable when a broad commentary on current events is being carried out. After breaking news spreads across Twitter, the "topical focus of incoming tweets" may make the user pay attention to this breaking story [6]. For example, Mendoza et al. [16] investigated the behavior of Twitter users under an emergency situation, namely the 2010 earthquake in Chile. They analyzed the Twitter activity in the hours and days following the disaster as well as certain social phenomena like the dissemination of false rumors and confirmed news.

Studies suggest that citizens are increasingly participating in the "observation, selection, filtering, distribution and interpretation of events" and that digital technologies increase the presence of ambient news [13]. Domingo et al. [17] speak of "participatory journalism." A study by Pew Internet in 2010 showed that news is becoming a social experience and "participatory activity" since users increasingly post their own stories as well as experiences and reactions to current events [13, 18].

In this study, the Twitter activity by news services from Germany, the USA and the UK, one week before and one week after the selected triggering events—the terrorist attacks in Paris on 7th of January 2015, in Paris on 13th of November 2015, and in Brussels on 22nd of March 2016, is being investigated. The aim of this investigation is to identify the differences between top news services from the different countries in breaking news coverage via Twitter as well as its further dissemination by users through retweets.

2 Methods

For the purpose of this study we applied methods known from similar investigations on Twitter activity. The importance of social networks was recognized by social scientists long time ago [19]. The modern communication, especially social media, enhanced the role of networks in marketing [20, 21], information dissemination [22, 23], search [24], and expertise discovery [25, 26]. Twitter has already proved to be a suitable social medium for investigation of news dissemination and commentary on breaking news. Gahran [27] emphasized Twitter's immediate penetration and strong ability to spread such news. According to Farhi [20], Twitter is a "tool with speed and brevity that are ideal for pushing scoops and breaking news to readers" [3]. Breaking news play an important role in the "24-hour news culture" [28] and Twitter can provide users with this kind of news without them having to search for them on news' websites [5]. The breaking news that were chosen as triggering events for the current study are the terrorist attacks in January 2015 in Paris aimed primarily at the offices of the satirical weekly newspaper Charlie Hebdo, the series of coordinated terrorist attacks in November 2015 in Paris including suicide bombings and mass shootings outside the Stade de France, in Bataclan Theatre and several Cafes, and the terrorist attacks in March 2016 in Brussels that occurred at the Brussels airport and the Maalbeek metro station in the city center.

2.1   Applied Indicators

Despite sending messages, or "tweeting," Twitter enables users to "like" and "retweet" messages of (other) users. If users consider a tweet as interesting, they can forward it to their own followers by "retweeting" the original message [29]. The meaning of retweets (RTs) can vary [29]. Without RTs the original message would only reach limited number of users (namely, one's own followers). Despite spreading the original message through the network, a RT can be interpreted as an "endorsement for message and sender," or, when additional commentary is retweeted, more a commentary of current news rather than its dissemination [6]. Any retweeted tweet can be expected to reach an average of 1,000 Twitter users [9, 30]. Messages are usually retweeted when users find a message particularly interesting and worth sharing with others, therefore, RTs may reflect what "the Twitter community considers interesting on a global scale" [30].

Furthermore, a well-connected user with active followers is more likely to be retweeted [9, 30–32]. Other factors that may influence the amount of retweets (retweetability) are besides the number of followers and followees, the age of the account, the number of favorite tweets as well as the number and frequency of tweets [30, 32]. However, other studies contradicted the assumption that popular users with large numbers of followers have more influence on Twitter [33, 34]. According to Zhao et al. [35], Twitter users tweet less on world events, however, they do actively retweet such news. In our study, the retweetability of tweets on the triggering events posted by different news accounts is analyzed as an indicator of attention from the community.

While tweeting, an author can include links directed at other users by typing "@" and the respective user name. These directed links might represent "anything from intimate friendships to common interests, or even a passion for breaking news or celebrity gossip" [33]. During analysis of collected data, indicators were found that some of news agencies include directed links in their tweets. Some of these mentions are directed at accounts of celebrities that the news is about; other are directed at followers with whom the news agency is communicating. For this study, mentions indicating a "conversation" between the news account and users were included as variable.

2.2   News Accounts

Armstrong and Gao [3] examined how Twitter is used as a content dissemination tool by news agencies. In their study, they looked at tweets of nine news organizations during a 4-month period, in order to determine how individuals, links, news headlines and subject areas were employed within the 140-character limits. In our study the tweeting activity of 15 news services accounts from three different countries during a 2-week period was investigated. The focus is set on information dissemination of concrete breaking news and not on general characteristics of news distribution, therefore, a shorter observation time of two weeks appears sufficient.

The main Twitter accounts of most popular online news agencies from Germany [36], the USA [37] and UK [38] were investigated. The included German news services are *Bild*, *Frankfurter Allgemeine Zeitung*, *Süddeutsche Zeitung*, *Die Welt*, and *Zeit Online*. The investigated British news services are *Daily Express*, *Daily Mirror*, *The Guardian*, *Daily Mail* and *Telegraph News*. Finally, the investigated online news services from the USA are *CBS*, *CNN*, *NBC*, *USA Today*, and *Yahoo*.

The Twitter accounts were found either on the news organization's website or through a search on the Twitter website for the official account. From the respective news accounts, all tweets from the week preceding the investigated event ("triggering event") and all tweets from the week after the event, as well as from the day of the event, were retrieved. Hence, for Charlie Hebdo terrorist attacks (7th of January) there were retrieved tweets posted from 31st of December 2014 until 15th of January 2015. An example for an advanced Twitter search for the British news agency Daily Mail Online is: *from: MailOnline since: 2014-12-30 until: 2015-01-16*. For the second triggering event, the terrorist attacks in Paris (13th of November), the timespan was set from 6th to 20th of November 2015. For the last triggering event, the terrorist attacks in Brussels (22nd of March), the timespan was set from 15th to 29th of March 2016. For this study all "live" tweets were retrieved, which are all published tweets in real-time order, and not only the "top" tweets limited to the most popular ones.

2.3   Research Questions

Based on the retrieved tweets with focus on the three triggering events, this study aims at answering four main research questions:

RQ1:   What are the differences between news services' accounts from Germany, the USA, and UK regarding (a) the number of tweets posted per day, (b) the average number of RTs per tweet, and (c) their distribution over the two weeks around the terrorist attacks?

RQ2:   What are the differences between news services' accounts from Germany, the USA, and UK regarding (a) the ratio of tweets reporting on the terrorist attacks, (b) the average number of RTs that the news on terrorist attacks received, and (c) their distribution over the week after the terrorist attacks?

RQ3:   What are the differences between news services' accounts from Germany, the USA, and UK regarding (a) the relationship between the topic of tweet being the terrorist attack and the number of RTs it gets, and (b) potential changes in this relationship during the week after the attack?

RQ4:   Regarding all previous research questions, is there a noticeable difference in outcomes between the three investigated triggering events, i.e. is the breaking news coverage and its dissemination constant for all three attacks or is there a tendency of increasing or decreasing attention that they get?

2.4   Data Processing

All tweets were retrieved using the python application *tweepy* and the Twitter-API, as well as manually using Twitter's advanced search interface. The database structure included a unique ID, the tweet itself, the news service, publication date, country, number of likes, number of RTs, whether the tweet is topically related to the triggering event ("topic of interest"), and whether the tweet is only an interaction with users. The tweets were topic-coded by two independent researchers. After processing with SPSS, the consolidated database included average counts for each news agency and for each one of the 15 days per event—the average number of tweets and RTs (RQ1) as well as the ratio of tweets on the topic of interest (RQ2). Furthermore, for the week after the attacks, there was calculated the difference between daily average of RTs of tweets on the "topic of interest" and for tweets on different, non-related topics. This difference was normalized by setting it in relation to the mean number of RTs for all tweets (on topic of interest and on others). This way it was possible to compare all three countries, which are characterized by different amounts of tweets and RTs per tweet. This RT-ratio shows whether there is a positive or a negative tendency in retweeting news services' tweets reporting on the triggering event compared to tweets on other topics (RQ2):

$$RT\_ratio_{topic} = \frac{\emptyset RT_{topic} - \emptyset RT_{others}}{\emptyset RT_{all}} \times 100\%$$

The significance of the difference in retweetability between tweets on topic of interest and tweets on other topics was further examined with the Mann-Whitney U-test and the median RT-values (in contrast to the mean values, medians are not skewed by extreme values) for the both topic groups ("topic of interest" and "other topics"). The Mann-Whitney U-test was developed as a test of stochastic equality [39]. It is a rank-based nonparametric test that can be used to determine if there are differences between two groups on a continuous dependent variable [40], in this case the number of RTs.

For the analysis of the influence that the topic of a tweet ("topic of interest") can have on its further dissemination by users through RTs (RQ3), Pearson's point-biserial correlation coefficient (r_{pb}) was computed. This coefficient is used to determine the strength of a linear relationship between one continuous variable and one nominal dichotomous variable. The effect sizes of Pearson's correlation coefficient were defined by Cohen [41] as small, medium, and large and are reflected by the values 0.1, 0.3, and 0.5, respectively. These estimations were included in the analysis of the size of the effect that the topic of interest potentially has on the retweetability. Furthermore, the coefficient of determination (r_{pb}^2) was calculated in order to determine the proportion of variance in one variable that can be explained by the other variable [42, 43]. The coefficient of determination was calculated as the percentage of variance in the number of RTs that can be explained by the variance in the topic of the tweet ($r_{pb}^2 \times 100$).

3 Results

The dataset included 55,944 Tweets posted by 15 news services' Twitter accounts from three countries. There were 13,580 tweets from two weeks around the Charlie Hebdo terrorist attacks, 21,379 tweets from the period around the Paris terrorist attacks, and 20,987 tweets from the period around the terrorist attacks in Brussels. In general, there were 13,819 tweets from German, 30,801 from British, and 11,326 tweets from US-American news services' Twitter accounts. The differences between the accounts from different countries will be investigated while analyzing the data in context of the four research questions.

3.1 General Differences Between News Services' Twitter Activity

The first research question concerns the general differences between the news services' Twitter activity from the three investigated countries and for the three investigated triggering events. The observed Twitter activity enfold seven days before and seven days after each triggering event.

The first investigated triggering event are the Charlie Hebdo terrorist attacks (Fig. 1). As for the German news services, the average number of tweets per day

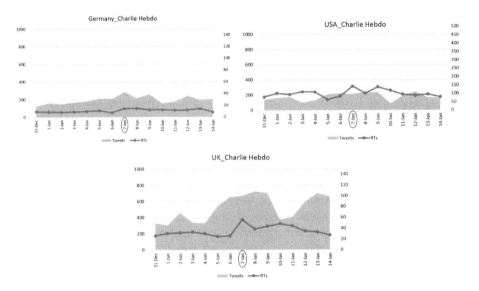

Fig. 1. Average number of tweets and of RTs per tweet within two weeks around the investigated triggering event *Charlie Hebdo* for German, USA and UK news services' Twitter accounts.

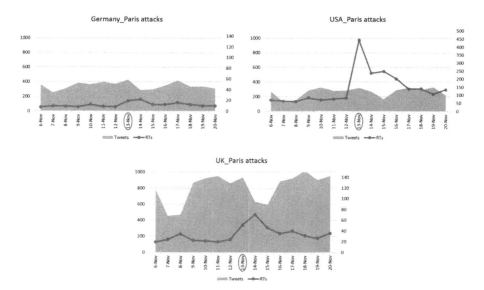

Fig. 2. Average number of tweets and of RTs per tweet within two weeks around the investigated triggering event *Paris attacks* for German, USA and UK news services' Twitter accounts.

ranged between 123 and 284 tweets, with a peak on the day of the event (7-Jan). Regarding the average retweetability, the number of RTs oscillated between 7.3 and 14.4 RTs/tweet with the highest value on the day after the event (8-Jan) and the day of the event (7-Jan) with 14.4 and 14.3 RTs/tweet respectively. As for the news services from the USA, they posted the least tweets. The average number of tweets per day ranged between 92 and 242 with a peak on 12-Jan (242 tweets) and on the day after the event (235 tweets). The lowest number of published tweets was given on Saturdays (3-Jan and 10-Jan) with 99 and 92 tweets respectively. However, the US-account have in average the highest number of RTs/tweet ranging between 63.6 and 143.33 RTs/tweet with a peak on the day of the event (7-Jan) with 143.3 RTs/tweet and two days after (9-Jan) with 138.8 RTs/tweet. The news account from UK published the highest average numbers of tweets per day, ranging between 305 and 724. There was a peak in number of published tweets on the two days following the event (8-Jan and 9-Jan) with 724 and 704 tweets respectively. The number of RTs/tweet ranged between 25 and 55.8, with a peak on the day of the event (7-Jan).

The Twitter activity and retweetability of news services around the time of Paris terrorist attacks is shown in Fig. 2. As for the news services from Germany, the average number of tweets per day increased when compared to the first triggering event, and ranged between 252 and 427 tweets per day. There was a peak in activity on the day of the event (13-Nov) and four days later (17-Nov) with 427 and 420 tweets respectively. The lowest numbers of tweets are given on 7-Nov and 14-Nov, which were Saturdays. The average number of RTs per tweet ranged between 7.24 and 21.7 with most RTs on the day after the event (14-Nov). Regarding the news services from the USA, the average number of tweets per day was between 126 and 331, which as well indicates an

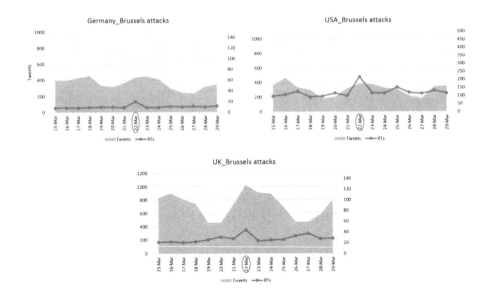

Fig. 3. Average number of tweets and of RTs per tweet within two weeks around the investigated triggering event *Brussels attacks* for German, USA and UK news services' Twitter accounts.

increase when compared to the first triggering event, with a peak on 19-Nov with 331 tweets, and lowest values on 7-Nov and 15-Nov (Saturday and Sunday). The numbers of RTs varied between 60.6 and 442.9 RTs/tweet with a very distinctive peak on the day of the event (13-Nov). Considering the news services from the UK, the average number of tweets per day was between 453 and 1,020 tweets, which is the highest from all investigated countries, with a peak on 18-Nov, and lowest values on 7-Nov and 8-Nov (Saturday and Sunday). The average number of RTs per tweet ranged between 19.2 and 70.7, with a peak on the day after the event (14-Nov) and the day of the event (13-Nov) with 70.7 and 51.4 RTs/tweets respectively.

Figure 3 depicts the Twitter activity and retweetability of news services' accounts around the time of Brussels terrorist attacks. As for the German news services, the average number of tweets was between 237 and 455, with peaks on 18-Mar and one day after the event (23-Mar) with 455 and 437 tweets respectively. The lowest average number of tweets per day was given on 26-Mar and 27-Mar (Saturday and Sunday). The average number of RTs ranged between 8.3 and 19.9 RTs/tweet, with a distinctive peak on the day of the event (22-Mar). The news services from the USA posted in average between 182 and 465 tweets per day, with a peak on 16-Mar and lowest values on 19-Mar, 20-Mar, 26-Mar and 27-Mar, which were the weekends. The average number of RTs ranged between 91.8 and 217.4 RTs/tweet, with a distinctive peak on the day of the event (22-Mar). As for the news services from UK, they published in average between 465 and 1,028 tweets/day, which is the highest number of all investigated countries and all three time periods. There was a peak in Twitter activity on the day of the event (22-Mar), whereas the lowest numbers of tweets were given for 19-Mar, 20-Mar and 26-Mar, 27-Mar. These were the weekends as well. The average number of retweeability was between 20.8 and 44.4 RTs/tweet with a distinctive peak on the day of the event (22-Mar).

3.2   Differences Between News Services Regarding the Reporting on the Triggering Event and the Retweetability Levels

The second research question regards the differences between the investigated news services' accounts considering the ratio of tweets on the topic of interest as well as the differences in retweetability of tweets on topic and tweets on other topics. For better inter-country comparability the differences were normalized (set into relation to the mean number of RTs of all tweets). Figure 4 shows the differences for the first investigated triggering event, the Charlie Hebdo terrorist attacks.

As for the news services from Germany (Fig. 4), the ratio of tweets on topic of interest ('Toi_ratio') during the week after the triggering event ranged between 53.7% and 28.45% of all tweets. The highest value was given on the 6th day after the event (13-Jan), followed by the 2nd and 3rd day after the event (9-Jan and 10-Jan) with 46.51% and 41.59% respectively. On the day of the event the ratio amounted to 37.32%. The lowest ratio was given on the 4th day (11-Jan, with 28.45%). The average difference in retweetability (difference in RTs between tweets about the attacks and tweets on other topic relative to the combined RTs-mean) of tweets on topic oscillated between +166.44% and −38.42%, with the highest positive difference on 11-Jan, followed by the day of the event with +128.9%. The lowest and the only one negative value was given on 13-Jan (−38.2%). Regarding the news services from the USA, the

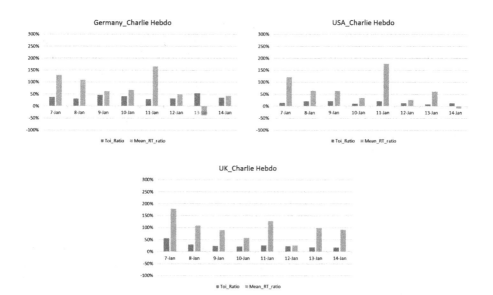

Fig. 4. The ratio of tweets on the triggering event ("toi") and the mean difference in retweeting tweets on topic of interest relative to the overall average number of RTs per tweet for the investigated triggering event *Charlie Hebdo* for German, USA and UK news services.

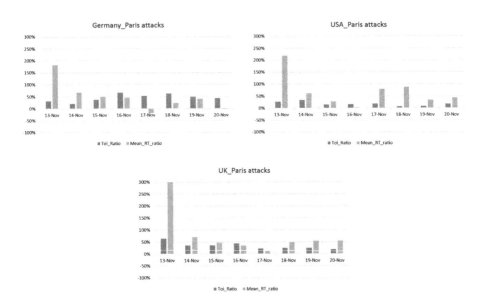

Fig. 5. The ratio of tweets on the triggering event ("toi") and the mean difference in retweeting tweets on topic of interest relative to the overall average number of RTs per tweet for the investigated triggering event *Paris attacks* for German, USA and UK news services.

topic of interest ratio ranged between 20.66% and 8.81% and was the lowest one of the three countries. There were peaks in the number of tweets on topic on two days after the event (8-Jan and 9-Jan) and on the 4th day (11-Jan), with slightly over 20%. The lowest ratio was given on 13-Jan. The mean difference in retweetability ranged between +177.8% and −8.54%. The highest positive difference in retweetability of tweets on topic of interest was given on the 4th day (11-Jan) and the day of the event (7-Jan), with +177.8% and +121.5% respectively. The lowest and only one negative value was given on 14-Jan (−8.54%). As for the news services from the UK, the topic of interest-ratio was between 55.32% and 17.4%, with the highest ratio on the day of the event (7-Jan), which then decreased over the week. The mean retweetability difference ranged between +179.4% and +26.1%, meaning that each day the tweets on topic got over-average number of RTs. The highest difference in retweetability was given on the day of the event (7-Jan) and on the 4th day (11-Jan) with +179.4% and +128.3% respectively.

Figure 5 shows the ratio of tweets on topic of interest and their retweetability for the second investigated triggering event, the Paris terrorist attacks. The German news services tweeted on this topic in around 66.7% to 20.2% of their tweets, with a peak between 3rd and 5th day after the event (16-Nov through 18-Nov). Surprisingly, the lowest ratio with 20.2% of tweets on topic was given on the first day after the event (14-Nov), followed by the day of the event (13-Nov) with 32.1%. The mean difference in retweetability of these tweets ranged between +181.8% and −18.5%, with highest positive difference on the day of the event (13-Nov) with +181.8% and two lowest, negative values on 17-Nov and 20-Nov with −18.5% and −1.42% respectively. As for the news services from the USA, the ratio of tweets on topic of interest was between 33.9% and 7.4%, with highest values on the first day after the event (14-Nov) and the day of the event (13-Nov), with 33.9% and 27.1% respectively, and lowest values on 5th and 6th day (18-Nov and 19-Nov) with 7.4% and 8.6% respectively. The mean retweetability difference lied between +220.1% and +2.7%, meaning that the retweetability of tweets on topic was over-average during the whole week after the triggering event. The highest values were given on the day of the event (13-Nov) with +220.1% over average and on the 5th day after the event (18-Nov) with +87.9%. The lowest difference in retweetability was given on the 3rd day after the event (16-Nov), with +2.7%. Regarding the news services from the UK, the topic of interest ratio ranged between 64.7% and 20.1% with the highest value on the day of the event (13-Nov) and the 3rd day after the event (16-Nov) with the ratios reaching 64.7% and 43.9% respectively. The lowest ratio was given on the 7th day after the event (20-Nov) and reached 20.1%. The mean difference in retweetability ranged between +299.5% and +13.4%. Again, all the values were over-average. The highest retweetability values were given on the first two days (13-Nov and 14-Nov) with +299.5% and +71.6% respectively. The lowest difference was given on the 4th day after the event (17-Nov) and reached 13.4%.

Figure 6 depicts the ratios of tweets on topic of interest and the mean difference in their retweetability for the last investigated triggering event, the Brussels terrorist attacks. The German news services tweeted on the topic of interest in between 62.2% and 1.16% of their tweets, with highest value on the day of the event (22-Mar), which decreased steadily over the week and reach the lowest ratio on the 7th day after the event (29-Mar). The mean difference in retweetability ranged between +80%

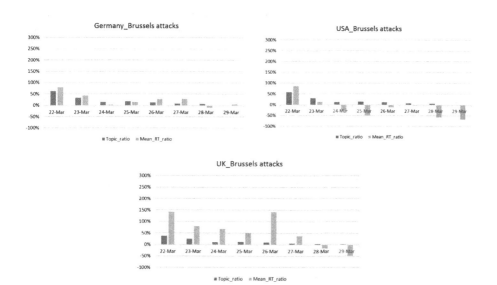

Fig. 6. The ratio of tweets on the triggering event ("toi") and the mean difference in retweeting tweets on topic of interest relative to the overall average number of RTs per tweet for the investigated triggering event *Brussels attacks* for German, USA and UK news services.

and −9.9%, with highest values on the first two days (22-Mar and 23-Mar) with 80% and 42.6% respectively, and the lowest, only one negative, value of −9.9% on the 6th day after the event (28-Mar). As for the news services from the USA, the ratio of tweets on topic of interest ranged between 58.1% and 0.9%, with highest value on the day of the event (22-Mar), decreasing over the week and reaching the lowest one on 29-Mar. The mean difference in retweetability ranged between +86.1% and −67.9%. The only over-average retweetability was given on the first two days (22-Mar and 23-Mar) with +86.1% and +14.2%. On the remaining days, the retweetability of tweets on topic was under-average. Considering the news services from the UK, the ratio of tweets on topic ranged between 37.8% and 1.4%, with the highest value during the first two days (22-Mar and 23-Mar), 37.8% and 25% respectively. The ratio decreased over the week after the event reaching the lowest value on 29-Mar. The mean difference in retweetability ranged between +142% and −47.9%. The highest value was given on the day of the event (22-Mar), steadily decreasing over the week and reaching negative values on 28-Mar (−16.6%) and 29-Mar (−47.9%).

The differences in retweetability of tweets on topic were further examined with the Mann-Whitney U-test (MWU). Tables 1 through 3 show the median number of RTs of tweets on topic of interest (toi_1) and of tweets on other non-related topics (toi_0), as well as the significance of these differences as computed with the MWU-test.

Table 1 presents the medians for each country and topic group as well as the significance outputs of the MWU-test for the first investigated triggering event, Charlie Hebdo terrorist attacks. Regarding the German news services accounts, for all investigated days, except for the 7th day, the differences in retweetability between tweets on topic of interest and of tweets on other topics were significant. The median of tweets on others topics oscillates between 4 and 6 RTs. The medians of tweets on topic were highest on the 1st and 5th day (16 RTs), and decreased on other days to 8.5–12 RTs. As for the news services from the USA, the differences were significant for the first three days and then again for the 5th and 6th day. For both topic groups the medians were the highest, compared to the other countries. The median number of tweets on other topics

Table 1. Difference in median retweetability of tweets on topic of interest (toi_1) and on other topics (toi_0) and their significance according to Mann-Whitney U-test for the triggering event *Charlie Hebdo*.

Charlie Hebdo	DE			USA			UK		
	toi_0	toi_1	Sig.	toi_0	toi_1	Sig.	toi_0	toi_1	Sig.
1st day	4	16	**	43	90	**	14	64	**
2nd day	4	12	**	32	67	**	15	43	**
3rd day	5	12	**	47	66	**	15	41	**
4th day	6	11	**	46	75.5	ns	22	41.5	**
5th day	4	16	**	27	77	*	20	50	**
6th day	6	10.5	**	34	48	**	17	30.5	**
7th day	5.5	8.5	ns	36	38.5	ns	15	30	**
8th day	4	10	**	37	55	ns	14	33.5	**

Table 2. Difference in median retweetability of tweets on topic of interest (toi_1) and on other topics (toi_0) and their significance according to Mann-Whitney U-test for the triggering event *Paris attacks*.

Paris attacks	DE			USA			UK		
	toi_0	toi_1	Sig.	toi_0	toi_1	Sig.	toi_0	toi_1	Sig.
1st day	5	34	**	37	388	**	11	110	**
2nd day	8	16	**	48	144	**	21	46.5	**
3rd day	6	10	**	76	110	*	20	38	**
4th day	6	9	**	53	93	**	15.5	21.5	**
5th day	9	11	ns	44	106	**	19.5	23.5	*
6th day	8	12	**	44	73	**	14.5	23	**
7th day	7	11	**	53.5	73	*	12	21	**
8th day	7	7	ns	53.5	122.5	**	15	27.5	**

was around 27 to 43 RTs, whereas for tweets on topic of interest between 38.5 and 90 RTs. Regarding news services from the UK, all differences between the both topic groups were significant, the medians of RTs for tweets on other topics were between 14 and 22 RTs, whereas for tweets on topic of interest between 30 and 64 RTs. For all countries, the medians for tweets on topic of interest were higher than for tweets on other topics through the whole week after the triggering event, however, they decreased at the end of the week.

Table 2 shows the outcomes for the second investigated triggering event, the Paris terrorist attacks. Regarding the German news services, the differences in retweetability between the two topic-groups were highly significant, except for the 5th and 8th day. Again, the retweetability medians of tweets on other topics were lower (between 5 and 9 RTs) than for tweets on topic of interest (between 7 and 34 RTs), however, they decreased to the end of the week. As for the USA, all differences were significant and the medians for tweets on topic of interest were even higher than for the first triggering event (between 73 and 388 RTs), tweets on other topics exhibited retweetability medians between 37 and 76 RTs. Regarding the news services from the UK, all differences were significant as well. The medians for tweets on topic of interest were between 21 and 110 RTs, whereas for tweets on other topics between 11 and 21 RTs.

Table 3 presents the retweetability medians and significance outcomes for the last investigated triggering event, the Brussels terrorist attacks. Here, the outcomes of MWU-test are way less significant than for other investigated triggering events. For Germany, there were significant differences on the first two days and on the 4th through 6th day. Furthermore, the differences were less distinctive when compared to the other triggering events. Tweets on topic of interest achieved the median retweetability score between 8 and 18 RTs, whereas the tweets on other topics between 5 and 8 RTs. As for the USA, the differences in retweetability were only significant for the 1st, 5th and 7th day. The first difference was very distinctive, with a median retweetability score of 155.5 for tweets on topic and of 49 for tweets on other topics. On the 5th day this difference got less noticeable (63 and 45 RTs respectively). On the 7th day, with least significant difference, the tweets on topic achieved less RTs than tweets on different

Table 3. Difference in median retweetability of tweets on topic of interest (toi_1) and on other topics (toi_0) and their significance according to Mann-Whitney U-test for the triggering event *Brussels attacks.*

Brussels attacks	DE			USA			UK		
	toi_0	toi_1	Sig.	toi_0	toi_1	Sig.	toi_0	toi_1	Sig.
1st day	5	18	**	49	155.5	**	8	35	**
2nd day	5	8	**	60	60	ns	9	17	**
3rd day	6	7	ns	57	52	ns	9	23	**
4th day	7	9	*	66	53	ns	8	20.5	**
5th day	7	10.5	*	45	63	*	13	29	**
6th day	8	13	*	58	67	ns	18	17.5	ns
7th day	6.5	8	ns	60	32	*	12	12	ns
8th day	7	11.5	ns	52	32	ns	13	09	ns

topics (32 and 60 RTs respectively). As for the UK, the differences in retweetability for the first five days were significant. However, a decrease in median scores is recognizable when compared to the previous two investigated events. The median retweetability scores for tweets on topic of interest were between 9 and 35 RTs, whereas for tweets on other topics between 8 and 18 RTs.

3.3   Inter-country Differences and Differences Between All Triggering Events Regarding Correlation Between Tweet's Topic and Its Retweetability

The third research question regards the differences between the investigated news services' accounts considering the correlation between the topic of the tweet and its retweetability. The focus of the analysis is also set on the comparison of the three triggering events (fourth research question). For this purpose, the point-biserial correlation between the "topic of interest" variable (coded as a binary variable) and the number of RTs (interval scaled variable) was computed. This correlation shows, whether the topic of the tweet (terrorist attacks) had influence on the number of received RTs and, if it did, how strong this effect was.

Regarding the first triggering event, Charlie Hebdo terrorist attacks, and the German news services, all values of point-biserial correlation between topic of the tweet and its retweetability are significant, except for the last two days. The effect sizes are medium on the 1st and 5th day, and small otherwise. As for the new services from the UK, the correlation is significant for all days except for the 6th day. The effect sizes are medium on the first two days and on the 5th day, and otherwise small. Regarding the new services from the USA, two significant correlations are given for the first three days and then for the 5th day. The effect sizes are medium only on the 5th day, and otherwise small.

For the second investigated triggering event, the Paris terrorist attacks, there are less significant values than for the first triggering event. As for the German news accounts, the correlation outcomes are significant for the first four days and for the 7th day. The

Table 4. Correlation between RTs and "topic of interest" computed with point-biserial correlation (r_{pb}) for the three triggering events. The thresholds for effect sizes: small (0.1), medium (0.3), and large (0.5), are color-coded (light-gray, medium-gray and dark-gray respectively).

	Charlie Hebdo			Paris Attacks			Brussels Attacks		
	DE	UK	USA	DE	UK	USA	DE	UK	USA
1st	.364**	.353**	.292**	.578**	.509**	.433**	.299**	.310**	.239**
2nd	.225**	.319**	.155*	.211**	.161**	.176**	.184**	.214**	.047
3rd	.282**	.228**	.159*	.234**	.177**	.073	.011	.123**	-.068
4th	.215**	.111*	.089	.129*	.103**	.004	.050	.085*	-.050
5th	.384**	.366**	.311**	-.048	.033	.166**	.101	.251**	-.019
6th	.132*	.048	.037	.099	.148**	.148*	.080	.049	-.005
7th	-.074	.119**	.098	.169**	.153**	.086	-.023	-.015	-.090
8th	.101	.187**	-.021	-.004	.045	.114	.004	-.021	-.037

correlation on the first day is of a large effect size. However, the correlations on the remaining days have only small effects. There is a very similar tendency for the news services from the UK. There is a significant correlation with large effect size on the first day and, after, there are significant correlations until the 4th day as well as on the 6th and 7th day with a small effect size. Regarding the news services from the USA, the correlations are significant on the first two days and on the 5th and 6th day. The correlation on the first day has a medium effect size, whereas on the remaining days only small one.

The last investigated triggering event, the Brussels terrorist attacks, exhibits the least significant correlations. For German accounts, the only significant correlations are given on the first two days, both of small effect sizes. As for the news services from the UK, the significant correlations are given for the first five days. The correlation on the first day is of a medium effect size, whereas on the remaining days of small one. The correlation on the 4th day does not even fall within the threshold of a small effect size (coefficient smaller than 0.1). Regarding the news services from the USA, there is only one significant correlation on the first day, with a small effect size.

Table 5 summarizes only the significant outcomes of the point-biserial correlations and includes the coefficients of determination (r_{pb}^2). These are the percentage values (square of the correlation r_{pb} multiplied by 100) that show what variance in the number of RTs can be explained by the variance in the topic of the tweet. For the first investigated event, the coefficient of determination was highest on the 5th day with 14.75% (Germany), 13.40% (UK) and 9.67% (USA), and on the first day with 13.25% (Germany), 12.46% (UK) and 8.53% (USA). As for the second investigated triggering event, there were less values with significance level under 0.05. The coefficient of determination was the highest for all three countries on the first day: 33.41% (Germany), 25.91% (UK) and 18.75% (USA). These values are also the highest for all three

Table 5. Coefficients of determination (r_{pb}^2) expressed as percentage values. Only significant values (p < .05) were used for the calculation (see Table 4).

	Charlie Hebdo			Paris Attacks			Brussels Attacks		
	DE	UK	USA	DE	UK	USA	DE	UK	USA
1^{sts}	13.25%	12.46%	8.53%	33.41%	25.91%	18.75%	8.94%	9.61%	5.71%
2nd	5.06%	10.18%	2.40%	4.45%	2.59%	3.10%	3.39%	4.58%	
3rd	7.95%	5.20%	2.53%	5.48%	3.13%			1.51%	
4th	4.62%	1.23%		1.66%	1.06%			0.72%	
5th	14.75%	13.40%	9.67%			2.76%		6.30%	
6th	1.74%				2.19%	2.19%			
7th		1.42%		2.86%	2.34%				
8th		3.50%							

investigated triggering events. As for the third triggering event, the most significant values are given for UK, followed by Germany with two significant values, and USA with only one. Here, the first day was marked with the highest coefficients of determination as well: 8.94% (Germany), 9.61% (UK) and 5.71% (the only one for the USA). These were, however, the lowest values compared to the other investigated triggering events.

3.4   Results in a Nutshell

The first research question concerned the general differences in Twitter activity between news services from Germany, UK and the USA. Indeed, it appears that the news services from the UK tweet the most, however, the most RTs per tweet are received by news services from the USA. As for Germany, the number of tweets per day was similar to the one of news accounts from the USA, but with a much lower number of RTs/tweet. In general, there was mostly a peak in Twitter activity on the day of the triggering event or on the day after, and a peak in RTs/tweet on the day of the triggering event for all countries. The lowest Twitter activity was usually observed on the weekends.

The second research question concerned the difference between countries in the amount of tweets on topic of interest as well as in their retweetability. From the three investigated countries, the news services from the USA posted in average the least tweets on the triggering event. The chronologically last triggering event, the Brussels terrorist attacks, got the lowest coverage when compared to the other two events. Regarding the retweetability of tweets on topic, it was again the lowest for the Brussels attacks. The differences in median retweetability were the highest and most significant after the Charlie Hebdo attacks, decreased after the Paris attacks, and were the lowest for the Brussels attacks. This indicates that with the time the differences in retweetability of tweets on topic of interest got minor and less significant.

The third research question regarded the differences between the three countries in the correlation between the topic of the tweet and its retweetability. This was also a further indicator for differences between the three triggering events (fourth research question). The observed tendency was similar to the analyses for the second research question. For the first triggering event, Charlie Hebdo terrorist attacks, the coefficients of determination were high on two separate days for all three countries. It was marked with significant correlations over several days with a medium or small effect sizes. For the second triggering event, the Paris terrorist attacks, there were fewer significant correlations with smaller effect sizes. The highest significant difference in retweetability was given on the day of the attacks. The last triggering event, the Brussels terrorist attacks, was marked with least correlations and relevant effect sizes only on the day of the attacks. For the USA the only significant correlation was given on the day of the attack and the coefficient of determination was smaller than after the other two triggering events. This tendency was recognizable for all three countries, but especially distinct for the news services from the USA. There appears to be a tendency of decreasing retweetability of tweets on triggering events being terrorist attacks. This is especially given for non-European news services (USA), but also recognizable for European news services (Germany and UK). The retweeting tendency moved from medium effects of tweet's topic on its retweetability over several days (first triggering event), to medium or large effects only on the day of the event followed by small effects on other days (second triggering event), and lastly, to small effects on the first day or first few days only (third triggering event).

4   Conclusion and Limitations

In this study we investigated news services' Twitter accounts from three countries and their Twitter activity around three terrorist attacks in Europe. Although there are differences in Twitter activity between the three countries regarding the average tweets posted per day and average number of RTs per tweet, there are some similarities regarding reporting on terrorist attacks and the reaction of the users. The relative number of tweets reporting on the terrorist attacks gets smaller with the time, it is especially distinctive for the last investigated event (Brussels attacks). The retweetability of such tweets gets lower with the time as well. The difference between tweets on concerned topic and other tweets fades. Even though there was a strong correlation between tweets on terrorist attacks for Charlie Hebdo over several days, there is almost no correlation for the last investigated event, Brussels attacks. This could indicate not only declining volume of reporting on such events, but also the lessening attention they get from the Twitter community.

In this study we considered only few variables (number of tweets, their categorization, and the number of RTs). Further research should consider other factors possibly influencing the Twitter activity, like the number of followers or the time since when the accounts are active. A multi-factor analysis could reveal further aspects influencing the retweetability of certain tweets. Furthermore, a more detailed topic analysis of tweets could reveal further differences between the countries as well as the investigated triggering vents. The fact that the news accounts from USA tweeted (relatively) least tweets on the event, however, that these tweets were mostly retweeted compared to other countries, requires a deeper analysis. Furthermore, the results indicate a deadening of the (Twitter) society towards news on terrorist attacks, which could by analyzed from a psychological perspective. Even though for the first terrorist attacks there was a continual attention in form of RTs over several days, for the latest ones there was just a minor reaction. After 24 h these were in fact no more than yesterday's news.

References

1. Jansen, B.J., Zhang, M., Sobel, K., Chowdury, A.: Twitter power: tweets as electronic word of mouth. J. Am. Soc. Inf. Sci. Technol. **60**, 2169–2188 (2009). doi:10.1002/ASI.V60:11
2. Fietkiewicz, K.J., Lins, E., Baran, K.S., Stock, W.G.: Inter-generational comparison of social media use: investigating the online behavior of different generational cohorts. In: 49th Hawaii International Conference on Systems Sciences, pp. 3829–3838. IEEE Computer Society, Washington, DC (2016). doi:10.1109/HICSS.2016.477
3. Armstrong, C.L., Gao, F.: Now tweet this: how news organizations use Twitter. Electron. News. **4**, 218–235 (2010). doi:10.1177/1931243110389457
4. Lenhart, A., Fox, S.: Twitter and status updating (2009). http://www.pewinternet.org/2009/02/12/twitter-and-status-updating/
5. Palser, B.: Hitting the tweet spot. Am. J. Rev., April/May 2009. http://ajrarchive.org/Article.asp?id=4737
6. Bruns, A., Burgees, J.: Research news discussion on Twitter: new methodologies. J. Stud. **13**, 801–814 (2012). doi:10.1080/1461670X.2012.664428
7. Letierce, J., Passant, A., Decker, S., Breslin, J.G.: Understanding how Twitter is used to spread scientific messages. In: WebSci Conference, Raleigh, NC, pp. 1–8 (2010)
8. Bruns, A.: The practice of news blogging. In: Bruns, A., Jacobs, J. (eds.) Uses of Blogs, pp. 11–22. Peter Lang, New York (2006)
9. Kwak, H., Lee, C., Park, H., Moon, S.: What is Twitter, a social network or a news media? Categories and subject descriptors. In: 19th International Conference on WWW, pp. 591–600. ACM, New Work (2010). doi:10.1145/1772690.1772751
10. Subašić, I., Berendt, B.: Peddling or creating? Investigating the role of Twitter in news reporting. In: Clough, P., Foley, C., Gurrin, C., Jones, G.J.F., Kraaij, W., Lee, H., Mudoch, V. (eds.) ECIR 2011. LNCS, vol. 6611, pp. 207–213. Springer, Heidelberg (2011). doi:10.1007/978-3-642-20161-5_21
11. Bruns, A.: Gatewatching: Collaborative Online News Production. Peter Lang, New York (2005)
12. Ettema, J.S.: New media and new mechanisms of public accountability. Journal. **10**, 319–321 (2009). doi:10.1177/1464884909102591
13. Hermida, A.: From TV to Twitter: how ambient news became ambient journalism. M/C J. **13**, 45–46 (2010). https://ssrn.com/abstract=1732603
14. Markopoulos, P., De Ruyter, B., Mackay, W.: Preface. In: Markopoulos, P., De Ruyter, B., Mackay, W. (eds.) Awareness Systems: Advances in Theory, Methodology and Design, pp. v–xiii. Springer, New York (2009). doi:10.1007/978-1-84882-477-5
15. Bruns, A.: Blogs, Wikipedia, Second Life, and Beyond: From Production to Produsage. Peter Lang, New York (2008)

16. Mendoza, M., Poblete, B., Castillo, C.: Twitter under crisis: can we trust what we RT? In: 1st Workshop on Social Media Analytics, pp. 71–79 (2010). doi:10.1145/1964858.1964869
17. Domingo, D., Quandt, T., Heinonen, A., Paulussen, S., Singer, J., Vujnovic, M.: Participatory journalism practices in the media and beyond: an international comparative study of initiatives in online newspaper. Journal. Pract. **2**, 326–342 (2008). doi:10.1080/17512780802281065
18. Purcell, K., Rainie, L., Mitchell, A., Rosenstiel, T., Olmstead, K.: Understanding the participatory news consumer (2010). http://www.pewinternet.org
19. Granovetter, M.S.: The strength of weak ties. Am. J. Sociol. **78**, 1360–1380 (1973)
20. Farhi, P.: The Twitter explosion. Am. Journal. Rev. **31**, 26–31 (2009)
21. Kempe, D., Kleinberg, J., Tardos, É.: Maximizing the spread of influence through a social network. In: International Conference on Knowledge Discovery and Data Mining, pp. 137–146. ACM, New York (2003). doi:10.1145/956755.956769
22. Gruhl, D., Guha, R., Liben-Nowell, D., Tomkins, A.: Information diffusion through blogspace. In: International WWW Conference, pp. 491–501. ACM, New York (2004). doi:10.1145/988672.988739
23. Wu, F., Huberman, B.A., Adamic, L.A., Tyler, J.R.: Information flow in social groups. Phys. A: Stat. Mech. Appl. **337**, 327–335 (2004). doi:10.1016/J.PHYSA.2004.01.030
24. Adamic, L., Adar, E.: How to search a social network. Soc. Netw. **27**, 187–203 (2005). doi:10.1016/j.socnet.2005.01.007
25. Davitz, J., Yu, J., Basu, S., Gutelius, D., Harris, A.: iLink: search and routing in social networks. In: International Conference on Knowledge Discovery and Data Mining, pp. 931–940. ACM, New York (2007). doi:10.1145/1281192.1281292
26. Lerman, K., Ghosh, R.: Information contagion: an empirical study of the spread of news on Digg and Twitter social networks. In: 4th International Conference on Weblogs Social Media, pp. 90–97. AAAI Press, Menlo Park (2010). doi:10.1146/ANNUREV.AN.03.100174.001431
27. Gahran, A.: Secondhand Twitter posse: how big is yours, and why should you care? (2008). http://www.poynter.org
28. Lewis, J., Cushion, S.: The thirst to be first. Journal. Pract. **3**, 304–318 (2009). doi:10.1080/17512780902798737
29. Boyd, D., Golder, S., Lotan, G.: Tweet, tweet, retweet: conversational aspects of retweeting on twitter. In: International Conference on System Sciences, pp. 1–10. IEEE Computer Society, Washington, DC (2010). doi:10.1109/HICSS.2010.412
30. Naveed, N., Gottron, T., Kunegis, J., Alhadi, A.C.: Bad news travel fast: a content-based analysis of interestingness on Twitter. In: 3rd International Web Science Conference, pp. 1–7. ACM, New York (2011). doi:10.1145/2527031.2527052
31. Hong, L., Dan, O., Davison, B.D.: Predicting popular messages in Twitter. In: International WWW Conference, pp. 57–58. ACM, New York (2011). doi:10.1145/1963192.1963222
32. Suh, B., Hong, L., Pirolli, P., Chi, E.H.: Want to be retweeted? Large scale analytics on factors impacting retweet in Twitter network. In: 2nd International Conference on Social Computing, pp. 177–184. IEEE Computer Society, Washington, DC (2010). doi:10.1109/SocialCom.2010.33
33. Cha, M., Haddai, H., Benevenuto, F., Gummadi, K.P.: Measuring user influence in Twitter: the million follower fallacy. In: 4th International Conference on Web and Social Media, pp. 10–17. AAAI Press, Menlo Park (2010). doi:10.1.1.167.192
34. Romero, D.M., Galuba, W., Asur, S., Huberman, B.A.: Influence and passivity in social media. In: 20th International Conference Companion on WWW, pp. 113–114. ACM, New York (2011). doi:10.1145/1963192.1963250

35. Zhao, W.X., Jiang, J., Weng, J., He, J., Lim, E.-P., Yan, H., Li, X.: Comparing Twitter and traditional media using topic models. In: Clough, P., Foley, C., Gurrin, C., Jones, G.J.F., Kraaij, W., Lee, H., Mudoch, V. (eds.) ECIR 2011. LNCS, vol. 6611, pp. 338–349. Springer, Heidelberg (2011). doi:10.1007/978-3-642-20161-5_34

36. Statista: Ranking der Top 20 Zeitungsportale nach der Anzahl der Besucher in Deutschland. de.statista.com/statistik/daten/studie/13032

37. PewResearchCenter: Digital: top 50 online news entities 2015. www.journalism.org

38. Online Newspapers: Top 50 English newspapers. www.onlinenewspapers.com

39. Mann, H.B., Whitney, D.R.: On a test of whether one of two random variables is stochastically larger than the other. Ann. Math. Stat. **18**, 50–60 (1947). doi:10.1214/aoms/1177730491

40. Laerd Statistics: Mann-Whitney U test using SPSS statistics. https://statistics.laerd.com

41. Cohen, J.: Statistical Power Analysis for the Behavioral Sciences. Lawrence Erlbaum, Hillsdale (1988)

42. Laerd Statistics: Point-biserial correlation using SPSS statistics. https://statistics.laerd.com

43. Sheskin, D.J.: Handbook of Parametric and Nonparametric Statistical Procedures. Chapman and Hall/CRC, New York (2003). doi:10.1201/9781420036268.CH28

e-Voting in America: Current Realities and Future Directions

Nathan Johnson[1(✉)], Brian M. Jones[2], and Kyle Clendenon[2]

[1] Western Carolina University, Cullowhee, NC, USA
jnjohnson@wcu.edu
[2] Tennessee Technological University, Cookeville, TN, USA
bjones@tntech.edu, kclendeno21@gmail.com

Abstract. This paper presents a snapshot of the current status of voting methodologies in the United States as of November 2016. The authors present the methodologies currently employed to facilitate voting including paper based and direct recording electronic systems. This is followed by a discussion of voter confidence in the election system where e-voting systems are utilized, particularly in the areas of auditing, security, influence, and human-computer interaction (HCI). The paper concludes with a brief summary of the future of e-voting, including what technology is on the horizon, and a discussion of future research directions.

Keywords: e-Voting · Human computer interaction · Election process · Voter confidence

1 Introduction

Ever since Alexander Hamilton first wrote about "the mode of appointment of the chief magistrate of the United States" in Federalist No. 67 [19], and George Washington was elected their first president in February 1789 [30], citizens of the United States (US) have been electing their governing officials. The president, governors, senators, congressional representatives, judges, mayors, and local officials have all been selected through the process of free and open voting.

Americans go to the polls nearly every year to vote for something, whether in local, state, or national elections. Although this exercise in democracy has been carried out unchanged since the early days of the republic, the method in which the votes are cast has not. In fact, as technology has advanced, so has the manner in which voters cast their vote. Technology has allowed the voting process to become more streamlined and efficient, and given rise to a variety of interfaces in which the voter may find themselves facing on Election Day. Along with these technological changes have come challenges in recording and tallying votes, and with these challenges, issues of trust in the voting system. Many of these challenges have presented themselves in the most recent US national election of President Donald J. Trump.

In the following pages, we review the different voting methodologies currently employed in the US and highlight the human computer interaction (HCI) considerations where appropriate. Next, we discuss how voter confidence in the election process

© Springer International Publishing AG 2017
G. Meiselwitz (Ed.): SCSM 2017, Part I, LNCS 10282, pp. 337–349, 2017.
DOI: 10.1007/978-3-319-58559-8_27

has been affected in terms of auditing, security, influence, finances, and HCI. Finally, we report on the future of voting technology, and offer further research direction.

2 Current Voting Systems Utilized in the United States

Voting systems in the US have varied from polling place to polling place over the years. These voting systems consist of various hardware, display devices, and methods for collecting and storing voting data (Roth [42]). In some states, such as New Mexico, Montana, and Maine, the voter encounters a system that Abraham Lincoln would find familiar - a paper ballot filled out and then counted by human hand. In three states, Washington, Oregon, and Colorado, and several counties in other states, voting is executed via the US Postal Service mail on paper ballot. In still other states, votes are cast and tallied on what are referred to as Direct Recording Electronic Systems (DRE), a completely electronic touchscreen and tallying system. Two systems, the punch card and mechanical lever, once mainstays across US polling places, have now been completely discontinued as methods for voting.

As of 2016, a mixture of these systems exist across the US, even differing from county to county within the same state in some cases. In addition, some of these systems allow for an audit of the actual vote and others do not depending on the system and the proprietary nature of the vendor supplying the system. In the following paragraphs, we detail how voters interact with the different voting systems currently used in the US [46].

2.1 Optically Scanned Paper Ballot System

When using paper ballot systems, voters typically mark their selections by filling in a space on a paper ballot (similar to an academic test scantron form). It is usually a box, oval, or circle that is completely colored in by the voter. Once all ballots are filled in and voting is complete, the ballots are electronically scanned and tallied to determine the number of votes cast for each candidate. Mail in voting occurs via this method in addition to traditional polling place voting. These ballots are typically auditable and able to be recounted by hand if necessary. As of 2016, nearly three-quarters of the US still uses this type of voting system [3].

2.2 Direct Record Electronic System

DREs are electronic systems that employ computers to capture votes immediately into an electronic memory module. There are various types of DRE systems, and interfaces may include touchscreens, electromechanical dials, and even buttons that are pushed to register the individual voter's selection. All votes are stored by the computer on a memory device (usually an internal hard drive). Some DRE systems are equipped with printers that allow a print out for the voter to confirm that their vote was inputted into the system as they wished before it is saved to the storage device. In addition, having a printout serves as a paper record of the vote providing an audit trail. However, not all

DRE systems are auditable and provide no means to determine if votes were missed, inaccurately tallied, or recounted.

2.3   Ballot Marking System

Ballot Marking systems are used to help disabled voters have easy access to voting technology. These devices generally use a combination of touchscreen and audio or other element such as gesture interaction, eye tracking, or other accessibility feature. These systems typically capture the vote on a paper ballot of some type, and the vote is later tabulated and recorded manually by humans. These types of systems are fully auditable and provide a method of recount.

2.4   Punch Card and Mechanical Lever Systems

These voting systems were once ubiquitous across the US and found in many polling locations, but as of the 2016 election season, they have been completely phased out [45]. These systems were retired after passage of the Help American's Vote Act (HAVA) in 2002, a response to issues discovered in the 2000 Presidential election where over a million ballots were not processed correctly [29]. Punch card voting systems utilized a paper card and a small device that allowed voters to punch holes in the ballot card corresponding to their desired vote. The pattern of holes punched indicated what candidate(s) the voter chose. Once the entire ballot card was completed, the voter then deposited it into a secure box to be tabulated later - either mechanically or by hand.

Punch card systems were not used as of the 2016 election cycle. Mechanical lever systems were first introduced in the last decade of the 1800s and were used in multiple jurisdictions across the states throughout the 20th century [32]. Voters utilizing mechanical voting machines would enter a booth and slide a mechanical lever to one side revealing their voting choices. Voters would then pull knobs to make their choices. Once complete, the lever would be slid back to its original position and the votes would be cast [6]. Mechanical lever systems have not been used since the 2010 election cycle.

In Table 1 below, the different voting methods and voting audit availability by state are reported [46].

3   Voter Confidence in the e-Voting Process

Using a combination of the voting tools outlined in the previous section, US voters have regularly gone to the polls to vote for their respective candidates since the late 18th century. Although the number of Americans going to the polls since WWII has dropped by nearly half [26], the free exercise of voting and the notion of being governed at the consent of the voter has endured.

Although the process of elections have persisted throughout US history, every election cycle generates episodes of vote miscounts and recounts, voting machine problems, vote tampering, precinct worker misconduct, and instances of voter fraud

Table 1. Voting methods by state

State	Voting method	Auditable?	State	Voting method	Auditable?
AL	Optical scan paper ballot systems	Yes	MT	Optical scan paper ballot systems	Yes
AK	Mixed paper ballot and DRE systems	Yes	NE	Optical scan paper ballot systems	Yes
AZ	Mixed paper ballot and DRE systems	Yes	NV	DRE systems	Yes
AR	Mixed paper ballot and DRE systems	No	NH	Optical scan paper ballot systems	Yes
CA	Mixed paper ballot and DRE systems	Yes	NJ	DRE systems	No
CO	Mixed paper ballot and DRE systems	Yes	NM	Optical scan paper ballot systems	Yes
CT	Optical scan paper ballot systems	Yes	NY	Optical scan paper ballot systems	Yes
DE	DRE Systems	No	NC	Mixed paper ballot and DRE systems	Yes
FL	Mixed paper ballot and DRE systems	No	ND	Optical scan paper ballot systems	Yes
GA	DRE systems	No	OH	Mixed paper ballot and DRE systems	Yes
HI	Mixed paper ballot and DRE systems	Yes	OK	Optical scan paper ballot systems	Yes
ID	Mixed paper ballot and DRE systems	Yes	OR	Optical scan paper ballot systems	Yes
IL	Mixed paper ballot and DRE systems	Yes	PA	Mixed paper ballot and DRE systems	No
IN	Mixed paper ballot and DRE systems	No	RI	Optical scan paper ballot systems	Yes
IA	Optical scan paper ballot systems	Yes	SC	DRE systems	No
KS	Mixed paper ballot and DRE systems	No	SD	Optical scan paper ballot systems	Yes
KY	Mixed paper ballot and DRE systems	No	TN	Mixed paper ballot and DRE systems	No
LA	DRE systems	No	TX	Mixed paper ballot and DRE systems	No
ME	Optical scan paper ballot systems	Yes	UT	DRE systems	Yes
MD	Optical scan paper ballot systems	Yes	VT	Optical scan paper ballot systems	Yes
MA	Optical scan paper ballot systems	Yes	VA	Mixed paper ballot and DRE systems	No

(continued)

Table 1. (*continued*)

State	Voting method	Auditable?	State	Voting method	Auditable?
MI	Optical scan paper ballot systems	Yes	WA	Mixed paper ballot and DRE systems	Yes
MN	Optical scan paper ballot systems	Yes	WV	Mixed paper ballot and DRE systems	Yes
MS	Mixed paper ballot and DRE systems	No	WI	Mixed paper ballot and DRE systems	Yes
MO	Mixed paper ballot and DRE systems	Yes	WY	Mixed paper ballot and DRE systems	Yes

Source: [46]

and/or disenfranchisement of a voting block. The most recent US presidential election was no different. For instance, in Connecticut, ballots were used that had the wrong candidate listed for the state legislature. Those ballots were used for over an hour before the error was caught [31]. In Georgia, North Carolina, and Pennsylvania it was reported that DREs were 'flipping' the vote from one presidential candidate to the other whenever the voter tried to select their favored candidate [9, 14, 44]. And in Michigan, scanning systems in over one-third of the all the voting precincts in Detroit recorded more votes than should have been possible for that particular precinct [28].

One of the impetuses for advancing e-voting technologies has been to streamline and strengthen the voting processes, while further empowering the citizenry [8]. For the most part, this has occurred. However, even with the passage of HAVA, and as the above reported scenarios from the most recent election cycle highlight, several considerations are still at play when discussing how confident the populace is in e-voting systems and methodologies. We believe that these considerations can be grouped into one of five broad categories: auditing, security, influence, finances, and HCI.

3.1 Auditing

A primary issue with e-voting on DRE machines is the potential lack of auditing the vote. While some e-voting machines allow for paper trails to be generated, others do not. Further, an auditing function is not required by the Federal Election Commission (FEC), although some states have enacted their own auditing rules. This lack of paper trail for every vote cast leaves the voter with the possibility of being "disenfranchised" if there is a contested election or some form of recount because there is no record of how they actually voted if they use a DRE that doesn't provide a paper receipt or is capable of a simple vote audit.

Complicating the issue is the fact that DREs are all proprietary pieces of machinery manufactured by a corporate entity. This reality carries with it the need for privacy and secrecy in testing and certification of the machinery. Both the tests and the results are often closely held secrets by the manufacturing entity, and tests only check for compliance with minimal FEC requirements. Further, any software running in the DRE that is considered commercially available is not required by the FEC to be tested [43].

3.2 Security

If auditing is the first issue that tops the list of voter concerns with DREs, security and integrity of the vote is a close second. Malicious tampering with a DRE system is a possibility both while the machine is in storage, or while it is actually being used to vote with. A report by the Congressional Research Service found that DREs are subject to a variety of nefarious attacks, particularly from malicious code [16]. These types of code (malware, viruses, Trojan horses, etc.) have been shown to be able to exploit themselves within machines and transmit to other linked machines. In addition, exploits based on basic memory buffer and encryption errors have been shown to be possible on certain vendors' machines [7].

One scenario of malicious tampering might find code being introduced physically via a bad actor while actually voting via some form of direct input or tampering. Another scenario sees the bad actor using innocent voters to carry out the attack on the DRE. For instance, some DREs require a "voter card" be used to activate the voting instance. These cards are reused by different voters throughout the election cycle. If one of these cards was stolen, compromised, and then reintroduced to the voting environment, unsuspecting voters might inadvertently introduce malicious code into the system. These so called "air gap" attacks have been demonstrated to be effective and quickly carried out. Attacks may do something as straight forward as altering vote tallies for particular candidates, or something more stealthy such as changing votes to specific candidate in a somewhat random fashion in order to disguise the nature of the attack. Even more sinister, some attacks might display one candidate on the screen, but record the vote for a different candidate [27, 48].

Other possible scenarios include compromising the central voting database used by the county or precinct that "programs" the DREs and collects the data from them as votes are tabulated. This intrusion could come physically or remotely as these central databases are often connected to the internet. Frustratingly, many of the DRE systems used around the US are running on software that only interfaces with now-extinct software such as Windows 2000 and Windows XP, the former of the two operating systems not having a security update in over six years.

A dilemma of security lies in the fact that every precinct and every state could be, and in some cases are, conducting their elections using different processes and systems. There are no set standards for security or nationwide policies that dictate how DREs are stored, activated, and used. Although, many have pointed to this very confusing and seemingly out of control arrangement, this decentralized and eclectic methodology for voting state by state, as part of the strength of the overall system. Because there are no set standards or common ways of conducting elections from state to state, it makes a coordinated attack on the entire system virtually impossible [33].

3.3 Influence

Another issue that surrounds e-voting is one of influence. As noted previously, DRE machines are acquired from a variety of vendors. The technology, software, and methodologies that these machines use to capture voter input may differ from county to county in the same state. Since each vendor has their own proprietary technology, issues surrounding trade secrets and industrial espionage make independent reviews of systems difficult [7]. Since a total air of secrecy surrounds these machines, voters are often left to wonder who is behind the companies that are providing the machines and doing the requisite testing to ensure they are working properly.

An informal interview with 20 recent voters showed that most felt fairly confident in the voting system in general; but when asked specifically about electronic voting, 3 of them expressed uncertainty in the "security" of their vote. They implied that it would be easy to change votes or simply not count votes, even with the checks and balances in place. Interestingly, 15 of the 20 participants felt that some undue influence was attempted on the most recent Presidential election. Most expressed that influence was always exerted in some way through money and power but that this year Russia might have also tried to influence the results.

We can see in the last US presidential election a prime example of the outside influence problem that voters have with electronic voting (and perhaps with voting in general in the US). Several news outlets, political blogs, and social media feeds reported on the connection between world-renown billionaire George Soros and the company Smartmatic that makes DREs. The story had little to no effect on the outcome of the election as no DREs from Smartmatic were used in the 2016 election cycle [10]. However, the story did highlight the potential for many voters to wonder if they could be confident that their vote was actually being cast for the candidate they wanted when using a DRE.

3.4   Finances

Many states took federal HAVA funding in 2002 to buy e-voting equipment, but have been unable to fund their replacements. Georgia, for instance, is using systems 10 years beyond their life expectancy and are not going to be able to replace them until the 2020s [41]. In 2007, the State of California announced that all of its DREs were to be pulled from service because they had failed simple security audits. Due to San Diego County's fraud, waste, and abuse rules, they were unable to dispose of the "useless" DREs and had to put them into storage. They have been paying the bill to store unused DREs ever since. Many of these voting systems come with annual "service" fees that cost the customer many times over what was paid for the original equipment. And still other systems are sold using antiquated technology inside such as ZipDrives, for which you can no longer even purchase media.

The problems and concerns facing e-voting in the US should probably be those of technology, security, and reliability [43]. Due to problems raised above surrounding auditing, security, influence and finance, e-voting has become a political football, a source of overall mistrust in the election process, headaches in the precincts where it is employed, and the go-to scapegoat for election night problems, voting challenges, and outcome disappointments.

3.5 HCI Considerations

In addition to the more intangible issues surrounding e-voting, there are also some physical and user interface considerations that must also be addressed for the electorate to continue using and supporting e-voting methods. Simple decisions regarding the design of e-voting interfaces can affect the outcomes of elections [47]. Seemingly simple design choices can affect how a voters choices are selected and recorded [13]. For this reason alone, it is vital that DRE interfaces are simple enough that it's very difficult for the voter to not understand how to use them [34]. Making DRE interfaces simple should help increase the public's acceptance of the technology [20]. In addition to simplicity, voters must feel that the e-voting system is usable. One of the main tenets making a computer system usable is its ability to make the user feel as though their use of the system will result in the intended effect [39], and if that effect is not achieved, there will be a mechanism for amending an action to achieve that effect [15].

Although we live in a techno-centric society, not everyone is computer literate or even wants to deal with technology [35, 36]. DREs should be designed with intuitiveness in mind, as users may not be accustomed to interfacing with technology. A recent study found that a significant number of voters in Georgia and Maryland, particularly those more advanced in years, required some form of assistance in order to successfully cast their votes [13].

In addition, age begins to affect other faculties such as vision and strength. Voters aged 52 and older make up 43% of the electorate in the US [17]. Since virtually every person begins to suffer some loss of visual acuity after the age of 40 [1], a clear and easy to read and comprehend visual interface should be a design priority. The size and location of menu items on an interface will impact both the speed and accuracy of a user's interaction [23–25]. Font sizes [37] and choice of color [12] are two interface options that should be available to voters. According to [40] legibility, or the typography and layout of the writing on the DRE screen, may increase the speed and accuracy of the voter's interpretation of what is on the screen. Letter spacing, type size, font, lighting, and other environmental factors all play a role in increasing legibility [42].

In short, HCI considerations should be taken into all future design decisions as new DRE technology is rolled out in polling places. Systems that are dynamically controllable, intuitively understood, and give the user options for input, legibility, and typography will be the most successful and accepted by the user.

4 Voter Confidence

One of the interesting outcomes of the 2000 presidential race was the outcry over the way voting was handled in the US. When the election between Al Gore and George Bush literally came down to recounted votes in Florida, the country thought it was in a constitutional crisis. Voters did not want to ever have a repeat of the Florida vote. HAVA was the government's response to what happened in Florida, and they hoped that the reforms proposed in the bill would modernize voting. To some extent it did, but by opening the door to doing away with traditional "paper" methods, new problems have arisen. The 2016 election cycle had people asking for paper trails and recounts, but in some cases it was impossible. There are even organizations, such as the Center for Hand-Counted Paper Ballots, whose sole purpose is to lobby for the paper ballot only to be used.

Previous research questions from studies, some posed nearly 20 years ago, regarding the future of e-voting still remain unanswered and are just as valid today. If e-voting systems are found to be problematic, should the results of current and previous electoral match-ups be questioned by the losing party? Should there be a set of national standards and voting machinery that everyone uses, thereby strengthening the process but weakening the decentralized nature of the system? Most of all, if voting irregularities persist with e-voting technologies, can the public's confidence in the electoral process be upheld [18, 42]?

5   The Future of e-Voting in the US

By the year 2020, many of the voting systems purchased across the counties and states using HAVA funds from 2002 will have reached their "end of life" and need to be replaced [5].

5.1   Emerging e-Voting Technology

In the near term, advancements are being made that could facilitate a number of new developments in how people vote. Los Angeles County, California has the interest and attention of researchers and election officials across the country as it attempts to overhaul its election technology. In contrast to established practice, the county is building its own electronic voting system after years of collecting voter input. Los Angeles election officials hope that by building a system better focused on the needs and preferences of voters, they can spur the voting technology marketplace to offer better solutions at a better value for the voting public. The results of this experiment could be very relevant to other states and localities as they look to replace their increasingly outdated voting technology [38].

Advancements in election technology also have the potential to streamline and simplify the experience of voters in other parts of the voting process, such as obtaining ballot information, registering to vote, verifying voter identity, and travelling to a polling location. Dr. R. Michael Alvarez, co-director of the CalTech/MIT Voting Technology Project, suggests that by 2028, voters will be registered to vote automatically when they obtain a driver's license. In addition, digitized voter rolls could provide streamlined voter identification, and could allow voters to vote at any polling location of their choosing [2].

5.2   Internet Based Voting

Looking further into the future, there is increasing pressure around the country to develop a secure, end-to-end verifiable, internet voting system [22]. The U.S. Government spent over a decade and more than 100 million dollars to develop such a system for military service-members stationed overseas. It abandoned this effort in 2014, after federal researchers concluded that mitigating the risks of internet voting was not feasible with current technology [21]. While such a system is still a possibility in the future, continued research and technical advancements will be necessary in areas such as digital protocols, systems engineering, interface design, and system availability and resiliency, among others, in order to make any internet voting system feasible for public elections [11]. The National Institute of Standards and Technology has indicated that it will continue to work with public and private entities in order to resolve these issues [4].

6   Conclusion and Research Implications

The future of e-Voting is fairly secure. The US will continue to use various methodologies for e-voting every time there is an election. E-voting will also continue to be used in democracies around the world as technologies continue to evolve.

One thing this study has revealed is the relative lack of academic research on the current e-voting landscape. Most of the research dates back to the middle of the first decade of the 21st century. The next presidential election will take place in the third decade of the 21st century and more current research is warranted. As we reflect on this past presidential election, scholars have both the opportunity and responsibility to offer insight into procedures and technology that will help ensure safe and valid elections.

Research that could bear fruit would be to look into standardizing the election process across all 50 states and county jurisdictions. Currently there is no single standard for all polling sites to follow. Whether or not this would improve or harm the system is ripe for further analysis.

References

1. Adult Vision: 41 to 60 years of age (n.d.). http://www.aoa.org/patients-and-public/good-vision-throughout-life/adult-vision-19-to-40-years-of-age/adult-vision-41-to-60-years-of-age?sso=y. Accessed 27 Dec 2016
2. Alvarez, R.M.: The future of voting. Wall Street J. (2016). http://www.wsj.com/articles/the-future-of-voting-1478272120
3. Barret, B.: America's electronic voting machines are scarily easy targets, 2 August 2016. https://www.wired.com/2016/08/americas-voting-machines-arent-ready-election/
4. Bass, J.: NIST activities on UOCAVA voting, 21 May 2012. https://www.nist.gov/itl/voting/nist-activities-uocava-voting. Accessed 30 Dec 2016
5. Bauer, R.F., Ginsberg, B.L.: The American voting experience: report and recommendations of the presidential commission on election administration. Technical report, pp. 01–112, January 2014. https://www.supportthevoter.gov/files/2014/01/Amer-Voting-Exper-final-draft-01-09-14-508.pdf
6. Bergin, B.: All your lever voting machine questions answered, 21 June 2013. http://www.wnyc.org/story/300838-your-lever-voting-machines-questions-answered-you-have-them-admit-it/?utm_source=sharedUrl&utm_medium=metatag&utm_campaign=sharedUrl. Accessed 21 Dec 2016

7. Bishop, M., Wagner, D.: Risks of e-voting. Commun. ACM **50** (2007). http://escholarship. org/uc/item/3dt089r1
8. Commission, E.: The information society for all (final report). Brussels: IST 2000 Programme (2000). http://ec.europa.eu/smart-regulation/evaluation/search/download.do;jsessionid=g1U q6EtTNoNIS7pmUYq4B2bmg8ftVJyKnTUNUgHzvAn4F3URMjq2!1168777535? documentId=2820
9. Dayton, R.: Voting Issues: Some Trump Voters Reporting Ballots Switching to Clinton, 8 November 2016. http://pittsburgh.cbslocal.com/2016/11/08/some-problems-reported-as-voters-head-to-polls/
10. Dewey, C.: What was fake on the internet this election: George Soros's voting machines. The Washington Post, 24 October 2016. https://www.washingtonpost.com/news/the-intersect/wp/2016/10/24/what-was-fake-on-the-internet-this-election-george-soross-voting-machines/
11. Dzieduszycka-Suinat, S., Murray, J., Kiniry, J., Zimmerman, D., Wagner, D., Robinson, P., Foltzer, A., Morina, S.: The future of voting: end-to-end verifiable internet voting-specification and feasibility study. US Vote Foundation (2015)
12. Edwards, A.: Computers and people with disabilities. In: Extra-Ordinary Human-Computer Interaction, pp. 19–43. Cambridge University Press, Cambridge (1995). http://dl.acm.org/ citation.cfm?id=215601
13. Evans, D., Paul, N.: Election security: perception and reality. IEEE Secur. Privacy Mag. **2** (1), 24–31 (2004)
14. Evans, J.: NAACP gets reports of problems with electronic voting machines in New Hanover County, 25 October 2016. http://www.wbtv.com/story/33467718/naacp-gets-reports-of-problems-with-electronic-voting-machines-in-new-hanover-county. Accessed 26 Dec 2016
15. Fairweather, B., Rogerson, S.: Interfaces for electronic voting: focus group evidence. Electron. Gov. Int. J. **2**(4), 369–383 (2005)
16. Fischer, E.: Election reform and electronic voting systems: analysis of security issues In: CRS Report for Congress No. RL32139. Congressional Research Service, Washington, D.C. (2003). https://epic.org/privacy/voting/crsreport.pdf
17. Fry, R.: Millennials match Baby Boomers as largest generation in U.S. electorate, but will they vote? 16 May 2016. http://www.pewresearch.org/fact-tank/2016/05/16/millennials-match-baby-boomers-as-largest-generation-in-u-s-electorate-but-will-they-vote/
18. Gritzalis, D.A.: Principles and requirements for a secure e-voting system. Comput. Secur. **21** (6), 539–556 (2002). https://doi.org/10.1016/S0167-4048(02)01014-3
19. Hamilton, A., Madison, J., Jay, J., Goldman, L.: The Federalist Papers. OUP Oxford (2008)
20. Henneman, R.L.: Design for usability: process, skills, and tools. Inf. Knowl. Syst. Manag. **1** (2), 133–144 (1999)
21. Internet voting, 4 September 2012. https://www.verifiedvoting.org/resources/internet-voting/
22. Jefferson, D.: If I can shop and bank online, why can't I vote online? 2 November 2011. https://www.verifiedvoting.org/resources/internet-voting/vote-online/
23. Johnson, N., Jones, B.: Is the color of your watch still giving you a fitt? Int. J. Inf. Bus. Manag. **8**(1), 1 (2016)
24. Jones, B.: On-line systems: control button design and characteristic effects on user learning and performance. In: American Conference on Information Systems 2004 Proceedings (2004)
25. Jones, B.M., McCoy, S.: Assessing the Effects of Web-Site Control Design on Single-Step Navigation. University of Pittsburgh, Pittsburgh (2003)
26. Keyssar, A.: The Right to Vote: The Contested History of Democracy in the United States. Basic Books, New York (2009)

27. Kohno, T., Stubblefield, A., Rubin, A.D., Wallach, D.S.: Analysis of an electronic voting system. In: Proceedings of 2004 IEEE Symposium on Security and Privacy, pp. 27–40. IEEE (2004). http://0-ieeexplore.ieee.org.wncln.wncln.org/xpls/abs_all.jsp?arnumber= 1301313

28. Kurth, J., Oosting, J.: Records: too many votes in 37% of Detroit's precincts, 13 December 2016. http://www.detroitnews.com/story/news/politics/2016/12/12/records-many-votes-detr oits-precincts/95363314/. Accessed 26 Dec 2016

29. Lovgren, S.: Are electronic voting machines reliable? Natl. Geograph. News, 1 November 2004. http://news.nationalgeographic.com/news/2004/11/1101_041101_election_voting. html

30. McDonald, F.: The Presidency of George Washington. University Press of Kansas, Lawrence (1974)

31. McKeever, J.: High turnout, long lines as people of Connecticut cast their votes, 8 November 2016. http://fox61.com/2016/11/08/connecticut-voters-cast-their-votes/

32. Mechanical Lever Machines (n.d.). http://www.fec.gov/pages/lever.htm. Accessed 21 Dec 2016

33. Mello-Stark, S.: Some states—including swing states—have flawed voting systems, 1 November 2016. http://www.vox.com/the-big-idea/2016/11/1/13486386/election-rigged- paper-trail-audit. Accessed 26 Dec 2016

34. Meyers, S.: The most important design guideline. IEEE Softw. **21**(4), 14–16 (2004)

35. Moeller, P.: Technology still a big disconnect for older Americans, 27 February 2012. http:// money.usnews.com/money/blogs/the-best-life/2012/02/27/technology-still-a-big-disconnect- for-older-americans. Accessed 27 Dec 2016

36. Morris, G., Scott, R., Woodward, A.: Polls Apart: A Future for Accessible Democracy (Electoral Commission). SCOPE, London (2002)

37. Nielsen, J.: Let users control font size. Jakob Nielsen's Alertbox, 19 August 2002

38. Norden, L., Famighetti, C.: America's voting technology crisis. The Atlantic, 15 September 2015. http://www.theatlantic.com/politics/archive/2015/09/americas-voting-technology-crisis/ 405262/

39. Preece, J., Rogers, Y., Sharp, H.: Interaction Design: Beyond Human-Computer Interaction. Wiley, New York (2002). https://www.mysciencework.com/publication/show/fbabc4fca2d 1da90150213ad37561404

40. Reynolds, L.: The legibility of printed scientific and technical information. In: Easterby, R., Zwaga, H. (eds.) Information Design. Wiley, Chichester (1984)

41. Riley, M., Robertson, J., Kocieniewski, D.: The computer voting revolution is already crappy, buggy, and obsolete. Bloomberg.com, 29 September 2016. https://www.bloomberg. com/features/2016-voting-technology/

42. Roth, S.K.: Disenfranchised by design: voting systems and the election process. Inf. Des. J. **9** (1), 29–38 (1998)

43. Simons, B.B.: Electronic voting systems: the good, the bad, and the stupid. ACM Queue **2** (7), 20–26 (2004)

44. Torres, K.: Georgia early voting machine suspected of "changing" votes, 27 October 2016. http://www.ajc.com/news/state–regional-govt–politics/georgia-voting-machine-suspected- flipping-presidential-votes/woKEUgpDDEyaw9o4J318XJ/. Accessed 26 Dec 2016

45. Voting Equipment in the United States (n.d.). https://www.verifiedvoting.org/resources/ voting-equipment/

46. Voting methods and equipment by state (n.d.). https://ballotpedia.org/Voting_methods_and_equipment_by_state. Accessed 21 Dec 2016
47. Wand, J.N., Shotts, K.W., Sekhon, J.S., Mebane Jr., W.R., Herron, M.C., Brady, H.E.: The butterfly did it: the aberrant vote for Buchanan in Palm Beach County, Florida. Am. Polit. Sci. Rev. 793–810 (2001)
48. Wertheimer, M.: Trusted agent report: diebold AccuVote-TS voting system. Prepared by: RABA Innovative Solution Cell (RiSC), 20 January 2004

Entrepreneurial Orientation and Open Innovation: Social Media as a Tool

Claudia Linde[(✉)]

Institute of Entrepreneurship and Business Development,
Lübeck University of Applied Sciences, Lübeck, Germany
Claudia.linde@fh-luebeck.de

Abstract. The implementation of open innovation depends on the proclivity for open innovation. The proclivity for open innovation and its tool social media is an attitude of the management. One factor that could affect the proclivity for open innovation is the entrepreneurial orientation (EO). The aim of this paper is to give a literature review and to develop a theoretical concept for the relationship between the EO and the proclivity for open innovation. Special focus lies upon the application of social media as a tool for open innovation.

Keywords: Social media · Open innovation · Proclivity for open innovation · Entrepreneurial orientation · SME

1 Introduction

Innovations are a necessity for companies to be competitive [1]. Only approximately 10% innovations are successful on the market. Therefore, the economic risk of the company is very high. Furthermore, companies are in a rising competition. Products have a shorter product life, so the companies are required to develop new products and to innovate faster [2]. This could be a problem specifically for small and medium-sized enterprises (SME). SMEs have lower personal and financial resources in comparison to large companies [3]. As a result, SMEs do not always have the multidisciplinary competencies in-house which are essential to innovate [4].

The strategy open innovation could be used to counter these challenges. With this strategy the company opens up their innovation process [5] by using different tools and methods for the integration of external actors and also for the exploitation of intellectual property [6]. Social media is a tool for the integration of external actors which could be used for the communication, networking and collaboration with diverse parties like users, suppliers, corporate partners and stakeholders [7]. Social media is very fast and mostly low-cost relative to the amount of people reached [8]. With social media as a tool of open innovation companies could integrate users into the different phases of their innovation process [9]. Social media does not only reach one specific user, instead the company could integrate a greater amount of users. This could lead to a lot of ideas articulating the needs of the different types of users [10, 11]. The ideas developed by the users could be selected and refined by the employees of the company and also by the users [12]. This way of idea generation could reduce the uncertainty

© Springer International Publishing AG 2017
G. Meiselwitz (Ed.): SCSM 2017, Part I, LNCS 10282, pp. 350–361, 2017.
DOI: 10.1007/978-3-319-58559-8_28

about the market as well as the risk of failed innovation, the time of market launch and cost of R&D. Moreover, ideas generated by users could be more successful because they are based on the needs of the users and the market [10, 13]. Although social media could be a possibility to handle the limited resources of SMEs, only 15% of German speaking companies use social media as a tool of open innovation [9].

Whether the implementation of social media as a tool for open innovation could be successful depends on the ability of the company to adapt its innovation process and on an appropriate industry [14]. Both factors influence the ability of an organization to adapt its innovation process. This paper focusses on the internal factors. The internal factors could be barriers for the implementation of open innovation and its tool social media [14].

One barrier could be an inappropriate culture and structure. An open culture and structure are necessary for employees to accept the new strategy and the implementation of social media as a tool. The management of the company directly influence the culture of the company. So, it is important that management enables an open culture, structure and environment. Furthermore, managers have to support the implementation of open innovation [12, 15, 16] and therefore, the proclivity for open innovation is a fundamental attitude of management [17]. Thus, it can be assumed that the decision for the implementation of open innovation, and social media as a tool for open innovation depends on the proclivity for open innovation [17].

The factors that have an impact on the proclivity for open innovation of the management are understudied [18–20]. Examined factors are, for example, the effect of entrepreneurial orientation (EO) and job characteristics like skill variety, task identity and autonomy [18–20].

So far, there are few studies which investigate the effect of the EO on the proclivity for open innovation [19, 20]. On the basis of existing studies on EO [19, 20] it could be proposed that there is a direct relationship between the concept of EO and proclivity for open innovation. EO depends on the attitude of the management and their intention to take risks, promote innovations and behave proactively [21, 22]. The strategic processes like open innovation in the company could be influenced by EO [23].

The existing studies do not distinguish between companies in a service and manufacturing sector. Further moderating factors which may influence the EO and the proclivity for open innovation could be more considered. The evaluation of the impact of EO on the proclivity to implement tools is also missing [19, 20]. This paper concentrates on SMEs. For this companies could the implementation of open innovation a positive possibility to handle their limited resources. SMEs mainly implement the outside-in process of the three open innovation processes. Especially in this outside-in process social media is a possible tool.

The aim of this paper is the development of a theoretical concept for the relationship between the EO and proclivity for open innovation based on a literature review on proclivity for open innovation as well as its tool social media and EO. The special focus lies on the application of social media as a tool for open innovation.

2 Theoretical Background

2.1 Proclivity for Open Innovation and the Application of the Tool Social Media

The proclivity for open innovation refers to the potential and willingness of the management to open up its innovation process [17, 19, 20]. This could be defined by the predisposition and attitude of the management to the application and implementation of open innovation [17].

Open innovation is a strategy for innovation management [10] with the aim to expand the company's innovative capability and activities. The environment surrounding the company is strategically taken into account and integrated into the innovation process [24]. The opposite strategy is closed innovation where companies generate ideas internally and the innovation process is closed for the environment. Companies that use open innovation as a strategy could have the chance to get competitive advantages by combining internal and external know-how in a beneficial and economic way [5, 25]. Advantages are, for example, a better fit to the needs of the users, reduction of the R&D costs as well as the time-to-market [10]. Open innovation contains three main processes: outside-in, inside-out and coupled process. The outside-in process integrates external actors in the internal innovation process [24]. With the inside-out process, internal intellectual property (IP) would be exploited for example through venturing, licensing or spin-offs. The combination of integration of external actors as well as exploitation of internal IP is the coupled process [24]. Especially in the outside-in process social media could be an important tool for the integration of external actors [9].

Social media is increasingly used for the interaction and also collaboration with a crowd [9]. The tool includes social networks, mobile communities, blogs, open-source-platforms, etc. [7], which allows organizations to actively ask their customers about needs and ideas. Another way is to analyze the communication of users on different themes that are of interest for the company [26]. Furthermore, the company gets contact to lead users who could offer specific information for problem solutions. This offers the opportunity for companies to obtain special information about the needs of users. The needs refer to an absent product at the market as well as an obsolete offer of the company [10]. In this context users are called co-innovators [27]. They can be included in all phases of the innovation process from the idea generation, product development, creation of a prototype and product as well as market tests. In addition, users can also be involved in the marketing and distribution, for example through advertising by users. Due to the early involvement of users in the innovation process, the market risk is considerably lower than in closed innovation strategies [10].

Until now, research on the implementation of open innovation has been increasingly focused on organizational and structural requirements, such as the absorptive capacity of the organization [28]. Little research has been done on the proclivity for open innovation [17–20, 29]. The research of social media is limited to its application to innovation especially during the phase of ideation [12], the impact of social media on co-creation [26] and social media as a method of open innovation during the different phases of the innovation process [12]. So far, social media as a tool for open innovation is hardly implemented in companies. Only 15% German speaking companies already use social media in R&D [9].

The decision to implement open innovation and apply social media in the open innovation process is commonly made top-down by management [16, 30]. Moreover, the configuration of organizational structures, processes and the innovation culture [31] as well as organizational innovations and strategic orientations are a responsibility of management [15]. The change of organizational structures and processes could only be successful if the management agrees with that change and pushes it forward [32]. Thus, only with a positive proclivity for open innovation management has the ability to apply open innovation and the tool social media [17].

The proclivity for open innovation depends on the attitude of management [17]. This raises the question of how the attitude of the management can be influenced so that they develop proclivity for open innovation. Factors which affect the proclivity for open innovation have been considered in fewer studies. One factor which affects the proclivity for open innovation is EO [19, 20]. EO is defined in the next section.

2.2   Entrepreneurial Orientation

The EO concept has its origin in strategic management. In the meantime, this concept is also of great importance in entrepreneurship [33]. The term EO was coined by Lumpkin and Dess [33, 34].

EO shapes the organization's policies and actions that enable entrepreneurial decisions and activities regardless of the age, size and sector of the company [35, 36]. Therefore, EO can be viewed as an entrepreneurial strategic process to achieve the vision and the generation of competitive advantages [35]. EO describes in which way a market entry with new products or services is implemented. Thus, it represents processes, activities and decision-making processes in which the new entry takes place [33].

EO is defined as entrepreneurial behavior [34] and depends on the degree to which the management is risk prone, open to innovation and behave proactively [21, 22]. Thus, an appropriate management personality can promote EO within the company [34], and consequently influence strategic processes in the organization [23]. This way, EO influences the degree of entrepreneurship throughout the organization [33].

According to Covin and Slevin [37], EO is characterized by three dimensions: innovation capability, the willingness to take risk and proactivity [37]. Innovation capability describes the ability of a company to pursue ideas and generate innovations [33], referring to different types of innovation. Companies with a high willingness to take risk are more likely to invest resources in projects with unknown results [38]. Proactivity marks a forward-looking attitude towards the pursuit of new opportunities, for instance entering new markets. This is contrary to passive behavior of a company, where no response to new possibilities is shown [33].

Existing research on the direct impact of EO on the proclivity for open innovation and the inside-out, outside-in and coupled-processes shows that EO has a positive effect on proclivity for open innovation [19, 20]. In studies to date, no distinction was made between different industry sectors. The sample of Ju et al. [19] consists of manufacturing SMEs and SMEs in the service sector. The internal, as well as the external framework conditions could be different in various industries, where the effect of EO on proclivity for open innovation can vary depending on these conditions [35, 39]. These studies should be specified. A further question is the evaluation of the impact of EO on proclivity for implementation of tools like social media [19, 20].

In the next section, a theoretical framework for the relationship between EO and proclivity for open innovation as well as the application of social media in the innovation process is developed.

3   Development of a Theoretical Framework

So far, only a few studies have researched the effect of EO on the proclivity for open innovation [19, 20]. Until now, the effect of EO on the three processes of open innovation (outside-in, inside-out and coupled process) was investigated in only one study. A positive effect on the proclivity in all three processes could be demonstrated [19]. Based on the results, the authors assume that the pursuit of the open innovation strategy in companies with a high EO is more successful than in companies with a low EO [20].

A high EO could enable a strategic reorientation and support a cultural change within a company [33, 40]. So EO could influence the implementation of open innovation as a strategy for innovation management [10]. The implementation of open innovation requires a rethinking of innovation management and a change of strategy when the innovation process has been previously closed. The decision for strategic change is distributed top-down [35]. Managers with an EO assess innovations in a positive way and perceive them as solutions for a necessary change [41]. It is necessary to adapt organizational structures and processes for the implementation of the open innovation strategy, typical factors influenced by management [15]. Only with agreement of the management the adaption could be successful [32].

One dimension of EO is the innovation capability, describing the ability of a company to pursue ideas and generate innovations [33]. The implementation of open innovation requires a high ability to innovate new products and also to change the internal innovation process. The organization and their structure have to adapt to the new strategy [42].

The next dimension of EO is willingness to take risks. The implementation of open innovation and also social media requires a high degree of openness and also willingness to take risk in the company. The company should consider which know-how should be published or protected. Social media applications cannot be well controlled because social media is highly dynamic [9] and thus increases uncertainty as well a risk of losing know-how. The use of open innovation may lead to additional costs for the company due to the enforcement, implementation and control of open innovation [10]. Especially for SMEs, these costs can be a barrier due to limited available financial resources [43].

The third dimension of EO is proactivity of management. Organizations with proactive management tend to be more alert to market trends and review new opportunities for the company [23]. With the implementation of social media the company could gain information about the needs of the users, for instance by could observing market trends. For successful implementation of open innovation, proactivity of management is required [17]. Proactivity is characterized by a forward-looking attitude towards the pursuit of new opportunities such as new market entries. Even if a company is not the first mover, it can be as proactive and innovative when it pursues new opportunities, take quick actions and react foresightedly [33]. This also relates to understanding and satisfaction of customer needs [44].

The dimensions of EO (innovation capability, the willingness to take risk and proactivity [37]) show attitudes of the management which could be seen as necessary for the implementation of open innovation. Therefore EO with the three dimensions (innovation capability, the willingness to take risk and proactivity [37]) could be seen as a precondition for the open innovation processes and as complementary strategies [19, 20].

On the basis of the existing studies on EO [19, 20] it could be proposed that there is a direct relationship between the concept of EO and the proclivity of open innovation. Although it cannot be assumed that all organizations implement open innovation and its three processes outside-in, inside-out and coupled process.

Most organizations implement the outside-in process [45]. Customers are primarily involved, followed by suppliers as well as governmental and commercial research institutes [46]. A study by van de Vrande et al. [43] shows that most SMEs involve their employees as a source of knowledge and their customers for knowledge generation. Rangus [17] assumes that employee integration, customer integration, external networking, and the outsourcing of R&D are relatively simple and appropriate activities to implement open innovation in SMEs [17, 29, 43].

Only a few SMEs implement formalized methods to use the inside-out process of open innovation [29, 43]. The reasons for this are the limited resources [3]. Frequently, they are unable to provide the necessary financing and contracts. Furthermore, it is common, that an innovation portfolio for risk compensation is not available. This refers to, for example, IP licensing, venturing and external investment [29, 43]. In order to identify and integrate innovations into the company, the company must employ appropriately qualified employees. In most cases SMEs do not have these employees. Another possibility is that they fear the loss of technological advantage. In the case of infringements of patents, SMEs have fewer opportunities to challenge them as do large companies [3].

The combination of the outside-in and the inside-out processes is the coupled process [24]. Based on the previous explanations it can be assumed that the implementation of the coupled process might be too complex for SMEs especially due to limited resources.

Therefore, it can be proposed that the EO has a positive effect on proclivity for open innovation within the outside-in, inside-out process and coupled process. But the application depends on the size and resources of the company.

Proposition 1: The EO of the management is positively related to the proclivity for open innovation in the context of the outside-in process.

Proposition 2: The EO is positively related to the proclivity for open innovation in the context of the inside-out process.

Proposition 3: The EO is positively related to the proclivity for open innovation in the context of the coupled process.

With social media as a tool for open innovation, companies could integrate users in the different phases of their innovation process. Especially in the outside-in process social media is an important tool for the integration of users. Each organization has to decide itself, to what extent innovation projects are useful for the application of open innovation tools. For this reason, consideration should also be given to the degree of openness of the company and thus to the publishing of internal know-how as well as IP via social media. Due to the possibilities of social media, the potential for know-how, creativity and the resulting possibility to generate innovation are endless [9]. Social media applications have high dynamics and cannot be completely managed and controlled [9], this requires a high degree of openness by the company and the management [28]. Companies operate under uncertainty and risk. Further risks can be the loss of know-how, an increased complexity in the process and also smaller differentiation from the competitors [46]. Therefore the management needs a high innovation capability, the willingness to take risk and proactivity, which are the dimensions of EO [37]. Furthermore, the proclivity for open innovation is necessary for the decision on the application of social media [17].

As a result, it can be proposed that EO and the proclivity for open innovation have a positive effect on the application of Social Media as a tool within the outside-in process and also in the coupled process.

Proposition 4: EO and the proclivity for open innovation are positively related to the application of social media within the outside-in process.

Proposition 5: EO and the proclivity for open innovation are positively related to the application of social media within the coupled process.

Open innovation cannot be implemented in every industry and company. It is necessary to examine whether the industry and thus the company is suited to adapt its innovation process to this approach [14]. Some industries are not suitable for an open innovation process, for example the military [10]. The internal as well as the external framework conditions could be different in various industries, whereby the effect of EO on the proclivity for open innovation varies, depending on these conditions [35, 39]. In the studies to date, no distinction was made between different sectors. For example Ju et al. [19] consider manufacturing SMEs and SMEs in the service sector.

Wales [47] also believes that many heterogeneous samples have been investigated in research to date. While these provide positive insights, studies in specific contexts can provide even more accurate information on the relationship between EO and different variables [47]. It can be assumed that the proclivity for open innovation differs in various industries. Therefore investigation should be made in a homogeneous sample from one industry.

Proposition 6: The proclivity for open innovation is different in various industries.

Technological turbulences are defined as rapid technological changes within an industry. Based on their results, Ju et al. [19] assume that SMEs in an industry with technological turbulences are concentrating more on the outside-in process to improve their own innovations. A high EO does not lead SMEs to establish the coupled process in technologically turbulent environments [19].

External factors like existing network structures, legal framework conditions and the environment could affect the opening of the innovation process [48]. It has already been confirmed empirically that external factors influence the effect of EO on company performances [39]. A corresponding effect for the relationship between EO and proclivity for open innovation can be proposed.

Proposition 7: Technological turbulences and external factors moderate the relationship between the EO and the proclivity for open innovation.

The organization's age and size can lead to different internal and external frame conditions [39].

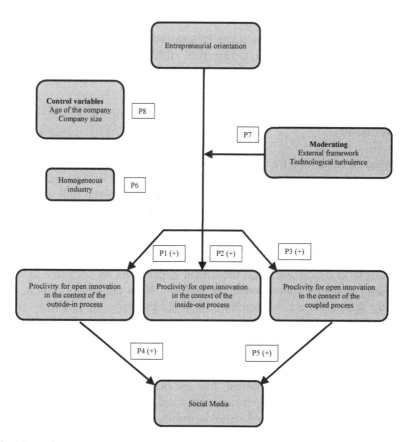

Fig. 1. Theoretical concept to the effect of EO on proclivity for open innovation and its tool social media

In order to implement open innovation, the corporate culture has to be open for innovation. This means that the culture provides the framework for the creation of innovations, while the employees can be creative, necessary spaces exist and something new would be regarded as something positive [2]. The cultural change is necessary, as otherwise the Not-Invented-Here (NIH)-syndrome may occur [10]. This is seen as the greatest barrier in the implementation of open innovation [24]. The syndrome occurs less often in young companies or in rapidly changing industries. Rather, it arises in older established companies with previously closed structures [5]. Therefore, it can be proposed that the company's age has an influence on the proclivity for open innovation.

Due to the company's size the existing financial and personal resources differ. SMEs have lower human and financial resources in comparison to large companies [3]. Because of these limited resources SMEs may not have the necessary multidisciplinary competencies in-house for the development of innovations [4]. Therefore it can be proposed that the company's size and age has an influence on the proclivity for open innovation.

Proposition 8: The relationship between EO and proclivity for open innovation should be controlled for the organization's size and age.

From the theoretical derivation, it can be assumed that EO has a positive effect on the proclivity for open innovation. However, differences can arise depending on internal and external frame conditions as shown in Fig. 1.

All propositions of this paper are shown in Fig. 1.

4   Conclusion

Initial studies have verified the positive effect of EO on the proclivity for open innovation. In one of these studies, this effect was also examined in three main processes [19, 20]. In the studies to date, no distinction was made between different industries [19, 20]. The internal as well as the external framework conditions can be differentiated in various industries, whereby the effect of EO on the proclivity for open innovation can be influenced [35, 39]. Also the moderating effects have to be considered.

In this paper a theoretical concept was developed. The propositions show that appropriateness to implement open innovation depends on the industry sector. Not every industry is suitable, for example the military. When the organization as well as the industry sector fits, a corresponding EO could influence the proclivity for open innovation. Thus, the management's attitude is a key factor for the implementation of open innovation. With proclivity for open innovation the company could be more inclined to implement social media as a tool. This could be a reason for the lower application of social media in German speaking companies.

The theoretical framework created, has not been empirically tested. Therefore, future research could test the theoretical concept and examine the impact of EO on the proclivity for open innovation and its tools within an industry. This also includes a further possibility to investigate the difference between large companies and SMEs. Since not all organizations implement all main processes of open innovation, future researches should also consider the impact on the individual processes. An interesting study would also be a comparison between different countries as well as between large companies and SMEs.

References

1. Pleschak, F., Sabisch, H.: Innovationsmanagement (in German). Schäffer-Poeschel Verlag, Stuttgart (1996)
2. Vahs, D., Brem, A.: Innovationsmanagement. Von der Idee zur erfolgreichen Vermarktung (in German), 4th revised and expanded edn. Schäffer-Poeschel Verlag, Stuttgart (2013)
3. Vanhaverbeke, W., Vermeersch, I., Zutter, S.: Open innovation in SMEs: how can small companies and start-ups benefit from open innovation strategies? Research report, Flanders DC study (2012)
4. Bianchi, M., Campodall'Orto, S., Frattini, F., Vercesi, P.: Enabling open innovation in small- and medium-sized enterprises: how to find alternative applications for your technologies. R&D Manag. **40**(4), 414–431 (2010)
5. Chesbrough, H.: Open innovation: a new paradigm for understanding industrial innovation. In: Chesbrough, H., Vanhaverbeke, W., West, J. (eds.) Open Innovation: Researching a New Paradigm, pp. 1–12. Oxford University Press, New York (2006)
6. Antikainen, M.J., Väätäjä, H.K.: Rewarding in open innovation communities – how to motivate members. Int. J. Entrep. Innov. Manag. **11**(4), 440–456 (2010)
7. Grabs, A., Bannour, K.M., Vogl, E.: Follow Me! Erfolgreiches Social Media Marketing mit Facebook, Twitter und Co. (in German), 3rd revised edn. Rheinwerk Verlag, Bonn (2015)
8. Hilker, C.: Erfolgreiche Social-Media-Strategien für die Zukunft. Mehr Profit durch Facebook, Twitter, Xing und Co. (in German). Linde Verlag Wien Ges.m.b.H., Wien (2012)
9. Rekece, R., Zimmermann, H.-D., Meili, C.: White Paper: Open Innovation Monitor 2012. Status Quo, Trends und Zukunftsperspektiven (in German). Die Innovationsgesellschaft mbH, St. Gallen (CH) (2012)
10. Reichwald, R., Piller, F.: Interaktive Wertschöpfung: Open Innovation, Individualisierung und neue Formen der Arbeitsteilung (in German), 2nd revised and expanded edn. Gabler GWV Fachverlage GmbH, Wiesbaden (2009)
11. Piller, F.T., Reichwald, R.: Wertschöpfungsprinzipien von Open Innovation. Information und Kommunikation in verteilten offenen Netzwerken (in German). In: Zerfaß, A., Möslein, K.M. (eds.) Kommunikation als Erfolgsfaktor im Innovationsmanagement: Strategien im Zeitalter der Open Innovation (in German), 1st edn, pp. 105–120. Gabler GWV Fachverlage GmbH, Wiesbaden (2009)
12. Mount, M., Martinez, M.G.: Social media: a tool for open innovation. Calif. Manag. Rev. **56**(4), 124–143 (2014)
13. Vanhaverbeke, W., van de Vrande, V., Chesbrough, H.: Understanding the advantages of open innovation practices in corporate venturing in terms of real options. Creat. Innov. Manag. **17**(4), 251–258 (2008)
14. Ili, S., Albers, A.: Chancen und Risiken von Open Innovation (in German). In: Ili, S. (ed.) Open Innovation. Prozesse, Methoden, Systeme, Kultur (in German), pp. 43–60. Symposium Publishing GmbH, Düsseldorf (2010)
15. Elenkov, D.S., Manev, I.M.: Top management leadership and influence on innovation: the role of sociocultural context. J. Manag. **31**(3), 381–402 (2005)

16. Burcharth, A.L., Knudsen, M.P., Søndergaard, H.A.: Neither invented nor shared here: the impact and management of attitudes for the adoption of open innovation practices. Technovation **34**, 149–161 (2014)
17. Rangus, K.: Proclivity for open innovation: construct development, determinants and outcomes. Doctoral dissertation, Ljubljana (2014)
18. Deegahawature, M.: Managers' inclination towards open innovation: effect of job characteristics. Eur. J. Bus. Manag. **6**(1), 8–16 (2014)
19. Ju, P.-H., Chen, D.-N., Yu, Y.-C., Wei, H.-L.: Relationships among open innovation processes, entrepreneurial orientation, and organizational performance of SMEs: the moderating role of technological turbulence. In: Kobyliński, A., Sobczak, A. (eds.) BIR 2013. LNBIP, vol. 158, pp. 140–160. Springer, Heidelberg (2013). doi:10.1007/978-3-642-40823-6_12
20. Hung, K.P., Chiang, Y.H.: Open innovation proclivity, entrepreneurial orientation, and perceived firm performance. Int. J. Technol. Manag. **52**(3/4), 257–274 (2010)
21. Covin, J.G., Slevin, D.P.: The influence of organization structure on the utility of an entrepreneurial top management style. J. Manag. Stud. **25**(13), 217–234 (1988)
22. Miller, D.: The correlates of entrepreneurship in three types of firms. Manag. Sci. **28**(7), 770–791 (1983)
23. Lumpkin, G., Cogliser, C.C., Schneider, D.R.: Understanding and measuring autonomy: an entrepreneurial orientation perspective. Entrep. Theory Pract. **33**(1), 47–69 (2009)
24. Gassmann, O., Enkel, E.: Open Innovation. Die Öffnung des Innovationsprozesses erhöht das Innovationspotenzial (in German). Z. Führ. Organ. **75**(3), 132–138 (2006)
25. Chesbrough, H.W.: Open Innovation. The New Imperative for Creating and Profiting from Technology. Harvard Business School Publishing Corporation, Boston (2003)
26. Piller, F., Vossen, A., Ihl, C.: From social media to social product development: the impact of social media on co-creation of innovation. Die Unternehm. **66**(1), 7–27 (2012)
27. Reichwald, R., Meyer, A., Engelmann, M., Walcher, D.: Der Kunde als Innovationspartner. Konsumenten integrieren, Flop-Raten reduzieren, Angebote verbessern (in German), 1st edn. Betriebswirtschaftlicher Verlag Dr. Th. Gabler GWV Fachverlage GmbH, Wiesbaden (2007)
28. da Mota Pedrosa, A., Välling, M., Boyd, B.: Knowledge related activities in open innovation: managers' characteristics and practices. Int. J. Technol. Manag. **61**(3/4), 254–273 (2013)
29. Rangus, K., Drnovšek, M., Di Minin, A.: Proclivity for open innovation: construct development and empirical validation. Innov. Manag. Policy Pract. **18**(2), 191–211 (2016)
30. Chesbrough, H., Crowther, A.K.: Beyond high tech: early adopters of open innovation in other industries. R&D Manag. **36**(3), 229–236 (2006)
31. Yadav, M.S., Prabhu, J.C., Chandy, R.K.: Managing the future: CEO attention and innovation outcomes. J. Mark. **71**, 84–101 (2007)
32. Saguy, S.I.: Academia-industry innovation interaction: paradigm shifts and avenues for the future. Procedia Food Sci. **1**, 1875–1882 (2011)
33. Lumpkin, G., Dess, G.G.: Clarifying the entrepreneurial orientation construct and linking it to performance. Acad. Manag. Rev. **21**(1), 135–172 (1996)
34. Yang, H., Dess, G.G.: Where do entrepreneurial orientations come from? An investigation on their social origin. Entrep. Firm Emerg. Growth **10**, 223–247 (2007)
35. Rauch, A., Wiklund, J., Lumpkin, G., Frese, M.: Entrepreneurial orientation and business performance: an assessment of past research and suggestions for the future. Entrep. Theory Pract. **33**(3), 761–787 (2009)
36. Covin, J.G., Wales, W.J.: The measurement of entrepreneurial orientation. Entrep. Theory Pract. **36**(4), 677–702 (2012)

37. Covin, J.G., Slevin, D.P.: The development and testing of an organizational-level entrepreneurship scale. In: Ronstadt, R., Hornaday, J.A., Peterson, R., Vesper, K.H. (eds.) Proceedings of the Sixth Annual Babson College Entrepreneurship Research Conference on Frontiers of Entrepreneurship Research 1986, pp. 628–639. P&R Publications, Waltham (1986)
38. Wiklund, J., Shepherd, D.: Knowledge-based resources, entrepreneurial orientation, and the performance of small and medium-sized businesses. Strateg. Manag. J. **24**, 1307–1314 (2003)
39. Wiklund, J., Shepherd, D.: Entrepreneurial orientation and small business performance: a configurational approach. J. Bus. Ventur. **20**, 71–91 (2005)
40. Covin, J.G., Slevin, D.P.: A conceptual model of entrepreneurship as firm behavior. Entrep. Theory Pract. **16**(1), 7–25 (1991)
41. Damanpour, F., Schneider, M.: Characteristics of innovation and innovation adoption in public organizations: assessing the role of managers. J. Public Adm. Res. Theory **19**(3), 495–522 (2008)
42. Elmquist, M., Fredberg, T., Ollila, S.: Exploring the field of open innovation. Eur. J. Innov. Manag. **12**(3), 326–345 (2009)
43. van de Vrande, V., Jong, J.P., Vanhaverbeke, W., Rochemont, M.: Open innovation in SMEs: trends, motives and management challenges. Technovation **29**, 423–437 (2009)
44. Vora, D., Vora, J., Polley, D.: Applying entrepreneurial orientation to a medium sized firm. Int. J. Entrep. Behav. Res. **18**(3), 352–379 (2012)
45. Enkel, E., Gassmann, O.: Neue Ideenquellen erschließen – Die Chancen von Open Innovation (in German). Mark. Rev. St. Gallen **26**(2), 6–11 (2009)
46. Enkel, E.: Chancen und Risiken von Open Innovation (in German). In: Zerfaß, A., Möslein, K.M. (eds.) Kommunikation als Erfolgsfaktor im Innovationsmanagement: Strategien im Zeitalter der Open Innovation (in German), 1st edn, pp. 177–192. Gabler GWV Fachverlage GmbH, Wiesbaden (2009)
47. Wales, W.J.: Entrepreneurial orientation: a review and synthesis of promising research directions. Int. Small Bus. J. **34**(1), 1–15 (2016)
48. Torkkeli, M.T., Kock, C.J., Salmi, P.A.: The "open innovation" paradigm: a contingency perspective. J. Ind. Eng. Manag. **2**(1), 176–207 (2009)

For Those About to Rock – Social Media Best Practices from Wacken Open Air

Christian W. Scheiner[1(✉)] and Nick Hüper[2]

[1] Institute of Entrepreneurship and Business Development,
Universität zu Lübeck, Lübeck, Germany
christian.scheiner@uni-luebeck.de
[2] International Concert Service, Wacken, Germany
nick@ics-int.com

Abstract. Social media has become the communication channel of choice when companies and organizations are confronted with crisis situations or emerging events. Within this study, a single crisis situation is examined. The metal festival Wacken Open Air from 2015, organized by International Concert Service, has been chosen as a case study where heavy rain falls before the event led to a crisis event. The study gives insights into the usage of social media by International Concert Service and offers best practice examples of how to handle such difficult situations.

Keywords: Wacken Open Air · Social media · Best practice · Crisis management · Crisis communication · Facebook · Twitter · International Concert Service · Heavy metal

1 Introduction

For every metal fan the Wacken Open Air has become a fixed date in the calendar, not only for the majority of German fans but also for the thousands of guests coming from all over the world. There are certainly not many places and events on this planet where you can see this many people genuinely enjoying themselves by breaking out of the limits and boundaries of their everyday lives.

In order to create an unforgettable experience, the festival does not only offer an outstanding line-up and performance of bands but it has also developed an extensive number of services in order to create a great experience for its fans.

As any major event taking place in the open space, storms and heavy rainfalls pose a serious risk to the festival organization as they may easily create emergency situations or crises and even lead to a cancellation of the event. In 2016, two major festivals, the Southside Festival and the Hurricane festival, had to be partially or completely cancelled for that reason. Preparing for crisis situations is therefore an essential task for festival organizers. Key component in handling such an emergency event is the crisis communication, which helps to prevent harm for festival visitors, to inform all stakeholders properly, and to avoid brand damage. Social media has become the communication channel of choice when organizations are confronted with such emerging events and crisis situations [1].

© Springer International Publishing AG 2017
G. Meiselwitz (Ed.): SCSM 2017, Part I, LNCS 10282, pp. 362–378, 2017.
DOI: 10.1007/978-3-319-58559-8_29

Within this study, the social media behavior of International Concert Service (ICS) as organizer of the Wacken Open Air is examined to illustrate social media best practices in such crisis situations.

2 Theoretical Background

2.1 Social Media

Following Kaplan and Haenlein, social media can be defined as "a group of Internet-based applications that build on the ideological and technological foundations of Web 2.0, and that allow the creation and exchange of user-generated content" [2, p. 61]. Social Media serves therewith as an umbrella term, under which different applications and services such as Facebook, Twitter, Instagram and YouTube are subsumed [2].

Given its rapid and widespread adoption during the last decades, social media has changed the way how companies interact with their customers and target groups. While individuals were formerly limited to merely consume information presented by companies, they can now interact directly with companies and also among each other, and can contribute in a democratized system in information generation, creation and distribution [3]. Given the degree of diffusion and the technological possibilities of social media combined with its comparable cost-effectiveness, Scheiner et al. [4] conclude that companies "can now quite literally reach a worldwide audience at the push of a button" [4, p. 438].

2.2 Crisis Communication

Coombs [5] defines a crisis as the "perception of an unpredictable event that threatens important expectancies of stakeholders and can seriously impact an organization's performance and generate negative outcomes" [5, pp. 2–3].

In light of a crisis, organizations can generally respond by attacking the individual or group that claims that a crisis is given (attack the accuser), denying the existence of a crisis (denial), downplaying the organizational responsibility for the crisis (excuse), minimizing and ignoring harmful consequences as well as attributing blame on victims (justification), taking actions to chum up with stakeholder (ingratiation), seeking to correct consequences (corrective action), and taking full responsibility for the crisis and its outcomes (full apology) [6].

Before choosing a response type, organizations have to consider how external viewers evaluate the organization's responsibility for the given situation. When stakeholders see the main responsibility in the organization, for instance when major repeated accidents occur, strategies such as minimizing and denying are not advisable. Natural disasters on the other hand are located outside the sphere of influence of organizations which allows organizations to choose from a wider spectrum of response strategies [6].

2.3 Crisis Communication and Social Media

In crisis situations, it is of utter importance to instantly distribute critically valuable information to as many people as possible. Social media allows companies and organizations to reach these goals at a reasonable cost in comparison to traditional media. It also possesses however several drawbacks and problematic issues to consider such as inaccurate and false information, misuse of social media, technological limitations, and potential costs [7]. There is also research indicating that in general social media is still not the most influential medium in a crisis situation. Etter and Verstergaard [8] examined for instance how different public sources influenced the perception of a crisis and how different sources interact with each other. They found that news media still remains the biggest influential factor of public discourse and affects the crisis framing on Facebook. Hence, the general public framing occurred in their case merely via news media. Despite the downsides of social media as well as the relativizing findings in the context of its meaning, the advantages of social media combined with the huge user numbers made it the choice of communication for organizations when facing a crisis [1].

With the rise of social media within the last decades, a growing body of guidelines and research has emerged to support organizations in times of crises and to explain patterns of user activity on social media.

Guidelines have been mainly developed by social media companies, industry associations as well as national and supranational institutions. Facebook as provider of the biggest and most influential social network suggests a seven step procedure to handle a crisis properly [9]. First, the cause for the emerging or given crisis has to be understood by assessing the nature of the problem. Second, the validity of feedback has to be evaluated. Third, the companies should unmistakably demonstrate that they take the complaints and issues seriously. Therein, it is necessary to keep conversations going by posting true facts, maintaining a consistent, conversational tone, and avoiding jargon. Fourth, a crisis response team should be established in order to ensure that complaints are addressed in a timely manner and responses are given by knowledgeable people. Fifth, organizations should transfer the communication from the Facebook page to Facebook Messenger or email to resolve the complaints or if the issue concerns a small but vocal group it is advisable to create a separate Facebook Page. Sixth, companies should thank people for their support and their positive comments on their Wall or should repost those- with their permission - to counter negative comments. Seventh, when the crisis is based on a valid problem, this problem has to be resolved swiftly. While resolving the issue, organizations keep the people informed about the progress. When a solution is found, critics should be involved in the communication plan [9].

The International Air Transport Association (IATA) as an example for the industry association represents 268 airlines and helps to formulate and to establish industry standards and policies [10]. In this role, and following the experience with the crash of a Boing 777 at San Francisco Airport where more than 44,000 tweets were posted within 30 min, IATA developed a crisis communication guideline that describes how to behave in emergencies and crises [11]. "Airlines, and other parties directly involved in an accident or major incident, no longer have the luxury to confirm information and wait for internal clearances before issuing some form of public statement – or at least an acknowledgement that they are aware of the initial reports and responding appropriately" [11, p. 10]. IATA, therefore, offers general recommendations for crisis situations and specific instructions for using major social media. From a general perspective, all social media used by an airline has to be integrated in the communication response. Airlines also need to ensure that the crisis communication can be initiated instantly, even if the administration rights for different social media accounts are distributed across several level within the organization. Monitoring of online communications about the company and the incident illustrates another essential element in an effective communication. The decision whether to use social media and if so, what is communicated, should be decided by senior level members. Airlines should remind their members of the organization follow the social media guidelines of the company and that members of the management team limit their comments to approved messages. Regarding the specific instructions for social media, IATA goes so far as to recommend concrete tweets ("First tweet – Aircraft accident: #(flight number)alert. We are investigating reports of an incident involving flight xxx (origin) to (destination). More information shortly." "Second tweet – Aircraft accident: #(flight number)alert. (Airline) regrets flight xxx (origin) to (destination) involved in an accident at (location). Response teams mobilized. More information will follow." [11, p. 35].

Guidelines for the adequate use of social media during crises have also been developed within national and supranational institutions. The German Federal Ministry of the Interior points out that the general guiding principle of crisis communication have to be considered in the use of social media. These are openness, transparency, honesty, consistency, and dialogue orientation [12]. In its guidelines, the Federal Ministry of the Interior [12] places an emphasis on the importance of activities before a crisis occurs. Accordingly, it is necessary to establish a broad reach through sophisticated community management and editorial work. In keeping information sovereignty during crisis situations, the Federal Ministry of the Interior underlines that passivity is not an option and should be completely avoided. Hence, it is better to communicate even uncertain information rather than not to inform the general public. Yet, uncertain information should be identified as such in order to increase credibility. In addition, social media is not only valuable before and during a crisis but also in the aftermath, where feedback should be collected in order to further improve the handling of future crisis.

Given the importance of social media for organizations, not only practical guidelines have been developed to support organizations, but also academic researchers have started to examine social media systematically to increase the understanding of an adequate crisis behavior. Stieglitz et al. [13] examined the crisis communication on Twitter of Qantas, an Australian carrier for long-haul air travel, in two different crisis situations; namely flight disruptions and cancellations caused by the eruption of the Chilean volcano Puyehue in 2011 and a global cancellation of all flights as a response to an industrial action. They found that the foreseeability of an event affects the magnitude of the Twitter discussions. The volcano eruptions influenced the air traffic gradually and could be foreseen to some extent. The grounding however impacted Qantas air traffic immediately and came as a complete surprise to customers and the public. The management decision caused therefore more engagement than the volcano eruption. There was also a difference in the content shared via Twitter. While tweets in the context of the volcano eruption were characterized by an information sharing behavior, tweets in the case of the global grounding were centered on Qantas management decisions and their consequences for the company and for the Australian industrial relations policies.

Hsu and Lawrence [14] examined the influence of social media on the shareholder value. They found a positive connection between online word-of-mouth and stock returns while stock returns decreased with the level of negative online word-of-mouth. This effect also increased with the growth of online word-of-mouth. Hsu and Lawrance [14] further observed that only 18 percent of the companies engaged at all in online conversations following product recalls; probably due to the fact that the majority of the product recalls do not pose a serious danger for the consumers and a proactive approach would lead to more severe consequences. Also, weaker brands seem to be more affected by negative online word-of-mouth as a result of product recalls than stronger brands.

Ehnis et al. [15] looked at the role of the Berlin police as an emergency management agency during the crisis situation related to the 1st of May and examined its relationships with other groups such as media organizations, commercial organizations, political groups, unions, and individuals in crisis situations. Ehnis et al. [15] found that the police tweeted comparably low volumes of factual information about the event. The tweets were however intensively re-tweeted due to the trustworthiness of the information coming from the Berlin police. Hence, the police used Twitter more as a megaphone to distribute knowledge rather than starting a dialogue with public.

Stieglitz and Krüger [1] analyzed the dynamics and sentiments of the Twitter discussions during a Toyota crisis. They found that discussions can be subcategorized into peaks and quiet stages where the volume of tweets differs. The increase was mainly initiated by new information released in relation to the issue. Interestingly, the users kept their numerical level of postings during peaks even. Therefore, it was not the amount of tweets but the total number of users that was responsible for the shift from quiet stages into peaks. Also sentiment-expressions did not increase in both stages, only the polarization of sentiments changed. During peaks, more positive and negative sentiment words were used than in quiet stages. Stieglitz and Krüger [1] found also indications that power-tweeters used sentiment words more frequently than average users and propose, based on that finding, that the average user is influenced by power-tweeters.

Park et al. [16] chose a similar research approach and investigated a crisis of Domino's Pizza. They found that bad news diffuse more quickly than other types of information. With an increase in bad news, the negative sentiments softened in the discussion. Based on their findings they recommend - in a crisis situation or an emerging event - to react quickly, admit the mistakes made, and apologize in an appropriate manner.

3   Metalheads

As the social media activity of the Wacken Open Air during a crisis situation is examined within this study, it should be taken into consideration that the target audience of the festival and therewith of this study consists of a highly specific group, heavy metal fans, or using the Wacken Open Air term: 'metalheads'.

Within the last decades, research on music preferences has attracted a lot of attention, and researchers have examined therein heavy metal, its fans and their perception by the public in various ways.

Concerning the perception of heavy metal, several studies showed that listeners and fans of heavy metal are confronted with several stereotypes. Heavy metals fans are for instance often perceived as working-class members of motorcycle gangs [17]. This perception, however, cannot be confirmed in reality. Although there are heavy metal fans who belong to the working-class and are members of motorcycle gangs, heavy metals fans can be found in any social class and the percentage of fans who own a motorcycle is rather small [17].

Next to a social status bias, also a physical attractiveness bias has been identified. Zillmann and Bathia [18] conducted an experiment to identify the effect of musical preference on the desirability of a potential heterosexual date. They found that the attractiveness of men increased when heavy metal was given as musical preference, while women were seen as less attractive and less sophisticated. This effect was, however, only given when the musical preference between participant and the potential dates differed. When the study participant and the opposite-gender peer shared the same musical preference, the attractiveness perception increased.

Heavy metal is also associated by the public with a higher acceptability of suicide due to its lyrics. Yet, Stack et al. [19] noticed the major shortcoming of ignoring religiosity in previous studies showing a connection between heavy metal and suicide. When Stack et al. [19] included religiosity into the model, the relationship between heavy metal and suicide became non-significant. They concluded, subsequently, that it is religiosity that defines the acceptability of suicide, not heavy metal.

Heavy metal is also often associated with explicit videos containing violence, (illegal) drug use, sexuality or eroticism. Based on a literature review, North and Hargeaves [20] conclude that "any figure that summate data across genres must be treated with caution. Rap and rock music do tend to feature more deleterious content than other genres [...] However, the especially contentious nature of rap and rock relative to other musical styles is not always so apparent as stereotypes of these might suggest" [p. 164].

Researchers have also focused on the linkage between personality of an individual and the preferred music style. Adrian North [21] conducted the probably most influential research in this context with a sample of 36,518 participants. Participants were in average 28.13 years old and lived in Australia and New Zealand (1,503), North America (10,223), and Europe (24,792). North [21] found that metal fans showed – in contrast to previous studies - no rebellious worldview, that the creative scores were not closely related to liking heavy metal, that metalheads have a small negative relation to hard-working, that they are not outgoing but gentle and at ease. Based on his findings he concludes that the "general public has held a stereotype of heavy metal fans being suicidally depressed and being a danger to themselves and society in general, but they are quite delicate things. Aside from their age, they're basically the same kind of person [as a classical music fan]. Lots of heavy metal fans will tell you that they also like Wagner, because it's big, loud and brash. There's also a sense of theater in both heavy rock and classical music, and I suspect that this is what they're really trying to get at when they listen" [22].

4   Wacken Open Air

This study has chosen Wacken Open Air as a sample subject to illustrate how effective crisis communication at a major event can be conducted. Wacken Open Air is the biggest heavy metal festival in the world and the second biggest festival in Germany. Since 2008 each year 75,000 fans attend the festival and join the journey to the little village of Wacken in Schleswig-Holstein in Germany with less than 2,000 inhabitants to make it the center of heavy metal for three full days.

Each year the festival is sold out weeks in advance and it has become more and more difficult to buy tickets for this highly anticipated event. While in 2008 tickets were still available 17 weeks before the festival, in 2015 the tickets were sold in the first 10 h.

In 1990, Wacken Open Air took place for the first time with 5th Avenue, Axe' n'Sex, Motoslug, Sacret Season, Skyline, and Wizzard as festival line. Since these early days the line-up has grown to more than 140 bands in 2016 having Judas Priest, Savatage, Trans-Siberian Orchestra, In Flames, Subway to Sally, U.D.O., or Rob Zombie as headliners of the festival.

Wacken Open Air attracts both young and old. In average 26% of the festival visitors are between 18 and 25 years old, 17% are between 26 and 29 years old, and 55,4% are 30 years and older.

The festival is also known for being one of the most peaceful. Attendants and inhabitants of Wacken enjoy the festival together and create an unforgettable experience.

5   Bring Down the Rain

In 2015 the uncontrollable happened. Days before the festival heavy rainfall set in. The rain was so strong that on the first arrival day, July 28, some areas of the festival area were impassable. The visitors, who were already at the campsite or near the festival site, were asked to follow the instructions of the stewards and to park and camp in the same place [23]. Later that day, the situation became even more problematic. International Concert Service issued a news update asking all visitors to use public transport or if this was not possible to travel with as few cars as possible. Visitors were also asked to park space-savingly [24]. With the ongoing heavy rainfall the situation worsened further and no end could be expected soon. Jaspher Ahrendt, social media manager at International Concert Service, described the situation as following: "Just a few moments ago we had another heavy downpour – it looked like all of Heaven's floodgates had been open at once" [24]. Despite the weather forecast indicating better weather conditions, the heavy rainfall continued also on July 29.

The large amounts of rain could not be possibly be absorbed by the underground or handled otherwise. As a consequence, and despite all efforts, the festival area became completely soaked and turned into an ocean of mud. Campsites were flooded and driveways as well as walkways were no longer passable. Cars got stuck in the mud blocking access and emergency routes. Tents, which were already set up, sunk in the mud and festival visitors got stuck in traffic jams near the festival area. Thus, visitors

Fig. 1. Mudland (Source: International Concert Service).

were informed that it would not be possible to get them all on the festival area, but that people had to park at interims positions and to spend the nights there in the cars. Fans who had yet not headed to Wacken were asked to postpone their arrival or find another accommodation for the night [25] as "every minute helps us and the ground" [26].

The situation did not improve also on July 30.. Due to the extreme conditions, it was not even possible to get to Wacken by car. Visitors were advised to wait a little bit longer or to use public transport [27]. Although the weather had improved and the downpours had stopped, another challenge emerged on the last night of the festival. Due to a clear sky, the night on August 1 was expected to be ice cold [28].

Summing up all events during the festival, Helge Rudolph, the online communication manger, concluded: "Mud, rain, cold nights [...] the now closed chapter of the 26th Wacken Open Air has been a festival of extremes" [29] (Fig. 1).

6   Cowboys from Hell

Considering the horrible weather conditions before and during the arrival as well as the situation at the camping sites and the festival area, the organizers of Wacken Open Air were clearly confronted with a crisis situation.

Apart from handling the crisis situations and finding solutions to newly occurring problems at the site, it was of utter importance to initiate a proper crisis communication. A core team, the Cowboys from Hell, comprising Jasper Ahrendt, Social Media Manager, Helge Rudolph, Online Communication Manager, and Nick Hüper, Head of

Communications (one of the authors of this article), assumed responsibility and took on the task. A common understanding or six principles served the cowboys from hell as guiding lights for the crisis communication:

- Provide all relevant groups with the latest information!
- Be transparent, accurate, and concise in the communication!
- Do everything to improve the situation at the festival site!
- Strengthen the sense of community among all visitors!
- Keep up the good mood of all visitors!
- Don't sugar-coat!

Three different social media platform were used during this crisis communication: Facebook, Twitter, and the Wacken Festival smartphone application. In the following, each social media platform will be highlighted.

6.1   Facebook

Wacken Open Air has approximately 490,000 followers on the social network site Facebook, which makes it the biggest social media platform for International Concert Service. A research conducted by the PEW Research Center found that 79 percent of all Internet users use Facebook. 88 percent of the people at the age of 18 to 29 use it, 84 percent of 30 to 49, 72 percent of people at 50 to 64, and 62 percent who are 65 and older. It is therewith not only the most popular social media platform but also the social media of choice for the target group of Wacken Open Air [30]. Facebook is also important for International Concert Service because of the community they have developed there over the last decades, which includes power users that act as open leaders and moderators. During the crisis, these community members supported the activities of International Concert Service and helped therewith to spread information and keep the spirits up.

Figures 2 and 3 show the number of users reached in total and organically in 2015 compared to 2014. The course of events is clearly mirrored by the figures. On the first day of arrival, the figures of 2015 and 2014 resemble each other. With the worsening situation at the festival site in 2015, the corresponding number of users reached increases dramatically peaking on arrival day 3 (July 29) to 641,938 total and 170,831 organic views. Afterwards, the views decline but remain above those of 2014.

As a crisis situation is examined, it is further interesting to study the positive feedback on posts with respect to the engagement on Facebook as a proxy for the general reaction of visitors. In general, it is noteworthy that the number of likes in 2015 is u-shaped. Shares and comments follow however again the previous pattern of users reached.

When comparing 2015 and 2014, it is remarkable that 2015 has significantly higher number of likes on the first two arrival days, that a higher tendency to comment can be detected, and that the number of shares exceeds the value in 2014 up to the first day of the festival (see Fig. 4).

When considering the reach, the engagement and the reactions of users, the outstanding role of Facebook for Wacken Open Air becomes clearly visible. It helped to

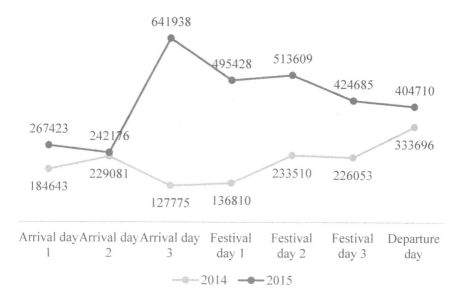

Fig. 2. Users reached (total)

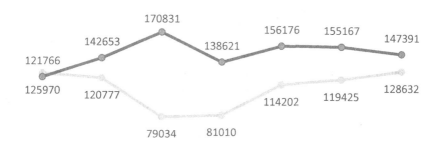

Fig. 3. Users reached (organic)

inform visitors and to establish or foster a process where festival visitors helped each other. At the same time, it is impressive to see that the number of positive feedback in 2015 was higher than in 2014 whilst the festival experience was interfered by bad weather conditions.

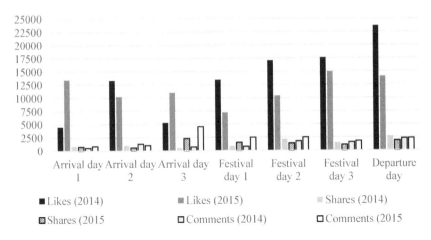

Fig. 4. Positive feedback

6.2 Twitter

Approximately 72,000 people follow Wacken Open Air on Twitter, which makes it the second biggest social media channel for International Concert Services. Even if Twitter is predestined to instantly distribute information, there are several shortcomings for Wacken Open Air, which diminished its importance during the crisis. First, the limitation of possible characters in tweets made it problematic to use it as an effective channel for sharing critically valuable information. Second, its reach is lower in comparison to Facebook. Third, the Wacken Open Air festival community prefers to use Facebook and to gather relevant information there, which can be explained by the age structure of festival visitors. While more than 50 percent of visitors are 30-year old and older, Twitter is generally used by only 23 percent of people at the age of 30 to 49 years and by 21 percent of people at 50 to 64 [30].

Figure 5 shows the development of impressions per day during the arrival period (July 27 to July 29) and during the festival (July 30 to August 1) as well as from the

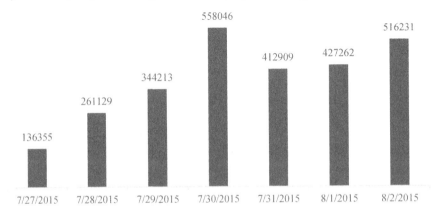

Fig. 5. Impressions per day

departure day (August 2). The impressions mirror the developments during this time and correspond to the pattern of Facebook. On July 27 only a small group of visitors prepared themselves to get to Wacken or were already at the campsite. When the situation became more problematic and more people started to head to Wacken, the impressions increased and reached a peak with 558,046 impressions on July 30, the day before the official start of Wacken Open Air. Afterwards, the impressions declined to 412,909 on August 1 and increased gradually to 516,231 until August 2.

The activity on Twitter in terms of responses, retweets, likes and clicked links (URLs) shows the same pattern (see Fig. 6). It is notable that followers on twitter were in general more interested in getting information (URLs) and less intrigued in starting a dialogue (Responses). The use of Twitter by visitors was therewith mainly for information seeking purposes which is understandable under the given situations. It is also interesting that the number of likes stayed almost stable with the exception of July 28.

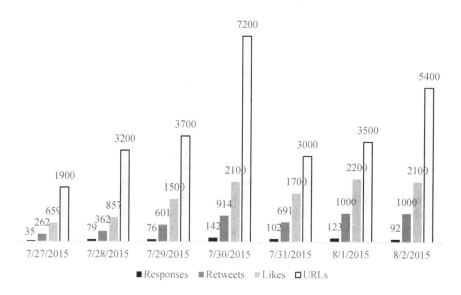

Fig. 6. Engagement per day

Given the impressions per day as well as the activity volume, it can be concluded that, despite its shortcomings, Twitter played an important role in the crisis situation. Information was shared fast and reached a wide audience.

6.3 Wacken Open Air App

Since 2010 International Concert Service used a smartphone application. 2015 was the first year to use the application with a push-notification. As any festival app, the Wacken Open Air application contains useful information such as the running order, news, maps, or bands and billing.

The most important function of the application was however the recently included push-notification. Having this function, International Concert Service could instantly provide all metalheads with valuable information and news during the crisis situation. Push-notifications had a maximal length of 140 letters and contained a link to the website of Wacken Open Air, where further information was available. In contrast to Facebook and Twitter, the application offered a highly targeted communication with a marginal spreading loss as it can be assumed that only those people download this service, who are actually visiting a festival. The application also contained a monitoring function showing the speed of information distribution. The application contained however at this point no geo-tagging function which made it impossible to differentiate between people who were already at the campsite, those who were on their way to Wacken, and finally those who were still at home preparing to start. Given their actual situation, each group possessed a different information need. Those at the festival site needed information of how to cope with the conditions on-site. The ones on the way to Wacken were mainly interested in the current traffic situation and the possibility to access the festival area. Still others, who were still preparing, needed to know whether to postpone the journey or to head to the festival site. With the missing geo-tagging function, the push-notifications could not be targeted at each group individually but all messages were sent to all users of the application.

More than 55,000 visitors (73 percent of all visitors) had downloaded the application. Eleven English push-notifications were sent during the festival (see Table 1). 90 percent were reached within 10 min after a notification was released. Hence, between 42,260 and 47,920 people were reached by the push-notification (see Fig. 7).

The Wacken Open Air application proved to be an immensely useful tool in this crisis situation in order to distribute critically valuable knowledge and to reach large parts of the festival visitors fast. The pattern of the Wacken Open Air application differs from those of Facebook and Twitter as the reach increased continuously and did not decrease on July 31. This can probably be explained by the different use of Facebook and Twitter compared to the Wacken Open Air application. While Facebook and Twitter had to be accessed in order to get the information, the application was automatically informing all visitors, who had downloaded it.

6.4   #Zusammenrücken/#Movetogether

Two guiding principles ("Strengthen the sense of community among all visitors!" and "Keep up the good mood of all visitors!") focus on the social dynamic at the festival. On July 28 when the situation became more and more problematic, the crisis communication team decided to start using the hashtags #movetogether in English messages and #zusammenrücken in German messages across all different social media channels.

The decision was not taken by the idea to create a monitoring and filter element for International Concert Service and metalheads alike but precisely in order to address these two guiding principles. Focusing on this aspect became extremely important at that time, as it became clear that the given weather conditions would impact the festival even if the heavy rain was to stop immediately.

Table 1. Push-notifications

Date	Number	Message
28.07.2015	1	Important!!! Wichtig!!! Please read the travel information in the news!
28.07.2015	2	Important weather and travel update! Please check the news and tell your friends!
28.07.2015	3	Update 3: Parking and Camping! Read and share this very important update!
29.07.2015	4	Urgent update for everyone who has already entered the holy ground! Please get your festival wristband immediately!
29.07.2015	5	Information on opening and stage times Bullhead City!
29.07.2015	6	Urgent request for all of you who have not yet started their journey and will travel by car: Please postpone your arrival to Thursday!
29.07.2015	7	Please do not come today! We will not be able to get all of you onto the festival area tonight!
29.07.2015	8	Alternative to the Carpark in Itzehoe! We can now offer another interim solution
29.07.2015	9	If you are at the festival: Please get your wristbands tonight! The wristband exchange is opened around the clock!
30.07.2015	10	Important: Only use public transportation to get to the festival today! Shuttles will be free of charge! Share this with everyone out there!
01.08.2015	11	We will have a very cold night due to the clear sky. Please put on warm clothes and take care of each other!

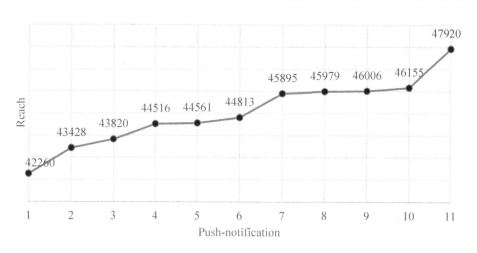

Fig. 7. Reach per push-notification

Right from its first use, #movetogether and #zusammenrücken became the motto among visitors, organizers, and crisis helpers at the festival site and an accurate description of what could be observed.

Fig. 8. Spontaneous helpfulness (Source: International Concert Service)

There is one specific facet that especially mirrors the atmosphere at the festival site. Due to the heavy rainfall and the mud, at least for the first hours it became impossible for handicapped people to access the festival site or even to get the necessary wristband. When other metalheads became aware of it, they rushed to help and carry the handicapped fans to the wristband stations and to the festival site (see Fig. 8).

Although the importance of using both hashtags was not fully reflected on social media platforms, #zusammenrücken and #movetogether served its purpose just fine.

7 Conclusion – See You in Wacken – Rain or Shine

Heavy rain, mud, and cold nights set the circumstances of Wacken Open Air 2015. It would have been no surprise if these conditions had negatively affected the 'festival experience and had caused negative reactions by the festival visitors.

Yet, the contrary was the case. On social media, Wacken Open Air received more positive reactions than in the year before and thus the festival experience remain intact. The main reason for this can surely be found in the involvement and behavior of everyone. Be it farmers from the area helping to get cars out of the mud, International Concert Service with all their efforts and activities, or (and most importantly) the festival visitors themselves helping each other and keeping their good mood.

The provided insights into the activities of the crisis communication team show that social media platforms are important tools to handle crisis situations. People use social media for information seeking purposes, sharing information, and finding solutions to given challenges. Concerning the activities of the crisis communication team, the predefined guiding principles helped the team not only to stay focused but also to successfully manage the situation from a communication perspective.

Another important key insight is the use of both hashtags #zusammenrücken and #movetogether. Even if their importance is not reflected on social media in terms of their usage in posts and tweets, just using them helped to strengthen the sense of community at the festival site and motivated people to keep their spirits up.

In total, Wacken Open Air 2015 will be remembered as a great festival with horrible weather and extraordinary fans or in the words of International Concert Service:

"Considering the horrible weather conditions before and during your arrival and the difficult situation on the ground of the camping sites and the festival area, your support, understanding, and unshakable positive humour have literally blown us away.

You have confirmed our awareness that: We can only organise the greatest metal fest on this planet with your help year after year!" [29].

Acknowledgement. The authors would like to thank Jasper Ahrendt for his support!

References

1. Stieglitz, S., Krüger, N.: Analysis of sentiments in corporate Twitter communication – a case study on an issue of Toyota. In: ACIS 2011 Proceedings (2011). http://aisel.aisnet.org/acis2011/29. Accessed 4 Feb 2017
2. Kaplan, A.M., Haenlein, M.: Users of the world, unite! The challenges and opportunities of social media. Bus. Horiz. **53**(1), 59–68 (2010)
3. Trefzger, T.F., Baccarella, C.V., Scheiner, C.W., Voigt, K.-I.: Hold the line! The challenge of being a premium brand in the social media era. In: Meiselwitz, G. (ed.) SCSM 2016. LNCS, vol. 9742, pp. 461–471. Springer, Cham (2016). doi:10.1007/978-3-319-39910-2_43
4. Scheiner, C.W., Krämer, K., Baccarella, C.V.: Cruel intentions? – The role of moral awareness, moral disengagement, and regulatory focus in the unethical use of social media by entrepreneurs. In: Meiselwitz, G. (ed.) SCSM 2016. LNCS, vol. 9742, pp. 437–448. Springer, Cham (2016). doi:10.1007/978-3-319-39910-2_41
5. Coombs, W.T.: Ongoing Crisis Communication: Planning, Managing, and Responding, 2nd edn. Sage, Los Angeles (2007)
6. Coombs, T.: An analytic framework for crisis situations: better responses from a better understanding of the situation. J. Public Relat. Res. **10**(3), 177–191 (1998)
7. Lindsay, B.: Social media and disasters: current uses, future options, and policy considerations. Congr. Res. Serv. (2011). http://fas.org/sgp/crs/homesec/R41987.pdf. Accessed 1 Feb 2016
8. Etter, M., Vestergaard, A.: Facebook and the public framing of a corporate crisis. Corp. Commun. Int. J. **20**(2), 163–177 (2015)
9. Social Media Crisis Response Guidelines (2011). https://www.facebook-studio.com/fbassets/media/753/FacebookSocialMediaCrisisGuidelines.pdf. Accessed 1 Feb 2017
10. IATA - About us (2017). http://www.iata.org/about/Pages/index.aspx. Accessed 4 Feb 2017
11. IATA Crisis Communications in the Digital Age – A Guide to "Best Practice" for the Aviation Industry (2016). http://www.iata.org/publications/Documents/crisis-communications-guidelines.pdf. Accessed 9 Feb 2017

12. Leitfaden Krisenkommunikation (2015). http://www.bmi.bund.de/SharedDocs/Downloads/DE/Broschueren/2014/leitfaden-krisenkommunikation.pdf;jsessionid=5B16430359DFDBF9C183E616DFDDDB90.2_cid364?__blob=publicationFile. Accessed 8 Feb 2017

13. Stieglitz, S., Bruns, A., Krüger, N.: Enterprise-related crisis communication on Twitter. In: Proceedings der 12. Internationalen Tagung Wirtschaftsinformatik (WI 2015), pp. 917–932 (2015). http://www.wi2015.uni-osnabrueck.de/Files/WI_2015_Tagungsband.pdf. Accessed 4 Feb 2017

14. Hsu, L., Lawrence, B.: The role of social media and brand equity during a product recall crisis: a shareholder value perspective. Int. J. Res. Mark. 33(1), 59–77 (2016)

15. Ehnis, C., Mirbabaie M., Bunker, D., Stieglitz, S.: The role of social media network participants in extreme events. In: Proceedings of the 25th Australasian Conference on Information Systems (2014). https://aut.researchgateway.ac.nz/handle/10292/8056. Accessed 6 Feb 2017

16. Park, J., Cha, M., Kim, H., Jaeseung, J.: Managing bad news in social media: a case study on domino's pizza crisis. In: Proceedings of the Sixth International AAAI Conference on Weblogs and Social Media (2012). http://mia.kaist.ac.kr/wp-content/uploads/2010/11/2012-06-icwsm-domino.pdf. Accessed 4 Feb 2017

17. Weinstein, D.: Heavy Metal: A Cultural Sociology. New Lexington Press, Indiana (1991)

18. Zillman, D., Bhatia, A.: Effects of associating with musical genres on heterosexual attraction. Comput. Res. 16(2), 263–288 (1989)

19. Stack, S., Gundlach, J., Reeves, J.L.: Heavy metal, religiosity, and suicide acceptability. Suicide Life Threat. Behav. 24(1), 15–23 (1994)

20. North, A., Hargreaves, D.: The Social and Applied Psychology of Music. Oxford University Press, Oxford (2008)

21. North, A.: Individual differences in musical taste. Am. J. Psychol. 123(2), 199–208 (2010)

22. Collingwood, J.: Preferred Music Style is Tied to Personality (2016). https://psychcentral.com/lib/preferred-music-style-is-tied-to-personality/. Accessed 5 Feb 2017

23. Ahrendt, J.: Parking and Camping (2015). http://www.wacken.com/en/news/news/news-detail/update-3-parking-and-camping/. Accessed 7 Feb 2017

24. Ahrendt, J.: Important!!! Weather Conditions and Urgent Travel Information (2015). http://www.wacken.com/en/news/news/news-detail/important-weather-conditions-and-urgent-travel-information/. Accessed 7 Feb 2017

25. Ahrendt, J.: Please do not Come Today! (2015). http://www.wacken.com/en/news/news/news-detail/please-do-not-come-today/. Accessed 6 Feb 2017

26. Ahrendt, J.: Arrival: If possible, please postpone your arrival until tomorrow (2015). http://www.wacken.com/en/news/news/news-detail/arrival-if-possible-please-postpone-your-arrival-until-tomorrow/. Accessed 6 Feb 2017

27. Rudolph, H.: Summary: Everything You Need to Know about the Arrival at Wacken (2015). http://www.wacken.com/en/news/news/news-detail/summary-everything-you-need-to-know-about-the-arrival-at-wacken/. Accessed 6 Feb 2017

28. Ahrendt, J.: It's Going to be a Cold Night (2015). http://www.wacken.com/en/news/news/news-detail/its-going-to-be-a-cold-night/. Accessed 6 Feb

29. Rudolph, H.: The W:O:A 2015 is History (2015). http://www.wacken.com/en/news/news/news-detail/the-woa-2015-is-history/. Accessed 8 Feb 2017

30. Greenwood, S., Perrin, A., Duggan, M.: Social Media Update 2016 (2016). http://assets.pewresearch.org/wp-content/uploads/sites/14/2016/11/10132827/PI_2016.11.11_Social-Media-Update_FINAL.pdf. Accessed 7 Feb 2017

Do Social Bots (Still) Act Different to Humans? – Comparing Metrics of Social Bots with Those of Humans

Stefan Stieglitz[(✉)], Florian Brachten, Davina Berthelé, Mira Schlaus, Chrissoula Venetopoulou, and Daniel Veutgen

Professional Communication in Electronic Media/Social Media, Department of Computer Science and Applied Cognitive Science, University of Duisburg-Essen, Duisburg, Germany
`stieglitz@connected-organization.de`

Abstract. As a consequence of the growing relevance of social media and improved algorithms and techniques, social bots have become a widely recognized phenomenon. Social bots can disrupt or influence online discourse in social media in many ways (e.g. spreading spam or astroturfing). In this paper, we compare 771 social bots with 693 human accounts. Our analysis is based on a Twitter data set concerning the U.S. election in 2016. Our study shows that human Twitter users and bot accounts differ in many ways. E.g. we found differences regarding the number of follower and the retweets per day of an account, as well as between the used links per day and the retweets per day. Our findings are helpful to identify social bots and to get insights about the impact of social bots in public social media communication.

Keywords: Social bots · Impact · Twitter · Follower · U.S. election

1 Introduction

Social media such as Facebook or Twitter offer new ways to publicly discuss political issues and to spread information in order to reach people and possibly influence their opinion [1]. Social media provides the infrastructure to easily share and produce content such as text, links or images. In this environment bots can spread information to human users even without being disclosed as pieces of software [2, 3]. Bots are defined as "software designed to act in ways that are similar to how a person would act in the social space" [4].

Be it the Brexit, the Arab Spring, Brazilian Protests or elections – social bots increasingly participate in communication on public social media. One goal they are following might be to influence political debates [5, 6]. Among others, political actors and governments might use social bots to manipulate the public opinion, to heat up debates or to muddy political issues [7]. During the second debate of the U.S. electional campaign 2016, one out of three of the 2,4 million pro-Trump-tweets were produced by social bots, whereas pro-Clinton-bots produced one out of four tweets of the overall 720.00 pro-Clinton-tweets [7]. Data about the 2016 U.S. election revealed that the

© Springer International Publishing AG 2017
G. Meiselwitz (Ed.): SCSM 2017, Part I, LNCS 10282, pp. 379–395, 2017.
DOI: 10.1007/978-3-319-58559-8_30

activity of automated pro-Clinton-accounts increased over time but never reached the traffic of automated pro-Trump-accounts. Overall, there were five times as many automated pro-Trump-tweets as automated pro-Clinton-tweets [8].

This example illustrates the high relevance of social bots and the need to conduct research in this field. The phenomenon of bots is nothing new though. As Ferrara et al. [9] point out, bots exist since the beginnings of computers. The term 'bot' is used to describe "a software designed to automate a task in a computing system" [4]. Social bots, as a more particular kind of bots produce or share content and interact with humans on social media, trying to mimic human behavior [10–12]. Even more specific, the term political (social) bots is used to describe "automated accounts that are active on public policy issues, elections, and political crisis" [6].

In practice, social bots can follow different goals. On the one hand, they can perform tasks such as (re)posting news or automatically share updates (e.g. about the weather) in a conversational (human) tone. On the other hand, bots could be used to imitate human behavior and to spread incorrect information, spam or viruses.

Often these bot profiles lack basic account information like name or profile pictures. Whereas regular users get access from front-end websites, bots obtain access through a site's application programming interface (API) [6]. As the API of Twitter is especially accessible, many social bots (respectively their creators) focus on this platform.

With more than 310 million active users and over 500 million tweets a day, Twitter is one of the biggest social media platforms in the world [13]. Twitter allows users to post and read messages ("tweets"), each restricted to a maximum of 140 characters. To create posts and to share messages of other users ("retweet") are amongst the main features [14]. Moreover, users can subscribe ("follow") other Twitter profiles and can be followed by others ("friends"). Following a user does not have to be reciprocal. A user can follow another user and thus receives this user' public posts which encourages to follow users one doesn't know in person even if those don't follow back [15]. While it is possible to restrict visibility of posts to users oneself approves, about 90% of the Twitter users make their content public for everybody [16] and thereby enable researchers and companies to gather and analyze personal data [17]. At the same time Twitter becomes interesting for spammers and others looking to spread their messages and possibly to influence users [18]. However, until now it is unclear how social bots act in social media and if it is different to human behaviour [17].

As research shows, social bots have been used in the political context (e.g. in 2016 in the Brexit vote and the presidential election in the United States). Also, in the forefront of the election of a new government in Germany 2017 politicians have begun a debate about the use of social bots in election campaigns. However, it remains unclear (a) if social bots actually have an influence on human users and (b) if so, how strong this influence is. For example, even though the Brexit campaign seemed to be subject of social bot activity, it has to be considered that Twitter is not used by the whole population in the same way (e.g. young people use it more intensively) [5]. The impact of social bots therefore remains unclear.

Our objective is thus to investigate the behaviour of social bots and compare it to the way human users act in the same data set. The aim is to reveal differences between those two groups and to garner insights into their behavior thus inferring the impact and providing further contribution in the research field of social bots.

Following, we first present prior research about the potential influence bots could have. Moreover, different approaches to identify bots and characteristics of users who are susceptible for bots will be explained. The Computers as Social Actors framework (CASA) [19] is presented to point out an important mechanism that plays a role in Human-Computer-Interaction (HCI). Furthermore, we explain our research design and present the results of our study. Finally, the implications of our findings are reported and discussed. The paper ends with a conclusion.

2   Related Work

Online Influence of Bots. Twitter and other social media platforms enable users to reach and possibly influence other users (and vice versa) through the networks' structure [20]. Political actors as well as actors from other fields, such as marketing, therefore have an interest to better understand or even influence social media communication [20]. In order to detect the influence of Twitter users, several factors can be considered. E.g. the more followers a user has, the more potential receivers of a message exist. The user is possibly more often mentioned and cited (or "re-tweeted") by other users and can therefore be considered a being influential [21].

As much as 61.5% of total web traffic is produced by bots [4] though it is important to note, that this number includes not only social bots but all kinds of automated processes – as well those outside of social media. As such social bots may serve as a channel to spread information in an efficient manner because several accounts are able to spread the same information or opinion without having to be controlled by a human. As studies show social bots can be used to influence political communication [5]. To reach this goal, bots can follow different strategies:

1. **Mimic human behavior:** in this context, Misener [25] emphasizes that bots try to simulate all online activities of real users with the aim of appearing human to blend in. Consequently, it may be harder to detect those social bot accounts that behave like human actors. One can assume that bot accounts that simulate human behavior very well, are hard to identify by third parties and might more efficiently influence communication [26].

2. **Overstate trends:** by using special hashtags or combining various hashtags, social bots can distort the weight of certain opinions covered by these hashtags. A widespread way trying to manipulate trends in social networks is to selectively attack the parameters that are collected purely quantitatively. These are, for example, 'likes' and shares on Facebook and the frequency of hashtags on Twitter. In this sense bots do not need to produce new content, they just multiply existing content.

3. **Astroturfing:** Another possibility of influencing the perception of users is astroturfing. According to Zhang et al. [27] astroturfing describes the practice of trying to create the impression of widely-supported ideas or opinions although they don't have support of a majority. The usage of astroturfing in a political context has been

shown multiple times [28]. Traditionally, astroturfing is conducted by public relations institutions or lobbying organisations [29]. However, since the rise of social media, astroturfing became a popular tool for organizations or single persons to create the impression of grassroots movements in the Internet [28]. Just like astroturfing, 'smoke screening' and misdirecting have been used in political contexts, as for example the Syrian civil war [4]. The practices describe the overlapping of a topic with spam or non-related content to distract the attention and to aggravate the finding of information.

Offline Influence of Bots. The question of just how big the offline influence is and whether there is an offline influence at all is another important aspect to address. Even if there is an influence online, it is still unclear if this influence could carry over to the behaviour outside of the Internet (e.g. regarding voting behavior during elections or buying decisions). The offline influence detection problem addresses these questions. The difficulty lies in the identification of users who may be influential in real life based on Twitter accounts and related data [21]. According to Cossu et al. [21] features predicting online influence, like number of followers or retweets, are inefficient to solve this problem. There are a few studies, which try to capture the offline impact of bots. Aiello et al. [26] outline that influence seems to depend on trust – an aspect which is related to the mimicking of human behaviour exhibited by social bots. Also the position in a social graph [30] seems to have an impact on influence. In addition, Cossu et al. [23] point out that the language used in tweets has an impact on the offline influence. Studies concerning the interdependence between popularity and influence in social media clarify that popularity is not a requirement of being influential and vice-versa [16]. It is thus that the awareness of communicating with a bot causes a decreasing influence. A massive influence of trends cannot be equated with effective manipulation. For this reason, there is a danger of overestimation of bot influence [5]. Hegelich [5] points out that all studies argue that someone does not change his political conviction just because of reading a message in social media. He however sees a subtler manipulation as very probable [5]. The author names the potential influence "Bot-Effekt" and illustrates that its impact in theory could be very large but is difficult to prove empirically [26].

Threats. In spite of the aforementioned difficulties, researches tried to measure influence, especially threats which may be caused by social bots. Findings suggest, risks for private information and the stock market as well as manipulated behavior [9, 10]. If social bots infiltrate social media, they can easily collect user data from connected (human) accounts. This has been demonstrated by Boshmaf et al. [10] who infiltrated users on Facebook and could collect sensible and monetary valuable private data like email addresses, phone numbers, and profile information. Moreover, they succeeded in collecting the same amount of data related to Facebook friends of the infiltrated user. If a network is infiltrated, social bots can manipulate the users' perception [9], for example by using astroturfing or smoke screening. According to Chu et al. [31] most spam messages on Twitter are generated by bots, whereas only a small amount is generated by human accounts. Moreover, the authors discovered that tweets by bots contained a higher number of external hyperlinks. Some bots generated tweets even contained more than one link. Many of these bot accounts shared and retweeted spam links. Grier et al. [32] and Gao et al. [33] also discovered large spam attacks by bots. Human accounts, in general, try to avoid and refuse to interact with spam [32].

As described, social bots can focus on 'negative actions' of certain kinds, like manipulation [9], stealing and misuse of private information [10], astroturfing [28] or smoke screening [4].

Identification of Bots. Since the advent of social bots, researchers developed several ways to identify bots in social media. Previous scientific approaches can be grouped into different categories: Concepts were based on network information [34–36] machine learning [9, 12, 31, 37], crowdsourcing [38] or a mixture of the attempts [39].

In contrast to the assumption of Xie et al. [35] as well as Paradise et al. [36], Boshmaf et al. [10] found that humans do not refuse to interact with bots. As a result, network information does not seem to deliver satisfying disclosure for the identification of potential bots. In contrast a detailed consideration of machine learning features seems to be more a more promising approach. For instance, Chu et al. [31] selected the parameters automation of tweeting, presence of spam, duplicate tweets, aggressive following behavior, originality of tweets and tweets with unrelated links as features. Chu et al. found that in contrast to human accounts, bots have less follower than friends, generate less tweets, tweet more often via API-based tools and use more URLs in their tweets.

Meanwhile, it is possible for some bots to avoid simple bot recognition algorithms. These more sophisticated bots for example try to keep a balanced relationship between friends and followers to avoid Twitter from deleting them because of the limit the platform stipulates on the ratio of followers over friends [31]. Furthermore, these bots simulate breaks and sleeping times and can even slightly modify messages, so that the semantic content is still the same, but automatic text programs do not recognize these texts as identical [5].

User Interaction with Bots. The Computers as Social Actors (CASA) framework focuses on interaction between humans and computers. Thereby, the framework helps to investigate and understand the possible differences or similarities between bots and humans [22]. The framework is derived from many studies examining human responses to a variety of media and is based on Media Equation-Theory which postulates that humans are treating computers as if they were real people [40]. Research showed that human-computer-interaction has important emotional [41] and behavioral outcomes [42] e.g. that humans do see bot accounts as more likeable or trustworthy if these bots exhibit empathy or that humans act despiteful when they feel betrayed by a computer. It was also demonstrated that theories from social science as well as experiments on human-human-interaction were reproducible in human-computer-interaction [19]. The same human scripts that guide human-human interaction are used [43] and cues that reveal asocial nature of a computer are ignored. In summary, humans interact with computers in similar ways as they interact with other humans which is also the case, when only restricted social cues are available [22].

More recent studies focus on bots as actors [14, 44, 45]. For example, Edward et al. [14] demonstrated that bots are perceived as credible, attractive, competent in communication, and interactional all of which are characteristics normally associated with humans.

Furthermore, Edwards et al. [22] conducted a two-part study to explore the differences in perception of communication quality between a human agent and a bot. They focused on the areas of cognitive elaboration, information seeking and learning outcomes. The authors could show that humans indicate similar levels of information seeking, cognitive elaboration, affective learning, and motivation behaviors when they receive information from a bot compared to a human user. Results suggest that participants learned the same from either a bot or a human agent. These findings are in accordance with the CASA framework which implies that organizations and individuals who use a bot to influence social media in different ways can be successful. In this case bots appeared to be just as efficient as a human agent for specific information [22]. This shows that automated accounts in general have the ability to evoke human affect towards them. This should go even further in regard to social bots as these try to mimic human behavior and thus could act unnoticed and try to improve their chances of affecting the social graph [12, 25]. However one recent study did not find that mimicking human behavior increased the chance having an influence [4]. The authors analyzed how the content of tweets by a social botnet differs from regular users in the same data set. They conducted a content analysis of tweets from Arabic and English Twitter users as well as from a social botnet and found that over 50% of the tweets generated by the botnet and approximately one third of the tweets from regular users contained news. Moreover, there was a difference in the expression of opinions in tweets. Arabic Twitter users expressed their opinion in 45% of their tweets, English Twitter users in 25.8%, while 12.4% of tweets from the botnet were opinion-related tweets. The authors conclude that it is ambiguous if social bots try to mimic human behavior which differs from previous research.

Research Gap and Hypotheses. Abokhodair et al. [4] note that an effective analysis should be able to differentiate the participation of humans from bot behavior. Consequently, to identify bots it is necessary to know what kind of differences exist. Studies show that differences exist in the number of followers and friends, the tweeting behavior and frequency, and in the integration of external URLs in tweets [31].

In order to contribute to this, we compare the behavior of bots and humans in the same Twitter data set. Deeper knowledge about the differences may contribute to the exploration of the bots' impact and facilitate future identification of bots.

Our first hypothesis deals with fundamental differences between bot and human accounts. We presume that there are differences concerning standard features, which can also be used to predict the online influence, like number of followers or retweets [21]. As previous studies show, bot accounts are often organized in a network-like structure and retweet more often than humans [9, 24]. Because of this, we assume that bot accounts retweet each other more often than human accounts. Beyond that Chu et al. [31] postulate that retweeting indicates a lack of originality and that bots post more external links. Therefore, our first hypotheses are:

H1a: Bot accounts have a lower number of followers than human accounts.
H1b: Bot accounts have a higher number of retweets than human accounts.
H1c: Bot accounts have a lower number of @ in Tweets than human accounts.
H1d: Bot accounts have a higher number of links than human accounts.

Cossu et al. [21], postulate that an account is more influential when it has more followers and is retweeted often. Therefore, we infer a relationship between these features and presume that:

H2a: The number of followers of a bot account is positively related to the number of retweets of this account.

H2b: The number of follower of a human account is positively related to the number of retweets of this account.

Because of the relationship between spam, hyperlinks and bots which was emphasized by Chu et al. [31], Grier et al. [32] and Gao et al. [33], as our third hypothesis, we expect:

H3: There is a positive relationship between tweeted links per day and retweets per day which differs between bot and human accounts.

According to Aiello et al. [26] who showed a relationship between activity and popularity, we indicate the following hypothesis:

H4: The more tweets are created per week, the more followers are generated.

3   Method

To test our hypotheses we gathered a data set of 6.5 million tweets via the Stream API. The set was collected from 31st of October 2016 to 6th of November 2016 – the last week before the presidential election in the United States. The data set contains tweets with either the term "Hillary Clinton" or "Donald Trump" – the both candidates running for presidency. The reason for collecting this specific data was, that to test our hypotheses we had to ensure that we could analyze a data set with a sufficient amount of bot accounts. As Howard and Kollanyi [6] showed for the Brexit and Mustafaraj and Metaxas [46] and Forelle et al. [47] for elections in America and Venezuela respectively, political events seem to be a regular aim for the use of bot accounts. Furthermore, to analyze a recent dataset (and thus take into account possible recent developments of bot account strategies) we chose the US election as a background for our dataset. The meta-data of Twitter contained information like the content of the tweet, the date and time when the tweet was posted, the authors name, description and ID, the number of followers and friends, the source from which the tweets were send and the physical location. Our goal was to identify approximately 100 humans and 100 bots for each day. In the following, the procedure of identification is explained stepwise.

Identifications of Bots. To identify bot accounts in our dataset we chose to exclude all accounts of which we could say with a high certainty that these were human accounts.

Our aim was to maintain tweets from users with a high probability to be a social bot. The first step was to exclude all verified user accounts. The next step was to exclude all accounts with less than 500 followers. As our aim was to identify social bots which may have an influence on people, 500 seemed like a fitting threshold to include only those bot accounts that could reach a significant number of people. The third step was to have a closer look on the source from which the tweets were posted. Most of the social bots are auto piloted and generate their tweets via unregistered API-based tools [31]. Because of this, all sources containing "Twitter" in the URL were excluded. Hereby, all sources which are normally used by humans were left out: This can be mobile applications like Twitter for tablets and mobile phones or the Twitter web client. We could reproduce that many of the remaining sources include social bot software which controlled the bot accounts. In the next step, we created a variable to show the relationship between the friends and followers of every user. For this calculation, the number of friends was divided by the number of followers. This friends-follower-ratio indicates if a user has more friends than followers. Previous literature proposes that this ratio should be high for bots and well-balanced for humans [31]. This means that bots normally have a lot more friends than followers. Thus, all accounts with a lower friend-follower-ratio than 150% were excluded. In the last step, all tweets of a user at one day were counted to have the number of tweets per day for every user. Prior research concerning Twitter data and social bots shows that bots have a much higher tweet per day rate than humans [15, 18, 31]. Therefore, all tweets of users with a lower tweet-per-day-rate than 10 were excluded to ensure that only active users, which could possibly be influential, remain.

Identification of Humans. To compare the bot accounts with human accounts we had in return to assure that the comparable sample only contained accounts controlled by humans with a comparable reach. The process of identification consisted of six steps. At first, all verified users were excluded to make sure that there were no organizations or news sites in the data set anymore. Second, all users which had less than 500 followers were excluded to make sure that only humans with a relatively high reach (and thus possibly influence) were considered. For the third step, only those sources which were most likely used exclusively by humans were chosen: "Twitter for iPhone" and "Twitter for Android". These tweets were posted via mobile phones and thus with a strong probability to come from a human as the application of bots on a mobile phone is much more difficult than using the API from a desktop-computer. In the next step, the friend-follower-ratio was calculated. As said before, humans tend to have a well-balanced ratio between accounts they follow and accounts which follow them. For that reason, we assumed that humans in our data set should have a friend-follower ratio of nearly 100% (meaning that they have an equal number of friends and followers). Therefore, all tweets from users which had a ratio of more than 105% or less than 95% were excluded. The next step to identify human accounts was to exclude all tweets from users which had the term "bot" in their author description which lead to the exclusion of accounts which were obviously automated (e.g. accounts that posted weather data). In the last step the sum of all tweets per day for every human was calculated and all humans which had less than ten tweets per day were excluded.

Description of the sample. Following the described steps we were able to identify approximately 100 active bots for every day (Table 1). Summed up, there were 270 different bots which posted 19,390 tweets on seven days, at which not every bot posted tweets every day. Table 2 shows how many bots were active on how many days in the covered week. Table 3 shows how many tweets the 1,175 identified human accounts posted on each day. In the whole week humans posted 62,365 tweets at least 500 identified humans were active each day (except for the 31st of October) (Table 4). To have a comparable number of bots and humans we decided to decrease the set of humans further. Therefore, we randomly selected nearly 100 humans for each day to compare them to approximately 100 bots. The final sample consisted of 693 identified human accounts which posted 12,699 tweets.

Table 1. Distribution of bot-tweets

Days	Bots	Tweets
31-Oct	99	2,551
1-Nov	108	3,254
2-Nov	116	3,298
3-Nov	104	2,696
4-Nov	112	1,953
5-Nov	100	2,621
6-Nov	131	3,017

Table 2. Frequency of bot activity

Number of bots	Number of days
30	7
11	6
23	5
23	4
33	3
42	2
109	1

Table 3. Distribution of human tweets

Day	Humans	Tweets
31-Oct	94	1,247
1-Nov	535	10,606
2-Nov	588	11,536
3-Nov	480	9,577
4-Nov	606	11,103
5-Nov	554	11,200
6-Nov	370	7,096

Table 4. Frequency of human activity

Number of humans	Number of days
35	7
89	6
119	5
123	4
160	3
222	2
427	1

Used Variables. Besides the aforementioned variables, which were used for the identification of accounts, further variables to test the hypotheses were required. The following variables were used.

— Author ID   — FF-Ratio

— Tweets per day   — Mentions per day (@ per day)

— Tweets per week   — Mentions/Tweet-Ratio (@/Tweet-Ratio)

— Retweets per day   — Links per day

— Retweets per week   — Link/Tweet-Ratio

— Retweet/Tweet-Ratio   — Author name

— Friends   — Date

— Followers   — Type (bot or human)

Preliminary Calculations. To calculate the statistical analyses IBM SPSS Statistics Version 23.0 was used. In order to determine the statistical significance, a confidence interval of 95% was used.

4   Results

Descriptive Statistics. The 771 identified bots on average generated 25.15 (SD = 20.19) tweets per day. In contrast the 693 humans generated only 18.32 (SD = 11.32) tweets per day. However, the humans had way more retweets per day (M = 15,921.55, SD = 19,108.23) than bots (M = 1,381.16, SD = 5,850.18). The ratio from average tweets to re-tweets was 85.45 (SD = 361.01) for bots and 897.05 (SD = 1,053.91) for humans. This means that on average every tweet of a bot was retweeted approximately 85 times, whereas a tweet of a human was retweeted almost 900 times. The average number of followers in our sample was 1,241.76 (SD = 655.25) for bots and 5,056.95 (SD = 7,278.91) for humans. The average friends count from bots was at 2,896.42 friends (SD = 1371.73) whereas humans had 5,022.51 friends on average (SD = 7,137.26). The ratio between mentions via @ per day and tweets per day show that bots used approximately one @ every second tweet (M = .42, SD = .66). In contrast humans used at least one @ in every tweet they posted (M = 1.2, SD = .24). Moreover, bots posted one or more links in every tweet (M = 1.24, SD = .6) whereas humans used less links per tweet (M = .88, SD = .22).

Hypothesis Testing. To test the first hypothesis we compared the mean values of bots and humans for the variables 'Followers', 'Retweets per day', '@ per day' and 'Links per day'. Results of Hypotheses 1a–1d are displayed in Table 5. Table 5 shows support for Hypotheses 1a, c, and d. As neither the sampling distribution was normal, nor the variances were equal, the nonparametric Mann-Whitney U test was used for comparison. Hypothesis 1a (bot accounts have a lower number of followers than human accounts), was supported ($p < .001$). The same applies to Hypothesis 1c - bot accounts have a lower number of @-characters in tweets than human accounts ($p < .001$), and Hypothesis 1d, tweets created by bot accounts have a higher number of links in their

Table 5. Means comparisons for Hypotheses 1a to 1d

	U	M	
		Bots	Humans
Followers	20.06*	522.32	966.34
Retweets per day	28.89*	431.14	1067.78
@ per day	28.76*	441.15	1056.65
Links per day	8.62*	822.75	632.09

*Note: *p < .001*

tweets than tweets by human accounts (p < .001). For hypothesis 1b on the other hand (bot accounts have a higher number of retweets than human accounts) the opposite was true. The Mann-Whitney U test showed a significant effect (p < .001), but with respect to the mean values, against the assumption – in our sample humans exhibited a larger number of retweets than bots.

Hypothesis 2 assumed a relationship between the number of followers and the number of retweets for an account. We tested this for bots and humans for each day individually. Hypothesis 2a focused on this relation at bot accounts, whereas 2b focused on human accounts. Sampling distribution was not normal, wherefore Spearman's rank correlation was calculated instead of a Pearson correlation. Table 6 shows the results of the correlation for each of the seven days. Hypothesis 2a and 2b are partially confirmation. Within the seven days, a correlation for bots was found on four days, and on five days for humans. There was a significant correlation for bot accounts for the 1st November (p = .009), 2nd November (p = .019), 3rd November (p = .006) and 6th November (p = .009). For human accounts a significant correlation on the 1st November (p = .004), 2nd November (p < .001), 4th November (p = .021), 5th November (p < .001) and 6th November (p = .001) was found. Interestingly, the strongest overall correlation which was found in the human sample on November 2nd was a negative one, meaning that the more follower an account has, the less retweets it got. Since only a few days showed a significant effect, a correlation was calculated for the whole week. It showed a significant moderate correlation for bot accounts (r_s = .12, p = .001) but not for human accounts.

Table 6. Correlations of followers and retweets for each day from 30th Oct. – 6th Nov.

	Bots		Humans	
	N	rs	N	rs
October 30th	99	.01	93	−.16
November 1st	108	.25**	100	.28**
November 2nd	116	.22*	101	−.46***
November 3rd	104	.27**	100	.17
November 4th	113	.07	100	.23*
November 5th	100	.06	100	.34***
November 6th	131	.23**	99	.32***

*Note: *p < .05, **p < .01, ***p < .001*

Hypothesis 3 claims a relationship between links per day and retweets per day. The third hypothesis was tested employing a correlation analysis between these two variables. This hypothesis was supported. As for the calculations of hypotheses 2a and 2b, sampling distribution was not normal leading to the use of Spearman's rank correlation. In both groups, humans (rs (693) = .33, $p < .001$) and bots (rs (771) = .16, $p < .001$), a significant effect was found for a moderate correlation the group of human accounts and a small correlation in the group of bot accounts.

The assumption "the more tweets were created per week, the more followers are generated" was tested in Hypothesis 4. To test the fourth hypothesis, a regression analysis with tweets per week and their number of followers was performed. Calculations showed no significant relationship for human accounts. However, for bot accounts, there is a significant if small correlation (F (1, 769) = 5.01, $p = .025$) with $R^2 = .006$. The number of followers increases with $\beta = .41$ for each tweet.

5   Discussion

The aim of this paper is to show differences between human and bot accounts to infer the impact of bots. The dataset of the US election was selected, because it is known that the candidates have used bots [6, 7]. Following, results as well as implications and limitations are discussed.

Interpretation of Results. The first hypothesis considers fundamental differences between human and bot accounts concerning standard features. The human and bot accounts differ in all examined features – number of follower, number of retweets, number of mentions, and number of links. This result comply with previous findings [21, 31]. Hypothesis 1a is supported which means that bot accounts have less followers than human accounts. This result matches with those of Chu et al. [31] who point out that bots have less followers than friends and that humans have a balanced follower-friend-ratio. Whereas humans have a reciprocal relationship, it seems that bots try to gain attention by adding friends and hope to be followed back. Further, we assumed that bot accounts garnered more retweets than human accounts. However, for our sample the opposite is true. Hence, Hypothesis 1b is not supported. This contradicts previous findings [9] which found that especially by retweeting each other, bots try to gain influence [24]. A possible explanation could be that human users in general are able to identify bot accounts and therefore those are retweeted less frequently. The assumption that bots use less @-characters than humans was supported (H1c). This can also be linked to the results of Chu et al. [31]. They suppose that bots generated less tweets and therefore bots may use less @-characters. The hypothesis that bot accounts use a higher number of links in their tweets than human accounts was also supported (H1d). This result coincides with the findings of Chu et al. [31]. It can be assumed that bots use links more frequently because they aim at spreading information and thus want to generate influence. Also, by using links the bot accounts don't need to produce original content in their tweets but could just link to a source with current information. The programming of those bots could be more easy.

Another assumption was that the number of followers of a bot account is related to the number of retweets of this account (H2a), as well as the notion that the number of followers of a human account is related to the number of retweets of this account (H2b). For some days, this assumption was supported. Regarding the U.S. election, no special event (e.g. a TV-debate) took place which might have explained these fluctuations. Regarding the entire week, only a relationship between the number of followers and retweets of the bot accounts could be found. This indicates that the more followers a bot has the more he is being retweeted or vice versa. The rejection of the hypothesis for human accounts could be attributed to the content of a tweet and it seems that the relation of followers and retweets is not important for human accounts. One can anticipate that the content of human accounts is more valuable because humans use more emotional words as Abokhodair et al. [4] showed.

Hypothesis 3 which assumed a relationship between tweeted links per day and retweets per day is supported. Studies showed that bots produce a great amount of spam [32]. It could thus be assumed that other bots retweet this spam and therefore the number of retweets rises with every new link. Since a correlation does not explain witch variable has impact and which is influenced it could be that the influence is in the opposite direction. As the relationship between links and retweets was stronger for the human accounts one possible explanation may be that (a) OSN users in general are able to differentiate between postings from human and bots accounts and (b) that links which are posted by a human account are perceived as more credible and trustworthy and therefore will be retweeted more often.

The results of hypothesis 4 show that bots generate one additional follower with almost every second tweet. These findings are similar to the results of Aiello et al. [26] who postulate that the activity of users influences their popularity. On Twitter the number of followers of a profile can, among other measures, express the popularity of a user. This could be a reason for the behavior of bots of producing a large amount of tweets [6]. The fourth hypothesis could not be supported for human accounts, though. Here, a possible explanation may be, that humans generate followers based on different features such as the content. In contrast to bot accounts humans may post more emotional tweets and express their opinions which may lead others to follow them as opposed to the pure quantity of their tweets.

6 Conclusion, Limitations, and Future Research

Conclusion. In this paper, we compared 771 identified bots accounts with 693 identified regular users of the same data set. As one of the first studies, we compared human and bot accounts from the same data set. Prior research mostly focused on bots in one data set and compared them to features taken from literature. Our goal was to understand how different aspects differ between the two groups to better assess the influence that social bots might have on human users on Twitter. According to prior research, important differences in the two groups' standard features likes followers, friends and retweeting behaviour exist. Moreover, coherences between features like followers and retweeting-behavior, the number of links used in tweets and the number of retweets in one day were reported. In our analyses, the hypothesis concerning the relation between followers and retweeting behavior was partially supported – one can see that there is a relation between these two features but this does not count for all investigated days in our data set. One important finding was that bots generated a new follower with every second tweet which may justify and explain the purpose behind an extremely high bot activity.

Furthermore, bots are often considered to operate on and within a network of several bot accounts as such limiting the impact of a single account but that is certainly able to produce a certain amount of content in OSNs over time. Summing everything up, one can say that widespread features were considered, compared and set into relation. First insights are unveiled regarding the number of tweets that are necessary to gain more followers. Against the backdrop of influencing users in OSNs, these findings are important to characterize the acting of Social Bots and to enlighten their intentions.

Limitations. Our findings are limited by the reduction of data. We focused on examining approximately 100 bot accounts for every day of the seven days. This temporal restriction accompanies another limitation – it is uncertain how the identified bots and human accounts act over a longer time period such as the complete US presidential campaign. This could lead to very active bots not attaining any focus in the investigation at hand and thus underestimating a possible impact. Beyond that human accounts were gathered via random samples for every investigated day. Moreover, the focus in this investigation lays on quantitative data. This implies that the content of a tweet is not considered. However, content and choice of words can possibly explain why some tweets are hyped or an account is followed by many others.

Future Research. The identification method used in our paper could be tested and refinded further. In turn our analyses can be carried out after applying different identification methods (e.g. from a machine learning perspective). Future research should also dig deeper on the meaning of URLs in tweets as our findings indicate that there is a relationship between posting links and retweeting a tweet. Furthermore, it would be interesting to take a profound insight into differences between professed bots which state themselves as bots and hidden bots which try to obscure their identity. In a third step these bots could be compared to human users.

References

1. Dang-Xuan, L., Stieglitz, S.: Impact and diffusion of sentiment in political communication–an empirical analysis of political weblogs. In: AAAI Conference on Weblogs and Social Media, pp. 3500–3509 (2012)
2. Bruns, A., Stieglitz, S.: Twitter data: what do they represent? IT - Inf. Technol. **56**, 240–245 (2014)
3. Bruns, A., Stieglitz, S.: Metrics for understanding communication on Twitter. In: Weller, K., Bruns, A., Burgess, J., Marth, M., Puschmann, C. (eds.) Twitter and Society, pp. 68–82. Peter Lang, New York (2014)

4. Abokhodair, N., Yoo, D., McDonald, D.W.: Dissecting a social Botnet. In: Proceedings of 18th ACM Conference on Computer Supported Cooperative Work and Social Computing - CSCW 2015, pp. 839–851 (2015)
5. Hegelich, S.: Invasion der Meinungs-Roboter. Anal. und Argumente, Konrad-Adenauer-Stiftung **221**, 2–9 (2016)
6. Howard, P.N., Kollanyi, B.: Bots, #StrongerIn, and #Brexit: Computational Propaganda during the UK-EU Referendum (2016)
7. Kollanyi, B., Howard, P.N., Woolley, S.C.: Bots and automation over Twitter during the second U.S. presidential debate. In: Comprop Data Memo, vol. 2 (2016)
8. Kollanyi, B., Howard, P.N., Woolley, S.C.: Bots and automation over Twitter during the U. S. Election, Oxford (2016)
9. Ferrara, E., Varol, O., Davis, C., Menczer, F., Flammini, A.: The rise of social bots. Commun. ACM **59**, 96–104 (2016)
10. Boshmaf, Y., Muslukhov, I., Beznosov, K., Ripeanu, M.: Design and analysis of a social botnet. Comput. Netw. **57**, 556–578 (2013)
11. Lee, K., Eoff, B.D., Caverlee, J.: Seven months with the devils: a long-term study of content polluters on Twitter. In: ICWSM 2011, pp. 185–192 (2011)
12. Wagner, C., Mitter, S., Körner, C., Strohmaier, M.: When social bots attack: modeling susceptibility of users in online social networks. In: CEUR Workshop Proceedings (2012)
13. IPO: Twitter. https://www.sec.gov/Archives/edgar/data/1418091/000119312513390321/d564001ds1.htm
14. Edwards, C., Edwards, A., Spence, P.R., Shelton, A.K.: Is that a bot running the social media feed? Testing the differences in perceptions of communication quality for a human agent and a bot agent on Twitter. In: Computers in Human Behavior, pp. 372–376 (2014)
15. Wald, R., Khoshgoftaar, T.M., Napolitano, A., Sumner, C.: Which users reply to and interact with Twitter social bots. In: Proceedings - International Conference on Tools with Artificial Intelligence, ICTAI (2013)
16. Cha, M., Haddai, H., Benevenuto, F., Gummadi, K.P.: Measuring user influence in Twitter: the million follower fallacy. In: International AAAI Conference on Weblogs and Social Media, pp. 10–17 (2010)
17. Freitas, C.A., Benevenuto, F., Ghosh, S., Veloso, A.: Reverse engineering socialbot infiltration strategies in Twitter. In: Proceedings of 2015 IEEE/ACM International Conference on Advances in Social Networks Analysis and Mining, pp. 25–32 (2015)
18. Wald, R., Khoshgoftaar, T.M., Napolitano, A., Sumner, C.: Predicting susceptibility to social bots on Twitter. In: Proceedings of 2013 IEEE 14th International Conference on Information Reuse and Integration, IRI 2013, pp. 135–144. IEEE (2013)
19. Nass, C., Moon, Y.: Machines and mindlessness: social responses to computers. J. Soc. Issues **56**, 81–103 (2000)
20. Messias, J., Schmidt, L., Oliveira, R.A.R., Benevenuto, F.: You followed my bot! Transforming robots into influential users in Twitter. First Monday **18** (2013)
21. Cossu, J.-V., Labatut, V., Dugué, N.: A review of features for the discrimination of Twitter users: application to the prediction of offline influence. Soc. Netw. Anal. Min. **6**, 1–23 (2016)
22. Edwards, C., Spence, P.R., Gentile, C.J., Edwards, A., Edwards, A.: How much Klout do you have … A test of system generated cues on source credibility. Comput. Human Behav. **29**, A12–A16 (2013)
23. Cossu, J.V., Dugue, N., Labatut, V.: Detecting real-world influence through Twitter. In: Proceedings - 2nd European Network Intelligence Conference, ENIC 2015, pp. 83–90 (2015)

24. Danish, M., Dugué, N., Perez, A.: On the importance of considering social capitalism when measuring influence on Twitter. In: International Conference on Behavioral, Economic, and Socio-Cultural Computing (BESC 2014), pp. 1-7, Shanghai (2014)
25. Misener, D.: Rise of the social bots: they could be influencing you online. http://www.cbc.ca/news/technology/rise-of-the-socialbots-they-could-be-influencing-you-online-1.981796
26. Aiello, L.M., Deplano, M., Schifanella, R., Ruffo, G.: People are strange when you're a stranger: impact and influence of bots on social networks. In: ICWSM 2012 - Proceedings of 6th International AAAI Conference on Weblogs and Social Media, pp. 10–17 (2012)
27. Zhang, J., Carpenter, D., Ko, M.: Online astroturfing: a theoretical perspective. In: 19th American Conference on Information Systems, AMCIS 2013, vol. 4, pp. 2559–2565 (2013)
28. Ratkiewicz, J., Conover, M., Meiss, M., Gonçalves, B., Patil, S., Flammini, A., Menczer, F.: Truthy: mapping the spread of astroturf in microblog streams. In: Proceedings of 20th International Conference Companion World Wide Web (WWW 2011), pp. 249–252 (2011)
29. McNutt, J.G.: Researching advocacy groups: internet sources for research about public interest groups and social movement organizations. J. Policy Pract. **9**, 308–312 (2010)
30. Ilyas, M.U., Radha, H.: Identifying influential nodes in online social networks using principal component centrality. In: Proceedings of 2011 IEEE International Conference on Communications, pp. 1–5 (2011)
31. Chu, Z., Gianvecchio, S., Wang, H., Jajodia, S.: Detecting automation of Twitter accounts: are you a human, bot, or cyborg? IEEE Trans. Dependable Secure Comput. **9**, 811–824 (2012)
32. Grier, C., Thomas, K., Paxson, V., Zhang, M.: @spam: The underground on 140 characters or less. In: Proceedings of 17th ACM Conference on Computer and Communications Security, pp. 27–37 (2010)
33. Gao, H., Hu, J., Wilson, C., Li, Z., Chen, Y., Zhao, B.Y.: Detecting and characterizing social spam campaigns. In: Proceedings of 10th ACM SIGCOMM Conference on Internet Measurement, pp. 35–47 (2010)
34. Cao, Q., Sirivianos, M., Yang, X., Pregueiro, T.: Aiding the detection of fake accounts in large scale social online services. In: NSDI 2012 – Proceedings of 9th USENIX Conference on Networked Systems Design and Implementation, vol. 15 (2012)
35. Xie, Y., Yu, F., Ke, Q., Abadi, M., Gillum, E., Vitaldevaria, K., Walter, J., Huang, J., Mao, Z.M.: Innocent by association: early recognition of legitimate users. In: Proceedings of 2012 Computer and Communications Security, pp. 353–364 (2012)
36. Paradise, A., Puzis, R., Shabtai, A.: Anti-reconnaissance tools: detecting targeted socialbots. IEEE Internet Comput. **18**, 11–19 (2014)
37. Davis, C.A., Varol, O., Ferrara, E., Flammini, A., Menczer, F.: BotOrNot: a system to evaluate social bots. In: Proceedings of 25th International Conference Companion World Wide Web, 1602.009, pp. 273–274 (2016)
38. Wang, G., Mohanlal, M., Wilson, C., Wang, X., Metzger, M., Zheng, H., Zhao, B.Y.: Social turing tests: crowdsourcing sybil detection. In: 20th Network and Distributed System Security Symposium (2012)
39. Alvisi, L., Clement, A., Epasto, A., Lattanzi, S., Panconesi, A.: SoK: the evolution of sybil defense via social networks. In: Proceedings - IEEE Symposium on Security and Privacy, pp. 382–396 (2013)
40. Reeves, B., Nass, C.: The media equation: how people treat computers, television, and new media (1996)
41. Brave, S., Nass, C., Hutchinson, K.: Computers that care: investigating the effects of orientation of emotion exhibited by an embodied computer agent. Int. J. Hum. Comput. Stud. **62**(2), 161–178 (2005)

42. Ferdig, R.E., Mishra, P.: Emotional responses to computers: experiences in unfairness, anger, and spite. J. Educ. Multimed. Hypermedia **13**, 143–161 (2004)
43. Kim, Y., Sundar, S.S.: Anthropomorphism of computers: is it mindful or mindless? Comput. Hum. Behav. **28**, 241–250 (2012)
44. Lee, K.M., Park, N., Song, H.: Can a robot be perceived as a developing creature? Hum. Commun. Res. **31**, 538–563 (2005)
45. Stoll, B., Edwards, C., Edwards, A.: "Why aren't you a sassy little thing": the effects of robot-enacted guilt trips on credibility and consensus in a negotiation. Commun. Stud. **67**, 530–547 (2016)
46. Mustafaraj, E., Metaxas, P.: From obscurity to prominence in minutes: political speech and real-time search. In: WebSci 2010: Extending the Frontiers of Society On-Line, p. 317 (2010)
47. Forelle, M.C., Howard, P.N., Monroy-Hernandez, A., Savage, S.: Political bots and the manipulation of public opinion in Venezuela. In: Social Science Research Network. SSRN Scholarly, Rochester, NY (2015). Paper ID 2635800

A Twitter Analysis of an Integrated E-Activism Campaign: #FeesMustFall - A South African Case Study

Abraham G. van der Vyver$^{(\boxtimes)}$

Monash South Africa, 144 Peter Road Ruimsig,
Johannesburg 1725, South Africa
braam.vandervyver@monash.edu

Abstract. The announcement by South African public universities that study fees will in 2017 be increased by 11.5% triggered the most widespread student riots since the apartheid years. The protests dubbed #FeesMustFall on Twitter began in 2015. This paper deals with tweets that were collected during the second wave of the campaign that played itself out during October–November 2016. The researcher purposefully sampled 300 tweets from citizen journalists and 150 tweets from professional journalists. Thematic analysis was manually conducted on the collected tweets. Codes were applied to the raw data as summary indicators for later analysis.

It was found that the citizen journalists who are not bound to the ethical constraints of a newsroom enjoyed a lot more freedom of expression than their counterparts in the official media. It is also not difficult for them to scoop the formal media with up-to-the minute tweets or to generate more metajournalism.

Keywords: E-democracy · Political engagement · E-activism · Citizen journalism · Professional journalism

1 Introduction

The announcement by South African public universities that study fees will in 2017 be increased by 11.5% triggered the most widespread student riots since the apartheid years which ended in 1994. The 2016 protests formed the second wave of such protests, the first wave taking place a year earlier in October 2015.

Dludla [1] posted the following report in Times Live:

"Students barricaded the entrances at University of Cape Town (UCT) and refused to leave, while their peers at Johannesburg's University of the Witwatersrand, where protests dubbed #FeesMustFall on Twitter began on Oct. 13, overturned vehicles driving into the campus, local media reported."

The University of Witwatersrand, hereafter referred to as Wits responded with a news release by Linda Jarvis, CFO at Wits, in which she explains that "We are mindful of the current economic climate and the financial strain on students and families. In light of this and following extensive consultations with the SRC and other University structures, we have reduced the average tuition fee for 2016 from 11% to 10.5%, and

© Springer International Publishing AG 2017
G. Meiselwitz (Ed.): SCSM 2017, Part I, LNCS 10282, pp. 396–410, 2017.
DOI: 10.1007/978-3-319-58559-8_31

the upfront fee increase from 10% to 6%" She also announced that residence fees will rise by 9.4% and international student fees by 10.7% [2]. Although the protests were peaceful and unofficial, Wits nevertheless cancelled all lectures and academic activities for October 14 [2].

According to Kekana [3] the police was called in to deal with the riots on most campuses. She reported that "(t)he SRC [of Wits] has posted videos on its social media pages of police forcibly removing a small group of students from a university entrance they had blocked. Dludla [1] reported that "Twenty-three UCT students were arrested, and police said they would face charges of disrupting the peace." Kekana [3] quoted an SRC member, Shaeera Kalla, who complained about the excessive force used by the police. At the time of the writing of this article, one year after the first wave of protests started, Kalla was recovering in hospital after being hit in the back by 13 rubber bullets fired by the police [4].

The protests quickly spread to other public universities. Dludla [1] reported the following:

> Police fired stun grenades to disperse protesters at Rhodes University in Grahamstown in the southeast. UCT and Rhodes University remain closed, while students at Fort Hare University in Eastern Cape also joined the protests. Stellenbosch University authorities obtained a court interdict to bar protests, as students gathered in groups on the campus east of Cape Town.

Dludla [1] quoted Francis Petersen, UCT's acting Vice-Chancellor who had the following to say: "The situation yesterday and today is very, very problematic for us. Some examinations could not take place and work was disrupted everywhere on campus."

In response to the protests, Dr. Blade Nzimande, the Minister for Higher Education and Training and vice chancellors agreed on a 6% cap on fee increases [5]. This offer was rejected by protesting students who demanded a 0% fee increase [5].

The spiral of violence resumed on 20 September 2016 Nzimande announced that it would be left to the public universities to determine their own fee increases but that it was recommended that increases don't exceed 8%. Gasa and Dougan [6] reported in The Daily Maverick that "(w)hen Nzimande announced that households earning below R600,000 per annum would be exempt from paying the 8% fee increment required by tertiary institutions, he also said government would subsidise the shortfall resulting from lack of funds."

The announcement generated a negative response from most of the student bodies at public universities.

> #FeesMustFall protesters immediately made their dissatisfaction known. Protesters shut down a number of the country's universities by blocking entrances, disrupting lectures, burning facilities and clashing with private security companies and police. At one of the chaotic campaign's lowest points, cleaner Celumusa Ntuli died after inhaling fumes from a fire extinguisher, released by protesting students inside a Wits University residence. Days later, footage of policemen firing rounds of rubber bullets at Rhodes University students went viral. Across the country, campuses burned and learning ground to a halt.
> Gasa and Dougan [6]

The studies of thousands of students are funded by the National Student Financial Aid Scheme (Nsfas). According to Saltmarsh [7] "(m)any have recently pointed out that greater student debt isn't even of much economic benefit to the government, as it will have to absorb all unpaid debt." This is not the only financial loss that the taxpayer is burdened with. Tax money is also used to fund the rebuilding and reparations to university property that was destroyed during the campaign. This assumption is confirmed in the Business Day of 24 December 2016 in which a figure of R24 billion of outstanding debt is disclosed.

2 Literature Review

The advent of the Internet and the subsequent rise of the social media have dramatically impacted on many disciplines and activities. According to Sivitanides and Shah [8] "(t)he world is in the midst of a digital revolution. The new tools of social media have reinvented social activism." In 2012 the Pew Research Center's Internet and American Life Project found that "the use of social media is becoming a feature of political and civic engagement for many Americans. Some 60% of American adults use either social networking sites like Facebook or Twitter to engage in some form of civil activism" [9]. This trend have caught on in South Africa where Facebook and Twitter campaigns have been launched as platforms of discourse in the case of high profile political and or polemical events and/or controversies. The Nkandla-debacle around the security upgrades at the president's personal homestead, the #RhodesMustFall campaign and the criminal case against the paralimpian, Oscar Pistorius illustrate this finding.

Uldam and Vestergaard [10] postulate that "(c)ivic activism has always produced tension between citizens who promote new and challenging demands and the responses of official institutions that typically lag behind the arc of change. In many cases, official responses are not simply slow; they may be repressive."

Cammaerts [11] is of the opinion that a strong linkage exists between social media and the formation and functioning of activism campaigns. He advanced that "social media platforms and the communicative practices they enable can potentially become constitutive of the construction of collective identities and have become highly relevant in view of disseminating, communicating, recording, and archiving a variety of movement discourses and deeds" (Cammaerts [11]).

The role of the social media is, however, not restricted to the dissemination and documentation of information. It also serves as a coordinating trigger for physical action. In that respect Alkhouja [12] emphasized that "dissidents need to mobilize protestors and push more people to streets in order to challenge the state's authority and alter the status quo. To this goal, Social Media served as a strategic effectual tool for activists." The Egyptian activist, Wael Ghonim is used by Giglio [13] as an example of an activist who implemented a page as a managerial as well as a motivational tool.

[Ghonim] "implored his Facebook fans to spread word of the protest to people on the ground, and he and other activists constantly coordinated efforts, combining online savvy with the street activism long practiced by the country's democracy movements. Ghonim seemed to view the page both as a kind of central command and a rallying point—getting people past 'the psychological barrier'"
Giglio [13]

Salter and Kay [14] related how students at the University of the West of England (UWE) in the UK undertook protests against the British government's cuts to educational funding in the higher education sector. "The occupation at UWE began on 22 November 2010 at 15:00 when a group of students took over the main cafe-bar area of the University. The initial motivation for the occupation was University management's decision to effectively demote up to 80 principal lecturers, readers and professors as part of an ongoing programme of cuts at the University [14] The authors explain that "Social media were utilised according to the specific capacities of each particular form. As the occupiers put it in the focus group, 'different things work differently—Facebook within UWE, encrypted email lists within the core occupation, Twitter between occupations, YouTube for wider society' " [14].

The protests didn't occur without conflict among the protesters. Salter and Kay [14] reported that "as one occupier, 'White', put it, there was a split between those more interested in 'process', and those more interested in 'protest'."

The protest patterns at UWE showed a remarkable resemblance with those in South Africa. According to Salter [15] it was also triggered by the government's intentions to raise fees "to subject education to the whimsical will of the 'market'- by charging young people £9000 ($14000) per year to be educated." Demonstrations and occupations were published on Facebook and Twitter while video chat technologies and secure email lists were used to announce strategies [15]. Salter [15] mentioned that during these wildcat protests routes were spontaneously determined making it difficult for the law enforcement officials to intervene. This was in stark contrast with the UK tradition of analogue protests where the protests were coordinated with the police [15].

In Portugal a major case study in activism developed on March 12th, 2011 namely the "Geração à Rasca" protests. It was followed by a social movement, the March 12th Movement (M12M). Rosas [16] gave the following explanation of the two initiatives: "The first was that the massive protests that erupted in the country's major cities, and that enrolled more than 500,000 people from all ages, backgrounds and status, were not mobilized by unions, political parties, or traditional social movements, but by four young university graduates" [16]. He elaborated as follows:

> these protests were not organized and coordinated through traditional offline organizations or grassroots movements, but through the Internet and some of its Web 2.0 technologies, in particular social media tools like Facebook and YouTube. How this could happen in a country where nonconventional politics were almost reserved to unions and to corporative interests was, indeed, puzzling, as it was puzzling why it happened in 2011 and not before. [16]

Alkhouja [12] warned that online activism does not necessarily translate to physical protests. Gladwell [17] underscored this aspect by postulating that "activism in the cyber space encourages what he calls 'slacktivism,' or superficial, minimal effort in support of causes which restrains physical onground activism."

This linkage between communication and active protests are illustrated and investigated in the "FeesMustFall campaign.

3 Methodology

The researcher decided to follow a qualitative approach for this study. Since literally thousands of tweets were posted during this lengthy campaign the researcher engaged in purposive sampling. In a purposive sample, you sample from a population with a particular purpose in mind. This technique is also known as purposeful sampling. According to Palinkas *et al.* "[p]urposeful sampling is widely used in qualitative research for the identification and selection of information-rich cases related to the phenomenon of interest [18].

The sample that the researcher construed also served as the first level of data analysis. Coyne [19] described this method as follows: "The full range and variation in a category rather than a variable is sought to guide the emerging theory. Thus the data control the further sampling and this means that data analysis and sampling are done concurrently. It is variation according to the emerging categories, rather than phenomenal variation or any other kind of variations described earlier."

The researcher purposefully sampled 300 tweets from citizen journalists and 150 tweets from professional journalists during the second wave of the campaign that played itself out during October – November 2016. A professional journalist is, for the purpose of this study, an individual who earns an income from producing content from a media outlet. "Citizen journalism is defined by a number of attributes which make it distinct from professional journalism, including unpaid work, absence of professional training, and often unedited publication of content, and may feature plain language, distinct story selection and news judgment, especially hyper-local issues, free accessibility, and interactivity" [20].

Thematic analysis was manually conducted on the collected tweets. Namey et al. [21] summarised thematic analysis by saying that it goes further than just counting words or phrases by identifying and describing intrinsic latent and explicit salient ideas. Codes identified for ideas and themes are then applied to the raw data as summary indicators for later analysis.

4 Results of Twitter Analysis

4.1 Citizen Journalists

The citizen journalists who are not bound by the ethical constraints of a newsroom enjoyed a lot more freedom of expression than their counterparts who worked in the official media. It is also not difficult for them to scoop their more illustrious competitors in the newsrooms with up-to-the minute tweets. Goode [22] raised what he called "the most vexing question about the boundaries of citizen journalism" namely "whether we should restrict its definition to practices in which citizens act as content creators, producing original news material." This question relates to other ways citizens express an opinion or make a contribution to the news environment e.g. by "rating, commenting, tagging and reposting," all acts of contribution that is seen as "considerably less significant than 'real' citizen journalism" [22]. Goode [22] offered the following clarification: "if a user posts a comment on an existing news story but, in doing so, brings to light new knowledge about that event or topic, then it is not clear that this contribution can be classified only as 'metajournalism'" [22]. Features such as hashtags and retweeting help spread news and information faster than other media, whether in normal or crisis situations, and get people with shared interests closer to each other [23]. As such, a broad conception of citizen journalism appears warranted on the proviso that the important democratic function of bringing new knowledge into the public sphere is not downgraded as equivalent to secondary commentary" [22].

Scoops. The following examples illustrate how a scoop (publishing news first) can be achieved with micro news or mainstream news.

> Students scream from their res at UKZN Westville @News24 [micro news]
>
> #UKZN Westville a warzone again [mainstream news]
>
> Night vigil is about to start. Mobilisation taking place in South Campus Auditorium [micro news].
>
> Police are moving in, closer to Knockndo residence entrance, firing rubber bullets [micro news]
>
> Situation tense #Wits students defying curfew, chanting outside residence. Police patroling. Roads barricaded [macro news]
>
> The #UKZN student services building is on fire [mainstream news].
>
> Protesters use big umbrellas as a shields from the rubber bullets at #VUT #Fees2017 [mainstream news].

Personal Emotions. Tweets can also be used to convey personal emotions, something that a journalist can't freely do. Respect, loathing, doubt, hate, and regret are depicted in the following tweets:

> I respect TUT students such bravery!!!
>
> So students pulled #FeesMustFall thru their asses in #Braamfontein Thugs, hooligans, arsonists, criminals. Lock them up without bail!
>
> Our successful efforts in maintaining a non-violent **#FeesMustFall** campaign for 2 years has been compromised. Its time to reflect. #NMMU
>
> #FeesMustFall. I hate the police man Ths is no lngr a protest, but its revolution. Lts fyt4 our Ryts #BlacklifeMatters.
>
> Had the state responded last year to the **#FeesMustFall** movement, today we wouldn't be saying rest in power, #BenjaminPhehla

Personal Characteristics. Tweets can be focused on personal characteristics.

> @SAPoliceService are showing great restraint in the **#FeesMustFall** clashes. They are being attacked, having rocks and bottles hurled at them.

Macro Themes. Macro themes were at the order of the day. Leadership, poverty, parenting, blame, standards, counselling.

The absence of leadership on #FeesMustFall is a major concern.

There is no leadership. He is dancing in India. He can't explain to them why no #FeesMustFall since presidency so compromised.

(The tweet refers to President Zuma dancing during a state visit to India).

#FeesMustFall protest way too big for VCs or even @DrBladeNzimande. Where is the Prez & DP? The country is burning & no leadership! Shocking

It's though for me to argue against #FeesMustFall because I don't understand extreme poverty and the desperation that come with it.

30% pass has filled our varsities with utter morons. How is government to blame for varsity being expensive? #FeesMustFall? Please explain

(The tweet refers to the 30% pass standard set for matric)

"More than just a fight for free education, this is a fight for their future"

Zille blames SA's failed parenting for Fallists' behaviour around #FeesMustFall

My people, we all need counselling after these Wits cruel acts. I know we don't believe in it, but we need it.

Public Figures. The tweets identified the names of the major players that the tweeters felt should be held accountable and/or could provide a solution.

Apart from President Zuma, deputy-president Ramaphosa, the Minister of Higher Education, Dr. Blade Nzimande, and the previous leader of the opposition, Helen Zille, who also feature in the tweets cited *supra* more names of high profile individuals appear in the sample.

Moseneke, former deputy Chief Justice, says #FeesMustFall is legitimate!

Do students risk alienating previous supporters of the **#FeesMustFall** campaign? Was #AdamHabib's mistake trying to be a friend instead of VC?

Habib is the Vice-Chancellor of Witwatersrand University (Wits).

Celebrities who were not involved in the campaign were also mentioned in the tweets.

Tell me, didn't Oscar Pistorius get bail? Mcebo Dlamini denied bail? Why? The regime fears those who preach ideas even more than murderous!

Hillary Clinton just said there will be no tuition bill for families earning less then $120k pa. We are still fighting for #FeesMustFall

Salute to Cassper for showing support for the **#FeesMustFall** movement in his performance!
#MTVMAMA2016

The tweet refers to Cassper Nyovest, a well-known South African rap artist.

Major Ideologies. Major ideologies were raised and even juxtaposed as can be seen in the following tweets:

So students want a communist solution for a personal capitalist outcome.

Zuma "#FeesMustFall a sign of a healthy democracy", mxim. Protests are a sign of bad governance

Political or Polemic Issues. The Twitter handle has also been used to address other political and polemic issues that were not directly linked to the #FeesMustFall campaign. The Chief Parliamentary Whip of the ANC, Jackson Mtembu was cited in the following tweet that raised the eyebrows of members of the ruling party:

Jackson Mthembu says he called for NEC members to resign enmasse. Says the ANC under Zuma is worse than the apartheid government.

Mthembu never denied the content.

It was inevitable that the Nkandla issue would come up. The R246 million spent on security and installations and improvements to President Zuma's private residence at Nkandla led to a prolonged series of investigations and a Constitutional Court Case.

S.A has had 22 years of democracy n yet they haven't set structure's 4free education but spend money on inkandla…mxm

Social media is responsible for what is happening in #Braamfontein right now.

Strategy. Our successful efforts in maintaining a non-violent #FeesMustFall campaign for 2 years has been compromised. Its time to reflect. #NMMU

Logic. Some of the tweets contained logical arguments.

Zuma "#FeesMustFall a sign of a healthy democracy", mxim. Protests are a sign of bad governance

The government says you are the future leaders of this country yet they won't invest in your education. The irony. **#FeesMustFall**

Remember FREE and QUALITY don't get along. Free Education for all? C'mon SA let's be realistic, we can't afford that

60 Billion lost in Corruption annually while providing free education would only be 45 Billion mhh! we really have to strike

The leader of a Communist Party rubbishing a demand for free education? What kind of communists are these?

Philosophy.

"If only our pain bothered you as much as our protests" - Shaun King

Ethics. The ethical stance of some of the journalists was also queried.

Barry Bateman has long chosen sides when it comes to #FeesMustFall, he has long thrown objectivity as a journalist when it comes to it.

Bateman is a senior reporter at EWN.

Detail. Many of the Twitterati emphasized detail in their tweets. The following tweets illustrate this point.

The campaign focusing on FEE FREE, DECOLONISED & QUALITY EDUCATION! Not just FREE EDUCATION!

Condemnation. Students arrested must face a litany of charges & expelled for such foolish acts. Criminals belong in jail not university.

Arson is a serious crime though… We can't condone burning buildings. It is highly unacceptable

Convenient smoke screen for those "students" that know they wont pass their studies, so they go on the rampage and call it #feesmustfall

Support. The Twittersphere was flooded with support for the protesters.

Comrades solder on. We are with you.

Unexpected Themes. Unexpected themes that point to lateral thinking appear from time to time in tweets.

#FeesMustFall is a great initiative, not only will it benefit the students, but it will benefit the ones paying Lobola in a few years.

Lobola is a "bride price, traditionally one paid with cattle [24]. Nowadays, it is more often than not paid in cash.

Negative Responses. The tweets contained a fair amount of criticism levelled against the actions that were triggered by the campaign.

Burning buildings is not the answer

Misguided revolutionary behaviour doesn't reflect any desire to grow and learn at a place of higher learning.

Geographic Distribution of the Tweets. The geographic spread of the campaign to all public universities are reflected in the tweets.

Coordination. Chamber of Mines invites Wits #FeesMustFall leaders to a meeting http://ift.tt/2e5XvbE #feesmustfall #vulavula

Let's stand together as we #OccupyTreasury tomorrow. We leave Hatfield at 9 am from Prospect Str.

Rumours. Rumours thrive on social platforms. They are often strategically implemented. The following example illustrate the point:

Now they're saying lecturers could be retrenched because of #FeesMustFall. Now that's scary. Our best lecturers will leave the country.

Confusion. If its not silly unconstitutional curfews then it's trigger happy policeman & useless bouncers. Where the hell are we?

Jest. There was also no shortage of jest.

#ExcusesForBeingSingle I don't have time, I'm busy striking on #FeesMustFall

#FeesMustFall public leader #DlaminiDlamini, who demands university shutdown, wants to write a test tomorrow?

4.2   Professional Journalists

As mentioned *supra* the professional journalists are often scooped by citizen journalists. This does not only apply to text but also to video footage that is captured with private phones. This does, however, not mean that the professional journalists passively accept this phenomenon. They run Twitter accounts, both in their formal and private capacity, and compete aggressively for scoops in cyberspace.

Ritter [25] distinguishes between legacy and neoteric journalist. He found that:

Many legacy journalists often hold off on publishing information via social media for strategic reasons, contradicting any perception that social media is a live, continuously updating, complete categorization of news events. Legacy journalists interviewed here drew attention to the struggle they face when choosing to break a story via social media instead of using the traditional medium. There was a clear distinction of opinions between legacy and neoteric journalists. Neoteric journalists view social media as an extension of the traditional medium. Simply stated, it is a way to keep viewers, readers, and listeners updated in the interim.

The researcher captured tweets from a wide array of professional journalists from across the journalism spectre. Not all of work for the conventional media. Some of them are freelance journalists, others are in public relations or work for lobbying agencies. The media represented in the sample vary from mainstream television and radio stations, influential newspapers, university publications, as well as media monitoring houses.

Scoops. The following good news story was tweeted by a blogger:

UNISA management to contribute R10 million to support students who need funding.

The radio stations with their regular news bulletins and "breaking news stories" are better positioned to compete for scoops. Power FM tweeted the following reference to a story that dominated their news bulletins:

Protesting TUT students have attempted to set a police Nyala (armoured vehicle) on fire.

A court reporter from Business Day tweeted "Court releases eight Wits students arrested for public violence." If s/he had to wait for the printed version to be finalized, the story would have lost its news value.

News24 tweeted when one of their journalists were hit by two rubber bullets at the Wits campus.

Journalist colleague hit with a rubber bullet. Lots of journos have started wearing helmets during …

The tweet illustrates how close to the action the journalists venture to get the big story.

Promotion. As can be expected, professional journalists often use tweets to direct the attention of the Twitterati to their writings on higher order topics. Judith February and Patrick Bond, both columnists for the electronic newspaper, The Daily Maverick serve as examples:

My piece in the DAILY MAVERICK on #feesmustfall, the public discourse and the balancing of rights: www.dailymaverick.co.za/opinionista/2016-10-23-where-is-the-middle-ground-in-south-african-debate

#FeesMustFall demand reflects sound fiscal logic, not 'ultra-leftism'

A new column by PATRICK BOND

Politicizing. Tweets are also used by the media to politicize an issue. A prominent anti-government Sunday paper tweeted the viewpoint of a radical newcomer to the parliamentary scene. Julius Malema is the leader of theEconomic Freedom Fighters.

Malema says the EFF is 100% behind students, "they must never surrender or retreat."

Comparison. Australian model: students get interest free loan and only pay back when employed and according to salary. Could it work in SA? #feesmustfall

Derick Watts, celebrity TV anchor of the investigative TV-program, Carte Blanche, explained the model in the tweet.

Analysis. Theuns Eloff is the Chairman of Higher Education South Africa. His tweet refers to an analysis on Fallism.

It read:

What lies behind Fallism? @politicsweb http://www.politicsweb.co.za/opinion/what-lies-behind-fallism…. **#FEESMUSTFALL** IS MERELY THE EARS OF THE HIPPOPOTAMUS*

Medical advice. #FeesMustFall: Four tips to protect your eyes during a protest http://bit.ly/2dhhdEL by our @pontsho_pilane

Satire. A leading South African satirist, Evita Bezuidenhout, highlighted a comical dimension of the protests.

Why do our police who are in the service of the people appear on the Wits campus dressed like extras from a Star Wars film?

Cartoons added more satire and truth to the discourse. The following cartoon relates to the large scale destruction of university property by the protesters.

4.3   The Grey Area

There is however a grey area where professional journalists can tweet in their personal capacity.

The Twitter profile of one of the most influential journalists in the country, Adriaan Basson, reads:

"Netwerk24 editor-in-chief/hoofredakteur. Author of 'Zuma Exposed' (Jonathan Ball). Digital first.
Views are my own."

During the storming of the parliament by more than a 1000 students during the campaign

Basson tweeted in his personal capacity that it is both a sad and historic day in South Africa's educational history.

The tweet was in his mother tongue, Afrikaans.

4.4   Metajournalism

The tweet that generated the most metajournalism was not posted by a professional journalist but by a politician who occasionally produces editorial columns and comments. Dali Mpofu is a practicing senior advocate as well as the deputy leader of the Economic Freedom Fighters. His tweet read:\

Calling progressive lawyers willing to assist with #FeesMustFall matters in all affected university towns.

Volunteers pls contact me urgently.

Mpofu issues an appeal for volunteerism to all lawyers in or near universities to assist with legal advice to student protesters who have been/may be arrested during the protests. It generated 61 conversations, 1300 retweets, and 684 likes. This tweet illustrates the power as well as diversity of the Twitter platform.

Among the conventional media a journalist from the Mail and Guardian triggered the most metajournalism.

Pauli van Wyk generated 36 conversations, 201 retweets, and 112 likes. Two other interest groups, The Social Justice Movement and the Freemarket Foundation fared better.

The most metajournalism in the sample was generated by the following tweet:

A child of the ANC Arrested by the ANC Fighting for what the ANC promised Cry the beloved ANC.

The tweet plays on the iconic novel, Cry the beloved country that was written by Alan Paton. It triggered 51 conversations, 1700 retweets, and 827 likes. It was posted by a citizen journalist.

Another tweet from an unidentified citizen journalist rendered 897 retweets and got 315 likes. It compared one of the student activists with the Paralympian, Oscar Pistorius, who is doing jail time for the murder of his girlfriend. It read:

Tell me, didn't Oscar Pistorius get bail? Mcebo Dlamini denied bail? Why?

The regime fears those who preach ideas even more than murderous!

5   Conclusion

It is clear from the findings that the Twittersphere is a major battleground where citizen journalists compete for scoops with professional journalists. Although the citizen journalists are not hampered by the ethical codes that restrict the professional journalists, the professional journalists can tweet under their own names. This matter will in all probability in the near future be tested in the courts.

Analysing the tweets during and after selection creates the feeling that the researcher is viewing the transcriptions of thousands of mini-interviews. The content is often rich, and the participants diverse in their views. The myriad of themes that feature, many of them ôf an unexpected nature, underscores the high levels of creativity that are unleashed by a campaign of this nature. This researcher postulates that the more political and/or polemical the issue that is tweeted about, the wider the array of themes that it will propagate.

An analysis of the metajournalism indicated that the leading citizen journalists generated more conversations, likes, and retweets than their professional counterparts. This can probably be subscribed to the fact that the tweets also served an operational function and were not only posted to distribute news. The other important aspect is the vast amount of metajournalism that was generated by the interest groups. In future the interest groups may be classified and analyzed as a separate group.

References

1. Dludla, N.: Police arrest 23 as students protest tuition fee-hike plan. Times Live (2016). http://www.timeslive.co.za/local/2015/10/20/Police-arrest-23-as-students-protest-tuition-fee-hike-plan. Accessed 20 Oct 2015
2. Connect. Why is Wits raising its fees. Citizen (2015). http://connect.citizen.co.za/news/25760/why-is-wits-raising-its-fees/3
3. Kekana, M.: Open Stellenbosch to fight proposed tuition fee hike, EWN (2016). http://ewn.co.za/2015/10/16/Open-Stellenbosch-to-fight-proposed-fee-hike. Accessed 16 Oct 2015
4. Pather, R., Whittles, G.: Cops who shot Shaeera Kalla to be subject of investigation. Mail & Guardian, 20 October 2016
5. Areff, A., Ngoepe, K., Gqirana, T.: Students reject 6% cap on fee increase, call for 0% increase. News24 (2016). http://www.news24.com/SouthAfrica/News/Students-reject-6-cap-on-fee-increase-call-for-0-increase-20151020
6. Gasa, S., Dougan, L.: #FeesMustFall 2016: where to from here? (2016). https://www.dailymaverick.co.za/article/2016-10-05-feesmustfall-2016-where-to-from-here/
7. Saltmarsh, C.: Unpaid debt is a valuable investment for the government. Forgetoday (2015). http://forgetoday.com/press/unpaid-student-debt-is-a-valuable-investment-for-the-government/. Accessed 24 July 2015
8. Sivitanides, M., Shah, V.: The era of digital activism. In: Conference for Information Systems Applied Research, 2011 CONISAR Proceedings, Wilmington, North Carolina, USA (2011)
9. Rainie, L., Smith, A., Lehman, K., Brady, H., Verba, S.: Social Media and Political Engagement (2012). http://www.pewinternet.org/2012/10/19/social-media-and-political-engagement/
10. Uldam, J., Vestergaard, A. (eds.): Civic Engagement and Social Media Political Participation Beyond Protest. Palgrave Macmillan, New York (2016)
11. Cammaerts, B.: Technologies of self-mediation: affordances and constraints of social media for protest movements. In: Uldam, J., Vestergaard, A. (eds.) Civic Engagement and Social Media Political Participation Beyond Protest. Palgrave Macmillan, New York (2015)

12. Alkhouja, M.: Social media for political change: the activists, governments, and firms triangle of powers during the Arab movement. In: Solo, A.G.M. (ed.) Handbook of Research on Political Activism in the Information Age. IGI Global, Hershey (2014)
13. Giglio, M.: The Facebook freedom fighter. Newsweek **157**(8), 14 (2011)
14. Salter, L., Kay, J.B.: The UWE occupation. Soc. Mov. Stud. **10**(4), 423–429 (2011). http://dx.doi.org/10.1080/14742837.2011.614112
15. Salter, L.: Emergent social movements in online media and states of crisis. In: McCaughey, M. (ed.) Cyberactivism on the Participatory Web. Routledge, New York (2014)
16. Rosas, R.: Protesting in a cultural frame: how social media was used by Portuguese "Geração à Rasca" activists and the M12M movement. In: Solo, A.G.M. (ed.) Handbook of Research on Political Activism in the Information Age. IGI Global, Hershey (2014)
17. Gladwell, M.: Annals of Innovation: Small Change: Why the Revolution will not be Tweeted. The New Yorker (2010). http://www.newyorker.com/reporting/2010/10/04/101004fa_fact_gladwell. Accessed 4 Oct 2010
18. Palinkas, L.A., Horwitz, S.M., Green, C.A., Wisdom, J.P., Duan, N., Hoagwood, K.: Purposeful sampling for qualitative data collection and analysis in mixed method implementation research. Adm. Policy Ment. Health Ment. Health Serv. Res. **42**(5), 533–544 (2013). doi:10.1007/s10488-013-0528-y
19. Coyne, I.T.: Sampling in qualitative research. Purposeful and theoretical sampling; merging or clear boundaries? J. Adv. Nurs. **26**, 623–630 (1997)
20. Harper, A.: Citizen journalism vs. professional journalism. In: Journalism: The Future (n.d.). https://journalismthefuture.wordpress.com/citizen-journalism-vs-professional-journalism/
21. Namey, E., Guest, G., Thairu, L., Johnson, L.: Data reduction techniques for large qualitative data sets. In: Guest, G., MacQueen, K.M. (eds.) Handbook for Teambased Qualitative Research, pp. 137–162. Rowman & Littlefield Pub Incorporated, Lanham (2008)
22. Goode, L.: Social news, citizen journalism and democracy. New Media Soc. **11**(8), 1287–1305 (2009)
23. Boyd, D., Golder, S., Lotan, G.: Tweet, tweet, retweet: conversational aspects of retweeting on Twitter. In: HICSS-43. IEEE, Kauai, 6 January 2010
24. https://en.oxforddictionaries.com/
25. Ritter, M.: The socially challenged: exploring obstacles to social media integration in newsrooms. Glob. Media J. **13**(24), 2–15 (2015)

Author Index

Printed in the United States
By Bookmasters